Seeing Like a Citizen

NEW AFRICAN HISTORIES

SERIES EDITORS: JEAN ALLMAN, ALLEN ISAACMAN, AND DEREK R. PETERSON

David William Cohen and E. S. Atieno Odhiambo, *The Risks of Knowledge*

Belinda Bozzoli, *Theatres of Struggle and the End of Apartheid*

Gary Kynoch, *We Are Fighting the World*

Stephanie Newell, *The Forger's Tale*

Jacob A. Tropp, *Natures of Colonial Change*

Jan Bender Shetler, *Imagining Serengeti*

Cheikh Anta Babou, *Fighting the Greater Jihad*

Marc Epprecht, *Heterosexual Africa?*

Marissa J. Moorman, *Intonations*

Karen E. Flint, *Healing Traditions*

Derek R. Peterson and Giacomo Macola, editors, *Recasting the Past*

Moses E. Ochonu, *Colonial Meltdown*

Emily S. Burrill, Richard L. Roberts, and Elizabeth Thornberry, editors, *Domestic Violence and the Law in Colonial and Postcolonial Africa*

Daniel R. Magaziner, *The Law and the Prophets*

Emily Lynn Osborn, *Our New Husbands Are Here*

Robert Trent Vinson, *The Americans Are Coming!*

James R. Brennan, *Taifa*

Benjamin N. Lawrance and Richard L. Roberts, editors, *Trafficking in Slavery's Wake*

David M. Gordon, *Invisible Agents*

Allen F. Isaacman and Barbara S. Isaacman, *Dams, Displacement, and the Delusion of Development*

Stephanie Newell, *The Power to Name*

Gibril R. Cole, *The Krio of West Africa*

Matthew M. Heaton, *Black Skin, White Coats*

Meredith Terretta, *Nation of Outlaws, State of Violence*

Paolo Israel, *In Step with the Times*

Michelle R. Moyd, *Violent Intermediaries*

Abosede A. George, *Making Modern Girls*

Alicia C. Decker, *In Idi Amin's Shadow*

Rachel Jean-Baptiste, *Conjugal Rights*

Shobana Shankar, *Who Shall Enter Paradise?*

Emily S. Burrill, *States of Marriage*

Todd Cleveland, *Diamonds in the Rough*

Carina E. Ray, *Crossing the Color Line*

Sarah Van Beurden, *Authentically African*

Giacomo Macola, *The Gun in Central Africa*

Lynn Schler, *Nation on Board*

Julie MacArthur, *Cartography and the Political Imagination*

Abou B. Bamba, *African Miracle, African Mirage*

Daniel Magaziner, *The Art of Life in South Africa*

Paul Ocobock, *An Uncertain Age*

Keren Weitzberg, *We Do Not Have Borders*

Nuno Domingos, *Football and Colonialism*

Jeffrey S. Ahlman, *Living with Nkrumahism*

Bianca Murillo, *Market Encounters*

Laura Fair, *Reel Pleasures*

Thomas F. McDow, *Buying Time*

Jon Soske, *Internal Frontiers*

Elizabeth W. Giorgis, *Modernist Art in Ethiopia*

Matthew V. Bender, *Water Brings No Harm*

David Morton, *Age of Concrete*

Marissa J. Moorman, *Powerful Frequencies*

Ndubueze L. Mbah, *Emergent Masculinities*

Judith A. Byfield, *The Great Upheaval*

Patricia Hayes and Gary Minkley, editors, *Ambivalent*

Mari K. Webel, *The Politics of Disease Control*

Kara Moskowitz, *Seeing Like a Citizen*

Seeing Like a Citizen

Decolonization, Development, and the Making of Kenya, 1945–1980

Kara Moskowitz

OHIO UNIVERSITY PRESS ~ ATHENS, OHIO

Ohio University Press, Athens, Ohio 45701
ohioswallow.com

Printed in the United States of America
Ohio University Press books are printed on acid-free paper. ∞ ™

29 28 27 26 25 24 23 22 21 20 19 5 4 3 2 1

Library of Congress Cataloging-in-Publication Data

Names: Moskowitz, Kara, author.
Title: Seeing like a citizen : decolonization, development, and the making of Kenya, 1945-1980 / Kara Moskowitz.
Other titles: New African histories series.
Description: Athens, Ohio : Ohio University Press, 2019. | Series: New African histories | Includes bibliographical references and index.
Identifiers: LCCN 2019031504 | ISBN 9780821423950 (hardcover) | ISBN 9780821423967 (paperback) | ISBN 9780821446898 (pdf)
Subjects: LCSH: Decolonization–Kenya. | Economic development–Political aspects–Kenya. | Kenya–History–20th century. | Kenya–Politics and government–20th century.
Classification: LCC DT433.58 .M67 2019 | DDC 967.6204–dc23
LC record available at https://lccn.loc.gov/2019031504

Contents

Illustrations

FIGURES

MAPS

Acknowledgments

In some ways, this book is about the networks that tie unlikely people together and that often provide crucial support. Over the years of researching and writing, I have gained firsthand insight into the importance of such networks, benefiting from the care and generous critiques of friends and family. This book would not exist without them.

The research for this book began at Emory University as a dissertation project. I was fortunate to have a truly remarkable set of advisers, and each has continued to offer input and guidance. First and foremost, I must thank Clifton Crais, who has read this book so many times that I have long lost count. Clifton has been incredibly generous with his time. His incisive comments and questions have opened up new lines of thinking, and the book is richer and vastly more intellectually rigorous for it. I am also deeply grateful to Kristin Mann. Kristin's meticulousness with evidence, analysis, and writing is unmatched, and she offered me invaluable advice at every point. Peter Little pushed me to approach my work through a more social scientific lens, and his seemingly limitless knowledge of Kenya has been incredibly helpful.

At Emory, I was privileged to have the support of faculty members and fellow graduate students in the Department of History and at the Institute of African Studies. Mari Webel and Pamela Scully provided helpful comments on my work. I met Kristin Phillips in my last year at Emory, but since then she has offered her critical eye to many chapters of this book, and her comments have made the book immeasurably better. Jill Rosenthal has helped me to think about histories of development differently. She closely read drafts of multiple chapters and has been a caring friend throughout. Thanks also to Dinah Hannaford, Molly McCullers, Husseina Dinani, Jane Hooper, Nathan Suhr-Sytsma, Debjani Bhattacharyya, Aubrey Graham, Francis Musoni, Elizabeth Stice, John Steen, Jessica Reuther, and Abby Meert, each of whom shaped this book in little and big ways. Special thanks to Abby, who kindly scanned some archival documents for me.

In Kenya, I began my research at the National Archives, and I am grateful to all of the archivists there. I am especially indebted to Peterson Kithuka and Richard Ambani. Richard's relentlessness in searching for missing archival documents made my project much richer, and the energy he brought to the archives made it a more joyful place to work. Dave Zarembka and Gladys Kamonya welcomed a stranger into their Lumakanda home. They introduced me to my research assistants, and I both enjoyed and learned from our nightly discussions. Richard Kemboi, Oliver Kamave, and Ann Mbuga assisted with my interviews. They made the collection of oral histories a pleasure, and I am grateful to each of them. Roger and Ela Middleton-Soyemi opened their Nairobi flat to me countless times when I visited for short research trips, and I am so appreciative of their hospitality and friendship. Thanks to Paul McPhater and Manav Pathania for doing the same in London, always warmly welcoming me into their home during research trips. Thanks also to Allan Muchiri, Kimeli Korir, and Joseph Boit, each of whom helped at various stages of the research. I am most grateful to the many Kenyans who spoke with me for hours, often on multiple occasions. They patiently and thoughtfully answered my questions, shared their experiences and insights, and offered me bottomless cups of chai. This book would not be what it is without them. Special thanks to Florence and Alfred Machayo, who spoke with me for the better part of a day—a few times—and then insisted I stay for dinner.

Julia Bailey was the first to hear my ideas as I began this research, and she has offered insightful feedback to the end. Amanda Lewis and Caleb Owen also shaped my thinking as I was conducting research. Kenda Mutongi has been an enthusiastic supporter for many years. Thanks also to Lisa Lindsay, John Aerni-Flessner, Alice Wiemers, Carrie Ritter, and Priya Lal, each of whom offered advice and helpful critiques. I am especially grateful to Muey Saeteurn, who has become my virtual writing and accountability partner and has been instrumental in these last stages. I was fortunate to present this book's introduction at the University of the Western Cape, where I received helpful comments, especially from Leslie Witz, Phindezwa Mnyaka, and Ciraj Rassool. I presented a draft of chapter 2 at the African Studies Association meeting, and I am grateful to Richard Roberts for his generous comments.

Chapter 6 benefited from my participation in the National History Center's International Seminar on Decolonization. I am grateful to the organizers, William Roger Louis, Dane Kennedy, Jason Parker, and especially to Philippa Levine and the late Marilyn Johnson, each of whom offered such generous mentorship. Thanks also to my fellow seminar participants, who helped me think more expansively and comparatively and who commented on chapters of the book, particularly Charlotte Lydia Riley, Muriam Haleh Davis, Emily Baughan, Simon Stevens, and Arthur Asseraf.

The University of Toronto was my first postgraduate academic home. Though the position was temporary, the members of my two departments—Historical and Cultural Studies and the Centre for Critical Development Studies—welcomed me so warmly. Some of the conversations I had with faculty there helped reshape my thinking. Thank you especially to Dan Bender, Madhavi Kale, Julie MacArthur, and Paul Kingston. Since then, I have been lucky to call the University of Missouri-St. Louis (UMSL) my intellectual home. I could not ask for a more collegial and supportive department. Chapter 4, in particular, benefited from a stimulating discussion at our department colloquium. Thanks especially to Laura Westhoff for her unflagging encouragement, and to Deborah Cohen and Andrew Hurley. My students have also taught me more than they know, and I thank them for inspiring me to think about the histories I teach and study in different ways. Ann Wainscott's tireless leadership of a now defunct St. Louis writing group is truly missed, and she was largely responsible for some of my most productive periods.

The research for the original dissertation project was funded by the Andrew Mellon Fellowship in Original Sources and Emory University's Department of History and Laney Graduate School. Fulbright-Hays Group Projects Abroad and Foreign Language and Area Studies fellowships provided support for Swahili language study. The University of Missouri Research Board supported a semester of research leave, UMSL International Studies and Programs and the College of Arts and Sciences helped fund two research trips, and a UMSL Research Award supported mapmaking, editing, and indexing. I am grateful to these institutions for their financial support. Thank you to Brian Balsley for his cartography work and to Katie Van Heest for her close editing. My sincere gratitude to the editors at Ohio University Press for their encouragement and guidance. Thank you to Gill Berchowitz, Derek Peterson, Jean Allman, and Allen Isaacman. Thanks especially to Derek for pushing me out of my intellectual comfort zone. This project is much richer for his keen insights. My deepest thanks as well to the two anonymous readers, who provided such extensive, critical, and constructive feedback.

Thanks to my siblings—David, Rachel, and Daniel—who have always been my greatest supporters and coconspirators, and to Daniel, particularly, who proofread and critiqued portions of my work at all hours. I am especially grateful to my partner, Joe Martinez. Joe trekked all the way to Uasin Gishu to lend his professional photography skills to this project, and he is responsible for many of the photos in this book, including the lovely portraits. Joe also offered constant, on-site editing assistance, but I am most thankful to him for his immense generosity, patience, and support. It is my parents to whom I owe the greatest debt. Their encouragement and support have always been unwavering, and they first taught me to think deeply and critically about complex topics. This book is for them.

Abbreviations Used in Text

ADC	African District Council
CAB	Central Agricultural Board
DC	district commissioner
IBRD	International Bank for Reconstruction and Development
IDP	internally displaced person
IMF	International Monetary Fund
LDSB	Land Development and Settlement Board
LNC	Local Native Council
KADU	Kenya African Democratic Union
KANU	Kenya African National Union
KCC	Kenya Cooperative Creameries
KDB	Kenya Dairy Board
KES	Kenyan shillings
KFA	Kenya Farmers Association
KIA	Kenya Institute of Administration
KNFU	Kenya National Farmers Union
KPU	Kenya People's Union
MAS	Million Acre Scheme
MMB	Maize Marketing Board
NGO	nongovernmental organization
PC	provincial commissioner
PS	permanent secretary
RVP	Rift Valley Province
SFT	Settlement Fund Trustees
USAID	United States Agency for International Development

A Note on Currency and Geography

This study covers a period spanning two political regimes. One of the book's premises—that decolonization was a process, which neither started nor ended at independence—means that units of currency and geography were in flux. I have tried to simplify these while maintaining historical accuracy, making note of changes in either the text or the endnotes.

The currencies primarily used in this book are pounds sterling (£) and Kenyan shillings (/). In 1921, British East Africa made its currency pounds. Throughout the period that Kenya used pounds, there were twenty shillings to the pound. In 1966, independent Kenya introduced the Kenyan shilling at par. Until 1980, the value moved between seven and nine shillings to the US dollar. Though the Kenyan state abandoned the sterling standard, certain development plans continued using this currency, since the British remained a chief donor. Thus the reader will find economic projections and evaluations in pounds sterling well past 1966.

Geographical boundaries and nomenclature were also susceptible to change throughout the period of study. I lay out these changes fairly explicitly in the introduction and chapters 1 and 2. The Kenyan colonial state was a bifurcated state, and the white highlands, or scheduled areas, were administered separately from the native reserves. Additionally, boundaries changed frequently and were highly contested. Most importantly, Kenya has made use of changing terminology. Since independence, regions have become provinces, and districts and counties have existed at once but have not always covered the same area. Recently, former districts have become counties.

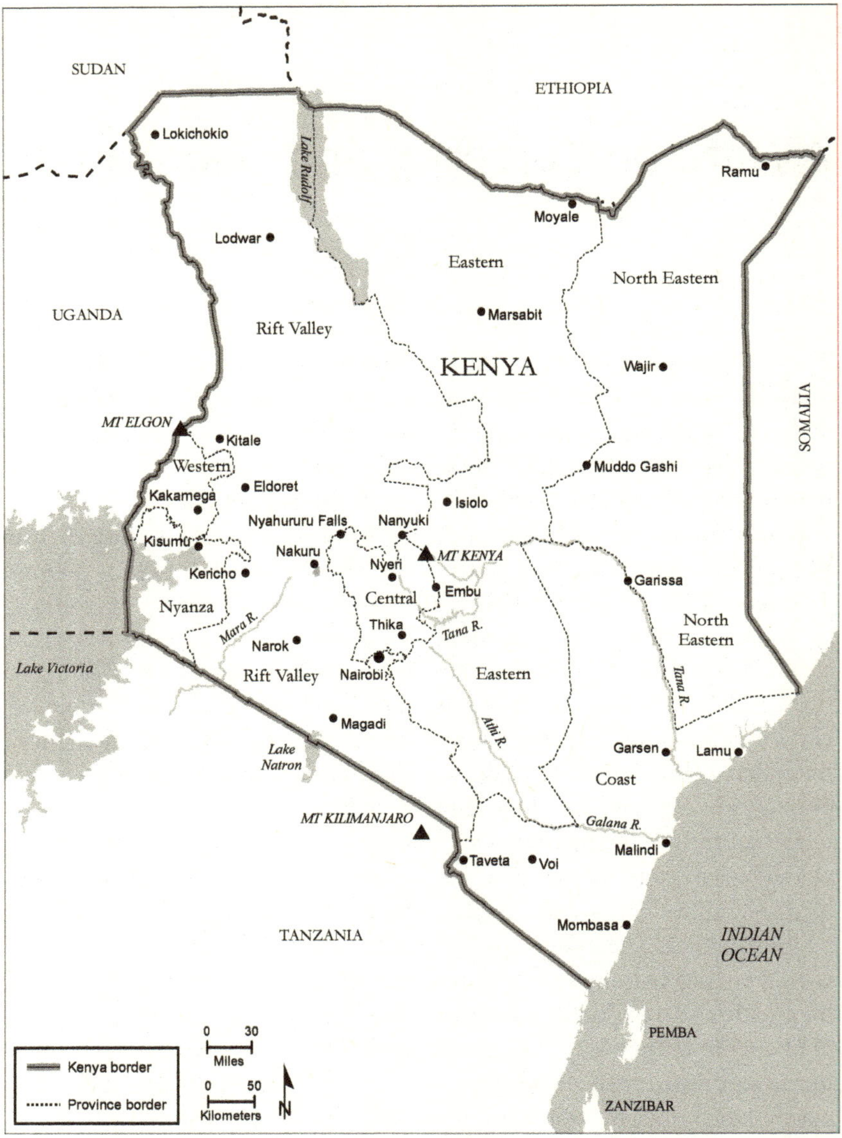

MAP A.1. Kenya, 1964. Map by Brian Edward Balsley, GISP.

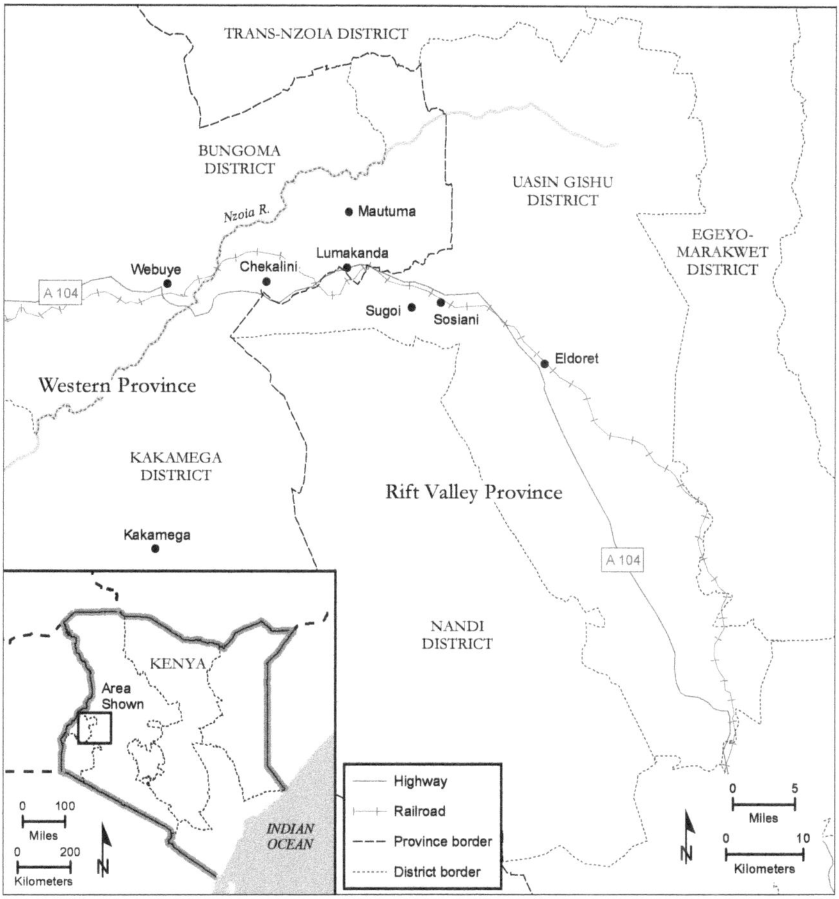

MAP A.2. Uasin Gishu, early postcolonial period. Map by Brian Edward Balsley, GISP.

Introduction

In 1961, a Kenyan farmer petitioned John F. Kennedy for an agricultural loan. "I want to practice proper farming," Zebedeo Omwando explained in his letter to the president, "but I do not know where to turn to get money."[1] American consul general Richard Freund replied some months later, affirming Kennedy's interest in the challenges facing Africa. "Unfortunately," Freund wrote, "it is not possible for President Kennedy personally to consider problems of individual citizens in foreign countries."[2]

Far from artless, Omwando's decision to solicit the US president for a small loan suggests political acumen and keen awareness of the shifting global context. Omwando penned his petition four months after Kennedy signed the executive order establishing the Peace Corps and shortly after the Kennedy Foundation financed the transportation of East African students to American universities. By 1961, transnational organizations and foreign nations had begun to fund development programs that disbursed loans to Kenyan farmers. Both international development and African decolonization had gained momentum at this point, and Kenya was in the midst of independence negotiations with the British. Zebedeo Omwando likely was not a naive actor but a shrewd one, attempting to make use of a newly available channel for accessing development resources and services such as credit, land, health care, education, and roads. He was neither alone in his broad ambitions to acquire development through political elites nor unique in his targeting of Kennedy as a potential political patron: White House correspondence just a month later records that in gratitude for American famine relief, a Kamba chief presented Kennedy with a walking stick, described as "a symbol of authority" in Kenya.[3]

Africans throughout the continent expected that independence would bring development. These expectations grew out of the postwar context and the passage of metropolitan development and welfare acts in the 1940s that expanded state-led development programs.[4] The promises of African nationalist leaders further contributed to widespread expectations for development. Postwar development programs and rising development rhetoric coincided with the establishment of the Bretton Woods institutions—the International Bank for Reconstruction and Development (IBRD; the original World Bank institution) and the International Monetary Fund (IMF).[5] The United Nations proclaimed the 1960s the "Development Decade," the same decade that witnessed the rapid decolonization of much of Africa.

In Kenya, independence negotiations began in 1960, and the most heated political debates revolved around the structure of the postcolonial government, which would determine who controlled the distribution of land and development. These were especially contentious issues. Only a small proportion of Kenyan land is suitable for intensive agriculture and grazing, European settlers had taken the most fertile regions during colonial rule, and different ethnic groups articulated competing claims for land. In 1962, prior to the resolution of these issues, the British colonial government and the World Bank began implementing the largest land transfer and resettlement program in Kenya's history—just one of many late colonial and early postcolonial programs aimed at restructuring tenure, redistributing land, and fostering agricultural development. These programs continued after Kenya gained independence on 12 December 1963, and they formed part of the broader emergence of mid-twentieth-century policies increasingly shaped by transnational institutions, which followed from land reform programs implemented in Latin America, the Middle East, and Southeast Asia.

By the mid-twentieth century, Kenyans had long relied on their relationships to access resources, and political institutions remained highly personalized. During decolonization, Kenyans directed some of their entreaties at international politicians like Kennedy, but more often they appealed to national or local actors. In late 1972, Kericho residents wrote to President Jomo Kenyatta, calling him "the eyes of our government," and asking for assistance with education and health care in the western Rift Valley highlands where they lived.[6] Hundreds of other Kenyans composed letters to the president also requesting aid, frequently addressing Kenyatta as "Father," while representing themselves as his, or the nation's, figurative children. In these petitions depicting Kenyatta as patriarch, Kenyans endeavored to strengthen their ties to a national actor with the ability to distribute resources.

Emboldened by the promises the changing setting held, and motivated by aspirations to improve their lives, new citizens actively sought aid from the ever-widening array of actors participating in development. In a trove of petitions from the 1960s and 1970s, Kenyans tested new and old political relationships alike, exploring which actors and institutions might offer the aid they desired. This extended beyond Kennedy and Kenyatta, to government ministers, members of Parliament, and local bureaucrats. When Kenyans sought assistance, they also turned to nonstate institutions, such as nongovernmental organizations (NGOs) or, locally, to ethnic elders, churches, and women's organizations.[7] Women's microfinance groups offered small loans, the very same service Zebedeo Omwando sent a petition all the way to America to request. NGOs provided famine relief, just as Kennedy did. Church groups offered scholarships for children's school fees, and local elders coordinated the building and funding of health centers, the very development Kericho residents petitioned Kenyatta about. To pursue development resources was to dive headfirst into an increasingly entangled web of political networks, which extended outward neither horizontally nor vertically, but unpredictably. Kenyans thus came to imagine themselves as members of global, national, and local political communities simultaneously.

Rural engagement in, and impact on, decolonizing development programming went far beyond solicitation, and beyond the strengthening and reworking of patron-client networks. Nonelite Kenyans also helped determine the outcomes of development interventions. While most Kenyans could not directly influence the development planning negotiated behind closed doors in Nairobi, London, Geneva, or Washington, they could affect the form and success of development programming on the ground in their communities. Sometimes, as with requests for aid, Kenyans took up pen and paper to draft letters to politicians or bureaucrats, requesting the creation of a much-needed program, the modification of an unsatisfactory one, or the termination of a particularly unpopular program. On occasion, Kenyan groups also took matters into their own hands. In the absence of adequate assistance, they created their own development by building local schools and hospitals without first receiving government authorization. In more exceptional instances, Kenyan communities vigorously obstructed the implementation of international programs by vandalizing development sites and disrupting progress. New citizens then used their experiences of development to construct and revise ideologies on political identity and political authority.

Clearly, decolonization and development were coterminous and coconstitutive historical processes.[8] Processes they truly were, occurring in fits and starts, heralding both continuities and changes, even after formal independence from British rule.[9] Given Kenya's overwhelmingly rural population and its economy's dependence on agricultural production, these processes unfolded in the countryside.[10] Development had national and transnational dimensions, to be sure, but centering on the actions and political imaginations of rural Kenyans—how they navigated the political transition, pursued access to aid, and sought to influence development programs in their own communities—exposes constraints on state power and reveals how average people fashioned citizenship in the postcolonial world.

After independence, the rural poor represented the vast majority of new African citizens and the main targets of development interventions. The 1960s offered extraordinary openings for political and economic innovation, as a recently established international development regime attempted to extend into the decolonizing world, and as transitional states set out to craft a new political order. This moment was primed for political experimentation, affording an expanding set of actors, who might have otherwise been more excluded, the ability to actively participate in political processes and development programming. The rural poor had a lot at stake; their material realities hung in the balance while politicians discussed development priorities and debated how to approach the distribution of state resources. Ordinary Africans intervened in these deliberations and, in doing so, helped to determine Kenya's development path.[11] Scholarship to date has highlighted—but perhaps overstated—the high-modernist logic of developmentalist states.[12] The discursive focus offers few insights into how development was carried out on the ground or how it shaped the material well-being of the poor, often consigning them to the backdrop.[13]

Most scholars have accepted that in the 1960s, international organizations transformed state actors into the exclusive agents of development and, in turn, presumed that these processes expanded and entrenched bureaucratic power.[14] It is often taken as axiomatic that during this period, the aim of development was economic growth.[15] In Kenya as elsewhere, neither development practice nor theory was ever coherent, fully constituted, or unanimously supported. Officials disagreed on how to achieve economic growth, and whether growth was even the ultimate goal, with some state actors arguing that wealth redistribution and economic equality were more telling indicators of societal health than gross domestic product (GDP).[16]

Rural Kenyans tended to link development to material prosperity as well as personal and communal well-being. Some expressed their ideas of development in abstract terms—as improvement, eradicating poverty, positive changes, or the introduction of new ideas.[17] Others defined development in terms of discrete, finite resources, such as land, or as having access to more intangible resources, such as education and health care.

The postcolonial state was divided over conflicting development models and limited by fiscal and personnel constraints. Unlike Frederick Cooper's widely cited notion of the "gatekeeper state"—which derives power and authority from regulating and distributing foreign aid—Kenya's independent state never achieved monopolistic, centralized control over the flow of aid or commodities.[18] Though the state might have been *an* agent of development, it was certainly not *the only* agent.[19] All developmentalist regimes did not inevitably produce a capacious bureaucracy that increased state power.[20] Indeed, in early postcolonial Kenya, Jomo Kenyatta's state governmentality lacked instrumental or institutional heft.

The 1960s development landscape brought together multitiered actors, transforming local development sites into cosmopolitan spaces.[21] Development programs were often internationally financed, state-led, and locally implemented.[22] Transnational institutions created the criteria, which privileged some, marginalized others, and delimited the possibilities of development. Central state actors shaped policies within—or without—the constrictions of donors. They also frequently distributed resources to rural supporters, who knew to negotiate developmental policy and implementation with the local elites and local bureaucrats facilitating the execution of development programs on the ground. At the same time, rural Kenyans sought alternatives to state-led aid offered by nongovernmental organizations and community institutions.[23]

Many scholars have suggested that nonstate actors and institutions did not come to play a pivotal role in development practice until much later. James Ferguson, for example, contends that two letters—one from Guinean boys to "the members of Europe" and another from a Zambian journalist to America—reveal "the limitations of the nation-state as the object of appeal or redress."[24] Ferguson suggests that this kind of invocation of a supranational moral order can be understood only as part of the neoliberal world. Yet these letters bear a striking resemblance to Omwando's letter to John F. Kennedy in 1961, revealing both continuity and rupture. During the 1960s, state, nonstate, and civil society actors, together, established new modes of governance and an international development order, which served as a forerunner to the neoliberalism of the 1990s.[25]

The early independent Kenyan state, similar to other states, was marked by its cleavages and contradictions. Perhaps the most consistent characteristic of the postcolonial state was its inconsistency.[26] Indeed, rural Kenyans often recounted the unreliability of the state—an intentional mode of governance, but also an unavoidable effect of the transition, part and parcel of political experimentations during decolonization. The government was financially constrained, and Kenyatta's ongoing efforts to centralize power produced conflicts between central and local administrations, generating contradictory outcomes—physically present local governments were intentionally underfunded and eventually incapacitated, and the overextended central state entered into rural lives episodically and unevenly.

At times, the state relied on local bureaucrats—settlement, agricultural, veterinary, medical, and community development officers, among others—to implement programs and act as representative conduits to rural areas. A government mandate to carry out development work did not, however, assuage the practical impediments that understaffed ministries and undertrained bureaucrats faced. State expectations tended to exceed bureaucratic capacity, particularly in rural contexts where officials were tasked with covering broad regions and hundreds of households, by either foot or bike. Pressured by their superiors to perform, local bureaucrats were often forced to make tough decisions. Some chose to visit their assigned communities only occasionally, while others decided to focus their energies on more developed households to create model farms ready to show off to touring notables. The successful rural execution of many programs depended greatly on individual bureaucrats. Given that the abilities, training, and commitment of these officials could range considerably, the local operations of a single program also varied. Kenyans thus experienced the provision of services and developmental assistance irregularly.

The rural sense of state unreliability emerges clearly in oral histories, with Kenyans describing how bureaucrats and elected officials carried out their work inconsistently. Some rural Kenyans described how members of Parliament visited during election cycles and then vanished. Many said that after giving out sugar and cooking fat in exchange for votes, *wabunge* (MPs) often disappeared, presumably somewhere into the distant capital, Nairobi.[27] While a number of Kenyans complained about the invisibility of rogue elected officials, others recounted the devotion and supportive presence of their MPs, illustrating the climate of unpredictability. They noted how representatives helped secure funding for local development programs.

During moments of crisis, members intervened on behalf of constituents, joining disaffected citizens to protest an unwanted development program or helping loan defaulters avoid eviction.

The *baraza* (local public meeting)[28] was the most reliable place to encounter government officials and make claims, but the outcomes were similarly unpredictable. Many Kenyans explained that they simply made their complaints and waited, unsure of the exact process for resolution. When communities aired their grievances at baraza, there was little telling whether they would receive a response. This created a feeling of inscrutability about how messages passed from rural areas to Nairobi government offices, and confusion about why some grievances were addressed while others were ignored. Frequently, Kenyan communities awaiting an official response never received one, only adding to the abstruseness, and transforming the space between rural communities and Nairobi into a kind of erratic void.

To compensate for this inconsistency, and to win the loyalties of the population, Nairobi officials attempted to depict the state as a translocal institution through continual symbolic representations.[29] The presence of important officials at groundbreaking and ribbon-cutting ceremonies was commonplace. Jomo Kenyatta's portrait was "all over," his voice could be heard on the radio nightly, and chiefs read the president's speeches aloud at baraza.[30] An Office of the President memorandum makes clear that such depictions were an intentional strategy, arguing that "to meet the needs of these people effectively, Government must be personalized in one individual who is easily accessible, sympathetic, understanding and authoritative."[31] In the view of the Office of the President, Jomo Kenyatta represented the perfect embodiment of the government. The countless petitions Kenyatta received, addressed to "*baba taifa*" (father of the nation), indicate that such representations could produce the desired outcomes.

An aura came to surround Kenyatta, and many Kenyans described him as an almost omniscient figure. William Serem, a Nandi pastoralist who initially supported the opposition party, recounted "meeting" Kenyatta: "When the president was coming, we were invited and we could only go to a place like Kapkong Primary School. We waited for him there. Even though we could not see him, it was our pleasure to see the president. We would go; we had met the president. Even if the president could go by air, it was our pleasure to look and clap."[32] Serem's account reveals the ubiquitous role Kenyatta came to play in many rural imaginaries, which might diverge from experiences with other state actors and with the unpredictability of policy implementation. In this setting, rural Kenyans came to understand individual actors as inconsistent conduits to state resources. They also came to understand the spatial reach of the state as selective and its workings as unreliable.

The postcolonial state was a bricolage of precolonial, colonial, and newly emerging modes of governmentality and political authority. Precolonial forms of patronage persisted, as personalized political networks continued to provide security, wealth, and prestige, though the terms of exchange in these relationships had altered. Former colonial officials transformed into development officers overnight.[33] The provincial administration—an administration of colonial origins—remained the most important government institution in local settings. While Kenyatta's image replaced Queen Elizabeth's, the khaki uniforms of local bureaucrats remained identical and continued to be integral to rural authority. Within subnational arenas, ethnic patriots debated and reworked moral ethnicities.[34] Throughout Kenya, new and old institutions—a blurred mix of state, parastatal, nongovernmental, and community—appeared and disappeared in local contexts, some changing dramatically during decolonization, others remaining more constant. Cooperatives, self-help groups, churches, and voluntary organizations—headed both by citizens and by nonnationals—took on legal, administrative, and developmental functions. Kenyans, in other words, were inundated with conflicting signs of power and authority.

These histories tell us not just about the inconsistencies of development provision, or the dissonance of the state, but, correspondingly, about the nature of postcolonial citizenship.[35] Sally Kogo's observations show how experiences of state unpredictability shaped rural political ideologies on the rights and duties of citizens, and on the obligations of the state. She remarked, "I wasn't disappointed in the *serikali* [government] because the place was bushy so it was understood that the government never knew that people were living there. So, it was our responsibility to go to the government and introduce ourselves, 'We have a place living somewhere there and we need your services.'"[36] At the time, Kogo lived in northern Uasin Gishu on a registered, titled, land-purchase cooperative, thirty-five miles from the district's capital of Eldoret, hardly the most remote or invisible location. This setting was marked by inconsistency, though, and some illegal squatter settlements became sites of development intervention, whereas some high-modernist development schemes became illegible to the very state actors who designed them. Kenya's director of Settlement, for example, had trouble confirming the regional location of a number of settlement schemes under his control in 1964.[37] This context obligated citizens to declare themselves, and their needs, to the government. In absence of such an announcement, state unpredictability often forced citizens to take on the labor of development themselves or seek assistance from other institutions, revealing the uneven set of rights, duties, and obligations accorded to Kenyans.

This book inverts James Scott's notion of "seeing like a state" to "seeing like a citizen." In Scott's depiction, monolithic states, with symmetric, ordered aesthetic visions, enacted massive social engineering plans, while "prostrate" civil societies lacked the capacity to resist.[38] Indeed, Sally Kogo's ideas about the connections between technocracy and development sound remarkably similar to Scott's, though from a citizen's perspective. A technocratic authoritarian state never materialized in Kenya, though a developmentalist one certainly did. In this setting, Kogo wanted to make herself "legible" to the state, not because it would make her more "manipulable," but because it might offer her access to resources.[39] Seeing like a citizen allows for a disaggregation of the state, and of citizens, exposing the limitations of high modernism as practice and theoretical framework. It pushes scholarly understanding beyond the dualistic, rudimentary narrative of states infringing on impotent citizens, and reveals, instead, the texture of a series of more complex political relationships.

Seeing like a citizen entails shifting the optical positioning, moving from the cartographer or surveyor's airplane flying above to the footpaths below, uncaptured by aerial photographs or miniaturized models. From that vantage, it is clear that the state was an internally varied, dissonant institution in the making, composed of dissenting actors. The view from below also reveals that citizenries' parallel never existed—no singular, generic, representative individual emerges.[40] Rather, quite the opposite. Seeing like a citizen exposes no standardized vision, but many visions, often in conflict, often irreconcilable. It reveals uniformity only in citizenship's unevenness, multivalence, and pluralism.[41]

Citizenship defines membership in a society, and it mediates the relationship between individual and community, setting expectations for how individuals gain rights, what duties they have, and what society is obligated to provide in return. In decolonizing Kenya, such expectations remained nebulous, and even the more clearly outlined citizenship expectations were inconsistently applied. National citizenship was neither claimed nor imposed, but rather negotiated, particularly the extent of belonging and protection that it offered. The transactional nature of citizenship drove the creation of new inequality, and not all citizens gained the equal "right to have rights."[42] Some Kenyans possessed greater ability to participate in the public sphere and to acquire rights, while others—still citizens—remained restricted to the margins of public arenas, their rights often more circumscribed, even though their duties tended to remain substantial. The incommensurate citizen-state relationships produced a spectrum of rights endowed to different individuals.

Citizenship's expansive framework—encompassing legal status; rights, entitlements, and duties; and a sense of identity and belonging—means that it can be enacted at various sites, on different terms, and that it is both open to contestation and prone to reconfiguration.[43] Through negotiations over development, Kenyan citizens, state officials, and development actors delineated a spectrum of national citizens' rights and duties, and an irregular set of state obligations, differentiated especially by ethnicity, gender, religion, region, and class. In the Rift Valley during decolonization, rights and duties tended to overshadow legal status, and to shape feelings of belonging in the new nation-state. Unresolved questions about the allocation of state resources, and who had rights to those resources, gained particular resonance. Ultimately, land resettlement played an outsized role in determining notions of citizenship, since many Kenyans expected land redistribution and conceived of land as an almost inherent right. Land access shaped feelings of national and ethnic rootedness at both an individual level and a communal level. Depending on the circumstances, landless individuals might feel excluded from both the nation and their ethnic community, and ethnic groups that made unsuccessful bids to land might protest their communal exclusion. Aside from land, Kenyans also expressed claims to education, health care, infrastructure, employment, and famine relief, often in the language of rights to personal security and self-determination, though national and subnational moral economies required they work hard to help themselves first. As with land, enduring exclusion from such services affected not only material realities but ideas about belonging.[44]

Though some believed citizenship granted every Kenyan inherent rights with minimal obligation to the nation, many Kenyan citizens willingly took on considerable duties. Kenyans tolerated state expectations that they contributed to nation-building, but they refused to accept that such duties could infringe upon their economic rights and liberties.[45] Thus, when state officials attempted to enact restrictive marketing policies in the name of national development, some Kenyan farmers—who interpreted these policies as unfairly limiting their individual economic freedoms—refused to adhere. In other instances, Kenyans—who advanced national development by providing free labor—used the fulfillment of their citizenly duties to try to obligate the state to contribute funding and resources to their programs. Some Kenyans even sought to take on citizenly duties, so they could become endowed with rights to state services. Nandi farmer Daniel Kebeney Bitok was landless and poor at independence. He said, "I wanted to be among the taxpayers, to attend the *baraza* [public meetings], to be educated on how to develop the nation. In return, the government should give me services."[46] At independence, the rights and duties of Kenyan citizens remained ill defined and in flux, and the forms of citizenship envisioned from below often countered those envisioned from above, provoking deliberation and negotiation at development sites.

Though citizenship in decolonizing Kenya was built through the promise of state resources, these promises were not delivered universally or equitably. As inequalities were remapped, Kenyans began expressing disparate ideas about citizenship in the new nation-state. Men who became landowners often defined being a *mwananchi* (citizen) in a possessive way—to be the owner of the land or the owner of the country. This idea underscores how citizenship came to be determined by rights to resources, particularly land—a resource that both materially and symbolically represented national belonging and a future premised on development.

Kenyans with limited access to land and development often felt those exclusions were tantamount to exclusion from citizenship. Women and landless men rarely used the language of rights, possession, or universalism, instead articulating their marginalization. Not only were most women excluded from landownership, but they were often barred from inhabiting public political spaces such as baraza, and they frequently recounted that rural bureaucrats refused to offer women the development services provided to men. Over the course of her adulthood, Eunice Tele Maiyo, a Nandi woman, lived on several different Rift Valley properties that her husband owned. As one of three co-wives, Maiyo lived only with her children and served as the farm caretaker. She participated in local groups and recounted meeting government officials through church. Despite this relatively privileged position, Maiyo defined citizens thus: "It was those who were among me, but it wasn't me."[47] Women's broad exclusion from development, especially landownership, and from actively participating in civic arenas, shaped a set of political philosophies that emphasized their denial of full citizenship rights.

Landless men, too, recalled feelings of marginalization. Daniel Kebeney Bitok, the Nandi man who described his desire to take on citizenly duties, squatted in the forest for over a decade before acquiring a small piece of land. He said, "Before I settled anywhere, I didn't recognize myself as a *mwananchi* [citizen]. But after getting this land, I called myself a mwananchi. I thought I belonged to somewhere else, not Kenya, before getting land."[48] Bitok understood his belonging within the nation as directly correlated to landownership. He conveyed how he wanted to be legible to the state, and he believed his legibility was dependent on a land title. Bitok added that after purchasing property, "it was easy for the government to trace my whereabouts, because of plot numbers, and to bring services to me."[49]

Because citizenship could act as an exclusionary and unpredictable framework, and because nonstate institutions offered some of the services that the state inconsistently provided, Kenyans also looked to local and international bodies to preserve old relationships, construct new ones, and to create alternate, pluralistic forms of citizenship. Often, marginalized Kenyans responded to their exclusion by turning inward, by drawing on kin and ethnic networks.[50] These relationships produced another set of expected rights and obligations, also negotiated and differentiated. Though ethnic institutions generally subordinated individual rights to the advancement of the whole, multiple animations of ethnicity and ethnic citizenship existed, derived from divergent ideas about morality, community, and belonging.

Among the Nandi, the most populous ethnic group in the Uasin Gishu region, communal claims to the fertile Rift Valley highlands—an important site of development—eclipsed almost all else. Moral economies continually evolved through debate and centered upon egalitarianism and reciprocity, encouraging Nandi communities, when able, to protect their members from insecurities. The *tiliet*—Nandi who call one another by relationship terms—enforced these codes of behavior.[51] Village elders and *kokwet* (neighborhood) leaders coordinated food donations to widows, the elderly, and the poor. The community, in turn, expected individuals to contribute to the common good, and Nandi proverbs reveal some citizen-society relationship norms. "Ta ng'enam tany chotin kongeet met" (When the hind legs hold a cow, it should support itself by standing on the front legs) reminded those who benefited from communal aid to give back. Indeed, when Nandi worked hard and contributed to shared success, they, too, could expect to prosper. The proverb "Makinamei beny birir ei buch" (One cannot touch the blood of an ox without eating the meat) confirmed that those who helped with slaughtering or communal work more generally would benefit individually as well.[52]

For the Nandi, as for other communities, ideas of authority and morality became highly contested during decolonization. Generational conflicts heightened as young, Western-educated nationalists entered politics, further upending the gerontocratic order. Christian elites continued to monopolize elected positions, but teetotaling evangelicals were ousted by less-rigid Catholics, who espoused populist politics. In the 1961 Legislative Council elections—contested by Jean-Marie Seroney and Shadrack Kimalel—Nandi voters demonstrated their investment in both ethnic and national politics. Seen as the establishment candidate and already suspect for his abstention from alcohol, voters criticized Kimalel on cultural terms. He was condemned for not undergoing the rite of circumcision and for marrying a widow.[53] Seroney—an unmarried youngster who had not built a house in Nandi—hardly fulfilled "customary" requirements. Yet, as a Catholic and a drinker, Seroney's candidacy signified dismantling the control of the deplored protestant elite and restoring traditional social relations around the beer pot. Indeed, when a Kimalel supporter called Seroney "*chemurandan*" (a pejorative term meaning variously lowly, filthy, a drunk), it only bolstered Seroney's lead.[54] The Nandi elected Seroney in a landslide. In doing so, they demanded space within the national public sphere and, simultaneously, reconsidered ethnic principles on expected sociality and good leadership.

Central to Seroney's long-standing popularity was his articulation of autochthonous ideas about land and belonging. While many ethnic patriots found such positions attractive, Seroney's platform also created tensions. By the time Seroney ran for elected office, the new Kalenjin ethnonym had gained resonance and relevance, bringing together the Nandi, Kipsigis, Tugen, Keiyo, Marakwet, Pokot, Sabaot, and Terik communities. Though the Kalenjin confederacy was founded on linguistic and cultural affinities, geography, and shared politics, divisions always existed. Many Kalenjin communities resented that missionaries used the Nandi language for translations of Bible passages and grammars.[55] The Kipsigis and the Nandi—the most populous and economically developed subgroups—fought for the first Bible translation to be completed in their respective dialects, and they also competed for the leadership of the Kalenjin. Though the Tugen ultimately won this contest, Daniel arap Moi's ascendance created a lasting schism.[56] Divisions were not limited to the educated elite or to intergroup political rivalries. Disagreements over boundaries, land claims, mobile women, resource allocation, and stock theft continually divided the Kalenjin, as did differences between highland and lowland communities, rural versus urban dwellers, and between Catholics and evangelicals.[57] Such tensions were always latent, and as they waxed and waned over the late colonial and early postcolonial periods, so, too, did popular attachment to this broader political subjectivity.

During this period, Kenyans began thinking not only beyond their particular villages and ethnic groups, but beyond their nation, to the continent and even to the world. Some rural Kenyans saw all black struggles as inherently connected, and thus felt obligated to support the antiapartheid movement and the American civil rights movement, regarding Nelson Mandela and Martin Luther King Jr. as leaders.[58] At this same time, some Kenyans recognized Kennedy and Nikita Khrushchev as patrons, along with other foreign donors and transnational institutions.[59] These more expansive political imaginations were the result not only of the provision of international development, but of improved media access and nationalist discourse.[60] The 1960 KANU manifesto critiqued apartheid as a component of its party platform, and Kenyatta spoke frequently about a united Africa.[61] Clearly, Kenyans participated in multiple publics and enacted subnational, national, and international citizenships simultaneously.

The political imagination of rural Kenyans might have been both narrower and broader than the geographic boundaries of the new nation-state as they looked both within and beyond their local communities to forge better futures. Ethnic patriots fortified their affinities, farmers formed links to black market traders, rural women made connections to create self-help groups, Kenyans of various backgrounds appealed to Jomo Kenyatta, and occasionally individuals—such as Omwando—petitioned international politicians. Over time, all of these actors started to possess firmer ideas about what constituted development, about the obligations of the government and other institutional bodies, and about the rights and responsibilities of citizens.

While there is a robust scholarship on the state and on rural resistance in colonial Kenya, there is little historical scholarship on Kenya's postcolonial politics.[62] Political scientists published the vast majority of research on independent Kenya in the 1970s and 1980s.[63] This literature focused almost exclusively on rural class differentiation, leaving many questions unanswered. Of the few historical works that examine Kenyan statecraft in the postcolonial era, most approach independent politics from elite perspectives.[64] Both the colonial and postcolonial historiographies have also centered primarily on ethnicity. Though ethnic identity has, undoubtedly, made a deep imprint on modern Kenya, it has never operated in isolation, but in conjunction with class, gender, kinship, generation, citizenship, and more.[65] Indeed, the coexistence of and subsequent tensions between these layered identities have contributed to the making of complex and contradictory political subjectivities. Building on Julie MacArthur's research on pluralist thinking, this study foregrounds the pluralist identities of ordinary Kenyans but expands the lens of analysis beyond the ethnos.[66] Examining identity at multiple scales and in multiple registers helps us to understand how Kenyans actually lived their lives and imagined their place in the world.

Uasin Gishu provides a particularly good case study for examining these questions. The district's population is, and was, multiethnic—composed of multiple subgroups of the Kalenjin, as well as Kikuyu, Luyia, Luo, and Kisii.

With the transition to independence, and the purchasing of former white settler farms, Uasin Gishu's population came to be marked by ethnic heterogeneity and by class diversity as wealthier Kenyans bought large farms in close proximity to smallholder settlement schemes and squatter villages.[67] During decolonization, Uasin Gishu was an important site of developmental intervention, and it thus became a site of resource competition and contested claims-making. Attending to the experiences of Uasin Gishu's residents not only reorients the scholarship away from ethnic paradigms and elite politics, but it reveals how a diverse set of Kenyans made claims by exploiting old connections while creating new ones, often drawing on multiple identities simultaneously.

UASIN GISHU AND THE WORLD

Uasin Gishu is a place that has at times been perceived as historically incidental.[68] The name Uasin Gishu comes from the eponymous Maasai subgroup (or *olosho*), who, during various periods, lived in the area.[69] It also denotes two geographical regions—a plateau on the northwestern edge of the Kenyan Rift Valley highlands and a district (later, a county) in modern Kenya.[70] While the plateau developed close to a million years ago when tectonic plates pulled apart forming the East African Rift, the district is a human invention of more recent, imperial origins. As such, the district's boundaries—and geographical scope—have proved susceptible to change. In contrast, since its emergence, the Rift Valley has remained a steady and striking score on the landscape, running thousands of miles and cutting across the entire length of Kenya. On either side of the valley lie Kenya's famously fecund highlands, of which Uasin Gishu is a part. Surrounded by numberless rolling hills, the flat grasslands of the Uasin Gishu plateau are visually and environmentally distinct, "a pastoralist's paradise."[71] The proximity of the two environments—fertile hills and drier plateau—has historically been complementary to agropastoral livelihoods and conducive to reciprocal trading relationships among agrarian and pastoralist communities.

Uasin Gishu constitutes the mooring for this book because it has been the mooring for a diverse and unique set of historical actors. With its fertile lands, assorted microecologies, and borderlands location, Uasin Gishu has unceasingly drawn varied groups whose encounters and innovations have propelled historical change. These same natural resources later transformed Uasin Gishu into a site of development intervention. More so than the region itself, the book centers on the changing people who have inhabited this place. Newcomers have not only sustained the region's pluralism but also generated its dynamic encounters—of trading and raiding, integration and division, cooperation and conflict.[72]

Uasin Gishu's longer ethnohistory molded the years that followed, with three main threads emerging.[73] First, Uasin Gishu was the site of successive migrations—from its precolonial past where the political economy depended upon mobile livelihoods, to its colonial past where European settlers and African labor migrants moved in, to the postcolonial era where resettlement programs and a developmentalist order brought new African residents and temporary foreign "experts." Second, these successive migrations have shaped contested, competing identities. Land is the final thread and must be read through the previous two: migration and political identity. Though people had been the means by which early African communities prospered, with colonial rule and the appropriation of Kenya's fertile highlands, land became the means by which communities aimed to sustain themselves, and the imagined ground upon which ethnic and national citizenships were adjudicated.

By the late first millennium, a group of Southern Nilotic peoples, who would later come to be called the Kalenjin, particularly the Nandi subgroup, migrated to the hills surrounding the Uasin Gishu plateau. They dwelled in small, scattered homesteads and assimilated the North Rift Cushites who preceded them.[74] Their neighbors would be Bantu and Nilotic, agriculturalist and pastoralist. The Nandi dual agropastoral economy meant they relied less on external trading relationships, and their military prowess and cattle raiding meant that they made some enemies, though they also cooperated with other communities.[75]

Nandi precolonial political institutions bore the marks of many East African societies. Leadership roles were not hereditary and were determined by seniority, gender, ambition, merit, and social position—based on personal attachments, obligations, and wealth. The *kokwet*, or neighborhood, was the most important political unit, and geographic proximity served as a foundation for Nandi relationships. The saying "Kii ibunegeey maat" (We get fire from each other) expresses the close bond of neighbors, who shared this vital element that warmed, illuminated, and nourished.[76] The Nandi had no chiefs. Decisions were made in councils, which any man could attend.[77] At this time, other Kalenjin groups called the Nandi the *Chemngal* (many words), on account of the vigorous deliberations that occurred.[78] Egalitarianism and mutuality underpinned Nandi moral ethnicity. These values, and the emphasis on spatiality, would remain central to Nandi ideologies, even after the political order transformed under colonial, then independent, rule.

Sometime before 1800, Maasai crossed the escarpments into the western highlands and took control of much of the plateau.[79] Throughout the nineteenth century, however, the power of the once supreme Maasai declined.[80] In the mid-nineteenth century, the Nandi recovered much of the land.[81] They also integrated the refugee prophets of the Maasai into their own group of diviners, the *orkoiik* (*orkoiyot*, sing.).[82] Nandi had long believed in the supernatural powers of orkoiik and relied on them for rainmaking, advising, and averting misfortune.[83] One Maasai prophet soon amassed a large following, eventually serving all Nandi. The rise of a paramount orkoiyot centralized politico-cosmological authority.[84]

The newfound success of the Nandi would be brief, but the 1880s represented their golden age. While prosperity shifted frequently in the Rift Valley, a symmetry of sorts remained in place until the end of the nineteenth century. Land, labor, and cattle—the hallmarks of precolonial East Africa—provided checks on power and accumulation.[85] While societies sought to accumulate cattle and land, they also had to accumulate dependents to herd the cattle, work the land, and defend both from others.[86] People would not labor without gaining a portion of the wealth, thus moderating stratification. Shared safety nets provided security in precarious settings. Fluid identities allowed the vulnerable to be absorbed into new communities. Cattle loaning safeguarded herds from epizootics, and diverse agricultural production and ecological systems provided some security from environmental failure. Trading allowed agriculturalists to convert produce into cattle, a more secure form of wealth. Herds, territory, and dependents inevitably expanded and contracted, but in times of crisis, highland residents could rely on their reciprocal relationships for survival.[87] While the political climate changed dramatically in the years to come, these social ideologies premised on egalitarianism, and expectations of protection would remain steadfast.

In the 1880s, highland safety nets began to break down. Bovine pleuropneumonia and rinderpest epidemics swept through East Africa in rapid, cyclical succession, ravaging herds to unprecedented degrees.[88] In the Rift Valley, drought, locusts, famine, smallpox, jiggers, and sleeping sickness followed.[89] Both human and cattle deaths are thought to have been immense.[90] The almost complete collapse of the stock economy transformed relationships of power and shifted patterns of accumulation to agricultural production.[91] This was especially destructive for the Maasai, and a little less so for the Nandi, though they too experienced much calamity.

The Nandi emerged from these disasters relatively unscathed, but this was just the first phase of catastrophe. In 1890, blaming the chief orkoiyot, Kimnyolei, for the misfortune, a group of Nandi assassinated him.[92] His

FIGURE A.1. Uasin Gishu railway, 2018. Photo courtesy of Joe Martinez.

murder portended greater catastrophe. Just before his death, Kimnyolei prophesied that foreigners would come to rule, and an iron snake spewing smoke would cut across Kenya from the Indian Ocean to Lake Victoria.[93] Despite his precise divination and dramatic death, Kimnyolei's legacy would be eclipsed by that of his son, Koitalel arap Samoei. Koitalel spearheaded the struggle against British conquest from 1895 to 1906, triggered by the extension of the railway line—the iron snake—into Nandi territory.[94]

The Nandi reacted to colonial incursion with intermittent raids, and the British reciprocated with punitive expeditions.[95] Despite early failures, colonial administrators continued to encroach on Nandi territory and to employ greater force.[96] By 1901 the railroad was completed, and the British were determined to finish their conquest as well.[97] For this, the new railway provided aid, transporting larger bodies of troops.[98] The railroad first traversed Nandi territory, provoking conflict, and eventually became one of the technologies buttressing British victory. Later, it would become a technology of extraction, exporting Uasin Gishu's commercial agricultural products.

The Nandi resisted conquest vehemently. The use of Nilotic age sets and Bantu territorial-clan organization helped foster broad cooperation.[99] Age sets cut across all Nandi communities, establishing males as elders, warriors, or boys, and *pororosiek* (military, territorial units) organized regiments. Both played an integral part in coordinating military action and mobilizing labor.[100] The wars with the Maasai and the rise of a chief orkoiyot further united the Nandi.[101] Yet, during conquest, these unifying forces proved to contain dangerous undersides. The Maasai recovered after their own decline by serving as levies in the increasingly lethal colonial army.[102] By the end of the resistance, the Nandi had incurred immense casualties—about seventeen hundred Nandi were killed, around 5 percent of the population.[103] The reliance on the orkoiyot's leadership concentrated authority. In December 1905, a British captain shot and killed Koitalel—likely unarmed under a truce—and by 1906, the Nandi had been defeated.[104]

Conquest's impact was considerable and enduring.[105] British rule devastated the highland equilibrium. In place of the system of managing risk through reciprocity and diverse agropastoral production, the British instituted indirect rule. The Crown Lands Ordinance established European rights to "unoccupied" or "uncultivated land."[106] The colonial state forced Kenyans into "native reserves," inhibiting their movement and curtailing their interactions with others. Both the Nandi practice of shifting cultivation and their land tenure system of occupancy rights relied on mobility and surplus land.[107] Kenyan ethnic identities became more fixed, cattle loaning practices were circumscribed, and agricultural trade was regulated. Societal stratification grew.

In 1908, Europeans began settling Uasin Gishu. Though immigration was an old phenomenon in the region, this was fundamentally different. Uasin Gishu became part of the scheduled areas, or "white highlands," where Europeans developed an economy based on the large-scale farming of cash crops. The location of the Nandi reserve, in an area less suitable to agropastoralism and separated from important grazing land and salt licks, brought hardships. The minimization of available land and coercive colonial policies—taxation and depasturization—drove Kenyans back to Uasin Gishu to work on European farms.[108] European settlers there used the Nandi as a labor reserve, establishing a system dependent upon "squatters" or labor-tenants.

Throughout the twentieth century, Europeans demanded increasing days of labor from squatters in exchange for worsening cultivation rights.[109] After World War I, the British took an additional 278 square kilometers of the Nandi reserve, displacing between 1,500 and 2,250 people. The area accounted for one-seventh of the reserve, and, as Nandi anger swelled, their identity became more indelibly attached to recovering land.[110] The cash-crop economy also became further entrenched in the interwar period, and European settlers in Uasin Gishu solicited the labor of the Kikuyu, new entrants to the region, as well as the Luyia, longtime neighbors of the

Kalenjin.[111] This migration, like that of European settlers, represented a historical process profoundly different from that of the precolonial era. The capitalist economy fostered competition rather than cooperation. Since conquest, reclamation, territoriality, and spatial logic had subsumed Nandi political thought. Land restitution, framed in autochthonous terms, invigorated Nandi patriotism, and they eyed the newcomers warily.

The events leading up to decolonization began in the 1930s and 1940s as African trade unionists went on strike, the British colonial state embraced developmentalist rule, African *askari* (soldiers) fought in World War II, and nationalists forced colonial officials to make concessions.[112] During the war, the British administration published newssheets and produced radio broadcasts in vernacular languages to recruit Africans.[113] Wartime radio correspondent John arap Chemallan coined the term "Kalenjin" at this time—derived from *kalenjok*, which means "I tell you" or "I say to you." Chemallan began each of his radio programs using this expression. The rising educated elite at Nairobi's Alliance High School took up the term, forming the Kalenjin Club in 1944.[114] The circulation of state media coincided with a general growth in publishing and broadcasting. In 1939, the Africa Inland Mission (AIM) published the first Nandi-language Bible.[115]

After the war, the linguistic work continued. Elite Nandi, Kipsigis, Tugen, Keiyo, Marakwet, Pokot, Sabaot, and Terik men formed a language committee to develop a standard orthography. Their broader goal was to achieve a "closer union" by making available common reading materials.[116] Postwar Kenya also saw the unmatched growth of vernacular media. In addition to the mission and government newspapers aimed at African audiences, Kenyans started some fifty-six newspapers in the decade following the war.[117] With the invention of the cheaper and longer-lasting transistor in 1948, African radio purchases skyrocketed.[118] The expansion of outlets allowed Kenyans to actively engage in new ethnic, national, and global public spheres.

Simultaneously, European settlers achieved greater prosperity in a booming economy, using profits to mechanize their farms and expel African laborers. The Mau Mau rebellion stemmed from these changes, as disenchanted Kikuyu men forced off highland farms returned to native reserves where they no longer possessed land rights. Mau Mau catalyzed major development intervention as the colonial state responded to unrest with land reform.[119] Land reform only heightened anxieties, as the emergence of a more permanent landed class—with individual registrations and titles—in turn created a more permanent landless one, comprising those denied the land security the program offered.

The Mau Mau Emergency drove other important historical changes. As a target site for state propaganda, the Rift Valley saw greater media expansion. By 1953, close to thirty-five hours of weekly broadcasting occurred in vernacular languages. The colonial government loaned out 350 radio sets and used a loudspeaker system to broadcast in urban areas.[120] These vernacular communications increasingly resonated with audiences in the 1950s, helping to spawn a new collectivity, the Kalenjin. Among the Kalenjin, media growth was especially pronounced. By 1957, there were 406 talk shows in the Kalenjin language, and the monthly paper, *Kalenjin*, had the largest circulation of any government newssheet.[121] This new ethnic appellation integrated but never replaced subgroups, allowing diverse identities to coexist with the corporate identity.[122] Though Kalenjin leaders drew on autochthonous language to galvanize their constituents, the uniform discourse disguised the continual challenges to communal cohesion. This diverse community made up of members with competing interests and ideologies was always inherently fragile.

Mau Mau also accelerated processes of decolonization, as the State of Emergency and a changing global setting pushed the British to leave. The British announced forthcoming independence in 1961, and Kenyan leaders and the British government began negotiations. The Kenya African National Union (KANU), which primarily represented the Kikuyu and the Luo, argued for a strong, national government. The Kenya African Democratic Union (KADU) represented the so-called minority ethnic groups, allied with European settlers, and had British government support. KADU advocated for *majimboism*—a complex federal-style government that allowed for regional autonomy and vested power in local governments.[123] At the close of the negotiations in 1963, the outcome remained ambiguous. The alliance with the settlers skewed power dynamics in favor of KADU, but the party did not possess the backing to win a popular vote. Though the final conference called for majimboism, Kenyan elections placed Jomo Kenyatta and KANU, overwhelmingly, in power. By 1964, Kenyatta had abolished the federal government structure, KADU had dissolved, and Kenya had become a de facto one-party state.[124] Though Kenya would remain under one-party rule for much of the next three decades, state actors and Kenyan citizens remained fiercely divided over whether and how resources should be redistributed.[125]

Decolonization entailed much more than political sovereignty.[126] In preparation for independence, the British colonial government, the World Bank, and others began implementing development programs, which facilitated a final stage of migration to Uasin Gishu. Not only did African families resettle through these programs, but new foreigners arrived too. They were more transient and less explicitly imperialist than their predecessors—development experts from the United Kingdom, the United States, West Germany, Norway, Japan, and Israel, among others.

Uasin Gishu's layered histories—as home to changing communities, as a space of diverse labor migration, and as a locale of land resettlement—set up this fertile district as a site of contestation. In Uasin Gishu, Kenyans debated how citizens became endowed with rights, aspiring political leaders gained or lost authority, and Kenyans reworked their ideas on justice and equality in a cosmopolitan context. For many Nandi, resistance to British conquest figured prominently in their ethnonationalist imagination, and ideas of autochthony and reparations underwrote Kalenjin postcolonial claims-making. For Uasin Gishu residents from other ethnic communities—particularly the Kikuyu and the Luyia—labor histories, national citizenship, and conflicting notions of territoriality substantiated competing claims. Yet the ethnic group represented but one community, one institution. The mid-twentieth century was marked by an uptick in ethnonationalism, by nationalism, and also by flourishing internationalism. As Kenyans made claims, and as they imagined and built a future, ethnic citizenships took on new significations, national citizenship became invigorated with multiple meanings, and global citizenships coalesced as well.

CHAPTER OUTLINE

This book centers on the 1960s and 1970s—two of Kenya's most formative decades for the establishment of development practice and a modern political order. What follows from this introduction does not progress in strict chronological order but represents a series of thematic studies with a narrative arc.[127] Every chapter examines development programs that politicians, development practitioners, and rural Kenyans considered significant. Each chapter also pieces together how these projects were conceived, contested, and reconfigured in local settings among a diverse set of actors, and each elucidates the emergence of postcolonial political practices.

The seven chapters that follow might be thought of in a series of groups. Chapters 1 through 3 deal with land, while chapters 4 and 5 turn to agricultural development, production, and marketing. Chapters 6 and 7 focus on nonagricultural development in the form of community development (primarily health care, education, and infrastructure) and industrial development. Each chapter extends from the local to the global. All of the chapters, additionally, work to show the breadth of rural Kenyan experiences, with an emphasis on growing inequality stemming from uneven access to development.

Since land and farming were (and are) fundamental to Kenyan imaginaries and to the Kenyan economy, the first five chapters focus on land and agricultural development. Chapters 1 through 3 center on Kenyans who sought land access during decolonization. Migration always entails ruptures and rebuilding, and, as Kenyans moved during decolonization, they constituted and reconstituted communities. The chapters on land, especially chapters 2 and 3, explore how identities evolved in this context, examining how ethnicity, class, and gender identities intersected and were reconfigured.

Chapter 1 explores Kenya's largest land resettlement program, the Million Acre Scheme. Between 1962 and 1967, this state-sponsored and internationally financed program settled close to half a million people on new farms. More than just a land transfer, this program included agricultural development, financing, marketing, and community planning. Land resettlement relied upon an enormous bureaucratic apparatus, which spanned three continents, involved a multitude of donors, and merited its own ministry within the Kenyan state. Even so, its high-modernist ambitions were frequently undermined in local settings. Land resettlement engendered contestations: both local and national elites subverted legislation to distribute land to their supporters. Ultimately, this contributed to a sense of state unpredictability and meant that Kenyans experienced land resettlement, and its connected agricultural aid, erratically and unevenly.

Chapter 2 continues to focus on the Million Acre Scheme but takes a bottom-up approach. While chapter 1 foregrounds institutional actors and land policy, chapter 2 provides comparative social histories of three settlement schemes, focusing on the experiences of settlers from different ethnic groups. The chapter illustrates how ethnic identity played a part in differentiating colonial and postcolonial experiences, and how ethnic ideologies shaped divergent strands of political thought about rights to land, political justice, and notions of belonging in the new nation. Even so, the chapter also exposes a surprising set of cleavages—not just interethnic but also intraethnic. In a context of land competition, political alliances and ethnic affinities were easily fractured, revealing competing geographic imaginations, incompatible ideas about land rights, and the localized contours of postcolonial debate. Kenyans drew on multiple political subjectivities not only to access land, but to make meaning of citizenship.

In spite of land resettlement programs, many Kenyans remained landless. Chapter 3 provides a historical account of those excluded from landownership—squatters and women. The chapter begins with an examination of state settlement programs aimed at squatters. Though these programs achieved one of their goals—tempering rural unrest—they still left many Kenyans without land. As opportunities closed, squatters often joined land-buying companies, pooling their money together to purchase plots privately. However, with little government oversight, the leaders of land-buying companies frequently defrauded their partners, leaving their names off title deeds and leaving squatters without land or their savings. The second part of chapter 3 turns to the position of women, who were excluded from land settlement opportunities and marginalized from exercising full ownership rights to family land or farm property. Even so, the chapter shows that these rights were negotiated through familial relationships and women's experiences differed considerably. The evidence, on the whole, demonstrates the complexity of land tenure and ownership in postcolonial Kenya—a setting where gradations of rights, and hence of citizenship, existed. The last section of the chapter explores how exclusion from state resources shaped political imaginaries—how landless Kenyans assessed the postcolonial state, crafted notions of citizenship, and evaluated independence.

Chapters 4 and 5 turn to agricultural development, with a focus on three interconnected issues—crop marketing, cooperative societies, and famine relief. These chapters continue to explore questions of citizenship and development, though they shift focus to debates over the economic duties of citizens. Both chapters also explore the ways in which rural Kenyans pushed back against ideas of citizenship that did not coincide with their own visions, and simultaneously demanded that the state take on greater obligations.

Chapter 4 examines cooperative development programs. The postcolonial Kenyan state tasked cooperatives with essential bureaucratic and authoritative functions and gave these organizations immense legal powers. Both the independent Kenyan state and transnational institutions encouraged the creation of cooperatives to provide farming services, regulate production, and ensure the payment of internationally financed loans and national agricultural taxes. Members were legally compelled to sell their crops to cooperative societies. The cooperatives sold these products on to state marketing boards, and then paid individual farmers after deducting loans and taxes. Through cooperatives, policymakers attempted to create a direct channel from rural farms to state markets, and to recast citizenly duty around rational economic conduct. State officials invoked an idea of civic duty where good Kenyans became devoted cooperative members and responsible borrowers. However, with almost unchecked power, cooperatives rarely served rural Kenyans, or the state, as planned. Thus Kenyan farmers asserted their rights as citizens to economic freedoms, refusing to engage with their cooperatives. Ultimately, local dissatisfaction catalyzed the fall of cooperative development, and the rise of postcolonial black market agricultural trade, with implications for both the Kenyan Treasury and Kenyan citizens.

In the mid-1960s, a drought precipitated a shortage of maize, Kenya's staple food. The drought quickly turned into a crisis of greater proportions than the dry weather warranted. Breakdowns in agricultural production and marketing proved to be a root cause as well. Kenyan farmers were avoiding the government-regulated market and, instead, selling maize into a "black market" that exported the product to Uganda and Tanzania. The subsequent relief efforts then became marred by a scandal. Daily newspaper coverage and a high-profile commission of inquiry revealed that state mishandling of American famine aid resulted from disorganization and cronyism, as politicians sold imported foodstuffs to their political networks. The maize crisis of 1964–66 brought questions about economic citizenship and state obligation to the forefront, and chapter 5 explores the public debate. Similar to cooperatives, through agricultural marketing policy the state fashioned ideas about citizenship, which prescribed particular forms of economic behavior. State actors envisioned Kenyans citizens not only as responsible borrowers but also as reliable and loyal producers who would sell exclusively to state markets. However, Kenyans contested the limits this citizenship placed on their economic autonomy and their agricultural profitability. Though they abjured a form of citizenship characterized by economic restrictions, many Kenyans imagined and enacted a form of citizenly duty that entailed building the nation by feeding it. They also expressed disappointment in a state that refused to take on the most basic obligation of providing famine relief.

Chapters 6 and 7 change directions, moving from agricultural development to community development and industrial development. Chapter 6 continues to explore questions of state obligation and postcolonial governance by examining negotiations over self-help. For community development programming, the independent Kenyan state drew on colonial strategies, which had also become increasingly popular in international development arenas. Kenyan government officials made self-help a central tenet of the state-citizen relationship, a relationship where the state helped only those who first helped themselves. Through self-help, state actors foisted responsibility for local development onto communities. This chapter shows that citizens keenly took up local projects, but in the process, they contested the development priorities of the state. Citizens and local groups shouldered immense burdens for contributing to their own development. When they refused to heed the advice of local officials, or to follow state protocol in building their institutions, rural communities asserted their rights to local autonomy and to enacting their own developmental visions. With the state often unable to contribute to these projects, elite Kenyans and nonstate organizations interceded, shaping expectations for more limited state obligations in the future. At the same time, in compelling communities to generate local development, self-help compounded regional and local inequalities as wealthier regions initiated more expensive projects and marginalized community members were excluded from planning processes.

Chapter 7 continues to examine contestations over development but explores a single project, a World Bank–funded paper factory. Between 1963 and 1978, squatters resisted this project. They refused to move from forestry locations, they uprooted trees intended as raw materials for the factory, and they sent delegations to President Kenyatta, demanding of him, "Are you planting trees or are you planting people?" Squatters were asking Kenyatta whether he supported a forest-and-paper industry program or a settlement program, since the two projects had been planned on the same land. This chapter focuses on the relationship between the rural squatters who resisted the project and the political elites who intervened, particularly President Kenyatta. Together, these two groups negotiated the modification of a major development program, and they worked out broader questions about political authority and political culture. In negotiating development, rural actors and political elites decided how resources would be distributed, and they entered into new patronage-based relationships. The chapter touches on many of the book's broader themes—local reformulations of development; conflicting visions of Kenya's economic and political future; contestation over citizens' differentiated rights to land and employment; and deliberations over the authority and legitimacy of leaders. In examining an internationally funded, state-led program that brought together a range of government ministries but also produced local level resistance, the Turbo Afforestation program offers a microcosm of the early postcolonial setting. It illustrates the range of actors that 1960s development brought together and the political issues these programs raised and resolved.

The conclusion provides a summary of the book's arguments, linking these histories to more recent national discussions and to the current politics of development. The chapter provides analysis of the 2010 Kenyan constitutional referendum and the two most recent national elections, which revived independence-era debates about whether the government structure should be centralized or devolved. These debates demonstrate that such questions remain fiercely contested as politicians continue to derive authority from controlling the allocation of development. The conclusion also tracks the longer outcomes of the decolonizing development programs explored in the body of the book, with attention to how they have been shaped by more intensive neoliberal policies. The chapter examines the indebtedness of rural landowners, the demise of self-help projects, and the collapse of the paper factory. Each contemporary appraisal reaffirms that the political and economic outcomes of decolonizing development projects were complex and ambivalent but also enduring. Though such programs often did not produce the desired results, development had profound material and political ramifications, extending inequalities and contributing to the creation of postcolonial political ideologies and practices.

A NOTE ON SOURCES AND METHODS

A single, inconspicuous sentence in a 1966 Ministry of Economic Planning and Development memorandum raises an important evidentiary problem for scholars of international development. The memo's author notes, "There were many approved development projects and schemes which had yet to be carried out."[128] While development plans provide rich insights into the thinking of technocrats, they tell us very little about how, and whether, development programs were implemented on the ground, or about how they were received, interpreted, and reworked by local people. The disjunctures between promises, plans, and practices, and the competing ideologies of different actors, tend to become flattened in reports composed to secure funding, exhibit success, and demonstrate consensus on best practices.

This book is based on two years of oral and archival research in Kenya, the United Kingdom, and the United States.[129] The various research sites speak to the cosmopolitan nature of rural Kenya, but also to the—at times—unlikely relationships that international development nurtured in the mid-twentieth century. Some of these places will be familiar to the reader, but many likely will not: Nairobi, Lumakanda, London, Tapsagoi, Washington, DC, Sosiani, Cambridge, Nakuru, Sugoi, Boston, Chekalini, Eldoret, Kakamega, College Park, Leseru, Oxford, Mautuma, Wheaton, and Webuye. These locations—from the Rift Valley highlands to Nairobi government buildings to the Western offices of transnational institutions—represent some of the many spaces that decolonizing development interventions brought together.

Oral histories are integral to this project, as they complicate the largely state-centric account in public records.[130] They also bring life to the historical narrative and contribute important insights into rural political imaginations. I spoke with 111 rural Kenyans at eight sites.[131] These interviews took place largely on the western border of Uasin Gishu County, but a good number took place in what is now Kakamega County.[132] The majority of people I spoke with were women, most were farmers, a few were former agricultural officials, some were squatters, some were landowners, and some were relatively wealthy, but the majority lived modest lives. They were Kalenjin (Nandi subgroup), Luyia (primarily the Maragoli subgroup), and Kikuyu, and they ranged in age from about sixty to one hundred. These actors participated in, shaped, and were shaped by numerous political, economic, and social institutions, such as self-help groups, women's associations, microfinancing organizations, ethnic groups, churches, cooperative societies, county councils, the Kenyan state, and the International Monetary Fund (IMF). Thus the rural Kenyans I spoke with engaged in various ways with many of the people who populated these institutions (and who populated the archival pages)—with chiefs, local bureaucrats, national politicians, the Kenyan president, Peace Corps volunteers, and World Bank officials, among many, many others. In writing, I have endeavored to simultaneously hold on to these different accounts, in the moments they neatly converged as well as in the moments they drifted apart. Both are revealing.

I always sought to have those I spoke with guide our discussion. I used an open-ended interview guide to better understand local histories through personal narratives. I drew on my archival research—both the information contained therein and that which was absent—to formulate the initial set of questions. I began with life histories and then moved on to questions about development.[133] I was especially interested in how Kenyans sought assistance—from the state, their communities, or NGOs. Next, I inquired about their social lives and local politics—how the lives of men and women differed, how they engaged with their ethnic communities, and how they accessed land, health care, agricultural assistance, and education. Last, I asked questions about the meaning of development and citizenship after independence. My questions evolved over time, as I gained a better understanding of the various ways the people I spoke with understood their own histories. I visited many people three, four, or five times to follow up on comments they had made, or to seek clarification about material I did not understand. These oral histories helped make clearer how rural decolonization unfolded on the ground.

As with archival documents, oral histories must be read against the grain. In some instances, the Kenyans I spoke with likely constructed narratives to elicit empathy. But in doing so, they were narrating what they had come to see as constituting injustice. In other instances, Kenyans narrated oral histories that contradicted one another, or contradicted archival evidence. These were often moments of critical importance because they revealed the contours of debate, sometimes about national politics or development policy, but just as often about disagreements over class, gender, labor, and

FIGURE A.2. Some of the interview subjects for this book. All photos courtesy of Joe Martinez.

William Serem, Leseru, 2018

Rael Serem, Leseru, 2018

Pauline Tum, Leseru, 2018

Jotham Njau Mwangi, Lumakanda, 2018

Nora Kasigene, Lumakanda, 2018

Karen Misavo, Lumakanda, 2018

Daniel Kebeney Bitok, Leseru, 2018

Ainea Alulu, Lumakanda, 2018

community belonging. Uasin Gishu has also been the site of interethnic violence, which shaped the memories of residents in different ways.[134] The reader will thus often find comparative analysis of rural experiences in place of a neat narrative.

This study also draws on a range of archival sources. In Kenya, where I spent the vast majority of my research time, I worked with records from a number of government ministries, including land and settlement, community development, local government, cooperatives, industry, natural resources, and the Office of the President. Within these folders, district and ministerial reports and development plans were deposited. I focused greater attention on uncovering more nuanced records that did not obscure debate, such as rural petitions to political leaders, local government meeting minutes, testimonies to national commissions of inquiry, and bureaucratic correspondence. Rural voices and ideas do not come through unmediated in these texts, even when rural Kenyans ostensibly represented themselves with petitions. The intended readers and the writers' motivations shape the epistolary content, language, and form.[135] Yet such petitions—like Omwando's to JFK—reveal the types of claims Kenyans believed they could make, offering important insights into their political ideologies.

At the US National Archives, the World Bank Group Archives, the Kennedy Library, the British National Archives, the special collections at Oxford, Cambridge, and the School of Oriental and African Studies, the Africa Inland Mission Regional Office Archives, and the Archives of the Billy Graham Center, I examined sources ranging from correspondence between British and Kenyan policymakers to NGO records and USAID documents. These records provided a largely top-down view, though they also provided evidence of contestations over development among a wider range of actors and of fractures within state bodies and transnational institutions. Drawing on multisited archival and oral sources offers a rich picture of engagement between these many actors.

1 "Can I Be One of Them?"

The Landscapes of Settlement in Decolonizing Kenya

A WAVE OF LETTERS BEGAN hitting the desks of Kenyan officials during the early 1960s. In one such letter, from June 1960, Ndugu Kariuki, a landless Kikuyu farmer, wrote to the Ministry of Agriculture and the district commissioner of Uasin Gishu: "I beg to submit this my application and forward my cries to you that, it is not so long since I heard you are giving some people 50 acres in Highland Farm, can I be one of them? Let me quote of all my trouble which it let me to apply for the above. My father has died long time ago when I was very young and he left me without anywhere to stay or any *shamba* [farm], and I am having my mother and big family. I started to work since 1940 and nothing I have saved due to miss any *shamba*."[1] Kariuki's letter resembled that of other Rift Valley land applicants at the time. Many petitions included biographical narratives about unfair impoverishment and extensive family obligations. The petitioners' descriptions of their destitution, in spite of hard work and family commitment, and the Swahili discourse of crying (*kulia*) for land illuminates popular ideas about the characteristics of a strong land applicant.[2] Writing his petition just as officials began negotiating land resettlement, Kariuki was clearly well aware of forthcoming political shifts. The popular notions he drew on to make his case as a land applicant were less attuned to the policy. Officials decided that poverty did not endow Kenyans with land rights, and those Kenyan politicians who advocated for the poor and for greater redistribution were increasingly sidelined.

During the same year that Kariuki penned his letter, the white highlands opened to African settlement. An order-in-council abolished the "Scheduled Areas" as a legal entity in Kenya, effectively ending racial restrictions. Also in 1960, the Kenya Legislative Council started debating land resettlement.[3] Kenyan representatives began "preliminary discussions" with the World Bank for a land settlement and development project in the highlands and, in August 1960, "the Bank indicated its willingness to consider this proposal."[4] A flurry of economic feasibility studies and land reform plans followed. Of the World Bank's early involvement, agricultural economist Willi Wapenhans would later say: "We made the loan to Kenya before independence, which was a fascinating thing. It sort of coincided with independence."[5] Indeed, Kenya's first independence conference took place the same year these land reform measures were initiated.

As Kenya was in the process of gaining formal sovereignty, an expanding set of external actors played a growing role in its affairs. By 1962, multiple states and institutions—Britain, West Germany, the World Bank, and the Colonial Development Corporation—had begun participating in the creation and enactment of Kenyan land settlement planning. Within Kenya, the inauguration of these programs required a modification of the administrative apparatus, giving rise to a dizzying number of agencies, ministries, and departments. Along with these new bodies, settlement involved a whole array of existing departments and branches—ranging from veterinary to hydraulics to survey—and also entailed the cooperation of "special-purpose government and quasi-government agricultural organizations," including local farm committees and statutory boards.[6]

In 1962, the largest resettlement program in Kenyan history—the Million Acre Scheme—began. While the Million Acre Scheme (MAS) represents perhaps the most technocratic of all the attempts to reimagine Kenya's geography, the high-modernist tropes of the policy, and of the historical literature, have obscured some of the contestations over its implementation.[7] On the ground, development plans were commonly undercut, both by Kenyans seeking land and by the state and development actors distributing it. In turn, citizens' access to resources became differentiated by their promise for contributing to development in the eyes of transnational actors, by their relationships to the local and ethnic elites allocating land, and by their knowledge of the program.

Land settlement embroiled so many actors and institutions because it entailed much more than the relocation of tens of thousands of Kenyan families, already a massive undertaking. Resettlement served as a land transfer program, a national development project, and a buyout plan for European settlers. The plans for Kenya's settlement schemes included the provision of agricultural aid, financial credit, and marketing assistance. Settlement involved the creation of new infrastructure, such as water pumps, roads, and fencing. It also required massive social engineering—the planning and constructing of town centers and the delivery of social services at new sites. For Kenyans like Ndugu Kariuki, exclusion from settlement might mean the loss of land, as well as the inability to access credit, piped water, farming assistance, and other agricultural services.

Though transnational, foreign, and national officials created settlement plans in far-off boardrooms, local Kenyan officials executed much of the program. They did so with little oversight, producing a disjuncture between planning and practice. Land resettlement made clear to rural Kenyans that multiple nodes of power existed. The highly localized implementation of these programs also produced vastly different experiences among Kenyan settlers.[8] Not only did material realities diverge from politicians' promises, but service provision occurred erratically and unevenly, contributing to a sense of state unpredictability.

This is the first of two chapters on the Million Acre Scheme. This chapter begins with an exploration of the legacies of colonialism and decolonization. Three seminal events—colonial dispossessions, postwar agricultural development programs, and Kenya's concession to purchase land from European settlers at market value—set the groundwork for postcolonial land reform. From there, the chapter turns to decolonizing settlement policy, with attention to settler selection and the extension programs that accompanied settlement. While international and national policy made deep imprints on the lives of rural Kenyans, institutional fractures existed. National politicians subverted policy, and local officials exercised largely unchecked influence on the ground.

DISPLACEMENT, DISPOSSESSION, AND DEVELOPMENT: COLONIAL LEGACIES

From conquest on, British colonialists displaced Kenyans. They founded a political economy based on the alienation of African lands for European use and, simultaneously, created a historically unprecedented land shortage. Despite this, colonial administrators refused to acknowledge the land problem for the first three decades of the twentieth century. In 1931, colonial officials admitted a problem existed, and they appointed a commission to formally investigate widespread grievances.[9] Though the state conceded the existence of a land shortage in theory, it conceded little else in practice, refusing Africans any rights to the highlands.[10] Throughout this period,

Kenyans in the highlands could gain only temporary usufruct rights as labor-tenants on European farms.

In the years following the commission, African land use became more constrained, not less. From the late 1930s through the 1950s, colonial legislation authorized European settlers to further restrict squatter livestock holdings and to demand greater days of labor in exchange for cultivation rights.[11] With meager plots, reduced herds, and few free days for personal farming, squatters in the white highlands found it increasingly difficult to meet their families' subsistence needs. In the postwar era, agricultural mechanization diminished the need for African labor, and European farmers expelled squatters. Both those disenchanted with labor conditions and those who lost their jobs returned to the reserves. Between 1946 and 1952, more than a hundred thousand Kikuyu squatters returned to central Kenya.[12] Squatters of other ethnicities also left the white highlands. Many Kalenjin living in Uasin Gishu today recount returning to the reserve or moving to other regions of Kenya. Some moved as far away as Uganda or Tanzania, in search of land and an escape from the oppressiveness of Kenyan colonialism.[13]

The Kikuyu example is the most well-known due to both the sheer quantity of squatters and the rebellion their repatriation set off. Kikuyu elites empowered under colonial rule did not allow former squatters returning to the reserves to exercise ancestral land rights, previously inalienable. The plight of the landless catalyzed rapid politicization in central Kenya, setting off the Mau Mau rebellion.

Amid the escalating violence, the British declared a State of Emergency in 1952 and enacted villagization—the forced relocation of almost the entire Kikuyu population to guarded villages.[14] Villagization paved the way for land reform measures, furnishing the opportunity for reordering the countryside and restructuring land tenure practices. In 1954, the colonial state initiated the Swynnerton Plan, the first large-scale land reform scheme in Kenyan history. The architects of the Swynnerton Plan believed the solution to Kenya's land issues and political problems lay in individual ownership and plot consolidation.[15] The planners attempted to eliminate the uncertainty and insecurity of "customary tenure." Instead, the Swynnerton Plan offered a system of registered land titles guaranteed by the state. The less overt but equally important aim was to create a new class of landed farmers. These farmers, colonial officials hoped, would form a conservative, African middle class with the same interests as white settlers and would thus curb political agitation.[16]

The new juridical regime grounded in individual property rights brought profound changes. Even though the Swynnerton Plan grew out of the repressive policies used to combat Mau Mau, the restructuring of land access and land tenure would have lasting implications for all of Kenya. British administrators extended the Swynnerton Plan beyond central Kenya to other regions, where chiefs converted land from communal tenure to individual holdings.[17] Ethnic elites throughout the colony excluded former squatters from land access. Investment in rural political networks had remained essential, and chiefs tended to allocate land to their loyal clients, most of whom had stayed in the reserves, and most of whom were senior men.[18] Land reform increased stratification with the further ascendance of an African elite and the more permanent dispossession of peasants.[19] The presumptions, goals, and outcomes of this first scheme would underpin future programs.

Despite the violence and draconian policies of the Emergency, with other shifts in the 1950s, Kenyans recognized mounting indications of forthcoming independence. As in many African settings, metropolitan powers found it difficult to justify colonial rule in the postwar period. They confronted growing dissent and were forced to make concessions to nationalists.[20] Consequently, some Kenyans began to expect both decolonization and land redistribution. These expectations altered political dynamics, creating intense competition for access to and control over a limited and valuable resource.

Ethnic elites began preparing for independence by bolstering communal claims to land. Kikuyu leaders, drawing on a moral ethnicity in which hard work merited reward, substantiated their land rights by highlighting the events of the past half-century.[21] They emphasized their agricultural labor in the highlands and their landlessness. In contrast, the Kalenjin, Maasai, and other minority ethnic groups made claims to the same lands on the basis of their precolonial occupation and their experiences of colonial injustice. Popular Nandi ideologies, in particular, centered increasingly on autochthony. The Nandi community focused on the restitution of lands that inspired the most emotive attachments from ethnic patriots and, simultaneously, on protecting the western highlands from Kikuyu infringement. Meanwhile, Luyia elites drew on both "nativism and cosmopolitan pluralism" to make claims to portions of the upper Rift.[22]

At this same time, a diverse set of elite political actors anticipated land resettlement. Kenyan politicians, British officials, World Bank representatives, and other development actors began discussing policy options. Western actors and an influential contingent of national politicians largely agreed that the Kenyan economy should continue to rely on agricultural exports. The colonial economy had not only revolved around plantation agriculture in the white highlands, but the colonial state created a political economy intended precisely to support the production and marketing of cash crops—coffee, tea, pyrethrum, sisal, and wattle.[23] As a result, in 1959, the scheduled areas produced 80 percent of Kenya's exportable surplus.[24] Though development agents and some state actors wanted to preserve this economy, they debated how best to balance the maintenance of the large estates they thought to be more profitable, while still settling the many poor, land-hungry Kenyans to forestall the unrest and instability they thought otherwise inevitable.[25]

Given that land played such a significant role in both Kenya's economy and politics, it also played a central role in independence negotiations, which commenced in 1960. The Lancaster House conferences combined deliberations over Jomo Kenyatta's release from prison, the framing of the constitution, the timing of independence, the British role in the transition, and the plan for land settlement. Land superseded other issues, producing unlikely alliances. The KADU coalition was founded on concern about Kikuyu-Luo hegemony and encroachment. The demographic strength of KANU's ethnic alliance, along with Kenyatta's popularity, ensured the party's electoral dominance. Yet Kenyatta's political ideologies aligned more closely with those of KADU leaders than with those of some of his own KANU allies. After independence, two opposing ideological factions emerged within KANU, one more conservative and one committed to radical redistribution.[26] Such questions had not been extensively deliberated ahead of independence, though they were broadly resolved by the constitution.[27] British actors refused to compromise a cornerstone of the agreement: that European farms in the highlands would be purchased for African settlement at market value on a willing buyer–willing seller basis.[28] In conceding this point, African delegates agreed to protect land valuations and private property rights, making it difficult to enact a program of redistribution without indebting the government or ruining its credit rating.

With a free market agreed upon, and the policy groundwork on land reform laid by the Swynnerton Plan, the colonial state initiated resettlement. British state actors hoped to carry out the majority of land reform prior to independence to control its implementation and, accordingly, to maintain the structures of the colonial economy. By independence in 1963, a great deal of settlement had already taken place. Most notably, the Million Acre Scheme began in 1962 and would conclude in 1967, transferring 1.17 million acres of land to Africans. Though the independence negotiations closed down many alternate possibilities for land resettlement, multitiered actors designed the program, selected settlers, and administered the schemes, and high-modernist plans were reworked on the ground.

FROM SUBJECT TO SETTLER: THE SELECTION PROCESS

As the brainchild of British administrators, the Million Acre Scheme sought to preserve the colonial economic framework and its "separate ethnic containers."[29] The original planners designed resettlement to occur adjacent to the colonially crafted ethnic boundaries of the reserves.[30] Resettlement programs provided pathways to landownership for those who had labored in the highlands as squatters, for those who inhabited the highlands prior to colonialism, and for those experiencing land shortages.[31] In other words, the Kikuyu—the so-called developers of the highlands, with high levels of landlessness—and the Kalenjin and other minority ethnic groups—the previous inhabitants of the highlands—could make claims for resettlement in the Rift Valley on a communal, territorial basis. Consequently, competition became more aggressive as ethnic leaders asserted communal rights to the highlands.

Aside from encouraging ethnic claims-making on autochthonous, developmentalist, and need-based terms, the Million Acre Scheme created two broad categories of applicants based on class. In policy grammar, "yeoman farmers" possessed agricultural knowledge and managerial experience, while "peasant settlers" simply needed land. Two main categories of plots coincided with the types of settlers. Low-density schemes consisted of larger plots. The emerging African elite—often first empowered under colonial indirect rule—were primarily the beneficiaries. Their privilege under colonialism enabled them to accumulate assets, thus providing them the financial means to purchase larger pieces of land. In contrast, on high-density schemes, "individual plot size was kept to the minimum" and intended for the landless and unemployed.[32]

The schemes of both the British government and the World Bank—the two largest settlement funders—mandated that yeoman farmers demonstrate agricultural experience and possess at least £500 for a down payment.[33] The British peasant scheme required that settlers be landless or "persons with an uneconomic sized holding."[34] In addition, British planners expected peasant settlers to "be able to provide their own working capital," noting that "it would be desirable for them to have at least £50 available."[35] Though peasant schemes were a political concession, British colonial administrators still privileged applicants with capital assets. In general, they favored applicants who would help sustain the status quo and preserve stability.[36] First and foremost, the British sought to safeguard the liberal underpinnings of the economy, especially the sanctity of individual property rights and the market-based valuation of land. In doing so, they reaffirmed existent class differences and reconfigured notions of citizenship. Capital investment became a prerequisite for accessing land, one of the promises of independence.

World Bank officials and British government actors agreed on many aspects of settlement: the fundamental distinctions between yeoman settlers and peasant settlers, the importance of yeoman settlers' management of larger holdings, and the need to conserve the land market. They disagreed in other respects. Unlike the British, World Bank officials were unwilling to make concessions to "non-progressive farmers," whom they saw as economically unproductive liabilities.[37] Thus the World Bank created more burdensome requirements for its peasant settlers, stipulating that applicants provide £100–150 for a down payment.[38] This large deposit put World Bank–funded land resettlement out of reach for most rural Kenyans, effectively rendering the Bank "peasant" scheme little more than pretense and creating some disquiet among members of the transitional Kenyan government. The 1963 minutes of a Ministry of Lands and Settlement meeting recorded the dissatisfaction of Tom Mboya, then minister of Justice and Constitutional Affairs. Mboya noted that he "did not see how the proposals in the memorandum would assist towards the alleviation of unemployment, since no landless and unemployed person could possibly find a sum as large as £25."[39] The large deposits precluded the landless and impoverished from qualifying for the very settlement schemes created for them.

Despite frustrations with the prohibitive down payments, such requirements remained in place. Other features of land resettlement were more short-lived. While colonial bureaucrats transferred a great deal of land in the first phases of settlement, decolonization empowered new actors. Independence negotiations codified a federal government where regions largely controlled land. Initially, regional and district governments held the authority for the selection of African settlers. By and large, local committees first made settler selections, and then the president of the Regional Assembly approved those choices.[40]

Less than a year after independence, in 1964, much of this changed. The opposition party, KADU, disbanded and crossed the aisle, transforming Kenya into a de facto one-party state. State actors abolished the federal independence constitution, centralized power, and revested regional land in the central government of the Republic of Kenya. Profound constitutional amendment heralded profound change in settler selection procedure. The central government took over responsibility for selection and declared resettlement compulsorily "non-tribal." This was a strategic maneuver to centralize power, though the Ministry of Lands and Settlement went to great lengths to justify the new policy, proclaiming it would resolve issues of "tribal favoritism," while ensuring "the interests of the economy and the security of the country."[41]

Rather than organize settlement around homogeneous ethnic groups on the borders of former native reserves, the new policy exclusively prioritized laborers residing on farms purchased for resettlement, regardless of ethnicity. The Kikuyu represented the largest group of resident laborers, even in a location as distant from central Kenya as Uasin Gishu. In 1960, the ethnic breakdown of African laborers in Uasin Gishu was 38.7 percent Kikuyu; 31.8 percent Kalenjin; 16.5 percent Luyia; and 13.0 percent Luo.[42] Between 1962 and 1964, Uasin Gishu settlement schemes had been largely reserved for the Kalenjin, though some areas that were formerly a part of Uasin Gishu had been excised to Kakamega District to settle landless Luyia. The new policy benefited landless Kikuyu laborers, previously excluded from settlement in Uasin Gishu.[43] Rather than assuaging tensions about favoritism, the policy exacerbated ethnic competition and antagonism, particularly in multiethnic areas.

Less than a month after the dissemination of a circular regarding the new protocol for settler selection, the regional government agent in Western Province bemoaned how "no local people can obtain plots." He added, "It is a well known fact that the majority of farm labour displaced by settlement schemes are aliens within the Region. . . . If such aliens are to be given priority for plots this will virtually exclude indigenous inhabitants of the Region from obtaining plots."[44] Instead of resolving concerns about ethnic preferential treatment, the prioritization of laborers inflamed feelings of injustice. Indeed, the regional agent went on to explicitly accuse the government of intentionally and unjustly favoring the Kikuyu. "I should like to take this opportunity," he wrote, "to point out that as far as settlement schemes in Central Region are concerned, settlement selection has so far been entirely on a tribal basis, contrary to Section 219 of the Constitution." He concluded, "It would seem that there is to be one law for the Kikuyu and another one for the rest of the country."[45] Many Kenyans believed selection favored outsiders, and they blamed the government for this bias.[46]

The privileging of farm laborers engendered discontent among non-Kikuyu, but it did not necessarily provide a direct or easy path to land for all ex-squatters. Former laborers' success as land applicants continued to rest on factors outside their control. If a European farmer remained in Kenya, or sold land privately, the employees might be displaced. However, if a European farmer sold land to the government, settlement selection favored the African laborers. Farm laborers' probability of selection also depended on whether their former employers recommended them to government officials. For example, the district commissioner of Kiambu replied to a letter from a European settler: "I thank you for your letter of the 12th August in which you wrote about land for your two employees. I have made a note of their names, and I will try and fix them up on a suitable settlement scheme in due course."[47] Though the archival record does not reveal whether the employees received land, oral histories suggest that departing white farmers deeply affected rural Kenyan land access. Kenyans selected for land resettlement on different schemes noted that when former employers endorsed their applications, selection committees gave laborers priority. Many Kenyans settled through the Million Acre Scheme attributed their selection to the actions of their former employers.[48] Conversely, without an employer's recommendation, Kenyans noted that their access to land resettlement was more proscribed.[49]

With resettlement policies, state and transnational institutions created and perpetuated structural inequalities, inhibiting some Kenyans from land opportunities and expanding class, ethnic, and gender disparities. Yet land resettlement entangled a wide range of actors who worked for and against the modernist plans of international development agencies and state institutions. National and local Kenyan actors played a growing role in determining settler selection, often by challenging donors' stipulations or undermining state directives. In other words, the practice of settlement on the ground often looked quite different from the initial plans.

Generally, once the government advertised a settlement scheme, aspiring landowners applied, either in person or through a written application.[50] Though applications differed, most required candidates to provide their name, address, age, occupation, marital status, number of children, farming experience, and details of assets.[51] The specific process after a prospective settler made an application depended on the funder, the type of scheme, and the location. It incorporated a range of bureaucrats, including settlement officers, agricultural officers, district commissioners, provincial officers, and local selection committees (of various compositions).[52]

The diverse actors involved in settlement enjoyed immense autonomy. Four years after the start of settlement, the selection procedure remained unstandardized.[53] Western provincial commissioner Paul Kipkorir Boit, among the first group of Africans appointed as Kenyan provincial commissioners, complained to the Ministry of Lands and Settlement in February 1965: "What those of us in the field want, or would like to see as far as allocation of plots is concerned, is a simple straightforward method which gives the potential candidates an impartial chance of obtaining a plot."[54] Similarly, on the house floor in 1965, Uasin Gishu MP Justin Kapting'ei Tuwei, who consistently advocated for the landless, criticized settlement, noting, "There is no uniform procedure as to how one gets a plot there and how much one pays for it."[55] Without such standard procedure, selection committees and local government bureaucrats possessed a great deal of latitude, and citizens unjustly excluded from land settlement often possessed little recourse.[56]

This paved the way for abuses, as settler selection decisions could be made without regard for land legislation. Individuals who possessed other pieces of land, for example, were settled on schemes intended for the landless.[57] Local elites also illegally received land allocations. Correspondence from the Ministry of Lands and Settlement in 1965 condemned how "persons who do not qualify, in accordance with the Government's ruling, to be considered for the schemes, have already been allocated plots, e.g. Chiefs, Sub-Chiefs, Teachers, County Councillors etc."[58] On some occasions, a single member of a local selection committee co-opted the entire process of selection and allocation by "picking chosen plots for his favoured applicants."[59]

Central government officials, too, contravened settlement policy. The district commissioner of Kakamega reported the occurrence of "the allocation of plots to prominent persons" in the Lugari settlement scheme. He added that "not only had we got instructions from Nairobi asking us to allocate plots to individuals, but some prominent persons make their way to the Settlement Offices in Lugari and Nzoia and indicate plots that they want allocated to themselves."[60] In perhaps the most egregious example, the Kenyan government used British aid money—earmarked for the landless—to allocate one-hundred-acre plots at subsidized rates to "a variety of eminent people including the President himself, the Minister of Settlement, his Permanent Secretary, a number of other senior officials, and in some cases, their wives and Members of Parliament."[61] Such occurrences reveal impropriety. But perhaps just as important, they reveal the disjuncture between planning and practice. State and local actors could undercut national and transnational authority in rural spaces, discarding accepted international development precepts. Such actions contributed to a general sense that the state acted as an unpredictable institution.

Despite the weighty requirements and the abuses in settler selection, many ordinary Kenyans did gain access to land through settlement. A number of schemes received more applications than plots available, as Kenyan families pooled their resources to fund a prospective settler. Support networks became essential to applying for land. Many settlers depended on their relatives' sponsorship to make a down payment.[62] Settlers also recounted living with family members who gave them an acre to plant, space to graze cattle, and a home for years at a time, while they waited to be chosen for settlement or to save enough money. Some had family who informed them about available land. Others gained access to land if they had a well-connected relative.

For both elite and nonelite Kenyans, social and political networks were integral to land access, revealing the limited reach of state agencies and international institutions at local sites. Negotiability tended to favor elite actors, who could exploit deep and multiple networks and navigate complicated bureaucratic terrains.[63] Even so, many landless Kenyans drew on their own networks and purchased farms through settlement, which provided them access to a whole host of additional agricultural development programs.

EXTENDING SETTLEMENT INTO DEVELOPMENT

State and development actors believed most Kenyan farmers "had very little or no education at all," and thus that Kenya's agricultural success depended on "an absolutely efficient Extension system."[64] Extension—additional agricultural aid and education—became a chief premise undergirding the policy during this first stage of settlement. The British were particularly convinced that Kenyan farmers required agricultural assistance, and they provided grants for these expensive services.[65] With this development funding, bureaucrats—colonial, then postcolonial—first carefully planned settlement sites, economies, and budgets. They next provided additional agricultural development and training programs aimed at reforming and maximizing the output of Kenyan farmers.

Land resettlement, with its requisite migrations, also set in motion major social changes. Tens of thousands of families—likely close to half a million people by 1970—moved to different parts of the nation to establish villages on former European estates.[66] These areas did not possess adequate resources for newly settled communities. There were few roads, few wells, often no schools or health centers. Thus the designers of the Million Acre Scheme saw, in this moment, an opportunity for infrastructural and social development. They created programs to help settlers construct new homes, build village institutions, and create roads. For this, however, the British refused to provide aid. In crafting these programs, state and development actors intended to aid Kenyans, but also to make them into nation-builders and good citizens.

High modernists might have been able to survey and map out settlements and towns, but ultimately, the untamable environment upended plans for uniformity (some farms were bigger or less square to adjust for marshy or rocky areas). In addition, technocrats created sites for schools and markets, or plans for roads, but local people put their own imprint on this planning when they walked, creating new footpaths, or when they made decisions in community building that contravened state plans.[67] Intentions and realities diverged, and the initial design of these sweeping programs often differed dramatically from the execution.

Long before Kenyan settlers arrived, technocrats planned each settlement site. Surveying, land valuation, and land purchase came first, then budgeting. Many bureaucrats did not visit the sites they designed, which resulted in planning errors.[68] Especially in the earliest years of settlement, officials were encouraged "to short-circuit wherever possible the normal channels" to finalize plans quickly, and to keep services to a "minimum."[69] Agricultural officers calculated the cost of production, estimated outputs and profits for each plot, and then submitted their budgets to agricultural committees.[70] Budgets were meant to ensure that smallholders could meet their subsistence needs, generate a specific net income, and repay settlement charges and loans.

In spite of this planning, just 10.7 percent of farms reached target incomes in the 1964–65 financial year, and by 1966–67, the number had grown only to 17.0 percent.[71] Though national and international policy guided budgeting, inexperienced local officers were given immense responsibilities for financial planning with little supervision. Since the initial years of settlement entailed much trial and error, even in the best of circumstances, budgets would have likely required modification.

Frequently, agricultural officers prepared settlement budgets based on misinformation. A chief technical officer from the Ministry of Agriculture complained in 1970 that "a good deal of the apparent failure of the One Million Acre Settlement Programme consists in the nature of the initial planning; the endless false assumptions on which budgeting was based and above all the inadequate infrastructure."[72] He noted as an example that watering points were too far, and farmers could take their cows only once a day, rather than two or three times. "As milk contains 75–80% of water," the officer added, "we could not tap the full potential of the high-grade dairy cows in Settlement. The most that could be expected under the circumstances was a yield of 1–2 gallons of milk from potential 5–6 gallon animals."[73] Without adequate water infrastructure, Kenyans could not meet the expected output. This instance shows that even with minor miscalculations, settlement planning produced profound ramifications for the labor and livelihoods of rural Kenyans.

Broadly speaking, bureaucrats' best-laid plans did not come to fruition. Atypical weather patterns and changing international markets also impacted agricultural profitability. In the 1960s, Kenya suffered through three major droughts. The year 1961 was particularly bad, "disastrous" in fact, in the words of the Rift Valley provincial commissioner.[74] Heavy rains followed drought and armyworms, causing damage to crops. European and African

FIGURE 1.1. Kenyan men cutting sisal on the coast, 1945. Photo courtesy of the British National Archives, CO 1069/137 (13).

areas of the Rift Valley required famine relief.[75] In 1965, drought struck again and "crops failed, cattle died, and a widespread famine" ensued.[76] By all accounts, 1969 was not as dire, but the "rains set in earlier than anticipated," then disappeared. The inconsistency meant lower crop yields than average.[77] For Kenyan settlers on new farms, and indeed for the newly independent nation, this could not have come at a worse time, as both citizen and state had to pay land and farming loans.

The international market also changed during the first decade of settlement. Technocrats planned many of the western highland settlement schemes for sisal—an agave plant that produces a fiber often used for making rope; or for pyrethrum—a flower that creates a natural insecticide. The market for both crops dropped dramatically soon afterward. In the 1960s, the introduction of synthetics almost completely displaced hard fibers from the global marketplace.[78] Settlers on the Lumakanda scheme, discussed in the next chapter, took out loans to purchase sisal plants. Soon after they arrived, the sisal price declined to such an extent that the crop was valueless. Some had already planted sisal and, consequently, had to take on the labor-intensive process of removing the plants, though they still had to pay the loans.[79] Like sisal, the demand for pyrethrum decreased with the rise of synthetics. In the late 1960s, a new group of potent yet safe artificial compounds came onto the market and precipitated a sharp drop in the price of

FIGURE 1.2. Kenyans picking pyrethrum in the Rift Valley, April 1961. Photo courtesy of Ivan Massar of Black Star for the World Bank. Country Photographs—Kenya, Loan 0256, Photographs, vol. 3, 1724745, Records of Office of External Affairs, WBGA.

pyrethrum.[80] In light of these market changes, many farmers in the northwest Rift Valley began producing maize and dairy, but these two crops were never as profitable as policymakers' projections for sisal and pyrethrum.

Kenyan farmers faced other challenges in the marketplace. They contended with international and national marketing restrictions and quotas. The International Coffee Organization first implemented quotas in the 1960s.[81] The Kenyan government put in place certain marketing quotas as well. Though the government continually amended these quotas, which ranged in their stringency, they still impacted smallholder production. In 1968, for instance, the Kenyan government announced that it would not purchase pyrethrum flowers over the quota and would penalize low-content flowers.[82] In response to the unfavorable economic conditions, a settlement officer noted that farmers "neglected" pyrethrum and turned their attention to different crops.[83]

Other unanticipated circumstances limited farmers' access to agricultural inputs, again disrupting the projections of planners. In the 1960s, a grade cattle shortage forced many farmers in settlement to go long periods without cattle.[84] Grade cattle yield more milk than indigenous cattle, and policymakers created settlement budgets based on the assumption that farmers would achieve grade dairy production quantities.[85] With a long wait list, many farmers could not meet these forecasts for years at a time. The availability and price of agricultural inputs also affected farmers' profits. In 1968, the CEO of the Central Agricultural Board noted his concern about the falling prices of agricultural goods and the rising prices of fertilizers and seeds. This trend only intensified when the government decreased its subsidies for fertilizers.[86] Affordable access to dairy cattle, fertilizers, seeds, and other agricultural inputs made a deep impact on farmers' incomes and upset the delicate budgets prepared for the schemes.

Though settlement did not run as planned, farmers likely would have had a difficult time meeting the budgets regardless. High-density plots were not only small, but they were expensive. At times, planners expected settlers to devote more than 70 percent of their income toward debt repayments.[87] This worsened a context in which many settlers had already dedicated most of their savings to buying their farms, leaving them with few resources for other expenses, investments, or emergencies.[88]

Technocrats did not just toil over the plans prior to settlers' arrival. Officials also created a series of interconnected extension programs for Kenyans after they settled. Extension services included agricultural and veterinary education and assistance. Agricultural education took place chiefly at farmer training centers and on experimental plots. During training center courses, instructors taught farmers agricultural methods such as planting techniques, fertilizer use, compost-making, artificial insemination, and tick control. Training centers also offered courses on nutrition, hygiene, and farm recordkeeping.[89] Agricultural instructors conducted similar trainings on experimental plots. On these local plots, the instructors demonstrated certain techniques. Some evidence suggests, though, that experimental plots were used to impress visitors.[90]

Bureaucrats tended to place greater weight on farmer education than the settlers did. The archival record contains myriad pronouncements on the importance of training programs and experimental plots. Agricultural officers spoke in great length and detail about this aspect of the program, making a direct connection between educational services and the accomplishments of settlement. Manasi Esipeya, a former Chekalini settlement officer, said that through agricultural education, the government "reformed those people who had never seen a grade cow, who had never seen a certified seed."[91] Esipeya, a secondary school graduate, began his agricultural career in the late colonial era in the sisal industry. By 1960, he had entered the colonial bureaucracy as the assistant records officer in the Department of Husbandry, and, just after independence, he became a settlement officer in the western highlands. As the above quotation suggests, Esipeya believed

FIGURE 1.3. Classroom instruction at a farmer training center, November 1960. Photo courtesy of Ivan Massar of Black Star for the World Bank. Country Photographs—Kenya, Loan 0256, Photographs, vol. 3, 1724745, Records of Office of External Affairs, WBGA.

high-modernist agricultural orthodoxy could transform Kenya's farmers. He evinced pride in his contribution to farmers' training and believed that settlement had "sustained the economy of the country."[92]

Settlers generally seemed more dubious. Those settlers who regarded these programs as beneficial often noted that such educational access had been unavailable to them in the colonial era.[93] Perhaps, then, the feelings of inclusion these programs fostered were just as important as the agricultural knowledge they delivered.[94] The majority of settlers, though, did not bring up these programs during interviews, which ranged widely on settlement programming. When asked about trainings, even those who attended had little to say, usually noting they were "helpful," while mentioning the course fees.[95]

Settlers held stronger opinions on the quality of extension services, likely because such services could deeply affect their household economies. For agricultural extension, instructors were directed to provide standardized recommendations about the exact acreage for each crop, what type of seeds to use, when to plant, and when to harvest. But settlement officers did not always follow the guidelines. In 1965, a deputy area settlement controller wrote that "several Settlement Officers are now giving conflicting advice to settlers. . . . Their instructions have been contrary to the standard recommendations of the Department of Agriculture."[96] Like many other

FIGURE 1.4. Outdoor instruction at a farmer training center, November 1960. Photo courtesy of Ivan Massar of Black Star for the World Bank. Country Photographs—Kenya, Loan 0256, Photographs, vol. 3, 1724745, Records of Office of External Affairs, WBGA.

development programs with top-down planning, technocrats had trouble controlling either the officers on the ground or the people targeted for development.

Compared to its agricultural counterpart, veterinary extension services required more intensive programming, especially with attention to disease control and the reproduction of grade cattle. Veterinary officers managed dips and spray races used to prevent tick-borne illnesses. They offered artificial insemination services to maintain grade stock and avoid interbreeding between grade and indigenous cattle. Such services required the physical presence of veterinary officers, though, in time, cooperative officials took over the management of these facilities. Despite veterinary programming, Kenyan settlers still lost cattle to preventable diseases.[97] Chemicals were not always kept at proper strength, and cattle became susceptible to epizootics. At other times, poorer settlers were reluctant to use these mandatory—but unenforced—veterinary services due to the expense.[98]

The shortage of technical staff further limited the services extension officers could provide. E. J. M. Rabu, assistant director of Agriculture, described the situation on the ground, noting that for every 139 farmers, there was one technical assistant, who might "visit only about 3–4 plots per day, all things being equal, that is the weather, his bicycle, and no interruption

FIGURE 1.5. Agricultural official provides instruction in artificial insemination, 1969. Photo courtesy of Per Gunvall for the World Bank. Country Photographs—Kenya, Loan 0256, Photographs, vol. 5, 30229054, Records of Office of External Affairs, WBGA.

at all from outside visitors. Visiting his farmers at this rate, he will take over 1½ month[s] before he goes back to the first plot he visited. In fact, in practice, he takes more than three months, before he has completed visiting every plot in his area."[99] Wilberforce Oyalo's firsthand account as an agricultural extension officer supports this description and provides further insights. Oyalo grew up on a small family farm in Bunyore. At independence, with his secondary education, he got a job in the Ministry of Agriculture and was initially assigned to Chekalini settlement. Chekalini covered an area of 10,699 acres and had close to 400 settlers.[100] Oyalo did not own a bicycle, and he recounted that he walked from plot to plot, using his farm notebook to instruct settlers.[101] Even the most conscientious and dedicated technical assistants found it difficult to visit every settlement farm in their charge. At times, extension workers chose to focus on "one or two good farms," simply because they could not cover their assigned region.[102]

The Kenyan state and its donors were more invested in offering extension services to "yeoman" farmers on low-density schemes, producing inequality. Despite twice the total acreage and the significantly greater number of farmers on high-density schemes, in some cases the state deployed roughly equal numbers of extension officers to both types of schemes.[103] These inadequacies multiplied in nonsettlement areas, where the presence of extension officers was only about a third of what it was on settlement schemes.[104]

Given the above, settlers possessed ambivalent and wide-ranging views on extension services. In theory, extension offered the state a conduit to rural areas. However, extension ultimately reproduced the same sense of state unpredictability that Kenyans encountered in so many other development arenas during the early postindependence period. Nandi farmer Kiptoo arap Maina recounted that agricultural extension services "went with the *wazungu* [Europeans]. I didn't even see their services. Because, those people were there, but they were very reluctant to do work."[105] In the colonial era, Maina moved frequently, between Uasin Gishu—where he worked for white farmers—the Nandi reserve, and Uganda. After independence, he sold his cattle to purchase land in Leseru, Uasin Gishu. Two factors likely shaped Maina's opinion of extension: his colonial experience working on a European farm and his purchase of land located outside a settlement scheme. The former meant that he had observed the colonial state fully leveraging its resources to assist white farmers, and the latter meant he had less access to extension services than Kenyans on state-run settlement schemes.

Even those settled on state schemes could encounter issues with extension services. Maragoli farmer Karen Misavo resided in the Lumakanda settlement scheme, and she, too, complained about extension, noting the unreliability of officers.[106] Like others, Misavo was particularly frustrated with the veterinary side of extension. Many of those services—such as artificial insemination or medical treatment—were time-sensitive, but the settlers could not rely on overburdened, understaffed veterinary assistants to arrive promptly. Misavo's dissatisfaction likely also grew out of the exclusions she experienced as a woman. Numerous women recounted that only men could speak with extension officers, or that they were completely barred from accessing extension services.[107]

Since extension relied so heavily on local officers, even the experiences of those with similar circumstances or backgrounds could vary dramatically. A number of settlers noted, for example, that technical assistants visited regularly, and that these programs were useful to them.[108] As with other development programs, rural Kenyans received extension services unevenly and possessed a range of attitudes on the programs and their local extension officers. Some farmers who encountered extension officers regularly contested the bureaucratic advice they received or tried to rework extension programming. When agricultural extension officers told settlers in

Sosiani that their land was good only for dairy cattle, they were skeptical. Sosiani settlers brought in maize seeds "to prove the agricultural extension officers wrong."[109] They did so successfully, and, going forward, maize was included in the crops the Department of Agriculture recommended. Despite this momentary disagreement, many Sosiani settlers believed extension was helpful, noting that officers ordered fertilizers and seeds, and taught settlers how to apply fertilizers and take soil samples. Other Kenyan farmers contested extension programming in distinctive ways, recounting how they ignored rules prohibiting them from bringing bulls into their settlements. They used the bulls instead of the expensive, but mandated, artificial insemination.[110]

In more extreme examples, communities requested the ouster of local officers. Such was the case in Chekalini in 1965 with Manasi Esipeya, the settlement officer who provided such a positive account of land settlement programming and its contribution to nation-building. In a letter addressed to Esipeya's superior, the senior settlement officer (SSO), the Chekalini cooperative society protested, "We don't want settlement officer of Chekalini Mr. T. M. Esipeya." The writers complained about Esipeya's "mistakes," which included failing to come through on his promise to give settlers cattle and plowing the communal experimental plot for personal use.[111] It is difficult to tease apart what specifically drove members of the cooperative society to write this letter, and whether politics or personality conflicts might have been at play. Given the response from the SSO, it seems that at least some of the complaints may have been unfounded. Some settlers in the neighboring Lumakanda scheme recalled that Esipeya collected loan payments and, in the mid-1960s, threatened defaulters with eviction, which created antagonism.[112] Indeed, just months after the Chekalini co-op sent their petition, settlement officials met in Eldoret to discuss the "relationships of officers with settlers," noting that due to forceful loan collections, rapport had deteriorated.[113] When settlers became frustrated with agricultural policy, they attempted to contest and rework development programs.

The architects of settlement originally planned for extension staffing to maintain a presence on each settlement for a period of two and a half years. By 1965, the Kenyan government saw this as a considerable underestimation and applied to the British to increase the period of supervision. In its application, the Kenyan Treasury noted that a reduction in the number of extension staff after two and a half years would be "dangerous and possibly disastrous," and such a course of action "would run the risk of a fall in agricultural output, the collapse of the schemes, and widespread failure on the part of the settlers to repay their loans."[114] Kenyans might have been ambivalent

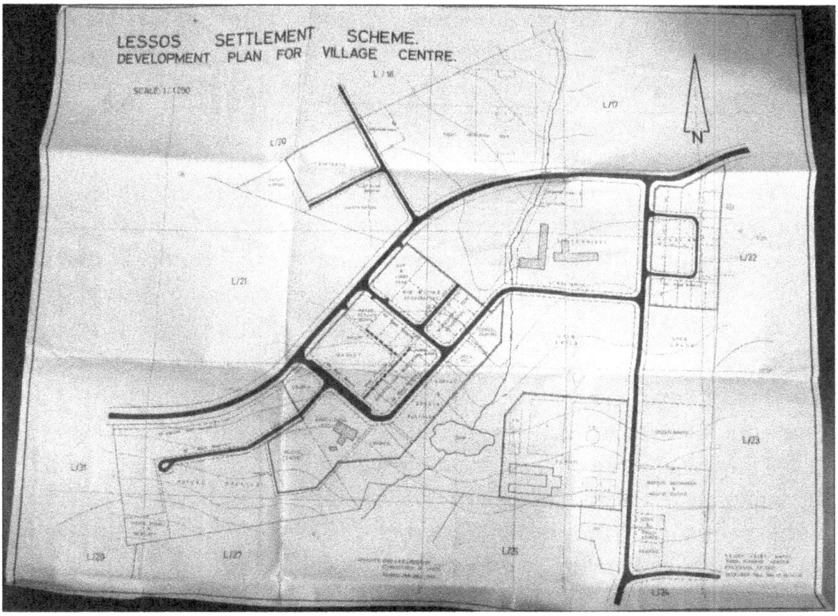

FIGURE 1.6. Diagram of town planning in Lessos settlement, 1962. Courtesy of the Kenya National Archives DC/ELD/1/10/9.

about extension, but the state put great faith in extension services and officers. Even so, the British became increasingly reluctant to continue funding expensive extension programs. Services diminished dramatically after the mid-1960s and extension officers had to cover increasingly large areas, producing greater doubt about the utility of these services, and a sense of state irregularity.[115]

The final aspect of settlement planning—which focused on community development—departed from the overt economic and agricultural emphasis of budgeting and extension. In dividing large farms, bureaucrats created settlements that lacked the necessary infrastructure for more densely populated communities, and thus obliged the government to take on town planning.[116] Officials demarcated spaces for markets, shops, schools, housing, and police, and settlement planners also determined the location of water supplies, drainage, and sanitation.[117] After settlers arrived, the state relied on their voluntary labor to carry out these plans. Kenyan settlers cleared land, built homes and latrines, and constructed villages, markets, roads, schools, and health centers. By 1968, seventy-six new villages had been established on settlement schemes.[118] While state bureaucrats set apart village sites in the initial stages of planning, often, years passed before a community had even the most rudimentary of institutions, such as schools or hospitals.

As with other aspects of settlement, town planning did not turn out to be the "relatively simple exercise" bureaucrats anticipated.[119] Funding constituted the biggest problem, largely because social service provision fell outside the purview of settlement. The British government prohibited Kenya from using settlement grant monies for educational, public health, or road services.[120] The settlement board possessed no funds to provide these services.[121] Different Kenyan government bodies attempted to defer responsibility, and these services remained chronically underfunded.[122] Throughout the 1960s, central state actors recommended to already overstretched local governments that they tax settlers to provide social services. In 1962, R. Tatton Brown, permanent secretary to the Ministry of Local Government, suggested that Kenyan county councils tax settlers fifty shillings per annum, charge them fees for veterinary and health services, and add further taxes for school-building. Even so, Brown admitted such charges would be a "heavy burden."[123] With settlers already encumbered by debt, they were often unable to make additional payments.

Ultimately, settlement schemes became a drain on local governments, which did not have the capacity to handle the large influx of people. Health authorities alleged, for example, that they traced infectious disease outbreaks to settlement schemes, which did not provide adequate medical services.[124] Some settlers had to walk between ten and fourteen miles to the nearest doctor.[125] In 1965, Uasin Gishu MP Justin Kapting'ei Tuwei asked the minister for Health and Housing, J. D. Otiende, why Uasin Gishu settlement schemes had been planned without health facilities. The minister replied that health services throughout the country were the responsibility of local authorities, and he could not name a single dispensary or health center that had been constructed in a Uasin Gishu scheme.[126] Settlers complained about the lack of health services too. A group from South Kinangop wrote to Kenyatta in 1963, "We got veterinary officer, agricultural officer, but no Doctor."[127] Settlers also pleaded for schools, water pumps, and roads, as those services were often insufficient in settlements.[128]

The execution of a massive, and immensely complicated, social engineering program depended on an already overstrained bureaucracy and a financially hamstrung set of local authorities. As a result, some settlers had limited access to important services, and, at times, overworked technocrats made mistakes. In the Sosiani scheme, similar to other settlements, residents recounted that there were no schools, health centers, or wells when they arrived. In this settlement, though, officials had forgotten to plan for such services and had not set aside any common land to construct community buildings. Ultimately, the community convinced one settler to give up his plot and move elsewhere so they could use the land for public institutions.[129]

Land settlement in Kenya introduced a series of interconnected programs to bolster agricultural production and build new communities. These services rarely worked exactly as officials envisioned. Planning errors meant farmers did not meet anticipated budgets, they did not always receive helpful extension services, and their villages possessed few amenities. Similar to many development projects, settlement generated contradictory experiences. While some aspects of the program—such as loan collection or agricultural training—could thrust an overbearing state onto Kenyan settlers, other elements of the program limited settlers' access to state services. Such incongruities contributed to the impression that the state acted unpredictably.

As the conclusion of the Million Acre Scheme neared, UK minister for Overseas Development, Barbara Castle, appointed a mission to advise on proposals for a further transfer of European farms in Kenya. The Stamp Mission's findings—that land transfer did not create economic development—contributed to major shifts in British policy.[130] The mission recommended the continuation of a land-purchase program, only after a two-year suspension and "at a much reduced level."[131] The British offered further assistance, though in a significantly different form from that first offered through the Million Acre Scheme. The UK no longer wanted to support the high-density settlement schemes, but rather specified that its aid would support low-density schemes, technical assistance, and development projects.[132] The Kenyan government opposed many of the mission's findings, noting that one of the main aims of settlement was "to meet a very strong political demand for some land ownership by smallholders."[133] By this time, though, Kenya was a de facto one-party state, and the radical wing of KANU—which had called for greater redistribution—had been marginalized. Kenyan officials agreed to accept more limited, and narrowly conceived, British aid.

The Stamp Mission marked the culmination of the era of large-scale land transfer targeted at smallholders. In its wake, the Kenyan state created the Haraka (meaning "fast" in Swahili) program, settling fourteen thousand landless people on thirty-seven schemes, composed of small farms only two and a half acres in size. In 1971, the government added the Shirika settlement program for large-scale cooperative farms. These programs signified watershed events. Gone were the days when the Kenyan state made profitable small farms available to families. Gone, too, were the days when the state attempted to provide the oversight and assistance initially envisioned. The stunted nature of the program, and the reluctance to address structural inequalities, perpetuated uneven landholdings in Uasin Gishu after independence. In 1980, the district contained 525 large farms, which covered 84 percent of the total land area.[134]

Even among the smallholders selected for settlement, these programs provided unequal access to state resources. In material terms, compared to nonsettlers, settlers had better extension and credit services, and oftentimes larger, more fertile landholdings. Though settlers had direct access to state agricultural development resources, these resources were provided unreliably, and their new communities often lacked other services—schools, hospitals, and roads. Nonetheless, settlement schemes provided poorer Kenyans with some of the best opportunities to purchase highland farms.

National politicians promised land resettlement and connected citizenship to landownership, and, simultaneously, ethnic elites made claims to land on behalf of their communities. At independence, residents of Uasin Gishu were thus well aware of both the land-buying prospects and the immense competition for land. As anticipation heightened, so, too, did tensions. Given the material and emotional significance of land, and its central role in decolonization, rural Kenyans made meaning of independence through land. They drew on colonial and postcolonial experiences—of displacement, shortage, labor, and settlement—and they drew also on ethnic and nationalist discourses pledging land redistribution.

2 "We Must Return to the Land That We Love"

Local Accounts and Life Histories in Three Settlement Schemes

> We all agreed that Uhuru would mean hard work. We also agreed that progress would mean sacrifice and discipline. Now, then, is the time to take the first step. We must begin from the base of our culture, the land. We must return to the land that we love. This is our greatest asset, and I now call on our people to complement the efforts and achievements of the Government . . . by exploiting to the full the soil of Kenya.
>
> —Jomo Kenyatta, 11 September 1964[1]

STATE ACTORS DEPICTED SETTLEMENT as broadly open to deserving Kenyans and linked participation in settlement to model citizenship. To this end, in 1962, Kenya's information services published a multilingual pamphlet, *Teach Yourself Citizenship for Self-Government*. The pamphlet included a section on purchasing land in the highlands, which explained the state institutions involved in land distribution, the funding available, the procedures for applying, and the selection process.[2]

By including a section on settlement, the pamphlet's writers suggested that understanding settlement signified a component of practicing good citizenship. The authors advised that the main qualifications for applying were the "ability to work hard to develop land, and lack of land elsewhere," adding that the applicant would also need "to deposit a proportion of the capital cost of the land and improvements." The pamphlet stressed that farmers were expected to toil faithfully "in order to increase the wealth of the country."[3] State actors attempted to fashion an idea of citizenship connected to land, setting out associated responsibilities, including learning about settlement programs and purchasing property. Similar to Kenyatta's pronouncements about the expected "contributions" of citizens, the pamphlet called upon the *wananchi* (citizens; sing. *mwananchi*) to build the nation, prescribing hard work as an essential citizenly duty.

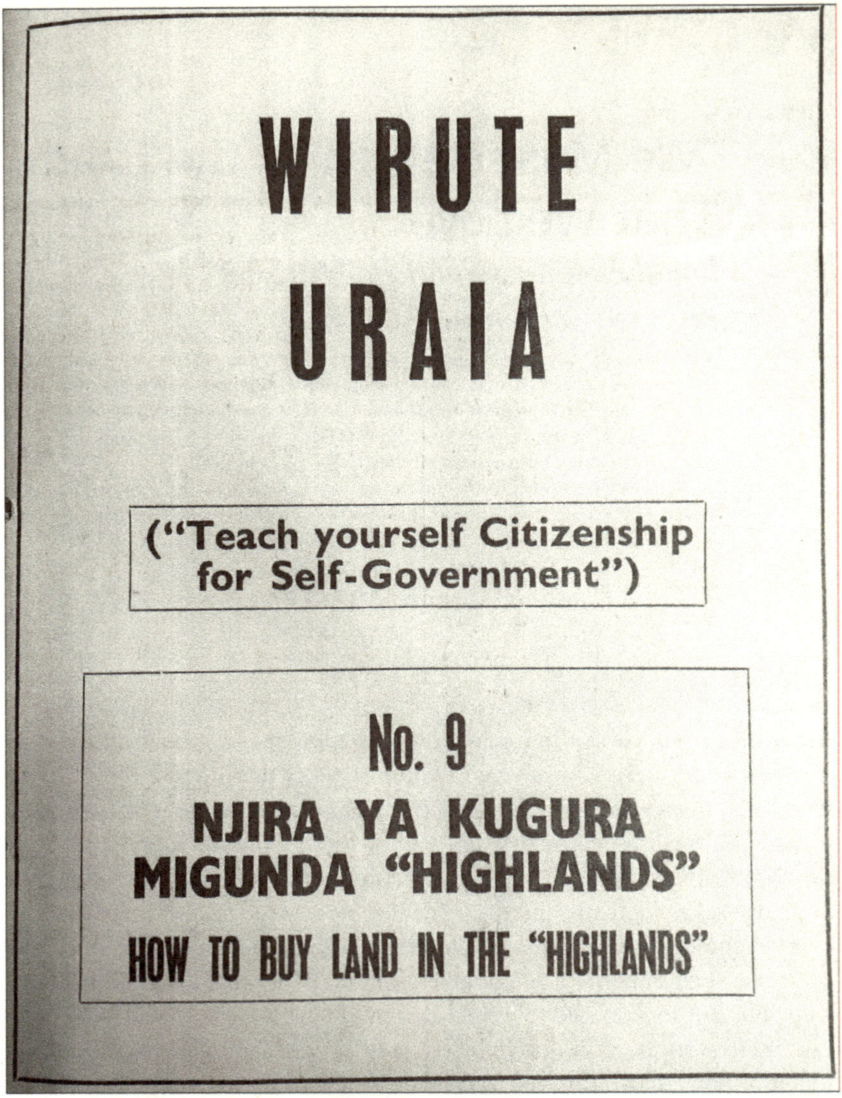
WIRUTE
URAIA
("Teach yourself Citizenship for Self-Government")
No. 9
NJIRA YA KUGURA MIGUNDA "HIGHLANDS"
HOW TO BUY LAND IN THE "HIGHLANDS"

FIGURE 2.1. *Teach Yourself Citizenship for Self-Government* (pamphlet, 1962). Courtesy of the Kenya National Archives DC/ELD/1/10/9.

Many rural Kenyans connected landownership to citizenship, but they also made meaning of settlement through additional lenses, often drawing on ethnic thought. Recognizing the influence of ethnic ideologies, the central government funneled some of its discourse through willing ethnic leaders. The former editorial staff of the *Kalenjin* newssheet was, in fact, tasked with translating *Teach Yourself Citizenship* into the Kalenjin language, and they helped the government to publish and distribute thirty thousand copies in Kalenjin-speaking areas.[4] National and ethnic citizenship became partly intertwined in the process. Yet ethnic identity differentiated colonial experiences and land access, and it colored unique expectations for land during decolonization. Particularly in multiethnic Uasin Gishu, where competition for land was intense, subnational strands of thought on rights to land and notions of belonging made deep impressions on prospective landowners.

Experiences of land resettlement could both reaffirm and undercut popular ideas about political subjectivity, in the process reconfiguring citizenship, ethnic identity, class, and gender. Because policymakers structured land reform for the poor on a communal basis, settlement schemes increased tensions between and within ethnic communities as Kenyans anxiously competed with one another for land. Once settled, Kenyans drew upon, blended, reinterpreted, and constructed ideas on authority and belonging.

SETTLEMENT SCENES

Kenya's landscape has been divided many times throughout its past. Longstanding disputes about political jurisdiction, national and subnational sovereignties, and individual and communal land rights have produced cartographic palimpsests. Each redrawing has added another layer, often leaving unaddressed the challenges foretold by remnant traces of the previous iteration.

In the precolonial era, borders—both those of territory and of identity—were flexible, continually morphing as communities migrated and settled, expanded and contracted, merged and divided. With the advent of colonial rule, British administrators set aside the highlands for European settlement and, simultaneously, consigned African communities to separate "native reserves." In this, they attempted to draw new, more rigid, ethnic and geographic borders. Drawing lines on maps differed considerably from the physical realization of such borders. The latter required policing an obstinate Kenyan population that refused to adhere to imperial geographic visions or legal decrees. Despite the unrelenting challenges of upholding newly invented borders, colonial officials continued to reimagine and

FIGURE 2.2. View of the Rift Valley, ca. 1896–99. Photo courtesy of the British National Archives CO 1069/185 (3a).

redraw them, particularly when they sought space for freshly arriving white settlers. With decolonization, this process continued; though, in this period, European settlers began departing. Not only did independence signify the construction of nation-state boundaries and new forms of national territoriality, but in Kenya, as with many other places, it also entailed the redrawing of internal boundaries.[5]

The northwest Rift Valley highlands experienced these recurrent cartographic alterations more so than many regions of Kenya. Uasin Gishu had been the site of continual migrations and shifting territorial control prior to conquest, and its location on the periphery of the European scheduled areas meant it was subject to frequent border modification. Not only had the region initially been part of the neighboring protectorate of Uganda, but in 1920, British administrators moved the border between the Nandi reserve and Uasin Gishu District, seizing one hundred square miles from the reserve to settle British veterans in the district.[6]

During independence negotiations, border modification resumed, and the Regional Boundaries Commission annexed portions of western Uasin Gishu District in Rift Valley Province for Kakamega District in Western

Province.[7] On both sides of this boundary, the Kenyan state engaged in further mapmaking, creating settlement schemes, now over a half-century old. The settlement projects here, which fell under the Million Acre Scheme, were neither the first nor the last rewriting of Kenya's countryside, though one of the more enduring.

The distance from Nairobi to the western Rift Valley is around two hundred miles. As one ascends the eastern escarpment, the dramatic landscape of the valley comes suddenly into view, with Mount Longonot visible in the distance. One continues on the highway past small towns and verdant scenery until reaching Nakuru, an old white highlands trading town, now the fourth-largest urban center in Kenya. After Nakuru, another hundred miles still remain before approaching Eldoret, the capital of Uasin Gishu and the fifth-biggest city in Kenya.

From Eldoret to Sosiani, a former settlement scheme, is just another nine miles, and the *matatu* (minibus) stop is fittingly named *maili tisa* (mile nine) for this relative distance. Maili tisa is an important transit point, since here the Kenya-Uganda highway meets the northward Eldoret-Kitale road. Trucks, matatus, and motorbikes park precariously along the highway; a string of kiosks dots the northern side of the road, and hawkers thrust biscuits, peanuts, cold drinks, and seasonal produce through the open windows of vehicles passing through.

Sosiani sits just to the south of the highway junction, one of many former settlement schemes in this area. Lumakanda, another former settlement site, is located on the northern side of the road, fifteen miles to the west. Yet the distance between the two feels much vaster. The environments differ visibly. Sosiani is drier and flatter, truly plateau land, while Lumakanda, undulating and lush, occupies an ecological crossroads where the plateau begins its descent into the Nyanza basin. Mautuma, a third scheme, sits just five miles north of Lumakanda. Provincial and district (now county) borders also separate the communities, as do the ethnic identities of their inhabitants—Nandi in Sosiani, Maragoli in Lumakanda, multiethnic (including Kikuyu) in Mautuma. These differences are no accident. They are a product of the layered cartographic renderings—first, the creation of the exclusive white highlands and separate African reserves; then the ethnically organized resettlement programs; and, most recently, political violence—each of which has reordered the landscape.

Lumakanda

Western Kenya, a region extending from Lake Victoria in the west to Mount Elgon in the east, has long been characterized by the interplay of its diverse

FIGURE 2.3. Lumakanda, 2013. Photo by author.

FIGURE 2.4. Sosiani, 2013. Photo by author.

communities. Precolonial tenure systems arose from this setting and its abundant fertile land. Male members of lineages collectively owned the land they lived on. Each individual man possessed usage rights and could make claims to the land he cleared, though grazing land was held communally.[8] When soils became depleted, families shifted their cultivation and moved to virgin lands.[9] By the nineteenth century, these practices had evolved. With population growth and the expansion of their neighbors, the communities of western Kenya established more fixed settlements.[10] When a European traveler arrived at the end of the nineteenth century, he remarked on the dense population of the area.[11]

Just a decade later, European colonial administrators created the North Kavirondo District to govern all the peoples they called the "Bantu Kavirondo." Though these peoples felt affinity for a multiplicity of interconnected identities and called themselves a variety of names, they never called themselves the Kavirondo. In the early colonial period, this area attracted few white settlers. Given its distance from both the capital and the port, the region was presumed unprofitable for export-oriented settler farming.[12] White missionaries, on the other hand, arrived soon after conquest. At the beginning of the twentieth century, Quaker missionaries first settled in western Kenya and began targeting the Maragoli people there for proselytization. It would be years before they had significant success, but over the course of the next few decades, many Maragoli would convert to Christianity.[13]

Shared resentment over colonial rule and colonial encroachment inspired the communities of western Kenya to come together to fashion a new, incorporative ethnic moniker, the Luyia, which gained popular resonance by the mid-1930s.[14] In spite of the collective name, within this pluralist group there remained divisions, borne from conflicting political ambitions and diverse colonial experiences, and thus, too, from divergent decolonizing aspirations. These competing visions came to a head in 1961 when the Regional Boundaries Commission offered Kenyans a platform to make territorial claims.[15] Among the Luyia, there was a consensus that they should appeal for their own region. The Luyia also generally agreed that this new region should integrate certain disputed areas to the north in Nandi, Uasin Gishu, and Trans Nzoia. The Maragoli represented the sole opponents to this plan, envisioning a Luyia region oriented to the south, which would situate the Maragoli more centrally.[16]

These claims not only divided the Luyia community, but they put Luyia in competition with the Kalenjin, who also made assertions to land in Nandi, Uasin Gishu, and Trans Nzoia. Indeed, the Kalenjin-Luyia conflict over this land threatened to destroy a fragile KADU alliance.[17] Ultimately, the Regional Boundaries Commission awarded the Luyia few of the additional territories they sought.[18] The commission excised some land from the western edge of the Kalenjin-dominated Uasin Gishu District to the Luyia-dominated Kakamega District. Administrators transferred this territory mainly to create settlements for the land-poor Luyia. By 1965, between 2,750 and 4,000 people lived in the area formerly a part of Uasin Gishu that had become part of Kakamega.[19]

Lumakanda settlement was one of those limited territorial concessions. In the colonial era, this region lay within the scheduled areas, home to European farms. Under the modified independence boundaries, the edge of the settlement sat flush with the boundary between Kakamega and Uasin Gishu. It also borders the Kenya-Uganda highway, providing access to an important transit network. Between 1963 and 1964, just over six hundred families settled on Lumakanda's 12,434 acres.

Lumakanda settlers identified as Maragoli, and almost all had resided in Maragoli locations prior to moving to the settlement. By the mid-twentieth century, Maragoliland had become "one of the most densely populated regions in Africa," which made it increasingly difficult for families there to sustain themselves on agriculture alone.[20] Men sought wage labor elsewhere, but unemployment remained a problem in both locations.[21] During decolonization, officials created settlement schemes for Maragoli to address these issues.

Among the Maragoli who settled in Lumakanda, some had worked as labor-tenants on European farms, and a number of men had also worked in urban areas for the colonial administration or as manual laborers. Despite their distance from home, labor migrants maintained strong ties to their family and friends in the Maragoli locations. The labor and migration histories of men varied, of course, and a number of those who became settlers had stayed in the reserve throughout the colonial period, close to kin, similar to most of the women who eventually became settlers. On the whole, Maragoli who had remained in the reserves were more reluctant to move. This disinclination grew out of concern over leaving the only home they had ever known—what they considered their "ancestral land"[22]—and from doubts over what decolonizing settlement programs would entail.

Located at the southernmost point of Luyia territory, the Maragoli locations were relatively distant from Lumakanda, about sixty miles. Maragoli were especially far, when compared with the locations of their Luyia counterparts, the Bukusu and the Kabras. Indeed, the creation of settlement schemes in this region for Maragoli intensified divisions between these communities.

Many Bukusu and Kabras had been laborers on European farms in the area and expected to be included in those settlements.[23] Maragoli settler Jamin Maneno Kihinga spent a decade and a half living in Nairobi, working as a clerk in the colonial administration before moving to Lumakanda in 1963. Kihinga recounted, "You know, this was a white highlands settlement. Bukusu and Kabras used to work for white settlers, and they used to depend on white settlers. So, when we arrived, they thought that the land belonged to them. . . . They used to say that Maragoli came with *mukurura*."[24] *Mukurura* is debris that washes up after a flood. The term illustrates Bukusu and Kabras sentiments about Maragoli settlement in Lumakanda.

Such tensions became inflamed at a number of settlement sites. In 1962, Uasin Gishu district commissioner J. G. Mackley noted that the decision to make the Lugari scheme exclusively available to the Maragoli and Bunyore had angered other Luyia subgroups. Mackley wrote, "The Bukusu, Tachoni and Kabras employees who have been on the Estate for many years naturally hope to be included in the Lugari Settlement Scheme and have sought to strengthen their claims by encouraging fellow tribesmen to enter and squat on the estate."[25] Despite their shared corporate ethnic identity, divisions existed among the Luyia. Competing territorial visions and irreconcilable ideas about rights to land and belonging came to a head at settlement sites.

On top of Luyia competition, members of the Maasai and Nandi communities asserted their rights to Lumakanda based on precolonial residency. They employed techniques similar to those of the Bukusu and Kabras to stake their claims. In 1965, J. O. Okeyo, district officer for Lugari, reported that some Maasai and Nandi families had "started moving in the [Lumakanda] Settlement Scheme illegally, they claim to have been told to do so by Chiefs and Sub-Chiefs."[26] Once there, the Maasai and Nandi built small huts and brought in their cattle. Okeyo added, "This move is becoming a threat to settlers in the area since they are looking at it as the beginning of the trouble."[27] Complex physical and imaginative geographies operated in multiethnic borderlands, and ethnic elites encouraged their constituents to make claims. Competition over settlement and development fractured political partnerships at local sites. Though general anxiety over Kikuyu dominance had fostered the creation of more expansive ethnic projects and multiethnic political coalitions, local politics exposed different fault lines, endangering delicate alliances.

Aside from concerns about leaving home, and the claims-making and antipathy of other communities, additional factors deterred some Maragoli from taking part in settlement. On occasion, Maragoli chiefs recruited so-called troublemakers to reduce their administrative problems. Throughout the 1960s, when the preponderance of settler selection occurred, Wilberforce Oyalo worked as a settlement officer in Chekalini, another majority Maragoli scheme, ten miles west of Lumakanda. He noted, "Some [chiefs] just said, 'This man has been troubling me. Let him go that way [to settlement] and perish there.'"[28] Alfred Machayo, a Maragoli civil servant, concurred with Oyalo's depiction. Machayo went to college in the United States. Upon returning to Kenya after independence, he took up a position in the Ministry of Agriculture, working in the Western and Rift Valley Provinces until 1967, when he became Kenya's chief agriculturalist.[29] Machayo recounted that in trying to "get rid of bad people" by sending them to settlement, chiefs dissuaded the more "suitable" prospective settlers from accepting land. As a result, rumors swirled that schemes were for criminals.[30] Machayo, for example, described how people in his village were surprised when he purchased a settlement plot, recounting his neighbors saying, "How does someone from university go to settlement?"[31]

Stories also circulated within the community about how the government intended to closely supervise settlement farms. These rumors began because new primary education programs included teachers' "schemes," or schedules, and the state also called settlement programs "schemes." Prospective settlers became convinced that as with teachers, the government would control their schedule, dictating when they woke up, milked their cows, and planted their maize. Prospective settlers from the Maragoli locations became concerned, additionally, about the land in settlement, which they heard was "so bushy," full of "wild animals," and difficult to clear.[32] Archival documentation suggests that "all sorts of rumours" about settlement spread throughout the country.[33] Certainly, many Kenyans held reservations about what this new program, first initiated by a distrusted colonial government, would entail.

Maragoli families did eventually fully settle the scheme in Lumakanda by the end of 1964. Machayo noted that because of the various discouragements, the state used a bit of "persuasion" to fill schemes.[34] Other evidence suggests state inducement occurred not only to convince the initially unenthused but also to influence settlers who tried to abscond. In 1963, Uasin Gishu's district commissioner wrote of the need to "hustle" rogue settlers back to their plots.[35] Given these circumstances, Maragoli willing to move had little trouble being selected for settlement. Those selected for Lumakanda received loans to buy approximately fifteen acres, two dairy cattle, maize seeds, and sisal plants.

Ainea Alulu settled in Lumakanda. Today, he is retired and spends much of his time at home, surrounded by multiple generations of family and the land he purchased in 1963. His house has a corrugated metal roof, a square wooden door, and small windows with wooden shutters.[36] Inside, it is tidy and furnished with the popular wooden-framed settees. The walls are decorated with old calendars handed out by politicians and a poster on hygiene from an NGO. The land is fertile but a little hilly. Cattle graze around the homestead, roosters occasionally squawk, and the radio persistently plays in the background. Sitting comfortably at home, Alulu exudes gentleness and happily speaks about the past. When one of his granddaughters starts to cry during our conversation, he comforts her, bringing the child onto his lap without thinking. Though he is generally serious and contemplative, occasionally, Alulu's hearty laugh punctuates his speaking as he recalls past events he finds amusing in retrospect.

Ainea Alulu's life history illustrates some of the broader biographical trends of Lumakanda residents—the difficulties of relying on farming for a livelihood in overpopulated Maragoliland, the important role that family and social networks played, and the relative ease with which willing Maragoli could be selected for settlement in the early 1960s. Alulu was born in 1940 in Kericho, where his *baba* (father) worked on a tea estate. He spent his childhood in Maragoli and, similar to other Lumakanda men interviewed, attended a Quaker primary school, Missionary Friends—Kaimosi. The proximity of missionary schools offered Maragoli greater access to education in the early to mid-twentieth century. Even so, education through primary school provided limited employment opportunities in the colonial era. Many Maragoli primary school graduates remained in the reserve to farm small plots of land or became migrant laborers, traveling to cities or European farms to work. Others, like Alulu, left Kenya altogether. Alulu moved to Uganda—not too distant from the Maragoli reserves—in the late 1950s, where he could have a farm.

Alulu said he did not expect land to become available in Kenya at independence, and he was still living in Uganda when officials started announcing settlement. Alulu recounted his surprise when he received a letter from his family saying that Kenyans were getting land. He stated that he had not planned to return to Kenya, but noted, "When I saw things moving, I decided to come back." Alulu traveled to Kenya and completed a settlement interview at his division. He did not recall the interview being burdensome, recounting that officials asked just a few questions, about his health, whether he deserved to get a piece of land, and if he had any other land. Soon after, Alulu was notified that he would get 14.5 acres and two dairy cattle in Lumakanda. He moved to the settlement in November 1963.

Alulu remarked that few Maragoli had been interested, because they thought the settlement schemes had "problems" and that, ultimately, people would be evicted. Other Maragoli settlers in Lumakanda similarly recounted that many people were either afraid of eviction or afraid settlement was a trick.[37] With these concerns, Maragoli drew upon the histories of the previous half-century in which colonial actors appropriated African land, ultimately exploiting and displacing African laborers. Maragoli reluctance to participate in settlement represented an articulation of their continued distrust of the colonial state. In addition to these misgivings, Lumakanda settlers, especially those who had never left the reserve, described fears about moving away from home. Though Alulu had lived in Uganda, he described how he also felt nervous, noting that he was "very courageous to come."[38] With many anxieties and few expectations, over time, most Lumakanda residents became appreciative of settlement, particularly with the economic benefits of their larger landholdings. Their proximity to both a road network and to agricultural extension services—with the divisional office headquartered in their scheme—also contributed to mostly positive assessments.[39] Alulu was generally satisfied that he made the right decision, noting that his brother had remained in Maragoli and regretted doing so.

Sosiani

By the late nineteenth century, a combination of age sets, local military regiments, patrilineal clans, and patrilocal extended families organized Nandi societies. But the most important social and political unit was a territorial one, the *koret* (parish or village). *Korotinwek* (pl.) served as the basic land unit and were structured by social ties and affinal relationships.[40] A council of elders (*kokwet*) headed and handled the affairs of each koret. According to colonial administrator Alfred C. Hollis's 1909 book, *The Nandi: Their Language and Folk-Lore*, the word *koret* meant not only "parish," but also "ground," "land," and "soil."[41] The homonym is suggestive of the important, and constitutive, relationship between Nandi identity and land.

Land was significant as a basic unit of social and political organization, as the resource agropastoralism depended upon, and as a cornerstone of Nandi cosmology. The spirits of dead ancestors—who resided underground—continued to play important roles in the lives of the living. Colonial occupation damaged this spiritual connection, and Nandi oral traditions of conquest emphasize the pain of being separated from their ancestors.[42] Nandi farmer Daniel Kebeney Bitok recounted a tradition similar to that narrated by others: "The *wazungu* [Europeans] were after the Nandi Hills land and told us to migrate to Kabiyet. We did not want to move away from our ancestors. We want to name our children after them. The wazungu assured us that our ancestors would follow us underground."[43] Bitok grew up working on a European estate around Tinderet in the Nandi Hills. The colonial state had seized this region from the Nandi for European settlement. As the site of the death of Koitalel arap Samoei, the leader of the Nandi anticolonial resistance, Tinderet elicited especially charged feelings.

The age sets and clans that cut across all Nandi provided linkages between geographically distant communities. Conquest transformed Nandi identity, though, and a politics of restitution became one of the critical factors animating ethnic solidarity. After Koitalel's death and the Nandi surrender, a 1907 colonial treaty laid out the boundaries of the Nandi reserve. Many Nandi were resentful of the loss of Tinderet, but the treaty guaranteed they would control the reserve in perpetuity. Just five years later, the British violated the agreement with the alienation of about seventeen square miles in Kaimosi. They did so again in 1919, when the colonial state alienated a further 130 square miles in Kipkarren to settle demobilized British soldiers.[44] Though the colonial government returned some of this land thereafter, the violations of the treaty and the loss of Tinderet symbolized broader injustices, and this land took on outsized importance.

In testimony given to the Kenya Land Commission in 1932, Nandi representative arap Chepkigen said, "At the time of the fighting the Government told us this was our boundary: The Europeans will be on that side of it and you will be on the other side of it. . . . The boundary has been pushed back until it no longer tallies with what we were shown before."[45] Thirty years later, during decolonization, Nandi leaders articulated these same land grievances. In August 1962, Kalenjin chiefs and the "people of Nandi district" wrote to the Regional Boundaries Commission: "Tinderet arouses more emotions among the Kalenjin in Nandi than any other area. The place is virtually sacred doubly so since their heroic King and Commander in Chief Samoei of revered memory was murdered there by a treacherous un-English act of an un-gallant English soldier when he went to surrender to the English in 1905 at the end of the so-called Nandi disturbances."[46] A politics of resentment and reparations had become central to Nandi identity.[47]

Other groups—both political allies and adversaries—made claims to this same land. Such contention tended to bolster Nandi ethnic affinity but could also prove incompatible to broader political projects. Nandi unity strengthened in opposition to perceived intrusion from the Kikuyu. Anxiety about Kikuyu-Luo dominance and encroachment also provided the basis for a shared politics among the Nandi, other Kalenjin subgroups, the Luyia, and the Maasai.[48] Yet, just as land politics and claims-making encouraged interethnic alliances, it also fractured them. The Nandi ethnonationalist project was founded upon a particular historical injustice and an assertion to land restitution. Nandi declarations of autochthony represented a fundamentally insular ideology. By drawing on autochthonous discourse, Nandi leaders attempted, in effect, to exclude not just the Kikuyu, but all other groups from making claims to territory they considered rightfully theirs. This included other Kalenjin subgroups, along with their KADU allies, the Luyia and the Maasai. Ultimately, the Nandi did not succeed in claiming Uasin Gishu. According to Kenya's national census in 1979, the Kalenjin made up 55 percent of Uasin Gishu's population, while the Kikuyu composed 19 percent and the Luyia 16 percent.[49] Among the Kalenjin living in Uasin Gishu, the majority were Nandi, but there were also significant numbers of Kipsigis and Keiyo. Though these groups inhabited different parts of the district, tensions have long simmered.[50]

In this charged, competitive setting, divisions emerged within the Nandi community as well. When Nandi contended with one another for land access, they drew on personal experiences of colonial oppression, and they relied on distinct political connections. Land aspirants asserted they were more deserving than their counterparts, and competition for land settlement revealed rifts within the Nandi community, especially between white highlands and native reserves residents. As with the intra-Luyia cleavages, the contested Nandi borderlands reveal a unique set of local political issues, irreconcilable with the thrust of regional and national politics.

Soon after being displaced at conquest, many Nandi returned to "the same fields that had been their ancestral homelands."[51] Throughout the first half of the twentieth century, growing numbers of Nandi moved to the scheduled areas. Colonial linguist and anthropologist G. W. B. Huntingford reported that the Nandi felt "fully entitled to live in the settled area because it was formerly occupied by them," and they regarded it "as little more than an extension of the Reserve and as a part of their tribal area."[52] By 1923, an estimated one-third of the Nandi population worked on European farms.[53]

For most Nandi, the greatest appeal to working in the highlands was access to grazing land. Nandi life centered around cattle. Wealth and social status were measured in cattle, and cattle were sacred in Nandi religion. The Nandi lexicon contains an abundance of words for types of cattle, markings of cattle, and cattle-specific terminology. Personal names are often derived from cattle terms (*Kimneny*, for instance, means "born when the cattle were at a salt lick"), and one of the most common daily prayers asks Asis, or God, to protect children and cattle ("Asis, kaasain tukua lakōk ak tuka"). With the delimiting and diminishing of their territory under colonial rule, the Nandi community relied on squatters in the highlands for additional land. The vast tracts of land allowed laborers to graze their own stock as well as those on loan to them from friends and family in the reserve through the *kaptich* system. By 1947, Nandi squatters—said to number 32,287—grazed about 40 percent of all the cattle in Uasin Gishu District.[54]

This was to be the zenith of Nandi stockholdings in the scheduled areas. As cereal prices declined following the Great Depression, white settlers shifted to stock farming and began limiting Nandi cattle.[55] In Uasin Gishu, as in other regions, the county council passed a resident laborers order in 1953, reducing the number of stock squatters could keep. Many Nandi continued to illegally hold excess stock, but, in 1957, "an intensive drive was launched to enforce the law," and colonial administrators impounded 5,374 cattle and 4,282 sheep.[56] In this setting, Nandi increasingly returned to the reserves, or moved to other parts of Kenya, and even to Uganda and Tanzania. Nandi farmer John Arusei described how he had worked in Moi's Bridge on a European farm for close to a decade, when "the *wazungu* [Europeans] acquired more cattle and drove squatter cattle away." He added, "After losing our cattle, we went back to Nandi [reserve]. The Kalenjin depend on cattle. Without cattle is without life."[57] Other Nandi interlocutors recounted similar migration stories after the enactment of cattle controls in the highlands.[58]

The cattle restrictions exacerbated already developing conflicts within the Nandi community. Colonial histories of mobility had produced cleavages between Nandi in the reserve and those in the scheduled areas. Stock restrictions circumscribed cattle loaning practices—essential to sustaining social relations between the reserves and scheduled areas—and thus, upset friendships and familial ties. Kaptich not only provided insurance against the loss of a herd to raids or epidemics, but the reciprocity of the system and the act of entrusting a friend with care for valued possessions strengthened relationships.[59] Without the cattle loaning system in place, and with tensions heightening as former squatters returned to the increasingly crowded reserve, some of these relationships frayed.

At this time, chiefs began subdividing communal land in Nandi for individual ownership. In doing so, they privileged the elite, denying land rights to many Nandi living outside the reserve and to women. The Nandi Local Native Council (LNC) passed a resolution in 1949, restricting enclosures to two acres and requiring prior authorization by chiefs and kokwet elders. This same resolution allowed chiefs, kokwet elders, members of the LNC, and other prominent individuals to keep larger plots they had already enclosed. In 1952, the Nandi District Land Committee passed an additional resolution denying Nandi employed outside the reserve the right to possess land in the reserve.[60] When elder elites in the reserve dispossessed highland laborers, the tensions that had begun to surface escalated.[61] As land shortages in the reserve increased, Nandi elites also intensified communal demands for the return of lost lands in Kaimosi and Kipkarren.[62]

These tensions became even more pronounced as land became available at decolonization. Nandi and non-Nandi—Kikuyu, Luyia, and Kalenjin, especially—vied for the same land, and so, too, did reserve Nandi and highland Nandi. A 1961 monthly report from one of the earliest schemes, Lessos, illustrates the mounting antagonism within the Nandi community. Lessos received five times more applicants than its capacity. A settlement officer noted that "those in the Reserve feel that if they are not careful, all the pets of the local European settlers will be found plots at their expense, while the latter feel that they have very little hope if all the selection is done through the Reserve Location Councils."[63] The Lessos selection committee eventually favored former laborers by skewing the selection point system.[64]

To make matters worse, in Lessos as in many other schemes, the Kenyan colonial government hired former European settlers to work as settlement officers. Nandi politician Jean-Marie Seroney derided this practice in the Legislative Council in June 1962:

> What disturbs me most about this scheme is that a former owner of this farm has been employed by the Government as a settlement officer. I could never imagine a more psychologically stupid appointment. Here is a *mzungu* [European] who sells his land to the Government because he has no confidence in Kenya, and then makes sure that he collects all his money—or at least he is assured of it, then wangles a job from Government with a salary, retains his house and then becomes a *mtumizi wa serikali* [government employee]. Then he is relied on by the Government to decide who is or is not fit to settle on this farm.[65]

Allowing European settlers to take up government posts, which positioned them to select settlers and manage settlements, provoked conflicts throughout Kenya. In South Kinangop (Central Province), settlers and clerks complained that two European officers treated them badly using "colonialism dictatorship laws." They warned, "In fact this is the time of all Kenya people White, Black or Red to work together and if one of these can't work using Democracy people will never cope with him."[66] While the petition illustrates frustration with the preservation of European authority, it also suggests that Kenyans felt empowered under the new political order, and European officials could soon experience the repercussions.

In Lessos, the selection committee—composed largely of former European employers—favored laborers, reinforcing the opinion held by reserve Nandi that selection was biased. Given that state policy allowed local officials immense latitude, on other occasions, committees privileged applicants from the reserve. The uncertainty created dissatisfaction and produced a general impression that settlement operated through favoritism. In turn, Nandi—both those in the scheduled areas and those in the reserve—protested to officials. The district commissioner of Kitale noted, for instance, how landless laborers in the highlands "complain that it is useless to apply to the District Commissioners of their District of origin, as they are not known there, and no one will speak for them when their applications come before the selection boards. They claim that only applicants in reserves, who are known to local officials have chances of being selected for a plot."[67] The district commissioner of Uasin Gishu agreed with this account, noting the "great danger that DC's from district of origin will tend to fill settlement vacancies with their home parishioners."[68] The composition of the committees could prejudice decisions, and settler selection often operated contrary to the dictates of land legislation.

The two Nandi factions had access to different nodes of colonial power, since reserve Nandi and highland Nandi had cultivated different sets of political relations in the colonial era. By placing these groups in competition with one another, development actors aggravated latent hostilities and created a setting rife with insecurity. This context, combined with ethnic discourse on imminent land restitution and a material need for land, drove Nandi to actively pursue settlement, often for years at a time. Becoming a landowner usually required multiple migrations and entailed drawing on extensive political and familial networks.

Such was the case, at least, for many of the Nandi who ultimately settled in Sosiani. At sixty-five hundred feet above sea level, Sosiani sits on a small strip of Uasin Gishu that extends out roughly twenty miles westward past the rest of the district's borders. It lies only about five miles away, on either side, from Kakamega District (now county) to the north and Nandi District (now county) to the south. In the colonial era, Sosiani had been part of Uasin Gishu District and the scheduled areas. Given its proximity to the Nandi reserve, and its conduciveness to pastoralism, many Nandi worked for European farmers in this region. The Nandi community generally regarded the northwest portion of Uasin Gishu as their rightful territory and expected this region would be returned. At independence, most of the settlement schemes in this area were designated for the Nandi, though significant numbers of Luyia and Kikuyu families settled in this region as well.

Sosiani was a relatively small scheme—just 5,307 acres and only ninety-seven settlers, who arrived between 1963 and 1965. The average plot size was 51.45 acres.[69] Sosiani settlers received larger plots, because technocrats graded the soil there as "category C," suitable only for grazing.[70] Planners thus designed the scheme solely for livestock and dairy production, though, later, officials approved maize production as well. Most settlers recounted that when applying for a plot, they registered their names with the Uasin Gishu district commissioner. In Sosiani's case, the settlement selection committee favored those with recommendations from European employers and chose the remainder by raffle. The involvement of the Uasin Gishu DC, as opposed to the Nandi DC, shaped the committee's decision to prioritize laborers over reserve dwellers.

In point of fact, almost every Sosiani settler had previously worked as a resident laborer on a European farm for at least a few years. Most had moved frequently—between various European farms and the Nandi reserve. At decolonization, the land poverty of Nandi laborers served as motivation to seek settlement. Communal bitterness over historical injustices further marshaled the pursuit of land. Sosiani settlers' life histories differed considerably from those of Lumakanda partially on account of these colonial experiences. Sosiani life histories reveal the rate of Nandi migration in the late colonial and early postcolonial periods, and a different set of tactics for accessing land.

Joseph arap Bir'geng, a Nandi man, was selected for one of the ninety-seven plots in Sosiani. Like Lumakanda settler Ainea Alulu, he still lives on the land he purchased through settlement over half a century ago. Bir'geng's land initially covered a little over fifty acres, but, recently, he sold part of this land. As he has grown older, some of his children have taken on the responsibility of managing the property, farming the land, and keeping the cattle. With the larger plots, Sosiani homesteads are farther apart. Still, Bir'geng's multigenerational farming household possesses a liveliness somewhat unbefitting of its bucolic location. Children, cattle, roosters, motorcycles, and radios continually disrupt momentary periods of silence. Now about ninety years old, Bir'geng is frail, soft-spoken, and a little hard of hearing. Even so, he has preserved specific memories of the late colonial and early postcolonial periods, and, like many Nandi, Bir'geng is a consummate storyteller who takes pleasure in recounting the past in lurid detail.[71]

Bir'geng was born in the Nandi reserve and spent his earliest years there. As with many Nandi of his generation, he never attended school. According to Africa Inland Mission (AIM) evangelists, the Nandi were "slow to respond to the Gospel."[72] In fact, the Church Mission Society, which first brought

Christianity to the Nandi reserve, packed up and left after just three years due to widespread antagonism. AIM followed, and, in 1914, over a decade after establishing itself in the region, the mission could point to little success. With their opposition to missionaries, though, Nandi had fewer educational opportunities than other Kenyan groups who converted earlier and more readily. The earliest Nandi government school opened in 1925 in Kapsabet, and it was the first broadly accepted educational institution, because the church was uninvolved.[73]

For most of his early childhood, Bir'geng remained in the reserve, where he worked on his family's farm helping to look after the cattle, a common job for Nandi boys. As a teen, Bir'geng moved to Uasin Gishu to seek employment. There he worked for a European farmer, planting pyrethrum. He stayed a couple of years and then returned to Nandi. In 1943, he moved to Uasin Gishu, again to work for a European farmer, this time to drive bulls and plow land. After three years or so, he returned to Nandi once again and remained there until just after independence. Bir'geng's recurrent migrations are reflective of broader Nandi migration patterns. Many Nandi continually moved between the scheduled areas and the reserve in the colonial era, with the proximity between the two encouraging mobility. When labor and political conditions evolved, and when commodity prices, economic opportunities, and politics shifted, Nandi would weigh their options and decide whether to move or stay. Indeed, Bir'geng's departure from the highlands in 1947 corresponds to the Nandi out-migration from the scheduled areas when Europeans enacted cattle restrictions.

From 1947 until independence, Bir'geng remained in the reserve. He did not receive an individual plot when Nandi chiefs subdivided communal land, so he farmed and kept cattle on his parents' land. Around independence, he recounted Nandi elders "going round saying the whites were leaving and land was ready to be bought." He then described the multiple steps he took to apply: "You go to the elders and you tell them your grievances, why you need the land, how you will make the *shamba* [farm] productive." This represented just a first step to getting an interview. Bir'geng remarked, "There was a difficulty with the interviews. You could not go direct. You had to be introduced. It was easier if you were known to the administration." Bir'geng recounted, additionally, the competitiveness of settlement selection, and how Kenyans often applied to multiple schemes before they had success. "People could apply here and then if they didn't get land, they could proceed to other places," he noted. His recollections coincide with other Nandi oral histories. In particular, Nandi already living in Uasin Gishu moved frequently to best position themselves for selection. They recounted squatting on former European farms they anticipated would become settlements, and they described moving in with family who lived close to settlement areas. In some ways, these repeated migrations paralleled the colonial era, when Nandi moved strategically every couple of years. Bir'geng was eventually selected for Sosiani, receiving a plot and four grade cattle in 1964. His land is flat, with some rocks and some swampy areas, but Bir'geng described it as "suitable."[74]

Given the competitiveness of the selection process for Nandi schemes, local political connections were essential. Nandi land applicants needed to understand the procedures in place and be willing to migrate continually in order to be selected. In a context of competition, Nandi moved strategically and drew extensively on familial, social, and political relationships to improve their chances for selection. This setting of uncertainty and contingency engendered insecurities and tensions. Even so, Bir'geng's somewhat tepid characterization of his land parallels the way many Nandi spoke about settlement, reflecting the communal response to territory that many expected and considered their own.

Mautuma

Like the Nandi, the Kikuyu had long traveled from their reserve to work for white settlers. They remained in the highlands for years, sometimes generations, and often more completely severed their ties with the reserve community. Beginning in the interwar era, Kikuyu squatters, like others, were subjected to increasingly restrictive laws. Most significantly, the 1937 Resident Native Laborers Ordinance (RNLO) allowed white settlers to dramatically curtail the acres squatters could cultivate, to limit squatter stock, to increase the number of days per year squatters worked on European farms, and to evict redundant or noncompliant squatters.[75] These amendments made clear that Kikuyu squatters had no rights to the highlands under colonial law, though they had believed they possessed customary rights of ownership for their kin and descendants (*githaka*). By the second half of the 1940s, the labor conditions in the highlands had become untenable, with squatter incomes declining precipitously, and with Europeans evicting rising numbers of Kikuyu. Kikuyu elites prohibited those squatters forced back to overcrowded central Kenya from exercising previously inalienable rights and, frequently, from getting "even an inch of land."[76]

While there is a vast literature on Kikuyu squatters in the highlands (the most populous group of resident laborers), much of this literature has focused on Kikuyu in the eastern highlands or on Mau Mau.[77] Despite the distance from central Kenya, Kikuyu represented the largest group of squatters in Uasin Gishu. As decolonization and land settlement got underway, many Kikuyu in the western highlands possessed few options for obtaining land. The planners of the Million Acre Scheme organized resettlement around ethnicity. They chose settlement sites that abutted the ethnically segregated native reserves, often annexing settlements into the reserves and selecting settlers with the corresponding ethnic background.[78] This design largely barred Kikuyu laborers in the northwest Rift—which did not border the Kikuyu native land units—from settlement.

In other words, as Kenya's land board purchased European estates to create new African villages, they dislocated Kikuyu laborers, who were deemed ineligible for settlement in the western highlands. By February 1962, administrators in Kikuyu districts reported "daily bus loads of vagrants being repatriated from outside," and noted the "worsening security situation occasioned by the large numbers of landless and jobless Kikuyu."[79] Beginning in 1962, other Kikuyu found themselves routed to transit camps, where they were supposed to reside for six to nine months awaiting more permanent settlement. Transit schemes offered neither access to adequate social services nor a direct path to settlement, and many Kikuyu families spent years in "unbearable conditions" at these camps.[80]

Countless Kikuyu who had worked and lived in Uasin Gishu wrote petitions seeking land in settlement schemes. In one instance, Paul Mwangi Kimani addressed a letter to Jomo Kenyatta on behalf of the Kikuyu families at Armstrong Farm in Ainabkoi, Uasin Gishu:

> But what I should let you know is that all the farms are taken by LDS [Land Development and Settlement] Board and Kalengine [*sic*] people have taken them, and we have no where to go or anything to do. So, that we ask you kindly to show us where to go and what to do.
>
> The reason why is that we can't let our children to diy [*sic*] day after day, because of hunger. After that on 17th Nov. 1964 our RGA [regional government agent] of Uasin Gish [*sic*] told us that we must go away before 17th Dec. 1964 because this Region belongs to Kalengine People only. So we have given note of one month to go away either to go to the moon or to the sea. We ask you to help us. We are over seven hundred people, either small plots or camp, if necessary. What shall we do when our RGA takes us away?[81]

Many Kikuyu who had been born in the Rift Valley, or lived there for decades, no longer possessed connections to central Kenya. Henry Magu

Kahigu lamented to his provincial commissioner, "I have lived in this province [Rift Valley] all my life and know not where my father came from," whereas Mwangi Njoroge and Stanley Mwangi Maina explained to the Rift Valley PC that no one in Fort Hall (central Kenya) "could recall us, nor give us any help and we had no relatives could be traced."[82] With land redistribution structured by ethnicity, civil servants offered Kikuyu little assistance. When the Uasin Gishu district commissioner replied to such letters, he noted there were no schemes for Kikuyu in the district, and they would have to look farther east.

After the passage of constitutional amendments in 1964, the central government controlled land, and settlement became determined by work history, not ethnicity. Suddenly, Kikuyu laborers in the western highlands who had worked at least four years were prioritized rather than excluded. Conversely, the Nandi—who had moved frequently and often not remained in the highlands consecutively—and the Maragoli—who had more often remained in the reserve—found their access to land diminished. This new form of selection heightened ethnic tensions. The Kalenjin and Luyia, who made communal territorial claims, saw the Kikuyu—already perceived as encroaching on the Rift Valley and as overly dominant in politics—benefit in their stead. The transition to a centralized, and more formalized, selection process was a product of the political maneuverings of a Kenyatta state bent on consolidating its power and advantaging the Kikuyu. Even so, much of the Million Acre Scheme had already been completed by this time.

Joseph Dugere Munge's life history offers insight into Kikuyu experiences in the western highlands. A landowner in what is now Kakamega County for over half a century, and with Rift Valley roots that go back eighty years, today Munge is one of few Kikuyu left in his village. Munge was born in 1937 in Kiambu, central Kenya. His family moved to the Rift Valley in 1939. When Munge was still a boy, he returned to Kiambu alone to attend an independent school. Kikuyu embraced Western education early on; they had greater access to schooling given the missionary presence and their proximity to Nairobi. In the mid-1930s, Kikuyu landlords and big farmers prospered with the rise of commodity prices. In turn, they expanded their acreages and evicted tenants and junior kin, who often became migrant laborers on white farms as a result. At this same time, Kikuyu school enrollments increased, and the growing number of squatters began opening small church and school outposts. "Independent," Kikuyu-run schools developed to meet the widespread demand for education, but they became popular because of their "strategic theory of education," which "trained students to deal with the rituals of government bureaucracy."[83] Munge completed six years of independent schooling and got his junior secretary certificate. It appears that independent education prepared Munge for employment in a colonial context. With his schooling, clerical and administrative job opportunities opened up. He first worked for the railway in Nairobi, where he also got married. Then, in 1958, he moved with his wife and young children back to the Rift Valley to manage a white farm.[84]

At independence, Munge recounted, "I didn't expect land. I didn't know what to do. I was just waiting." He first learned about settlement in 1963, when he heard about Lumakanda and "that people from Vihiga were being brought." Munge said he bided his time. He was not too nervous, because he knew he was not the only squatter and many people were talking about settlement. In 1964, after selection criteria had been modified, the European farm owner who had employed Munge gave his name to the district commissioner. Because Munge had worked on the farm for over four years, he was automatically prioritized for settlement. Further to Munge's benefit, his former employer worked as the settlement officer in nearby Lumakanda. As a result, he did not even complete an interview for his application. Munge remained on his employer's farm until he was settled on the Mautuma scheme in 1965 along with fellow laborers from the farm, and from two other white farms in the area.[85]

Similar to Lumakanda, Mautuma had been part of Uasin Gishu but was excised to Kakamega District during decolonization. It was formerly a large sisal estate, situated just five miles due north of Lumakanda. As a result, when state officials first planned Mautuma in 1963, they created the scheme for the Luyia, mostly Maragoli and Bunyore. In 1965, the government carried out an extension. Since the extension took place under a different constitution, and a different set of policies on settler selection, it included multiethnic settlers. In heterogeneous districts like Uasin Gishu, laborers came from a number of different ethnic communities. The ethnic composition of the newer Mautuma settlers paralleled that of the former laborers. Thus, Luyia, Kikuyu, and Kalenjin all became residents there. With the extension, Mautuma covered 10,367 acres and included 536 plots, roughly equivalent in size to Lumakanda, and about twice the acreage and five times the settlers of Sosiani.[86] Though the average plot size was eighteen acres, there were three different acreage categories—eleven, fifteen, and thirty-seven acres—so settler incomes varied considerably.[87]

Mautuma—like Lumakanda—was designed for maize and dairy, and most settlers, including Munge, got eleven or fifteen acres and two cattle. Unlike Lumakanda, Mautuma sat some distance from the main roads and had no extension officer on the scheme, two factors that negatively affected profits. Munge was generally content, as he compared the liberties landownership endowed him with to the restrictions and repression of colonialism. He said, "During the colonial period, we worked like slaves, but now, I have the freedom to do anything for myself."[88] Still, this positive interpretation of independence was tempered by later events.

The constitutional amendments wrought changes, ending regionalism, centralizing settler selection, and favoring former labor-tenants. Not only were settlers multiethnic, but they were chosen strictly on the basis of work history. Mautuma differed fundamentally from Lumakanda, where many settlers had never worked as squatters on European farms, and from Sosiani, which was homogeneously Nandi.

Comparing Settlement Histories

In the years after settlement, residents of Lumakanda, Sosiani, and Mautuma thought about the significance of their land, and the significance of independence, in vastly different terms. With few expectations for land at independence, Maragoli settlers were generally grateful. Wilberforce Oyalo—the extension officer we met in the previous chapter—worked and lived in Chekalini, one of the Luyia schemes excised to Kakamega. He asserted, "Those who came this way are better off than those who remained. If we were here longer, you could see even many people coming . . . for maize. Now we are the feeders [of the Maragoli]."[89] Almost all Lumakanda settlers proclaimed they were more prosperous than their family members who stayed behind. The reluctance they once felt had disappeared.

Nandi settlers, though, possessed greater ambivalence. Unlike Maragoli settlers, many Nandi recounted that settlement in Uasin Gishu had not made them better off than their relatives who remained in Nandi District, commenting that "their lives were almost the same."[90] Nandi expectations for settlement and for land restitution shaped their dispassionate evaluations of the postcolonial context. After independence, many Nandi continued to feel resentful about lands lost during colonialism and anger about outsiders' encroachment on the western highlands. An effective and emotionally resonant ethnonationalist campaign, built upon rights to the lands of Uasin Gishu and Tinderet, continued to be central to Nandi politics even after the conclusion of resettlement programming.

For the few Kikuyu left in the region, decolonizing land settlement is also marked by its ambivalence. Kikuyu in Uasin Gishu valued their land. However, their expectations for land and their experiences as vulnerable ethnic minorities in the northwest Rift moderated their appreciation. In 1969, for example, Kikuyu settler Samwel Ngugi wrote to Minister of State

Mbiyu Koinange on behalf of the Kikuyu community living in Turbo, Uasin Gishu: "There is tribalism between Kikuyu and Nandis. . . . Kikuyu who are living within Kaptabei Settlement Scheme are sleeping outside at present. Nandis have already burnt houses and beaten Kikuyu."[91] At tense political moments, Kikuyu found themselves targeted and some left. After violence in 1992, 1997, and 2007–8, Kikuyu departed in even greater numbers. Their understandings of settlement cannot but have been shaped by the devastating violence in this region. They often expressed how much better their lives were immediately after independence as compared to today.[92]

Settlers of various ethnic backgrounds also shared experiences. All the life histories confirm the importance of political networks—whether those networks were rooted in former European employers, chiefs in the reserves, the members of selection committees, or family members. Further, settlers—even those who had supported the KADU opposition—generally credited Kenyatta with giving them their *shamba* (farm). Likewise, many settlers' notions of Kenyan citizenship were shaped by their experiences accessing land. Interlocutors articulated notions of citizenly duties akin to those laid out in the *Teach Yourself Citizenship for Self-Government* pamphlet. Lumakanda settler Ainea Alulu recounted that he advanced nation-building efforts by practicing modern farming. Settlers generally spoke with pride about their hard work, in farming and in community development, which they saw as important contributions to Kenyan development. Male landowners on the whole equated citizenship with owning the country or the land.

While Kikuyu settlers in Mautuma defined the term "mwananchi" similarly, their notions of citizenship and nation-building have also been molded in response to their insecurities, and they commonly spoke specifically about belonging, peace, harmony, and cooperation.[93] In this case, Kikuyu ideologies serve as a reminder that Kenyan political philosophies coalesced from ethnic and national political thought but evolved continually, based on personal experiences and local politics.

In multiethnic, contested regions like Uasin Gishu, Kenyans drew on numerous political subjectivities, and on national and ethnic discourse, to make land claims and to make meaning of citizenship. High-density schemes aimed at the poor pitted local Kenyan groups, particularly ethnic groups, against one another for valued fertile land. On the ground, political coalitions and ethnic affinities easily became fractured, revealing competing territorial visions, irreconcilable ideas about land rights, and localized political fault lines.

While the Maragoli did not make specific claims to Lumakanda, they did live in one of the most densely populated regions of Kenya. On account of the distance and their distrust of the colonial government, when land became available at Lumakanda, many worried about leaving their communities and traveling to an unfamiliar place. Eventually, Maragoli families settled the scheme, though, in the process, they aggravated tensions with their Luyia allies, the Bukusu and Kabras who had expected resettlement. Despite their initial reluctance, most Lumakanda settlers came to see their land as one of the promises of independence fulfilled.

Similar to other communities with ties to the highlands, many Nandi imagined independence as inextricably connected to land redistribution. Communal declarations of ownership over Uasin Gishu bolstered Nandi claims. Competitiveness was multilayered, though, and not just interethnic but also intraethnic. The growing rivalry between Nandi in the reserve and Nandi outside the reserve heightened decolonizing anxieties over land, and Nandi also contended with other Kalenjin subgroups and with their Luyia allies. Complex, intermingled ethnic and national political thought became further convoluted when inflected by personal experience and local politics. Ultimately, the commonly held Nandi belief in their rights to western Uasin Gishu often meant that those who got land did not feel fully satisfied with settlement and independence.

Kikuyu farm-purchasing opportunities were initially limited in the western highlands. While the privileging of labor identity over ethnic identity in 1964 improved Kikuyu chances of selection for settlement, by that time many Kikuyu had already been displaced from the northwest Rift to transit camps, other highlands regions, central Kenya, or urban areas. Those who remained in Uasin Gishu seemed to expect they would eventually get land. Perhaps their optimism was a product of the Kikuyu domination of formal political arenas or of Kikuyu moral ethnicity, which rewarded hard work. Even so, their position as ethnic minorities produced feelings of vulnerability and unbelonging.

The next chapter turns to those excluded from land settlement. The landless, land-impoverished, and land-insecure were influenced by the same political ideologies and geographic visions as Uasin Gishu landowners. They, too, made sense of the historical moment and their place in it by employing ethnic and national discourses and by drawing on their individual experiences. Their notions of independence, governance, and citizenship became inflected especially by their experiences of land insecurity.

3 "The Land Was Ours, but It Was Not Mine"

Land Marginalization and the Political Imagination

> Kenya now faces the tenth-year anniversary of its independence. Surely, some have milked and enjoyed the fruits of uhuru. I am hungry and thirsty.
>
> —Squatter James K. Sitieney to the Office of the President, 1973[1]

IN A 1964 LETTER addressed to Pres. Jomo Kenyatta, two Kenyans complained that the poor had not received "even half" of the land distributed through settlement. "Now, if these acres are finished," they asked, "what will you give us we the needy?" The writers made claims to land based on their impoverishment. Given their continued landlessness, they also mused whether *uhuru* (independence) held any meaning: "We are surprised to be told that we received independence. . . . The poor voted to get a government which can eliminate bad things of the colonialists for them, yet things are getting worse than before."[2] The writing effused disillusionment.

Independence had come just mere months prior. Anticipation had been great, however, and many Kenyans expected land. Independence did not herald radical redistribution, and landownership continued to be inequitable. Those who remained landless or land-poor questioned whether uhuru had really arrived. Ten years later, as the epigraph illustrates, landless Kenyans were still asking similar questions—when, if ever, would they enjoy the fruits of freedom? In this they sought the resources of the state, particularly land.

That these expectations went unmet troubled the ideological promises of decolonization—promises of more equitable access to resources. While Kenyan subjects became citizens at independence, some did not gain full rights to landownership and property. Women, the poor, marginalized ethnicities, pastoralists, and uneducated Kenyans were often excluded from land access. This was not the decolonizing future many Kenyans had envisioned, and, for them, independence often held more symbolic than material meaning. The postcolonial era produced few tangible changes for those who remained landless, and the disappointments of this decolonizing continuity permeated political imaginaries.

Landlessness and land insecurity affected material circumstances and produced some of the deepest contours in rural thinking. Exclusion from state resources colored how Kenyans assessed the postcolonial government, fashioned notions of citizenship, and evaluated the significance of independence. Most Kenyans who became landowners during the 1960s—regardless of ethnicity—thought of independence as significant and conceptualized citizenship through the language of ownership, either of land or of nation. Landless men and women, on the other hand, often did not consider independence a significant milestone in their lives. Because of their marginalized position and because they were less visible to state actors, women and the landless experienced the postcolonial state as a highly unreliable institution. Frequently, they did not consider themselves citizens at all.

The first section of this chapter examines the decolonizing policy aimed at the landless. Squatter settlement programs offered new opportunities for landownership, but these programs dramatically curtailed the resources provided through settlement schemes and never sought to completely resolve landlessness. The remainder of the chapter turns to the perspectives of the land-insecure. The second part explores land-buying organizations—groups that pooled money to purchase land privately. These organizations went largely unregulated and often eventually further dispossessed the landless. From there, the chapter turns to women who were also structurally excluded from landownership opportunities, but often through different mechanisms than those used to marginalize men. Gendered inequalities excluded women from owning land and circumscribed their property rights and financial liberties, but family-level negotiations also created differences among households. In some circumstances, women experienced relative economic autonomy in their control of family land, household resources, and farm production. The final section analyzes how landlessness and land insecurity shaped conceptions of governance, citizenship, and independence.

SQUATTERS AND POSTCOLONIAL POLICY

By the postwar era, the problem of landlessness in Kenya was worsening. Throughout the first half of the twentieth century, the colonial state had continually appropriated fertile land for European settlers. In the 1950s, bureaucrats reversed colonial land tenure orthodoxies, offering certain Africans property rights. Chiefs in the reserves then allocated individual plots unequally, excluding large numbers of people. Simultaneously, the population was skyrocketing, exacerbating the problem.

This intractable setting became further complicated when nationalists and ethnic leaders began promising that independence would bring land redistribution. Indeed, the 1960 KANU Manifesto pledged, "Resettlement will, then, be KANU's foremost problem: resettlement not at the cost of the high standard of agriculture already attained, but definitely at the expense of absentee landlordism, of individuals owning large square miles while neighbouring African people jostle in small areas."[3] For some, particularly those selected for land settlement, independence lived up to those promises. Many others remained landless, however. By the 1966–67 financial year, the Million Acre Scheme—the largest land resettlement program in Kenyan history—had concluded. Settlement possibilities for the landless began closing down as the amount of land available for purchase with government support decreased dramatically.

Though some settlement programs targeted the landless and aimed to assuage squatters, these schemes offered an incomplete solution to a deeply rooted problem.[4] Kenyan policymakers had long known this, recognizing that there were "more squatters than land on which to settle" them.[5] In response, the independent government developed a new squatter policy in 1964. The state implemented "Operation Real Estate," a plan to evict all squatters using magistrates on the ground to quickly adjudicate cases.[6] A year later, when it had become clear that this action would not achieve its goals, Kenyatta appointed Z. B. Shimechero as special commissioner for squatters. He assigned the commissioner "to determine the extent of the squatter problem, to advise the Government on alternative measures for settlement or re-employment of squatters, and to advise the Government on the most expeditious way for the removal of illegal squatters."[7] After the failure of Operation Real Estate, and its grassroots, litigious strategy, the government experimented with a more cautious approach.

Under Shimechero's leadership, the Kenyan state reworked squatter policy, focusing initially on preventing the influx of new squatters and removing those who began squatting after 1 May 1965.[8] Another of Shimechero's first acts was quite basic—clarifying confusing terminology. The special commissioner recommended distinguishing between "genuine" squatters, those living on property to which they had no title, and those he labeled "resident labourers," who had, under colonial rule, been called squatters.[9] Following the introduction of this new nomenclature, Shimechero ordered the identification and registration of all squatters.[10] The proposed census-taking exercise paralleled the high-modernist planning for Kenyan settlement programs. Similar to settlement, though, planning and practice differed considerably, and the government found it nearly impossible to "trace" the "original homes" of squatters, or to differentiate between "genuine" and "non-genuine" squatters.[11] This represented a setback, as an indecipherable countryside was one more difficult to reorder.

Aside from the difficulty of counting populations intrinsically difficult to count, Shimechero's work was beset by bitter government divisions on the issue of squatters. Early estimates put the number of Kenyan squatters at seventy thousand families, or about half a million people. This number, the minister for Lands and Settlement noted, "considerably exceeds the number of families dealt with in the whole of the One Million Acre Settlement schemes."[12] Though Kenyan officials generally agreed that "the squatter problem" had to be addressed, they disagreed on exactly why and how. There was a consensus that a "crowd of landless / frustrated persons" threatened security, development, and public health.[13] On everything else, officials conflicted. KANU radicals, some of whom would later join the Kenya People's Union (KPU), championed squatters, arguing for real land redistribution and limits on accumulation.[14] These squatter advocates argued that the state had neglected the "genuine destitute," who were "roaming the country" in search of land.[15] They declared that squatters had "as much right as anyone else to expect a reasonable future from our Nation."[16] On the contrary, more conservative state actors suggested squatters were in positions of destitution on account of indolence. They argued that assisting squatters took away resources from "tens of thousands of other smallholders throughout Kenya who have shown initiative and are willing to put in a greater amount of their own effort."[17]

Official division fundamentally boiled down to two interconnected questions—first, whether all Kenyans had a right to own land; and, if not, whether squatters made deserving recipients of land. The independence negotiations, which maintained the land market and preserved large estates, provided a resounding response to the question of land rights. It was impossible for all Kenyans to become landowners without an explicitly redistributive policy founded on the apportionment of smaller, more evenly sized landholdings. Clearly, then, not all Kenyans had rights to own land. Thus, the debate centered on squatter merit, and officials deliberated whether Kenyans became squatters as a result of their own idleness or as a result of structural marginalization, and, also, whether settling squatters would contribute to Kenya's development. Even those policymakers who supported the landless tended to equivocate on the economic benefits of squatter settlement. Most proponents assumed squatters possessed little agricultural knowledge and that farming small plots of land was "not real development," but, nonetheless, "some kind of land settlement programme should be continued."[18] Such prevarication was commonplace, and state actors debated this issue throughout the 1960s and 1970s on shifting terms.

Regardless of the split in official opinion, the Kenyan constitution left lawmakers few legal options for removing squatters. In a 1966 note to the Ministry of Lands and Settlement, the state counsel warned: "At present no powers exist under which squatters could be forcibly removed to settlements schemes." He added that squatters could be "compulsorily cleared from private land" only after obtaining convictions and removal orders under the trespass act, a course of action that would have undoubtedly overrun the courts. Under the circumstances, the state counsel advised "persuasion, backed perhaps by transportation and loan facilities."[19] Without making attractive alternative land offers to squatters, this represented an unlikely solution.

Various challenges notwithstanding—the troublingly large number of squatters, the disagreements among officials, and the difficulties of moving squatters—Shimechero and his colleagues pressed forward. In 1966, after completing the bulk of squatter registration, a subcommittee of the Kenyan cabinet projected that the government could "absorb" 75 percent of the total squatter population through settlement programs providing squatters with small pieces of land and little else.[20] By September 1968, squatter registration efforts had essentially come to a close, amassing a total count of forty-six thousand families, with the largest numbers coming from the Central and Rift Valley Provinces. Together, the two provinces held more than half the country's squatters.[21] Even so, correspondence about the difficulties of identifying squatters and the improbability of some of the numbers indicate these statistics were likely inexact.[22]

Before the end of registration, and after much debate, state officials finally agreed on a new squatter policy. Ultimately, the state decided it was "better to settle many squatters at a low standard of living equivalent to that existing in rural areas rather than settle a few squatters at a reasonably high level of income."[23] Without further aid, development actors thought it was financially impossible "to embark on elaborate squatter schemes," and as a result, it would be necessary to introduce a "quick and low cost type of settlement."[24] This represented a radical policy change, but financial constraints, lack of available land, high unemployment rates, and concern about squatter unrest left government officials little choice.[25] Financial considerations served as one of the more compelling justifications for this form of squatter settlement, since it cost an estimated £30 to settle a squatter family, while it cost up to £250 for one family in "normal" settlement.[26]

Even with the revised plan, the earliest iteration was patchwork. Gradually, the Kenyan state created more formalized national policy for squatter settlement. In 1966, the special commissioner began *Haraka* (meaning "fast") schemes—the epitome of the new no-frills settlement strategy, complete with modestly sized plots and absent extension services. Through these efforts, by 1968, the special commissioner had placed 12,693 families, or 63,465 individuals, in settlements.[27] The 1970–74 national development plan also included the settlement of squatters in its objectives.[28] In 1971, the government created the *Shirika* program, for the "landless, unemployed, and destitute" to work on government-managed cooperative farms.[29] These programs, and squatter policy more broadly, contravened Kenya's earlier development plans—which stressed the allotment of individual landholdings that could provide net income, not just subsistence.

Despite squatter programs, landlessness and land poverty remained a widespread problem. Parceling a limited portion of Kenya's land into small, unsustainable pieces for a fraction of the squatter population would not resolve the issue. In absence of another solution, state officials often informally sanctioned illegal squatter villages. These settlements occupied a liminal space—both integrated into the national polity and excluded from it. On the one hand, illegal squatter settlements bore some of the hallmarks of Kenyan state intervention. Chiefs—members of the provincial administration—played an active role in illegal squatter villages. They encouraged squatter communities to elect village elders, who mediated between the locality and the government and resolved local conflicts internally.[30] The centrality of village elders to illegal squatter governance paralleled that of other settlements. Many Kenyans considered village elders the essence of the postcolonial government, because they were more physically present than any other official.[31] State actors engaged with illegal squatter communities in other ways as well. Squatters recalled officials from the Ministry of Agriculture providing them with fertilizer and seeds and local officials collecting their taxes.[32]

At the same time, certain aspects of illegal squatter life differed radically from areas of Kenya more wholly integrated into the national polity. Decision making in illegal squatter villages was often more communal and more localized than elsewhere, absent the high-modernist planning the state relied on in other communities. In squatter settlements, the local administration (composed of village elders and other local leaders), not the central state, subdivided the land, often in conversation with community members. Further, squatter communities were usually prohibited from erecting schools and health centers, local institutions that other communities actively built in the early postcolonial era.[33]

While state actors collected taxes from squatters, and even distributed agricultural inputs to them, squatters' exclusion from local social services revealed the limits of their citizenship. Squatter settlements were by no means invisible to state actors, but they were only partially included in state programs. For squatters, experiences of a sometimes present, sometimes absent state contributed to emerging ideas of state unpredictability. International donors also largely overlooked squatter communities. As a result of their exclusion from external patronage, some squatters possessed more localized, less cosmopolitan political imaginaries.

State policy aimed primarily to mollify squatters. Kenyan officials hoped to settle enough squatters to satisfy the landless, and, under certain circumstances, officials turned a blind eye to squatter settlements they considered unobjectionable. Even so, those Kenyans excluded from government programs actively sought out other land opportunities. The next section turns to a common course of action taken by those excluded from settlement—joining land-buying organizations.

"WHERE WILL THE CHASED ONES GO?"

As Kenyans watched the available land in state-led settlement shrink, they began forming cooperatives, companies, and partnerships to purchase land collectively on the free market.[34] These organizations offered another solution to landlessness, and the Kenyan state quietly supported collective farm-buying by minimizing the bureaucratic hurdles. A 1965 report on cooperative farming noted that "from 1963 to 1965, 349 farm purchasing societies were registered. Political instructions received under the then Ministry of Commerce and Industry encouraged registration with a minimum of formalities."[35] The report continued, "The majority of these newly registered societies have never been contacted by the departmental staff, simply because there was not sufficient staff to cope with the new development. But what is even more significant, there was a complete absence of any policy or regulations regarding the direction of this new type of cooperative society."[36] In a setting of bureaucratic and fiscal constraints, and of state unpredictability, private land-buying groups afforded Kenyans new opportunities.[37] Together, members could assemble a down payment and qualify for loans. In fact, by mid-1965, the vast majority of African capital expenditure on the free land market was channeled through these organizations, with individual outlay accounting for only 14 percent of the total.[38]

Without government regulation, though, the leaders of farm-buying partnerships could take advantage of members. Fraud ensued, especially in societies with shadow partners—partners who contributed to the down payment but whose names were not listed on the title deed. This occurred commonly and became a subject of discussion among government officials. A Central Agricultural Board paper noted how, frequently, Kenyans who wanted to buy large farms "collect contributions from 'shadow' partners, although, in effect, only the true purchaser is eventually registered as the proprietor of the farm."[39] Former agricultural officials recounted that many Kenyans were persuaded to go into farm-buying this way.[40] Wealthier owners often deceived poorer partners about their tenure status, eventually expelling these individuals from land they thought they owned. Shadow partners had no legal right to land they had donated money toward purchasing.

Hidden partnerships had profound effects on rural lives. In a letter to Tom Mboya, minister for Economic Planning and Development, two hidden partners lamented: "We bought lands in Uasin Gishu. Our problem is that we were not registered for the lands. Only our partners were registered. Now, the partners tell us that the Government does not recognize us, and some of them have begun to chase away some people."[41] As the letter continues, the writers expressed disbelief. "How will this be?" they demanded. "When the Europeans left, the Government gave out loans for people so that they could buy land. People sold their cattle and property so that they could buy land and raise their standard of living. Now, if they chase away other people, where will the chased ones go to, and they cannot go back to where they were chased from?"[42] This case represents just one of many where shadow partners lost land without legal recourse. In the process, Kenyans were often stripped of their assets and savings, which they had used to contribute to the land purchase.

At other times, shadow partners never even set foot on the land. In 1966, a member of a land-buying cooperative complained in a letter to the minister of Cooperatives and Social Services that since donating money to buy land, "a year and a half have elapsed and nothing so far has been done by the office bearers, in that they have neither bought a farm nor convened a General Meeting."[43] He added, "There is mounting indignation and worry among the members of the said Society as we are not informed of what progress has been made. We are of the view that our money is lying idle, if not wrongly spent."[44] Rural Kenyans frequently contributed to down payments, never to see their money or land again.

Indeed, the government received so many complaints that the commissioner of Cooperative Development placed an embargo on farm-buying cooperative registration in 1965.[45] By then, numerous farmers were already embroiled in these organizations, and the ramifications were lasting. Many Kenyans who purchased land through farm-buying cooperatives in the mid-1960s detailed the difficulties they encountered. Often, the land was not clearly subdivided, yet the leaders pressured members to pay loans. Without clear boundaries, partners might all pay equally, or they might pay for more land than they had. Many of those who joined farm-buying organizations recounted how leaders took their money, but members received only a fraction of the plots they had been promised.[46]

Kenyans were defrauded in various ways, and some deceptive organizers misled partners about the quality of the land. Just after independence, Sally Kogo and her Nandi family joined a multiethnic farm-buying organization in Ziwa, Uasin Gishu. The Kogos moved from Tinderet, where they possessed no land but farmed a small plot on loan from family. They wanted their own *shamba* (farm), and the Ziwa farm enticed Kogo and her husband because of the plot sizes. When they met the "spokesperson" advertising the farm, he emphasized the large plots but mentioned only in passing that sisal had been planted on the land previously. Upon arrival, Kogo was surprised to find that sisal—a crop whose market value declined dramatically in the 1960s—still covered the entire farm. Removing sisal is labor-intensive and time-consuming, and, as a result, her family was unable to plant maize the first season. She said she was "disappointed" and felt she had been "cheated."[47] After a couple of years, when different land became available, the Kogos left their farm and sold it. Others recounted purchasing unproductive land through a farm-buying cooperative and having to sell the farm after just a few years.[48]

Compared to settlers in the Million Acre Scheme, members of farm-buying organizations possessed few protections if their land was smaller or less fertile than expected. Million Acre Scheme settlers moved onto plots only after their settlements had undergone fairly extensive surveys—contour mapping, soil classification, land use analysis, and annual rainfall measures. Subsequently, planners demarcated and mapped the land, and then, only after the completion of these steps, did settlers arrive.[49] Though this system had its shortcomings, such preparatory work better safeguarded Kenyans from purchasing poor-quality or insufficiently sized land. Moreover, in cases where surveyors made errors, plotholders could submit complaints to agricultural technocrats.[50] Such a system was not in place for private purchases through land-buying organizations. Without surveys and with limited prospects for state intervention, members often had few options when they found their shamba infertile or smaller than expected.

Land and property loss within farm-buying organizations often had enduring repercussions. Kimeli arap Chepkwony's experience illustrates how fraught relationships within these organizations could result in permanent dispossession. Chepkwony was born in Kosirai, Nandi reserve, and remained there throughout the colonial period. Seeking a larger piece of land, at independence, Chepkwony moved to Uasin Gishu and purchased a plot through a farm-buying cooperative. After eight successful years in Uasin Gishu, Chepkwony decided to sell his land shares and move to a larger plot for his growing herd. He then migrated north to Trans Nzoia, where he purchased eighty acres of land through a different farm-buying cooperative, this one composed of two Kalenjin subgroups, the Nandi and the Sabaot. Chepkwony recounted that he used the land there to graze his sixty head of cattle, and also to grow wheat, maize, and finger millet.

Just a couple of years after moving to Trans Nzoia, Chepkwony lost his land and cattle during a conflict between the members of the cooperative. According to Chepkwony, in 1973, on the advice of a veterinary officer, the Nandi members of the cooperative built a cattle dip. Once finished, they refused to allow the Sabaot members to use the dip, because the Sabaot had not contributed to the construction. In response, the Sabaot destroyed the dip, and, soon after, many cattle died of east coast fever. Angry with the Sabaot for destroying the dip, the Nandi responded violently, and the police made a number of arrests. Chepkwony left the volatile area, and, during his absence, others moved onto his vacant land. In the aftermath, Chepkwony wandered the countryside, looking for somewhere to live. He hired a lawyer to get his land back, but to no avail. Eventually, he arrived close to his former land in Uasin Gishu, and an area chief directed him to the Kapkiruk illegal squatter settlement, where he continues to live to this day.[51] Tense relationships could develop in cooperatives, and there were vulnerabilities inherent to participation in a land-buying group. Without a title, Chepkwony could not legally prove he owned the land.

The settlement policy that disqualified many poor Kenyans, the squatter policy that did not adequately address landlessness, and the loan policy that barred average individual Kenyans from accessing credit all played a role in pushing Kenyans to seek out other land-buying opportunities. In the years after independence, these Kenyans experienced exclusion from the state programs that offered land, loans, infrastructure, and services. When they joined unregulated land-buying groups, Kenyans also faced exclusion from state protections, exposing them to theft and dispossession.

Despite the problems, by 1971, the state again encouraged cooperative farming, this time under government management through the Shirika program. With this program, the government attempted to keep larger estates intact, operating as a single commercial entity. The Settlement Fund Trustees owned the whole of these properties, but leased them to cooperative societies as individual units. Shirika settlers worked together as laborers on the majority of the undivided cooperative farmland, though each family also received a subsistence plot of about two and a half acres for personal use.[52]

The creation of this program in 1971 coincided with the abolishment of the Department of Squatters and signaled the beginning of another iteration of settlement policy, once again amending previous orthodoxies. Shirika represented an obvious contrast to earlier state policy on high-density settlement schemes, which had emphasized individual ownership. State officials not only devoted a large portion of the settlement budget in the 1970s to Shirika, but, in the 1974 to 1978 planning period, officials proposed using over two-thirds of the land purchased for settlement on Shirika.[53] The director of Settlement rationalized the priority given to Shirika by noting the program's ability "to satisfy both the inborn longings of individuals to own a piece of land of their own . . . and at the same time preserve a pattern of large scale farming."[54] Government officials justified this policy reversal by emphasizing how Shirika struck a balance between satiating Kenyan desires for land and state desires to maintain economies of scale in agricultural production.

Similar to other programs, Shirika in theory looked different from Shirika in practice. After reducing the area of the original farm in order to allocate subsistence plots, managers found they did not require the labor of all the new settlers. This left some settlers unemployed, with small plots deprived of extension services.[55] Shirika not only ran differently than predicted, but Kenyans also received this program less warmly than officials expected. Standing on the parliamentary floor in July 1974, Jean-Marie Seroney, the populist Nandi MP for Tinderet, voiced the concerns of many landless Kenyans. "I do not like to entertain the idea that there exists a Shirika Settlement Scheme," he declared.[56] Seroney then described how settlers on Shirika farms did not have enough land even to keep cattle—a major point of contention for pastoralist groups in Uasin Gishu—and how settlers were subject to the whims of the management. He concluded, "I personally feel that these people should be given more acres of land in Shirika Settlement schemes so that they can make a decent living."[57] In this, Seroney articulated the feelings of many rural Kenyans, who wanted larger plots, indisputable land rights, self-determination, and prosperity.[58]

Though Shirika protected poor Kenyans from the dispossession that so commonly occurred in land-buying societies, the program did little to satisfy what the director of Settlement had so evocatively described as "inborn longings." In fact, Shirika settlement looked awfully similar to the colonial labor system in the highlands, where Africans had spent most of their time working on farms they did not own in exchange for minimal payment and subsistence plots. Similar to land-buying groups, Shirika did not offer Kenyans permanent ownership. Further, the program did not provide Kenyan families enough land to keep cattle or to produce agricultural goods to sell. In other words, Shirika plots bore little resemblance to the fruits of freedom Kenyans had envisioned.

Unlike other squatter programs, Shirika inserted a domineering state into Kenyans' daily lives by overseeing their agricultural labor. Generally, landless Kenyans who resettled through group land purchases on the free market or through squatter programming experienced little state intervention, and thus greater land insecurity and more limited access to services and resources. The activeness of state involvement in Shirika contrasted with these other squatter programs, representing another instance of state unreliability.

"WOMEN WHO ARE NEVER ALLOWED TO BUY *SHAMBAS*"

At the beginning of 1963, two colonial officials corresponded about a landless widow with nine children. After the first official inquired whether they could provide the widow any assistance, the second responded, "I am afraid that there is no help that I can give to this wretched woman. The present directive is that plots must only be granted to male heads of families."[59] With this note, the correspondence concluded, making clear that women's access to settlement was restricted, and they possessed nominal rights to land. While women's exclusions broadly paralleled that of landless men, they were often marginalized through different state and societal mechanisms.

When the colonial government began resettlement, single women were ineligible to purchase land through these programs. For many Kenyan women, as for women across the continent, colonialism had meant greater labor obligations, weakened control over household management, and less secure land rights.[60] The land consolidation, partitioning, and titling processes that took place in the mid-twentieth century dispossessed and disenfranchised women. In Nandi, with land partitioning, men received titles but also sole inheritance rights. A system of use-rights that had previously included women transformed into one of male private ownership. The implications were profound—suddenly, Nandi women could be denied land access, previously inalienable, and their control over land and production diminished.[61] Other women had similar experiences. Over the course of the first six decades of the twentieth century, Luyia women's access to all forms of property, including land, became profoundly limited. These proscriptions ultimately served as social controls, forcing Luyia women to get married, and remain married, in order to access land.[62] Kikuyu women also saw their claims to land restricted as Kikuyu men redefined customary law.[63] At independence, colonial forms of marginalization were frequently compounded, particularly through exclusions from state resources and social services. By initially excluding women, resettlement programs perpetuated some of the gendered inequalities the colonial state had introduced and that ethnic elders had executed. Early postcolonial international development practice, then, helped prop up the authority of senior men in relation to women.

Accordingly, the "wretched" widow was just one of many in the same position.[64] Prospective female settlers had few advocates among bureaucrats and politicians, but one member of Parliament urged the government to offer women settlement opportunities. In 1966, Embakasi MP Mwangi Karungaru proclaimed, "One day the women of this country will not have any employment, and, in fact, nothing to keep them busy. Mr. Speaker, Sir, when this happens they will ask, 'Why are the men enjoying the fruits of this country, when we have been forgotten?'" Karungaru continued, "I am asking the Minister [for Lands and Settlement] whether he would consider allocating land to the women." After some heckling from his fellow members, Karungaru offered justification for his proposal: "Mr. Speaker, Sir, the reason which makes me suggest that the women should be given the opportunity to own their own plots of land is because these women do have dependents and they have to educate them." Karungaru's argument was premised on nation-building motherhood—nurturing the nation by nurturing its next generation. For other members, though, these sentiments were radical and a threat to familial structures. One member of Parliament cut in, "You are encouraging divorce." Karungaru responded, "I am not encouraging divorce, I am encouraging our children to enjoy the fruits of independence, because they are entitled to them."[65]

Astute widows made similar arguments for land on the basis of their motherhood. Wambui w/o [wife of] Muiruri of Ainabkoi—a farm laborer in the white highlands, widow, and mother of eight children—corresponded with her district commissioner at the beginning of 1963 about the discriminatory land policy. "I am surprised to see that I am not entitled to get any portion in areas where Land Development Scheme is going on," she wrote. "I would like to know whether you would advice [*sic*] me what I should do as I feel I ought to get the same share as I am the successor of my husband in the family."[66] In her petition, the widow demonstrated knowledge of settlement requirements, noting her experience as a laborer on a European farm, and highlighting, too, her position as head of household. Based on these qualifications, Wambui claimed the same entitlements as Kenyan men.

But women did not possess the same entitlements as men. The district commissioner replied that he expected to be able to "invite applications from widows like yourself next month."[67] By the next month, other widows from the same farm were still petitioning for land and the policy had yet to change. These widows made land claims on different terms than Wambui. Similar to many male petitioners, they emphasized their impoverishment, seeming to believe that poverty accorded Kenyans with rights to resources.[68] A group of widowed employees wrote, "We women with no husbands we have no where to go or money to settle new settlements because no body to help us and now many people have gone to build their homes, sir, when shall we go to build ours?"[69] To this petition, the district commissioner replied with less certainty: "I am hoping women without husbands will be able to apply for settlement soon."[70]

The Kenyan government did eventually change its policy of disqualifying single women from land settlement, though little changed on the ground. Despite legal amendment, discrimination remained embedded in the selection process. Poor women were seldom able to meet the stipulations for settlement. According to officials, they did not possess the agricultural knowledge necessary to become individual smallholders—a skill set measured largely by time spent laboring on European farms. Furthermore, women often did not have the capital for a down payment. Even when women could meet these qualifications, administrative procedures tended to ensure their continued exclusion. Similar to squatters, women tended to be less visible to the state. As the above petitions demonstrate, women wanted to make themselves legible to state actors in order to access land. However, they did not have labor cards or identity cards. Thus, women could neither prove that they had worked on European farms nor the location of their "home area"—two requirements for settlement selection.

The district officer of Vihiga called attention to these challenges in 1966. "I found it very difficult to identify some of these people, especially women because they had no Labour Cards," he noted. The officer thus relied on area subchiefs to designate deserving land applicants.[71] Though local officials exercised immense powers in settlement selection, they often favored elite men as a means of entering into relationships of mutual reciprocity. Not only did the settlement qualifications and selection procedures discriminate against women, but so, too, did local officers, who saw little advantage in assisting the politically and economically marginalized. Oral evidence supports the archival evidence on these practices. Almost universally, the Kenyans surveyed for this study could not recount single women purchasing land, even within settlement schemes initiated after women were legally allowed to apply.

Thus, six years after independence, women continued complaining about their lack of land access, and they increasingly addressed their grievances to more senior government offices. In a November 1968 petition, the Cherangani KANU women's wing "requested intervention" from the Office of the President and detailed their difficulties purchasing land. They wrote, "Among the residents of Cherangani we have widows and other women who are never allowed to buy *shambas* (farms) by the leaders in this area. We are always told that our time for buying the *shambas* is past though we have our money."[72] The archival file contained no reply. In response to vast exclusions, women sought new advocates to take on their claims, though these efforts produced only occasional successes.

Even those women who achieved land access through their husbands' ownership experienced state exclusion. Similar to men settled through squatter programming, women's access to state actors and to state resources was circumscribed. Just after independence, Solome Teregin, a Nandi woman, moved to Uasin Gishu with her family, where they purchased land through a farm-buying cooperative. While the family lived generally contentedly in the cooperative, Teregin recounted, "There were extension officers and veterinary officers, but I had no idea what they were doing. Only *wazee* [senior men] could call them."[73] Female settlers on other schemes, and of various ethnic backgrounds, had similar recollections, noting that women "were put aside when agricultural extension officers were teaching farming methods."[74] Even when women's families possessed land, they were excluded from the extension services that complemented property ownership.

Women's marginalization went beyond land settlement and extension services to property rights broadly.[75] Widows were particularly vulnerable, and the state provided few protections.[76] While widows were rarely permitted to inherit land, they had rights to hold and manage land until their sons came of age. In-laws often tried to push out the women maintaining land for male heirs.[77] Widows' land rights were jeopardized when they did not possess the necessary documentation. Men's names were on title deeds; most women did not have marriage certificates; and many did not realize that they needed their husbands' identity cards to prove their rights to the land.[78] Settlement schemes provided widows slightly greater security than on average, since the African court prepared a certificate of succession designating the heirs, officially vesting the land in the heirs' names.[79] Widows on settlement schemes still remained susceptible to dispossession, and when plots were transferred, officials primarily focused on ensuring farm productivity and loan recovery rather than on protecting women.[80]

With ambiguous land rights, complicated legal structures, and an intimidating court system, widows' property rights were insecure.[81] Some Kenyans characterized in-laws generally as "grabbers," noting that women needed the government to protect their land.[82] The archival record reveals that various male relatives took land. Yet when widows complained to the government, it was often to no avail. In 1964, Wambui w/o Gatungu wrote to President Kenyatta, "When my husband died, Gitau (my son) started selling this land at the same time. I had no idea that he was selling the land as he sold it secretly." She added with dismay, "I reported the matter to the Land Office at Kiambu, where they did but nothing." The archival folder contained no reply from the president. Despite describing her "great trouble" and how her son spent the money "uselessly," the law provided Wambui little recourse, as her son was the rightful heir.[83]

While written evidence consistently illustrates widows' precarity, the preponderance of oral histories collected for this study contradicts the documentary record. Women and men across different ethnicities commonly recounted how well Kenyan society took care of widows. Pauline Tum, a Nandi woman, emphasized how families supported widows. Tum moved frequently as a child and young adult—between multiethnic areas in Kakamega, Uasin Gishu, and Laikipia. While Tum had observed diverse communities caring for widows, her personal experience most deeply shaped her ideas. Tum's father passed away when she was young, and she described the significance of in-laws in such cases. Tum's uncle—her father's brother—took care of her family until her brother reached adulthood and took on the responsibility himself.[84] Many people noted that widows were respected and that the whole community helped them.[85]

Others highlighted the bureaucratic and legal safeguards in place. Nandi and Luyia settlers emphasized that land registration protected widows, ensuring they could hold property for their children.[86] Certainly, residing in settlement schemes provided widows greater security than on average, since settlers tended to have more documentation, a by-product of the bureaucratic machinations of international development. Though female settlers stressed widows' security, they simultaneously revealed women's limited land rights prospects in the early postcolonial era. In describing women's ability to act as interim managers, they made clear there was no opportunity for ownership.[87]

FIGURE 3.1. Women harvesting vegetables in the highlands, 1969. Photo courtesy of Per Gunvell for the World Bank. Country Photographs—Kenya, Loan 0256, Photographs, vol. 5, 30229054, Records of Office of External Affairs, WBGA.

The wide-ranging depictions of widows' security and rights underscore the ambiguities of legal pluralism and the diverse experiences of women in various localities. Oral histories indicate a strong public ideology, as well as pride, in caring for widows, but this may have been valued more in theory than in practice. Moral ethnicities generally obliged communities to look after the vulnerable. The Nandi concept of *tiliet*, a system that binds relations together, notionally endowed widows with the right to call upon an expansive set of kin in times of need. By publicly airing their problems through *kehenda mwoyo*, or "worries of the heart," Maragoli widows could impel men to "protect" them. As Kenda Mutongi has shown, however, the effectiveness of "worries of the heart" diminished in the postcolonial era, and widows became particularly susceptible to land theft by in-laws.[88] Though some widows certainly maintained control over family farms, many remained vulnerable to land seizures.

Kenya's land tenure system produced inequalities between men and women, but intimate relationships and local norms delineated a spectrum of rights that varied between families, communities, and regions. While some women enjoyed fairly secure rights to land, these were almost always usage rights rather than property rights. Indeed, within households, women's usage rights were rarely circumscribed, since women's labor was so central to Kenyan agricultural production.[89] These usage rights, however, provided women neither ownership rights nor sole rights to the products of their labor. When Rift Valley women recounted their experiences and ideas about property, they often revealed the complexities of rights.

Pauline Ngetich, for example, settled in Sosiani in 1965 with her husband, who had been a labor-tenant in the colonial era. Her husband's labor history satisfied official requirements, though Ngetich, too, possessed "farming knowledge" and a similar work history. Both state and Nandi tenets on property ownership prescribed that the title deed be in her husband's name as the male head of household. Even so, Ngetich was responsible for most of the farm labor, since her husband worked for Kenya Power and Lighting. Though she was pleased with the land in Sosiani, Ngetich recounted that in the 1960s and 1970s, husbands regarded their wives as "children" and women had "no freedom." She eloquently summed up her marginalized position in relation to the family farm by noting: "The land was ours, but it was not mine."[90] In this statement, Ngetich asserted that the land belonged to her family and was hers to work, but her husband's to own and her sons' to inherit.[91] The restrictions on women's land rights extended to other farm property as well, and Ngetich emphasized this point. She remarked, "When somebody was practicing poultry-keeping, those poultry were not hers. When she could actually sell some chicken to buy a sheep, the sheep would not belong to her. Even a cow."[92] Women's labor did not endow them with property rights or with rights to agricultural profits. Men frequently managed household income and controlled the marketing of profitable crops, while women managed produce harvested for family consumption. Some women described how their husbands made decisions about whether to buy cattle and sheep, and which goods to purchase for the home, such as cloth, sugar, or salt.[93] Others recalled having to consult their husbands before selling small amounts of maize or beans to make contributions to church groups.[94]

Yet families also negotiated these decisions based on personal circumstances. A number of women whose husbands lived off their farm recounted the opportunities for personal, managerial, and financial independence that opened up as a result. Lumakanda settler Fanike Chanzu's husband worked in an administrative position in Eldoret. She recounted how difficult it was to do all the farmwork by herself, waking up at five in the morning each day to milk the cows and deliver the milk to the dairy co-op. Chanzu said that her husband made the payments for their land loan at first, but, eventually, she took over that responsibility.[95] Male labor migration occurred fairly commonly, helping to diversify agricultural risk. While a husband's absence increased the wife's workload, it also boosted household incomes and often provided women greater freedoms. Similarly, at times, women in polygynous marriages had more control over their household economies. Some settlers recounted how polygynous men allowed trusted wives to farm family plots and manage finances.[96]

Financial arrangements differed, but most commonly male heads of household managed familial income and assets. Even so, women challenged men using a range of strategies and on various terms. In some circumstances, financial power obligated men to adequately provide for their families. In 1966, S. M. Kubai penned a petition to Kenyatta on behalf of a woman whose husband abandoned her: "Now she says that she is in great difficulty on children's expenses and also for her own expenses. Therefore she is seeking for *Mzee's* advice on this matter because she does not want to take her husband to the court before knowing his last decision."[97] Regardless of whether this constituted a compelling legal case, the letter asserted women's rights to family resources. Women challenged their husbands and male relatives in other ways as well—by hiding money from them, by insisting on making financial decisions alongside them, or by running away from marriages. Rural Kenyans clearly engaged in complex negotiations over household financial control.[98]

Undoubtedly, vast gendered inequalities existed in the early postcolonial period, but women's social, political, and economic experiences ranged dramatically. Two life histories serve to illustrate this. Eunice Birir now lives in Leseru, a sublocation in Uasin Gishu that borders Sosiani.[99] She was born in Trans Nzoia to Nandi parents. Birir's childhood was spent migrating between various European farms in Trans Nzoia and Uasin Gishu Districts, where her father and brothers worked. After the enactment of cattle restrictions in the 1950s, her family left the scheduled areas, squatting or using land on loan to them in Nandi. As independence approached, one of Birir's brothers moved in with some relatives to position himself for land in Ndalat, where a settlement was rumored to be opening shortly. The rumors proved true, and Birir's brother applied and received a plot. As he made plans to move, he convinced their parents to join him.

By then, Birir was married. With her parents and brother living elsewhere and unable to accommodate her growing household, Birir moved with her husband and children to western Kenya, where they hoped to secure a piece of land. Her brother-in-law lived on a European farm in the region, and he lent land to them for a few years. Then, Birir's parents—still living in Ndalat—notified the couple about a settlement opportunity close to them in Sosiani. After they were selected, Birir and her husband sold their cattle and asked for assistance from relatives to collect the deposit for a plot. They received forty-four acres and four dairy cattle.

Three years later, Birir's husband sold the Sosiani land without consulting her and moved their family to a farm farther northeast in Uasin Gishu. Birir mentioned that her husband had begun drinking more heavily by this time, but she said she could not make sense of his rash decision making. In moving her away from kin, though, Birir's husband limited her negotiating power within the marriage and household. Nandi social organization had long meant that wives lived in communities that included both their husbands' kin and their own. Patrilineal clans were geographically scattered, and local communities were organized by a host of connections based on friendship, kin, and affinal relationships. In times of need—including of marital strife—women could draw on their own local relationships for assistance. With the continual migrations and resettlements of the twentieth century, both Nandi women and men saw their proximity to their relations shift frequently.

For many Nandi women, tiliet relations were especially important as a safeguard. Not only did relations intervene during marital disagreements, but they provided women support with childbirth and childcare. As a result, when Birir's husband sold their land and purchased a more distant farm, she stayed in Ndalat with her parents to care for her newborn. When she eventually moved to the farm with her husband, their relationship continued to deteriorate. Already farther away from her kin, Birir's husband ensured she remained socially isolated by prohibiting her from joining a church or a women's group, two organizations that strengthened women's networks and provided them assistance. In addition, according to Birir, her husband would not listen to any of her advice, made poor financial decisions, and did not help with farmwork. While her husband stayed at the house, Birir took the cows out in the morning, came back to prepare lunch, and then collected the cattle in the afternoon. During weekends, she took her children to do tilling, sowing, weeding, or harvesting. Her husband continued to drink, and sometimes behaved violently when he was intoxicated.

Birir was unhappy in her marriage but, given the options, decided it was best to stay. They had children together, and he controlled their property and finances. Because her husband's name was on the title deed, if Birir left, she would forgo access to their land, and thus to the food she produced for her family. She worried how she would be able to care for her family and send her kids to school. Choosing to remain on the farm with her husband still produced anxiety. Birir recounted that her husband sometimes refused to pay the loans. When her firstborn son was old enough, he began assisting her financially, helping out with the loan or when she struggled to produce enough food. Birir said she constantly worried about eviction, asking: "Mimi na watoto tulienda wapi tena?" (Where were my children and I going again?) This rhetorical question alludes to her chronic migrations, and also to the fact that Birir saw her alternatives as profoundly limited.

Birir said she respected the law that her husband owned everything, because the land was registered under his name. She believed, however, that it was unfair for him to misuse what they had while others struggled. In this, she reflected both ethnic and national ideas about property rights as exclusively male. At the same time, in declaring the unjustness of her husband's poor work ethic, Birir articulated prevailing moral economies—both ethnic and national—about hard work. These moral economies took on new valences during decolonization. Given land shortages in the nation, Kenyans interpreted the underutilization of the scarce and sought-after resource as particularly egregious. Further, the independent state called upon all Kenyans to work hard to build the nation, especially through farming, and refusal to do so was often censured and depicted as unpatriotic. Though Birir's circumstances were particularly difficult, her life history holds much in common with other women during this period. Her financial and personal autonomy, freedom of political and social engagement, and access to resources were all restricted by the patriarchal structures of early independent Kenya. Her husband provided little for the family and she did the majority of the labor, yet she had no control over the financial resources of the household.[100]

Grace Nasimiyu's life history differs considerably from Eunice Birir's, though it also involves a troubled marital relationship. Born in Vihiga in 1937, Nasimiyu lived with her parents, helping them with farmwork until she married in 1952. She then moved onto a small piece of land with her husband in Kabras, his home area.[101] Intermarriage between Luyia subgroups—in this case, a Maragoli woman and a Kabras man—occurred regularly. Through intermarriages, women carried and imparted social intelligence and played an essential role in the production and reproduction of Luyia identity and community.[102] While intermarriage was common, marriage dissolutions were less common. However, just a handful of years later, in 1958, Nasimiyu and her husband divorced due to what she described—vaguely and euphemistically—as family differences. Marital disputes invariably occurred, but the social stigmas attached to divorce, and the economic hardships female divorcées faced, restrained divorce rates in the mid-twentieth century. In the rare cases when women sought divorce, the courts usually required proof of mistreatment, the husband's assent or the backing of a male relative, and the ability to repay most of the bride price.[103]

Following the divorce, Nasimiyu returned to her parents' home, where she later heard about settlement programs. Her parents encouraged her to apply for land, and her father offered to give her his identity card and the money for a down payment. Nasimiyu then went "crying" to the settlement officer, saying she had three children. The officer promised he would help. Good to his word, Nasimiyu received a plot in the Lumakanda settlement scheme in 1964. The assistance, from both her parents and the settlement officer, was essential to Nasimiyu's successful acquisition of land. Without her father's identity card and monetary contribution, Nasimiyu would not have qualified. Without the settlement officer's personal support, the selection committee would likely have overlooked Nasimiyu's application.

Even after becoming a landowner, Nasimiyu still confronted the challenges of caring for three small children and farming twenty-two acres by herself. She said, however, that it was not difficult because she was hardworking—a common discourse among successful farmers. Nasimiyu indicated that she received assistance from the community. Neighbors offered to care for her children when she needed, and she said that people worked together on each other's farms. Once her children grew up, they helped her as well. She recounted—like many other women but unlike Eunice Birir—the importance of her church and of the Maendeleo ya Wanawake (Progress for Women) organization. Both fostered communal support, and Maendeleo ya Wanawake provided women financial assistance through microlending. Nasimiyu did not believe she received any special help simply because she was a single mother. She said she always went to women first with her problems, but local leaders assisted her as well.[104] In settlement schemes, having the support of women's organizations, churches, neighbors, and village elders proved especially important for women living distant from kin.

Nasimiyu's circumstances were certainly exceptional. Very few Kenyans remembered single women who purchased land in settlement. State actors and development practitioners initially disqualified single women from resettlement programs. After the policy changed, local committees, headed by elite men, often continued to exclude women from landownership. Though many Kenyan men also had difficulty acquiring land, in the postcolonial era, men had always been eligible for land. Women, on the other hand, generally experienced wholesale exclusion from landownership.

Nasimiyu's success in acquiring land depended a great deal on the support of her father and the special assistance of one settlement officer. While many Kenyans relied on their networks to purchase land, men tended to have wider networks to draw on, and their social and familial connections often provided greater assistance. Despite this, Nasimiyu believed her rights were equivalent to any man's. When asked if women and men were equal, Nasimiyu replied curtly, "What men got [land], even me, I got."[105] With this statement, she declared that equal access to land corresponded to broader equality between women and men. Indeed, as a landowner, Nasimiyu's life experiences differed dramatically from those of women like Eunice Birir. Though both women worked hard in agricultural and domestic realms, Nasimiyu possessed much greater personal and financial autonomy.

"AFTER INDEPENDENCE, NOTHING LOOKED GOOD TO ME"

Many rural Kenyans imagined independence through land redistribution, but rural experiences acquiring land differed markedly. Landless and land-insecure men and women constructed ideas about government, citizenship, and independence in a context where the postcolonial state promised change but reproduced many of the inequalities of the colonial state. These inequalities and exclusions—along with ethnic and national ideologies—molded their political philosophies and engendered debates about justice in the postcolony.

While state officials discussed land policy through a technocratic lens—deliberating the most efficient economies of scale or the best agricultural techniques—the rural poor debated and evaluated land programs on different terms—on whether settlement had made Kenya more just. They often did so by drawing on personal experiences. In the late colonial and early postcolonial era, Sylvester Barngetung Sing'ari, a Nandi man, worked for a European farmer in Uasin Gishu. When the farmer eventually sold his land to the Kenyan military, most of the laborers—possessing limited options—stayed behind and squatted on the land. Though the area became state land, the military never made use of it, and Sing'ari has squatted there since 1972. To Sing'ari, in purchasing the land but not using it, government officials became the new group mistreating the poor. He explained, "I had a feeling that independence could bring equality, because people with property had been overpowering the poor. Those who have nothing, those people who were left behind, those people who were squatters, who were poor right from the beginning. I thought independence meant equality for us all."[106] The government's underutilization of land, while Kenyans remained landless, luridly symbolized the inequalities wrought by independence.[107]

Through land allocation and development, Kenyans assessed not only the extent of the country's inequality, but they also assessed government commitment to egalitarianism and fairness. Landless men described their disappointment in a government that they felt favored the wealthy. They also described the reverberating effects of exclusion from landownership. Forest squatters, in particular, complained that they did not receive extension services; that they had to travel to settlement schemes to get those services; and that the state did not provide development equally.[108] Kenyans used land, social services, and development to gauge whether the promises of independence had materialized, and to evaluate the state's dedication to fairness and equality.

While personal experiences of land and development shaped Kenyan thought, various scales of political imagination existed. Many rural Nandi made sense of landlessness by drawing on ethnic lines of thought critical of postcolonial inequality. Influenced by personal experiences and ethnic philosophies, they spoke of injustices and made vociferous communal territorial claims. Frederick Kemboi arap Tum Kaptulus was not able to purchase land on a settlement scheme and spent decades as a casual migrant laborer in Uasin Gishu. He explained, "I was disappointed in the government, because the people who owned property were given more on top of what they had. But others were being overlooked. And, therefore, to me, freedom meant nothing." Kaptulus did not just speak about his individual exclusion from land, but he articulated Nandi and Kalenjin ideas, remarking, "When they introduced *majimbo* [regionalism], majimbo meant our land would be returned to us. It meant the whole of the Rift Valley should be Kalenjin." He added that the Kalenjin sent some chiefs to Kenyatta, warning him not to allow "his children," the Kikuyu, to come west of Nakuru.[109] Kaptulus's sentiments reflected Nandi notions about autochthony, territoriality, and restitution, but they also incorporated personal disappointments.[110]

Kaptulus could draw on a rich corpus of Nandi patriotic discourse to make sense of his own experiences. With decolonization, a sense of urgency, borne from anxiety and opportunity, strengthened extant geographic imaginings. Jean-Marie Seroney proclaimed that all land in the Rift Valley belonged to the Kalenjin and the Maasai. In 1969, Seroney coauthored and distributed the "Nandi Hills Declaration," asserting Nandi land rights. The declaration stated that "every grain of soil and every square centimeter of land in Tindiret area generally and Nandi Hills Location in particular belongs, under God, to the Nandi people; and every non-Nandi . . . is a temporary tenant at the will of the Nandi." The declaration also outlined a territorially grounded ethnic citizenship, proclaiming that anyone who did not identify as Nandi should agree to live under Nandi law and custom and perform expected duties for the community, or leave the district, "lest he incurs the wrath and the undying enmity of the Nandi people."[111] Though the laws, customs, and duties were only vaguely referred to, the implications were clear—Nandi citizenship was a prerequisite for settlement on Nandi land. The declaration openly contradicted post-majimbo national citizenship, which delegitimized communal land claims.

Many members of the Nandi community celebrated Seroney for his ethnoterritorial work. A popular Kalenjin song composed in his honor included the refrain "Seroney kityo" (Who but Seroney alone / it is Seroney only!).[112] To some, Seroney became not just a hero but an innovator, the creator of a more revolutionary form of territorial ethnic nationalism. Pauline Tum spent years moving from farm to farm in Uasin Gishu as her husband worked as a migrant agricultural laborer on temporary contracts. She vividly recounted the importance of Seroney's leadership: "The Nandi recognized Seroney as a person who defended us, studied maps, defended our rights. He was defending the boundary of the Nandi."[113] As a woman and member of a then landless household, Tum was twice marginalized and thus especially enthusiastic about Seroney's activism. The declaration built upon and bolstered already existent and resonant political imaginations centered on land.

Land was flush with deeper meanings. Kenyans used land to evaluate their government's commitment to equality, and to strengthen ethnic identity and allegiance. They also used land to compose multivalent understandings of national citizenship and belonging. Male landowners frequently described being a *mwananchi* (citizen) in the language of ownership and belonging, of land and the nation.[114] In defining citizenship this way, male landowners articulated their belonging within the nation, and their rights to Kenya's most valuable resource—its land.

In contrast to landowners, women and landless men expressed ambivalence about early postcolonial citizenship. Women—from various ethnic groups and class backgrounds—tended to be less certain about the meaning of *mwananchi*, and to be more equivocal about whether they were citizens.[115] Many women gave reductive answers. *Mwananchi* meant to be a Kenyan.[116] Some women qualified their responses, noting they never went to school and were not well equipped to say.[117] When women did give fuller responses, they often articulated their exclusion.[118] Similar to property rights, some women saw their citizenship as mediated by male family members. Broadly speaking, women's access to land resettlement, development programming, and social services was restricted, diminishing their ability to engage with state officials.

Nonetheless, other women contended that they were citizens. Nora Kasigene believed so. Originally from Vihiga, Kasigene moved with her husband to the Lumakanda settlement in 1963. The resources and services that international aid made available to settlers, along with the scheme's proximity to a highway and to agricultural extension services, fostered feelings of inclusion within the national polity. Kasigene asserted, "Women were citizens. We were the same." She explained, "If the husband wanted to sell the cow, he had to talk with his wife about it. If she gave the okay, then the husband would sell." But, Kasigene added, "if the woman suggested they sell the cow, the husband would not tolerate it."[119] Her ideas illustrate how some women interpreted their roles in household economic management as equivalent to broader political empowerment and enfranchisement. At the same time, Kasigene highlights the unequal property rights of husband and wife, which paralleled the unequal rights of citizenship.

While other women shared Kasigene's views, not all were so sure. Rael Serem, a Nandi woman who lived in various parts of the Rift Valley before settling in Uasin Gishu, was more critical of women's position within postcolonial Kenya. She said, "Because I was living with my husband on this land, I was a mwananchi through my husband." Unlike Kasigene, Serem saw the inequalities within her marriage as equivalent to the gendered inequalities within Kenya. She described how men took their wives to be "like children," how women worked hard but owned nothing they produced, how they could not attend *baraza* (local public meetings), and how difficult it was for women to make claims for greater rights. These experiences shaped her evaluations of *uhuru* (independence): "Yes, we were really free. We got independence. But, still we were under our husbands. So, freedom was not there to us yet."[120] Women's liberties, consequent to their rights to land, labor, and property, were multilayered and nuanced, but certainly partial.

Landless men, like women, recounted feelings of uncertainty about citizenship, though men were more likely to voice their concern about the inequalities embedded within citizenship. In 1973, for example, a group of squatters of "mixed tribes" petitioned the Office of the President: "We feel part and parcel to Kenya Government. We also feel that we are entitled to the privileges which other 'Wananchi' are enjoying, even wild animals in Kenya are enjoying as they are allocated National Parks. What about we? Why have we been rejected and despised?"[121] The squatters argued that they were essential to the government and were entitled to state resources. They contended that fauna received greater privileges in the new nation than marginalized Kenyan citizens, criticizing the state for refusing them such rights.

Their position was a product of the discrepancy between state rhetoric on citizens' rights to resources and the lived experiences of landless Kenyans.

Frederick Kemboi arap Tum Kaptulus drew on his personal experiences of landlessness as well as ethnic lines of thought to make sense of the independent moment. Such ideas tended to conflict with national discourse. Kaptulus thus disputed the common description of *mwananchi*—the owner of the land. "Why did people say this?" he asked, continuing, "It is the child of the country." Here, he used the literal translation; *mwana* means "child," while *nchi* is "country." Kaptulus continued, "I wanted not to be the child, but to be the real owner."[122] In this, Kaptulus—like the above squatters—asserted the disappointments of postcolonial citizenship, where the state offered citizens neither real ownership of the land nor metaphorical ownership of the country but, instead, infantilized disenfranchised portions of the population.[123]

Continued landlessness and perpetuated structural inequalities also colored the ways in which Kenyans made sense of independence. While landowners commonly understood independence as a significant marker in their lives and in Kenyan history, the landless often recalled that not much changed. Many of the social, political, and economic realities of landless Kenyans remained similar before and after independence. Those searching for land often made extended and recurrent rural migrations. This held close parallels to the colonial era, when they moved from one European farm to another, or from rural locations to cities, in search of employment and security. These migrations produced feelings of displacement. Hence, landless Kenyans neither saw themselves as citizens nor did they articulate notions of citizenship centered on belonging. Compared to landowners, many squatters also had less access to government services, such as education and health care—additional promises of independence that had not materialized.[124] In other words, there was both a dramatic difference in how landowners and the landless conceptualized independence and a dramatic difference between their material experiences of independence.

Women often said their lives did not change after independence. They continued to be disenfranchised in spaces that stretched from their homes to that of the new nation-state. Nandi squatter Mary Kitur explained, "After independence, nothing looked good to me, because even before independence I was a squatter and at the moment I am still a squatter, so I do not see its importance." Kitur was displaced countless times. From 1976 up to today, she has been landless, squatting illegally first in a forest and, since 1984, in an illegal settlement in Uasin Gishu. Kitur formed her political ideologies in response to experiences of land insecurity, remarking, "As an independent country, I thought that every resident should be resettled and was supposed to be given enough resources by the government to be provided for equally." She added, "For anyone to be a true mwananchi, they should not be a squatter anywhere or lacking behind in development."[125] Kitur's gender limited her ability to acquire and control state and household resources, while her landlessness limited the state resources and services she could access. Both created feelings of exclusion and unbelonging. Kitur articulated a political philosophy on government obligation and citizens' rights inextricably tied to equitable resource distribution.

Landless men's and women's interpretations of independent politics were shaped by their colonial and postcolonial experiences, by ethnic ideologies, and by national discourse on citizenship. Their disappointment was, at times, deep—a product of the real hardships they endured, of ethnic ideologies about land restitution and justice, and of national politicians' unmet promises. Some land-insecure Kenyans recounted how they came to believe that independence would not effect change, at times triggering disengagement from political participation.[126]

Though settlement programs transferred much land from Europeans to Africans, policymakers never planned to make all Kenyans into property owners. Even so, anxiety about rural unrest motivated state officials to create squatter settlements to appease a portion of the landless population. These programs did not resolve the squatter problem and, in absence of a different solution, Kenyan officials often provided informal support to innocuous illegal squatter settlements.

As state-led settlement opportunities closed, Kenyans turned to other channels for land. Often, they formed land-buying groups, combining their resources to gather a down payment and qualify for loans. The Kenyan state sanctioned these organizations, largely because they required little bureaucratic or financial outlay. Without government oversight, however, leaders of land-buying groups frequently deceived their members, keeping their names off the title deeds and eventually leaving them landless and further impoverished.

Kenya's property rights regime also marginalized women. Not only were single women originally disqualified from settlement, but even after the policy changed, structural and procedural biases ensured women's continued exclusion. Kenyan women in various familial contexts with ranging land rights were susceptible to dispossession. Both widows maintaining property for their sons' inheritance and women laboring on family farmland occupied positions of vulnerability. Though patriarchal structures limited women's property rights, families often negotiated these rights at the household level, and women's experiences differed considerably.

In postcolonial Kenya, a spectrum of shifting and tenuous rights existed. While property rights protected some, they excluded many others from Kenya's most sought-after resource. Given the great expectations for land redistribution during decolonization, landlessness and land insecurity shaped political imaginaries, as marginalized Kenyans made sense of the postcolonial moment largely through their exclusion from accessing the resources of the state. In turn, many landless men and women articulated their disappointment with the early postcolonial government for its lack of commitment to equality, and some did not think of themselves as citizens. For them, independence signified little political or economic change.

The next chapter shifts back to settlement schemes to examine an attendant program—cooperative marketing societies. Though the objectives of cooperative marketing organizations differed from land-buying groups, in both cases, cooperatives received little regulatory attention, and dishonest leaders often defrauded members. Unlike farm-buying cooperatives, deception in marketing cooperatives did not produce landlessness, though it increased indebtedness.

4 "If I Was Evicted, Where Could I Go?"

Cooperative Development and Contestations over Economic Citizenship

On 8 May 1964, a cooperative society called Turbo Munyaka registered in Kenya.[1] It was just one of more than a thousand cooperatives in early postcolonial Kenya founded to channel produce to markets, manage farmers' financial accounts, and provide agricultural services.[2] It was also to be one of many cooperatives plagued by internal discord. In 1968, representatives of Turbo Munyaka penned a letter of complaint to the commissioner for Cooperative Development. The writers alleged that a co-op member named Makumi Muiru—whom they referred to as a "devilman"—attacked another member with a club and a spear, planted opium, was "in possession of witchcraft," threatened to cut farm elders with a *panga* (machete), and brewed liquor illegally.[3] For his part, Muiru denied all the charges and claimed the society discriminated against him.[4] He contended that other members destroyed his house and would not allow him to use communal cooperative property, such as the tractor.[5] After Muiru's letter, the archival paper trail abruptly stops, so it is here this vignette must end—outcome uncertain, though antipathy indisputable and seemingly irreconcilable. It was neither the first nor the last time members of Turbo Munyaka accused one another of misdeeds.[6]

A second cooperative case has a more apparent outcome, though a less clear beginning. Even so, the minutes of an April 1965 settlement staff meeting provide one start. They read, "It would be very desirable if an example were made of the worst settlers and that they were displaced, and their land re-allocated to persons who could make good use of it."[7] In various regions of Kenya, settlement officers held similar discussions about farmers with overdue agricultural loans—loans overseen by cooperative societies like Turbo Munyaka. By October 1966, a special committee had examined twenty-six cases involving "chronic defaulters," and "they recommended repossession of the plots in every case."[8] A series of evictions followed. On 28 February 1967, the committee recommended that another 107 farmers be evicted and their plots repossessed.[9] Three years had passed since independence. All the evictees had lived on their farms fewer than five years, and almost all were members of cooperative societies charged with collecting internationally financed loans and providing farming support.

Together, the two vignettes underscore that Kenyan cooperative societies possessed the trappings of both communes and parastatals. Composed of kith and kin, neighbors and friends, cooperatives embroiled intimate familial and social relationships in the broader political economy. Members were in daily contact with one another, but they also engaged with officials from the Kenyan state and international institutions, who delegated important developmental and administrative functions to these groups.

Both the colonial and the postcolonial states endowed these organizations and their leaders with such responsibilities because they believed cooperatives might expand local technical support and better connect farmers to state markets.[10] Technocrats envisaged cooperative societies distributing subsidized inputs such as seeds and fertilizers; managing communal property such as maize mills and cattle dips; and offering agricultural services such as artificial insemination. Individual members were legally compelled to sell their agricultural produce to their societies. The cooperatives were required to sell these products on to state marketing boards. Statutory boards paid the cooperative societies, who, in turn, paid the individual farmers after deducting fees and taxes.

It was the cooperative committee, not the general membership, that conducted this "real business" of the society.[11] While cooperative participants elected the committee leadership, the committee members were wholly entrusted with overseeing cooperative agricultural production and marketing, and with managing cooperative finances. In liaising between state and citizen, and in taking on these governing functions, cooperative committees represented an emerging form of civic life, one vested with enormous responsibilities.

In decolonizing Kenya, cooperative committees took on a new duty as debt collectors. Independence negotiations stipulated that resettlement programs—transferring land from European to African owners—could take place only through voluntary, "market value" sales. This requirement produced widespread indebtedness when Kenyans purchased land on credit from the state. It catalyzed, too, the incorporation of small-scale producers into global lending economies, as the Kenyan Treasury offered loans to citizens by taking on debt from international financial institutions and bilateral lenders. Accordingly, state and transnational policymakers became concerned with farmer loan delinquency, and the Settlement Fund Trustees suggested that "the success or failure of settlement hinges on the ability of settlers to repay their loans."[12] In this, they meant the success of the new property rights regime and the maintenance of Kenya's credit rating. Cooperatives offered an inexpensive solution, and the state designated these societies as credit brokers.[13] In doing so, government officials created a new site of state-building *outside* the state. The Kenyan state devolved power but remained an interventionist institution by proxy, entrusting community organizations to manage part of the economy.

Kenya's cooperative history challenges the oft-accepted notion that developmentalist states expanded, and exclusively relied upon, bureaucratic power.[14] In fact, cooperatives provided the understaffed bureaucratic machinery of Kenya's central state with an alternate governing institution. Fiscal constraints along with Kenyatta's ongoing efforts to centralize power meant that in Kenya, local governments were intentionally stymied and defunded, and the overstretched central state entered into rural lives irregularly. At times, Nairobi officials empowered community organizations such as cooperatives to administer development programs. In doing so, Kenyan policymakers attempted to respatialize state power by subordinating formal local governments to civil society.[15] Though the Kenyan state relied upon cooperatives, the state did little to monitor these groups. With limited oversight, the local elites who composed cooperative committees used societies for their own benefit at times, acting against the interests of the rural poor, who made up the vast majority of members.

Policymakers attempted to recast state power through cooperative development, and they also attempted to recast citizenship, with special attention to proper economic conduct. Kenyan citizens would not only be landowners, as the first three chapters showed, but dutiful cooperative members and responsible borrowers. While many Kenyans took pride in the former ideal, they felt less attached to the latter. Rural farmers, instead, asserted their rights as citizens to make independent economic decisions, particularly when they found cooperative control overbearing or cooperative leaders duplicitous. Thus many farmers abjured cooperatives, setting off a chain reaction extending from Kenyan producers to the international lenders who had funded resettlement.

These programs enmeshed the local with the national and the transnational. The first two sections provide a top-down examination of cooperative history. The chapter begins with an analysis of agricultural cooperatives in the colonial era, while the second part turns to independent policy and rhetoric on cooperatives, as Kenyatta repurposed cooperatives for a postcolonial setting. The following section moves to a mid-level examination of cooperatives in the dairy sector, illustrating how farmers made decisions about participating in cooperatives partly based on their experiences with statutory marketing boards and third-party service providers. The chapter then changes scope again, examining cooperatives from below, revealing conflicts within individual cooperative societies, and between cooperative committees and state actors. The final section provides a multitiered analysis of the decline of the cooperative movement. Through contestation over cooperative policy, rural Kenyans asserted their visions for good governance and individual economic liberties. State officials could neither effortlessly mold an obedient civil society nor a Kenyan citizenry. Both civic life and citizenship were newly emerging, and, in each, Kenyans asserted their rights to act autonomously.

COOPERATIVES AND COLONIALISM

Despite later postcolonial rhetoric emphasizing the traditionalism of communal labor, it was the cooperative marketing societies of European settlers that set the institutional groundwork for African cooperatives to come.[16] Soon after colonial conquest, as early as 1908, white settlers began founding cooperative societies.[17] Initially, these farmers formed European-only societies to collectively process their goods and better sell their products, in effect, monopolizing the export market.[18] Only in 1931 did the Kenya colonial government enact the first cooperative society ordinance. A process of registering national cooperatives followed. The most significant cooperative—the Kenya Farmers Association (Cooperative) Limited (KFA)—formed in 1923.[19]

The 1940s ushered in an era of cooperative expansion as the colonial state increasingly paid attention to African development and welfare. A 1944 government report promoted the extension of cooperatives to Africans. The colonial government established the Cooperative Department a year later, in 1945.[20] Soon after, African producers began establishing cooperative societies to market their produce. However, discriminatory practices remained in place, barring Africans from selling the most profitable products.[21] Many of the first African cooperatives struggled, since they marketed crops that generated less revenue.[22]

In the postwar era, the colonial state began amending agricultural marketing policies, gradually dismantling discrimination. Africans could begin growing cash crops but only under strict control. State actors continued protecting white settler agriculture from African competition while generating new revenue by levying taxes on African produce.[23] Cooperative societies allowed the colonial administration to achieve these aims. Cooperative membership became compulsory for farmers cultivating certain crops, and the state would issue growers' licenses only to cooperative members. More African farmers began growing crops such as coffee and pyrethrum, and thus became required to join cooperatives to market their produce legally. Kenyan farmers also began voluntarily forming dairy cooperative societies in the late 1940s and early 1950s, taking advantage of the benefits cooperative marketing afforded dairy producers. By 1952, the fifty-seven dairy societies represented the largest of the registered African cooperatives.[24]

Within a few years, colonial planners began debating whether to make membership in cooperative societies compulsory for the marketing of all agricultural produce.[25] Similar to other British colonial settings, the state found cooperative societies easier to control than individual producers, as cooperatives created a direct channel between farmers and government-regulated marketing boards. The state instituted cooperative policy to extend indirect rule into African economic arenas.[26] Though the colonial state was restructured in the postwar era, conceding to Africans greater self-determination in both politics and commerce, these reforms ensured the maintenance of a decentralized but interventionist state.

As a result, cooperative societies held increasing importance for state policy on agricultural production and marketing. Colonial officials began exerting pressure on African farmers to join cooperatives, and membership expanded dramatically in the second half of the 1950s. From 1956 to 1961, there was a nearly sixfold increase in the valued agricultural production of cooperatives and a growth rate averaging more than 40 percent per year.[27] African cooperatives produced coffee valued at £409,000 in 1956, and by 1961, they produced £3,005,000 worth of coffee. Cereal values moved from £110,000 to £168,000.[28] This greater revenue resulted from new opportunities for African producers to sell these crops legally, and from the growing number of cooperative societies that channeled African products directly to state marketing boards.

Despite the newfound enthusiasm for the cooperative sector, the colonial bureaucracy did not expand to match cooperative growth. In July 1947, there were only two trained inspectors in the Registrar of Cooperative Societies, and they were expected to monitor all twenty-nine newly formed societies.[29] By September 1947, sixty African cooperative societies had registered, and the Cooperative Department staff had increased to three inspectors and six subinspectors.[30] Five years later, in 1952, E. J. A. Leslie, the registrar of Cooperative Societies, wrote to the secretary for Agriculture that smaller societies were "incapable of managing their affairs."[31] Leslie asserted that the profits of cooperatives proved inadequate to cover even the cost of the limited clerical staff and suggested they "be wound up."[32] The colonial state would neither increase its cooperative administration to remedy this problem nor heed Leslie's advice.

Rather, colonial policymakers continued promoting cooperatives. State actors justified cooperative development in Kenya by emphasizing the suitability of cooperatives for an African setting. In 1955, M. X. Rodrigues, of the Registrar for Cooperatives, argued that co-ops would put a "brake on [the] moral deterioration" that competition and capitalism supposedly engendered, by providing "the practical environment wherein to practice the virtues of unselfishness, mutual help, honesty and trustworthiness."[33] In this, the registrar drew on relics of colonial ideology that deemed Africans incapable of capitalism.[34] Even as colonial officials revised these ideas, they maintained certain assumptions about the deficiencies of African economic logic. British colonialists conceptualized a paradoxical trajectory for imagined African protocapitalists. According to the administration, though cooperative societies facilitated integration into the market, they also slowed the moral decline that capitalism evidently precipitated in Africans. Unlike the rugged individualism revered for Westerners, colonial officials presumed that African farmers were not advanced enough to become outright capitalists, just communal ones.

Cooperatives served further rhetorical purposes for the colonial state. As other colonies moved toward independence and self-governance, Kenyan colonial officers discussed the utility of cooperatives "in preparing the people for more democratic forms of government."[35] For the colonial state, cooperatives represented a transitional panacea, bridging the African "communal past" with the democratic future. In March 1955, the registrar of cooperatives published a paper spelling out the virtues of cooperatives for democratic training. The registrar argued that cooperative members must be taught "to discriminate between the merits of rival candidates."[36] The paper went on to assert, "Without this experience at the lowest level it can scarcely be expected that electors will escape the many pitfalls laid in their way by demagogues seeking election to some important body."[37] The paper acknowledged future independence but concurrently asserted that Kenyans were unprepared for self-governance.

By the mid-1950s, colonial actors had begun lauding cooperatives for their ability to prepare Kenyans for democratic engagement. However, in 1952, registrar of cooperatives E. J. A. Leslie wrote that "uneducated" members were having a difficult time monitoring their cooperative finances and their cooperative leaders. The registrar noted, "The democratic control disappears and the secretary, to all intents and purposes, becomes a dictator over whom the only control is the occasional visit by an Inspector."[38] Leslie's comments suggest that cooperatives did not provide lessons in democracy but, rather, openings for opportunists. Even so, the colonial state made few policy changes, and added few staff to the meager Cooperative Department to better monitor cooperatives. This trend augured problems to come in the independent era.

Despite the early setbacks, in May 1962 the Ministry of Settlement began "considering the widespread extension of the Co-operative movement in farming."[39] Though Kenyan officials sought to extend cooperative development throughout all of Kenya, they planned for cooperatives to play especially important roles on resettlement schemes. Cooperatives would provide important agricultural services to help settlers meet their budgets, they would channel produce to markets, and they would collect loan repayments from members.

In many parts of the world, officials saw cooperatives, credit, and markets as a tripartite development solution.[40] The delegates who established the World Bank and International Monetary Fund at Bretton Woods in 1944 believed credit and markets encouraged discipline and accountability.[41] In the early 1960s, the UN Economic Commission commented on "the importance of the growth of co-operation in all African countries."[42] Decolonizing states throughout Africa augmented already existing cooperative programs, and they also drew ideas from various international examples.

For Kenya's cooperative policy, Israel was particularly influential.[43] In 1962, a group of Kenyan agricultural officials visited Israel, and, subsequently, Arie Amir, Israel's deputy minister of Agriculture, took two years' leave to become an adviser on Kenyan cooperative farming.[44] Amir pushed for Kenya to create a farming system akin to Israel's *moshavim*—cooperative settlements in which production and distribution were communal, but family life and home economics were individualistic.[45] Though Amir and his Kenyan acolytes—both KADU and KANU politicians—pressured the Ministry of Settlement to introduce moshavim, technocrats were not convinced.[46] As Kenya approached independence, an Israeli model had been introduced, but state and nonstate actors held reservations about its practical implications. Ultimately, as with other programs, proposed development models bore little resemblance to what transpired on the ground.

KENYATTA'S COOPERATIVES

Given the significance of cooperatives to Kenya's agricultural economy, the independent government continued to facilitate the sector's expansion. The state registered the Kenya National Federation of Cooperatives in 1964 to advise the government, and amended the Cooperative Societies Act in 1966 to give the commissioner for Cooperative Development greater powers. The year 1967 saw the founding of the national Cooperative College. In 1968, Kenya established a cooperative bank, which acted as the financial institution for cooperative organizations.[47]

Kenyan state actors approached bilateral donors about aiding cooperative development during the early postcolonial period. These solicitations led to the establishment of the Nordic Project for Cooperative Assistance in 1967, which provided help with staff, accounting systems, credit and banking services, and education.[48] American Peace Corps volunteers also began serving in cooperative management positions around this same time.[49] Both the British Overseas Development Administration and the United States Agency for International Development (USAID) granted money to nongovernmental organizations providing legal advice and assistance to cooperative societies.[50] While external partners supported the cooperative development sector, they often did so as a quasi extension of the Kenyan state, funding programs to monitor cooperative financing or to train cooperative leadership. Unlike other development programs, foreign aid for cooperatives rarely provided a direct path to resources. Though externally funded trainings afforded cooperative board members few overt material advantages, becoming trustees of development provided opportunities for economic gain.

In order to encourage Kenyan citizens to join the cooperative movement, the independent state drew on a diverse set of rhetorical devices—some old, some new. As in the colonial era, the government spilled a great deal of ink declaring cooperative agriculture's "direct roots in African tradition."[51] Kenyan state actors attempted to naturalize cooperatives by connecting them to a quixotic, precolonial past wherein farmers had worked communally. In 1964, a Department of Cooperative Development report proclaimed, "It is said that African farmers had been practicing co-operative farming long before co-operation with a capital 'C' was even thought of; that is to say they worked in groups on each other's fields."[52] The report implied that Kenyan farmers would effortlessly shift into the legally formalized cooperative societies the government promoted during decolonization. Immense differences existed between the mobilization of communal work and the marketing of crops through government-regulated cooperative societies, though.

Simultaneously, state actors highlighted that farmers—as members of these societies—would build the nation by working together, just as they had built their communities historically. A poster promoting the advantages of cooperatives showed two goats tethered to one another, each pulling in the opposite direction and trying, unsuccessfully, to reach different patches of grass. The next image depicted the goats working together, first moving toward one clump of grass and then toward the other.[53] The message was clear; Kenyans should work together. State records from the time were also peppered with manifestos on the importance of "co-operation."[54] In emphasizing cooperation, state actors attempted to brush past the hostilities of the independence negotiations, particularly the ethnic animosities that endured. In a 1971 speech, the permanent secretary for Cooperatives and Social Services, J. N. Oluoch, exemplified this logic: "Co-operatives by their very democratic nature should know and recognize no tribal bonds."[55] State actors used discourse that encouraged citizens to join the cooperative movement by tying it to tradition and nation-building, and they proffered cooperatives as a solution to lingering antagonism in the nation. In connecting cooperatives to a celebrated past and an optimistic future, state officials attempted to encourage farmers to join societies.

The Kenyan state also relied on both the persuasiveness of low-level bureaucrats and policy inducements to increase cooperative membership. Though the state could not legally force Kenyans to join voluntary organizations, state actors urged all Kenyans who resettled during decolonization to join the cooperatives on their schemes.[56] The vast majority of interviewees at six former settlement sites had believed they were required to join their cooperative societies. Maragoli settler Rastos Omamo said, for instance, that he helped start the cooperative in Lumakanda. Omamo recounted that the settlement officer, a state bureaucrat, approached him and a few others, telling them they should form a co-op and that everyone had to join.[57] The evidence suggests Kenyan settlers took this official counsel seriously. The state also encouraged Kenyans to create and join cooperatives through policy incentives. A government report proposed "having credit facilities made available to such groups [cooperatives] as against individuals."[58] The state provided cooperatives not only with credit that poor farmers could not access, but with subsidized agricultural services. Patrick Zieze, another Lumakanda cooperative member, recalled that government bureaucrats told him and his neighbors that if they worked together they could more easily access government services.[59] State actors emphasized the benefits of cooperatives, encouraging rural farmers to join.

Policy pressure and government rhetoric produced results. From 1963 to 1964, the number of registered cooperatives more than doubled and membership grew by more than fivefold.[60] The value of agricultural goods that cooperative societies produced increased by six times.[61] This growth continued throughout the 1960s. By 1967, Kenya had more than 1,030 cooperative societies, and, by 1969, registered societies totaled 1,850.[62] At the end of 1973, ten years after independence, the number of cooperatives had increased to 2,184, with a total membership of more than 620,000.[63]

Greater cooperative membership was only a means to an end. After the rapid expansion of cooperatives, officials expected these organizations to advance development. However, the discourse on cooperation and nation-building provided few solutions for molding Kenyan citizens into the economic agents the state envisaged. While many government officials took up optimistic cooperative rhetoric, some came to recognize its limitations. The commissioner for Cooperative Development wrote, for instance, "There is . . . a tendency in some circles to pay lip service to a co-operative ideal in matters of land settlement, without any real appreciation of the difficulties involved."[64] According to the commissioner, discourse had been emphasized at the expense of policy. In fact, the discourse obscured much of what was taking place on the ground. Though cooperative numbers had increased dramatically, in 1969, less than half of these societies were "active."[65] The dormancy of so many cooperatives emerged from a setting where the government pressured farmers to participate in cooperative development, and also from a setting where farmers had increasingly become disenchanted with the cooperative political economy.

Even for active societies, state discourse did not effortlessly produce a utopic setting of cooperation. Cooperative development required synergy among numerous groups with divergent interests, including rural farmers, cooperative leaders, local bureaucrats, statutory board members, and national officials. Frequently, these interactions created conflict, not unity. In 1967, the executive officer of the Kenya Dairy Board wrote to cooperative leaders about their "essential" role in policing illegal milk sales outside the exclusive contracts with the board. The officer concluded his letter on a hostile note: "I wish to know from each one of you whether you are prepared to impose fines on your members who might be arrested by my Board, taken to a court of law and convicted."[66] Cooperative leaders seemed both ill prepared and unconcerned with fining their members, as illegal sales—circumventing both cooperatives and marketing boards—continued, despite threats of arrest.

Cooperative leaders were also generally uninterested in training programs. In 1971, the cooperative assistant for Education noted that "the Cooperative Societies (Settlement) committee members and staff courses participation is growing worse day by day. The committee members have shown lack of interest in attending local courses."[67] In extolling cooperatives for cultivating and strengthening harmonious and productive relationships, officials had paid less attention to the challenges of unifying diverse groups. State actors presumed that citizens believed their duties in nation-building superseded their individual economic interests. This proved a miscalculation, as farmers increasingly made economic decisions based upon local factors, such as their personal relationships with other co-op members. Rural Kenyans began conceptualizing and enacting a form of citizenship that endowed them with economic liberties.

Notwithstanding the mounting evidence of conflict in cooperative partnerships, the postcolonial state—similar to the colonial state—provided little regulation and little help mediating among the various actors. The state lacked the qualified manpower to even staff its Cooperative Department. In 1963, about a month and a half before independence, Merlyn Davies, commissioner for Cooperative Development, noted that out of thirty-three cooperative officer positions, there were ten vacancies for which he "could not find suitable applicants to fill, in spite of lowering the standards required."[68] Training and support continued to be inadequate almost a decade later. A Nordic adviser noted in 1970 that ten cooperative officers monitored 130 settlement cooperative societies.[69] There was one cooperative officer—traveling on foot or by bicycle—for every thirteen schemes, most of which had thousands of residents and thousands of acres of land. The meager staff and almost unchecked powers of cooperative leaders would have vast implications.

DAIRY DILEMMAS

For centuries, residents of the northwest Rift Valley have grazed their herds on the Uasin Gishu plateau. This region remained cattle country in the postcolonial era. Many of the cooperatives there marketed dairy products, which brought statutory board officials, local bureaucrats, cooperative elites, third-party vendors, and Kenyan pastoralists into the same ambit. Dairy production depended on each of these actors faithfully carrying out their responsibilities. Any breakdowns could affect farmers' livelihoods.

As with most agricultural products in early postcolonial Kenya, a statutory board regulated the production and marketing of dairy. In contrast to other forms of agricultural production, dairy farming was often of a more collective nature and also heavily reliant on the services of nonstate actors. The investments dairy farmers made in cattle dips, for example, required communal donation, upkeep, and use. Further, unlike other agricultural products, the marketing of milk and cream required cooperative dairy farmers to combine their produce, and one member's poor product could spoil everyone's. Last, since dairy products are highly perishable, reliable transport was essential. As time passed, dairy farmers made decisions about whether and how to participate in their cooperative societies based on the policies of statutory boards, the reliability of third-party vendors, and the competence of other co-op dairy producers.

For milk cooperatives, the state instituted a system of marketing regulations similar to those created for other crops. The Dairy Industry Act Cap. 336 of 1958 set up the Kenya Dairy Board (KDB) with statutory control and the responsibility of "organizing, regulation and development of efficient production, marketing distribution and supply of dairy produce."[70] The dairy board legally prohibited selling milk without a license. Most milk producers sold to the KDB-licensed Kenya Cooperative Creameries (KCC), which then retailed the milk to the KDB.[71] Together, the Kenya Dairy Board and the Kenya Cooperative Creameries created a contract and quota system, which fixed the amount of milk individuals could sell. The intent was to ensure a regular supply of milk, but this policy disincentivized farmers and cooperative societies from producing to their full potential. Additionally, the KDB did not allocate quotas equally, creating dissatisfaction among farmers and cooperatives with low production allowances.[72] In 1970, in response to smallholders' frustrations, the Kenya Cooperative Creameries and the Kenya Dairy Board dismantled the quota system, and the price of milk simultaneously increased. By 1975, cooperative farmers supplied 40 percent of Kenya's total milk production.[73]

Dairy producers were affected not only by statutory board policy, but also by the availability and consistency of transport in their area. Given that milk production occurs daily, hiring a vehicle was an important, and substantial, expense. Some of the companies providing transportation proved undependable, leading to the adulteration of milk products. The Sosiani cooperative society lamented this issue in their application to purchase a tractor in 1972. "The means of transport that we have at the moment is not all reliable as we have some 3,000 kg. of milk downgraded monthly due to lateness in transportation. Most of the members however have complained about this loss of milk and some have started to apply for their own licence at KCC," they wrote.[74] Rural residents recounted similar stories. Chekalini settler and

FIGURE 4.1. Milking time, May 1972. Photo courtesy of James Pickerell for the World Bank. Country Photographs—Kenya, Loan 0303, Photographs, 1724753, Records of Office of External Affairs, WBGA.

agricultural official Alfred Machayo noted that the main company in the area, Great Rift Valley Transporters, sometimes arrived at 4 a.m., sometimes at midday.[75] Kiptoo arap Maina, a farmer and resident of Leseru—thirty miles to the east of Chekalini—had similar recollections about the transport company. Maina said the transport company sometimes did not come and the milk would spoil.[76] Government records support these oral accounts, as the Uasin Gishu District annual report of 1970 described "the poor service accorded" to cooperatives "by such companies as Great Rift Transporters."[77] Regardless of who was to blame, the KCC graded the milk delivered, and lower-grade milk earned less money, while spoiled milk earned no money at all. Inconsistent transport could thus decrease farmer incomes.

The success of dairy cooperatives also depended upon the production of each member. Many farmers recounted that the products of certain cooperative members depreciated the value of their milk. Some Lumakanda settlers spoke of the "*shida ya KCC* [the problem with the KCC]," noting that if even a single bucket of milk was not up to standard, the creamery would not pay out any money.[78] Other Lumakanda settlers confirmed this account, recounting that sharing a bucket became a problem in the cooperative, "because someone might have low-quality, dirty, watered-down milk, and it

FIGURE 4.2. A farmer transports his milk, May 1972. Photo courtesy of James Pickerell for the World Bank. Country Photographs—Kenya, Loan 0303, Photographs, 1724753, Records of Office of External Affairs, WBGA.

brought down the standard for everyone."[79] These experiences and their real economic impacts shaped farmers' marketing decisions.

Cooperative Societies for their part were empowered under the Cooperative Societies Act of 1966, not only to bind their members to supply all produce through the cooperative, but also to fine members for infringement.[80] Most societies included these stipulations in their bylaws. However, the combination of low milk quotas, inconsistent transport, poor milk production by fellow members, and the consequent lower-graded product and decreased profit caused many farmers to reconsider their options, whether or not they violated bylaws. A number of farmers began delivering milk on their own, outside their cooperative societies. H. E. Agimba, the assistant commissioner for Cooperative Development, commented to one cooperative officer, "There are quite a number of people from societies under you who deliver their milk direct to KCC. This as you realize, has put such societies in a very embarrassing situation whereby they cannot afford to repay their loans, maintain their cattle dips, etc. Yet such members keep on receiving services from the societies."[81] Individual direct deliveries of milk exacerbated already existing problems within cooperative societies.

When co-op milk production decreased, collective profits fell, loan payments dwindled, and cooperative services declined. These last two outcomes had further consequences. Lumakanda residents, for example, wrote to the commissioner of Cooperative Development about the deteriorating services in their society, asserting, "Dip Chemical to the dip No. 5 was since it was put there when this dip was opened in June 1972 has never been refilled, and the old water drained. . . . Water in the dip these days is nothing but mud."[82] Such negligence often led to additional complications for cooperative societies. When cooperatives did not manage dips properly, or when they did not compel farmers to use them, cattle epizootics occurred. Such was the case in Mautuma, where a substantial number of cattle died as a result of tick-borne illnesses. Making matters worse, the Mautuma cooperative could not always supply medicine to the veterinary scout, due to a lack of funds.[83] Many farmers held much of their wealth in cattle, and to lose a herd, or even a single cow, could be devastating. Disease also reduced milk output. The failings of any one aspect of cooperative management, or dairy production, then, could set off a series of other problems.

MISRULE, MISMANAGEMENT, MISCONDUCT

In April 1971, the Co-operative Bank of Kenya Limited denied a loan application from Turbo Munyaka—the same society with a purported "devilman" from the start of this chapter. The bank refused the application for close to two hundred thousand shillings because it was "not prepared to give a loan to repay another loan," and because it found the cooperative's financial position to be "weak."[84] These pecuniary woes exposed mismanagement, as did the various grievances about office bearers' indiscretions.[85] Some members alleged that officers sold collectively owned goods and used only a small portion of the profits to pay the cooperative's bills.[86] Others complained that cooperative leaders used society loan money to purchase personal goods.[87] In another instance, two different officials collected taxes from members but never brought the proceeds to the county council. One leader said that "the money got stolen," while the other simply "did not succeed in making the payment."[88] The above represents just a small sampling of one cooperative society's travails at the hands of what the district cooperative officer described as an "exploitative clique of officials."[89] Turbo Munyaka paints a picture of cooperative dysfunction. Though such issues were not uncommon in Kenya's early postcolonial cooperatives, rural Kenyans never tolerated them passively. In response, Kenyans contested corrupt cooperative leaders, condemned state inaction, and put forth different ideas of development and citizenship.

State officials hoped to integrate Kenyans into the economy through cooperatives, but this plan depended on innumerable actors behaving as the state envisioned. A Ministry of Cooperative Development report reveals government misconceptions about the straightforwardness of enacting such plans. "The Government of the newly independent country looked at Cooperatives as an ideal way to incorporate large numbers of *Wananchi* [citizens] into the National Development Process," Michael Chege Kuria wrote on behalf of the ministry.[90] On the whole, state actors seemed to believe it would be fairly simple to mold Kenyans into *wananchi*, and accordingly, into productive participants in national development.

Early on it became clear that this would not be the case, and neither the leaders of community organizations nor citizens would act as the state expected or directed. Kenya offered education programs for cooperative officers and members in an attempt to make them into nation-building wananchi. Even so, state confidence in cooperative officers' ability, devotion, and scrupulousness was often misguided. Cooperative leaders were thrust into positions with little to no experience.[91] On settlement schemes, the state expected cooperative societies to take over numerous government functions with little training, and within five years, co-ops were supposed to manage the entire scheme.[92] The state was well aware that not only were many cooperative officers unprepared to carry out their responsibilities, but cooperative boards were also understaffed. This remained the case for years. A Nordic adviser noted in 1972 that cooperatives had a "lack of qualified staff, only 1/3 of the societies have qualified farm managers, and only a few have qualified book-keepers / records / clerks."[93] This government correspondence concerning qualifications did not even broach how the self-interest of cooperative officers could affect their work.

By the mid- to late 1960s, some of the disadvantages of cooperative development had become clear. Though Kenyan state actors recognized the need to improve support and regulation, they still had to contend with the limitations of an overextended bureaucracy.[94] As a solution, government officials began advising individual cooperative societies to amalgamate with one another into cooperative unions. Officials hoped larger cooperatives would have greater capacity to manage themselves, and that the state could more ably monitor fewer cooperatives.[95] President Kenyatta espoused this line of thinking in 1964. He complained that there were "too many [cooperatives] . . . too small to do a good job for their members," arguing that smaller societies needed to join together to "become effective economic organizations."[96] Rural Kenyans possessed different ideas about how to improve cooperatives. Already displeased with the restrictions cooperatives placed on their economic autonomy, they had little interest in further distancing themselves from the cooperative leadership, or in entrusting strangers with their produce and profits.

Kenyans disregarded state advice and carried out the reverse action, reducing the size of their cooperatives. In the 1960s and 1970s, a number of cooperative societies broke away from unions and some cooperative societies split into smaller organizations. Kenyans justified the decision to divide their societies on the basis that unions and larger cooperatives held little accountability to members. In one instance in 1968, Sosiani cooperative split from Ndalat cooperative.[97] Interlocutors gave ranging explanations for the division, including desires for greater ownership and allegations that Ndalat leaders secretly sold members' farms.[98] The archival record simply explains the split as being on account of "social problems."[99] Various reasoning aside, splintering cooperatives signified rural resistance to state interference with local governance. In defying state guidance, rural Kenyans defended their individual and local autonomy, and asserted visions of a more scaled-down political economic apparatus. Though both officials and farmers had sought a solution to fraud and mismanagement, when state actors suggested cooperative unions, they misread the desires of rural Kenyans. Many Kenyans were happy to be good wananchi by becoming better integrated into a market economy, but they intended to do so on their own terms.

Irrespective of cooperative splits, issues with cooperative management continued throughout the 1960s and seem to have climaxed in the 1970s. Mautuma residents recounted a decline in cooperative services over the years. They noted that the cooperative was helpful at first. After a while, though, the management worsened, and members said they were not paid fairly for their produce.[100] The recollections of former cooperative members in other communities resonated with the Mautuma experience. Lumakanda residents recounted that the cooperative did not pay farmers enough, and regardless of how many times they changed leadership, the problems remained.[101] While low payments could result from mismanagement, they were also a product of the costliness of administering cooperative services.[102] In this context, many farmers started selling their produce outside their cooperatives.

Kenyans recounted being underpaid, and they also recounted that at times, cooperative leaders intentionally deceived members. Nandi farmer Mary Kitur moved to various locations in the Rift Valley before she became a squatter in Uasin Gishu. Soon after independence, her family settled on a farm and joined a cooperative society. Kitur described how the cooperative committee lied to members, saying that their production was only just enough to pay for land rates. She also remarked that they were not given receipts.[103] Kitur's account paralleled rural Kenyans in other communities, who noted that when farmers asked about their payments, the cooperative board would say they had not yet received a bank statement.[104] Other Uasin Gishu residents narrated even more dramatic experiences of theft, recounting how cooperative managers took off with the society's money and car.[105]

In some of these cases of alleged misconduct, society members asked government officers to carry out investigations. In 1967, three members of the Uasin Gishu Progressive Farmers Co-op Society wrote, "We are to ask you if the society being above named is different or a part from the others? Because no any investigations done since it was made a society in the time of three years. . . . Why?"[106] The petitioners added that despite a resolution, the cooperative had not held its annual general meeting. Noting the financial indiscretions of their cooperative manager, the letter writers asked, "Why doesn't the co-op officer of Eldoret ask this? And he was chosen to look for it?"[107] The petitioners sought state regulation. Other cooperative members also sought government intervention. Former Lumakanda co-op members recalled that people had to complain in order to convince the government to come and audit their organizations.[108] The localized nature of cooperatives further complicated efforts to police any misconduct. Members sometimes reported corrupt officers. However, because local residents ran co-ops, when members pursued punishment for cooperative officials, they might find themselves taking their relatives or friends to prison.[109] No simple solution existed, and, for some, their cooperative experiences served to repudiate state rhetoric of cooperation.

Though many rural farmers recounted malfeasance in oral histories, some Kenyans had more positive experiences, and certainly not all cooperative officers were corrupt men waiting to take advantage of guileless farmers. Sosiani settler Joseph arap Bir'geng said he thought his cooperative was helpful and the board members were active.[110] He added, "It took us a very short time to learn to work together because of the cooperative. Whatever the problem, we all chipped in."[111] Unlike the co-op members who recounted being cheated in Lumakanda and Mautuma, Bir'geng noted that Sosiani residents received receipts when they sold their produce to the cooperative. If anyone had complaints, they could go and discuss their issues with the board and other members. Most Sosiani settlers substantiated Bir'geng's positive account. Perhaps Sosiani's relative cooperative success can be partially attributed to its smaller size, and the importance of neighborhood sociality in Nandi culture. Through personal interactions and societal expectations of conduct, members could hold the leadership accountable, allowing the cooperative to function more democratically. Cooperatives were local institutions with immense variation, and their success often depended a great deal on the actions of a few leaders and on community relations.

Co-op members had a range of experiences, and they possessed a range of ideas about the appropriate roles for cooperatives in local development. In 1965, the assistant commissioner for Cooperative Development wrote to his commissioner about how the Lugari Farmers Cooperative was "heading for trouble."[112] The assistant commissioner explained that the co-op board members had visited his office to discuss purchasing a lorry (truck). To save money, he had directed the society to submit a loan application to purchase a tractor and trailer instead. In spite of this, the board members "bought a lorry before they left Nairobi and took it back with them against our advice."[113] Members of the cooperative—angry about unreliable transport, and about losing portions of their milk quota—had pressured leaders to purchase the lorry, or "their houses would be burned down."[114] Even after bureaucrats explained to cooperative members that a lorry was financially impracticable, "most of the members there insisted for the retention of this vehicle, and agreed to contribute."[115] In refusing to follow the assistant commissioner's advice, the cooperative members asserted their rights to self-determination.

The lorry provided the cooperative with a more reliable form of transport for their agricultural produce. It also provided them with autonomy and an emblem of prosperity. Ownership of a lorry symbolized the progress and development that many rural farmers desired and wanted to perform. State actors did not recognize this, however, and did not realize the significance of the will of the members. The inquiry concluded that the committee board members "did not exercise the prudence and diligence required of them in accordance with their By-laws," and that "appropriate action should be instituted against the persons concerned for the purchase of this vehicle, as it had involved the society in financial difficulties."[116] The cooperative members and state officials clearly possessed conflicting priorities and visions for development.

State officials intervened actively in a case where members seem to have agreed on their affairs. In other instances, the state allowed cooperative boards with immense powers to work largely unsupervised, creating opportunities for nefarious leaders to defraud members. Kenyans conceptualized state interference and state absence as issues of governance, and many rural Kenyans imagined both the bureaucrats assigned to monitor cooperatives and the cooperative committee as a part of the *serikali* (government).[117] Yet cooperatives were community organizations, occupying a liminal space. They engaged with, but operated partially outside, the sphere of the state. This ambiguity, along with disagreements about Kenya's nascent political economy, induced contestations. When cooperative societies resisted the state, they asserted divergent ideas about their finances and priorities and asserted their local autonomy. When members refused to sell their produce through their co-ops, they contested poor leadership. In this, Kenyan citizens also declared their individual economic liberties.

The aftermath of this last contestation would be the most enduring. In charging cooperatives with control of loan repayments, the Kenyan state entrusted undertrained and underregulated community organizations with managing portions of a broader credit system that extended all the way to bilateral and transnational donors and banking systems.

LAND LOANS AND INDEBTED FARMERS

In 1961, the British government agreed to make a grant to Kenya for one-third the land purchase price paid to European farmers departing from the scheduled areas. This arrangement required Kenya to take out a loan to meet the other two-thirds of the cost. The Kenyan government used the grant and loan money to purchase land from European farmers, paying half the purchase price in cash, and the remainder through three equal installments with a 5 percent interest rate. Kenyan farmers who purchased land in settlement schemes made a down payment to the Kenyan government and took out a loan to pay the balance. Government officials planned to use settler loan payments to repay state loans.[118] As a way of encouraging Kenyans to make payments, state actors crafted a concept of citizenly duty that entailed responsible borrowing. Kenyan debtors—many of whom had never taken out bank-backed loans and some of whom did not fully understand the terms—responded to this and other state incursions on their personal economic autonomy by asserting their rights as citizens to self-determination.

Because Kenya's credit depended on its farmers, the state attempted to monitor settlement finances closely, with the assistance of cooperative societies, government officers, and external development actors.[119] The Kenyan state required cooperatives to submit budgets and production plans. In registration applications, cooperative societies outlined their total acreage, the number of settlers, and the average plot size per person. They listed the crops contributing to the cooperative economy and the net target income. The application forms required cooperatives to break down these calculations further, listing the acres every farmer would devote to each crop and estimating the expenditures involved (such as transport, dip expenses, or wages for cooperative officers).[120] State officials believed settlement officers and Peace Corps volunteers would be "of great value" with budgeting and planning, and that they might analyze production shortfalls or examine loan repayment patterns.[121]

Despite this system, the assemblage of loans proved complicated for officials to manage and for Kenyans to navigate. Various ministries and departments simultaneously offered loans to the same individuals, often with little communication, allowing farmers to accumulate debt rapidly.[122] While the difficulty of paying back multiple loans contributed to the problem, growing debt was also a product of impossible lending terms. Some loans had high interest rates. The cereals loan, for example, had an interest rate of 8 percent charged each year the loan remained outstanding.[123] In certain circumstances, loan terms forced farmers to begin repayment before they had harvested a single crop.[124] Criticizing this practice in 1965, Uasin Gishu MP Justin Tuwei noted how some settlers "receive letters saying that they should have to pay for their plots before they have been given such plots in the settlement schemes. I do not know what makes this Ministry [of Settlement] rush to the new settlers who have not been living there, some of them have not even built their houses."[125] In other instances, bureaucrats grossly miscalculated farmers' expected income and, consequently, miscalculated the rate at which farmers could repay their loans.[126] Though profits were often much lower than initially projected, cooperative societies nonetheless deducted 50 percent of the expected, rather than the actual, income.[127] At times, farmers did not repay loans because school fees and taxes came due ahead of loan repayments, and families could not afford to pay all three.[128] Some settlers recounted developing tactics to avoid loan repayments deliberately.[129]

Loan arrears began as soon as settlement programs opened in Kenya. In the nine months prior to April 1962—a year and a half before independence but just after the start of settlement—the aggregate loan arrears almost doubled.[130] At the time, no agrarian loan officer existed, and the government worked to appoint one immediately. Even after creating a greater bureaucratic apparatus to monitor repayments, the pattern continued. By the end of 1970, settlers had paid only 54 percent of the total amount billed.[131]

The mismanagement of cooperative societies played a significant role in loan delinquency.[132] In response to mismanagement, corruption, and high deductions, members sold produce outside their cooperatives, in effect avoiding loan repayments.[133] On other occasions, cooperative societies did not properly deduct loan repayments or promptly send checks, or the leaders took the money for themselves. Evidence from various communities suggests that it was not just malfeasance, but maladministration affecting loan payments. In Mautuma, a settler complained that loan deductions did not appear on his bills. Upon further inspection, officials realized the cooperative officer had placed settlers' checks in his desk drawer, where they sat for two months.[134] Such delays in crediting payments toward accounts contributed to general confusion. Many settlers could not figure out how much they actually owed, and, in at least one case, a resourceful entrepreneur created a business charging settlers to calculate their debt.[135]

Across settlement, low loan repayments were a problem. The settlement schemes in the western Rift Valley were especially notorious for their poor repayment records. In 1966 and 1967, Turbo, Uasin Gishu, had the lowest loan repayment rates in all of Kenya. In the month of June 1966, Turbo-area settlers repaid only 28 percent of their loans. By June 1967, Turbo settlers showed some improvement, though their loan repayments had risen only to 38 percent.[136] This put the Kenyan government in a difficult position. Government correspondence in 1965 noted, "Since so much international finance (World Bank, West German and British) is involved in settlement, repayment will, more than any other single item, affect the country's credit ability for new loans."[137] Indeed, the Kenyan Treasury approached the British government in 1965 about a suspension on the repayment of land loans. The British refused. In 1966, Minister of Finance James Gichuru again contacted the British government about loan terms. In this same year, the Van Arkadie Mission, tasked with investigating land settlement, recommended the postponement of Kenyan government payments, but also the eviction of persistent defaulters.[138] Though the British did not reschedule the payments, they did give Kenya an interest-free loan of £18 million for the period between 1966 and 1970.

The director of Settlement created an investigations section in 1966 with a mandate to increase the rate of loan repayment. The section's first annual report reveals its didactic strategy. The report noted the investigations section's duty "to change the minds of settlers that land was not given for free but that settlers shall have to pay the arrears forthwith or run the risk of losing their plots."[139] With this education about suitable economic behavior and the importance of property rights, officials hoped to teach Kenyan settlers how to be proper economic citizens.

If settlers would not progress voluntarily, the state vowed to police their economic decision making more closely. For Kenyan bureaucrats, eviction represented the ultimate lesson for obstinate farmer-citizens. The investigations section began recommending expulsion of defaulters in its first year. In writing about these early evictions, the senior investigations officer blurred tutelage and battle, remarking: "Before the offensive was launched, defaulters believed that Warning Notices and Letters of Demand were meaningless scraps of paper."[140] Notwithstanding the truculent language, in actuality evictions occurred inconsistently. Some evicted settlers took advantage of state disorganization, reapplying "to be selected as replacements for re-settlement on the very same plots from which they have been evicted," clearly defeating the objective.[141] The initial set of evictions did frighten settlers enough to produce skyrocketing rates of loan payments in the months following.[142] Senior investigations officer T. K. Patel described the effects of these evictions as "electric" because of how "monies started flowing in at a higher rate."[143]

Not all bureaucrats were pleased with the results. At a meeting in Eldoret, settlement officers noted with concern that they had become a "villain of the peace." An officer complained that he could not "get within shooting distance of his settlers even to discuss the day to day affairs of settlement. They see him coming and they are OFF, and deep in the forest something sirs, so the morale of both settlers and settlement staff gets lower and lower."[144] Evictions had caused relations between settlers and settlement officers to deteriorate and threatened the general functioning of the schemes.

In response to complaints, the Office of the President announced a two-year moratorium on loan repayments and directed that the cases of the evicted be reconsidered.[145] Unlike the bureaucrats of the investigations unit, the president balanced pragmatism and populism to maintain authority. The quick policy turnabout created confusion, though. The moratorium, like the initial eviction policy, was riddled with inconsistencies. The *Daily Nation* reported on its front page in May 1967: "The decision to give settlers two years before they need to start repaying would apply to all who occupied not more than 100 acres of land."[146] The permanent secretary to the Treasury believed this reporting was inaccurate, and they had actually decided on a two-year moratorium to new settlers, not those already settled.[147] Meanwhile, the *East African Standard*, the other major daily, reported—in contrast to the intentions of the policy—that those who had more than one hundred acres would also be considered for loan moratorium.[148] Eventually, the government clarified its position, asserting that the moratorium applied only to new settlers, and evictees could not return to their former plots but could have their cases reviewed.[149]

Perhaps the most worrying implications of the loan reprieve were the hazy financial consequences. The new policy did not clearly set out how the moratoria affected repayments. Some believed the moratoria meant a deferment of payments for two years, in which case a loan repayable over ten years would become payable over twelve years, with a two-year gap in repayments. Others believed that moratorium policy meant the recalculation of the loan payments so that the period of the loan remained the same, but the repayments increased during the years in which they were made.[150] Once it became clear that the former was the case, the financial adviser to Settlement estimated it would cost the Treasury an additional £2.7 million by the end of 1968–69.[151] These numbers were eventually revised to half a million pounds, and the financial adviser projected the moratorium would cost the settlers more in the end as well.[152]

When evictions took place, they deeply affected families and communities. Lumakanda's cooperative society foundered early on, and former settlers preserved strong memories of the evictions, recounting their feelings of precarity. Even so, they did not take the expulsions idly. Instead, residents recounted seeking help from Member of Parliament Masinde Warengai, who visited them, and then spoke with Kenyatta to convince him not to evict the settlers.[153] Other evidence suggests that MPs all over the country interceded on behalf of their constituents. The permanent secretary of the Ministry of Lands and Settlement lamented, "Members of Parliament in some areas have urged those we had evicted on account of not paying up their due instalments to go back to their farms."[154] Though Kenyans frequently complained about absent representatives, many MPs intervened to protect their constituents from eviction. Land and land security were essential to political authority, and a general consensus formed on the unjustness of evictions.

Despite the public support, some rural Kenyans continued to fear eviction. For Maragoli farmer Patrick Zieze, settlement had initially been a godsend. Landless in his home location, Zieze had moved between Vihiga, the white highlands, and Nairobi, for years working different jobs. When he heard about the Lumakanda scheme, Zieze applied and was selected. After years of dislocation and insecurity, in 1963, Zieze and his family settled. In 1964, Zieze joined the Lumakanda cooperative, but problems with the cooperative and loan repayments arose immediately. He recounted, "We were being told we were paying the loan through the cooperative, but the officers were tricky and were not actually paying loans, just stealing money. . . . We could be given a paper which said they have deducted money for the loan, but when we went to the settlement office, we would find the loan had not been paid."[155] The ensuing threat of expulsions deeply affected Zieze: "Some people were given eviction notices because they were not able to pay for their loan. On my side, they could come and find me at home and tell me that they wanted their loan, and I tell them that I don't have money. And they tell me if you don't have money we are going, but when we come back we are going to sell your land. And, then they could add other fees to the loan. I was frightened because I was wondering, if I was evicted, where could I go?"[156] The evictions made a deep imprint on Zieze, upending the promises and possibilities of an independence marked by greater security and state protection.

The evidence suggests that many Kenyans felt compassion for indebted farmers and evictees, but some possessed more hard-line opinions on loan repayments. Joseph arap Bir'geng, the Nandi settler introduced in chapter 2, was part of the Sosiani co-op and did not have difficulties repaying his loans in the early postcolonial period. Perhaps because of his experience, Bir'geng expressed less sympathy for evictees. He likened the *shamba* (farm) to bride-price. If you do not pay, Bir'geng asserted, the wife's family takes her back. He added that it was the responsibility of the owner to pay back the loan, or the government could reclaim the land.[157] Here, he applied state rhetoric on citizenly duties to purchase land and make loan payments on time. Sosiani settlers like Bir'geng did not witness their neighbors, friends, or family being evicted. Because Sosiani residents owned more cattle than Lumakanda settlers, they possessed greater financial security and the ability to convert their cattle into cash if needed. Sosiani settlers could always sell their cattle, and, in addition, dairy farming provided frequent financial returns, so the possibility of eviction did not pose as great a threat.

Very few settlers borrowing money in the 1960s had ever been given a bank-backed loan, and these personal financial histories shaped the way farmers approached their repayment. The loans were, in large part, anathema to any financial arrangement in Kenyan economic history.[158] This economic history was certainly not without indebtedness, but borrowing and lending had worked flexibly in the past. Many settlers understood their thirty-year loan as granting them thirty years' time to pay. They did not realize they had to pay continually and promptly. Further, many rural Kenyans had no experience with raised interest rates, and the extent of their debt often came as a surprise. Misconceptions were the product of unfamiliarity, miscommunication, and the complexity of the credit system. Patrick Zieze, the Lumakanda settler nearly evicted, described the messages he received from state bureaucrats. He said that if you had money and wanted to pay all at once, the settlement officer would not allow it. Zieze recounted how officers used to ask, "'Pesa hizi zinakuuma [does this money pain you]?' This is something to pay slowly."[159]

State efforts to forge a citizenry composed of responsible borrowers were largely ineffective. This failure was not simply one of misunderstanding and miscommunication, but also one borne of contestation. Kenyans asserted their rights to economic liberties when they withdrew from cooperatives and when they chose how to spend their money. In refusing to repay their loans, they claimed the right to aspire to certain standards of living. Thus, they prioritized purchasing basic household goods, accessing important services such as health care and education, and participating in important social rites such as weddings, births, and funerals.[160] Most generally, they claimed the right to make their own financial decisions based on personal circumstances. As Zieze recounted, "We were paying what we felt we had."[161]

Claims-making and small victories aside, rural Kenyans would still have to settle their debts. Despite all the difficulties Kenyan farmers had repaying their loans, in 1967, the interest rate on land-purchase loans was raised to 7.5 percent.[162] Together, the evictions, followed by loan moratoriums, followed by the interest rate increase, reveal the tensions of statecraft. State officials and Kenyans debated how best to balance the economic rights and duties of citizens with nation-building, producing an erratic set of economic policies. While most state officials and Kenyans conceded that the loans would eventually need to be paid, they disagreed about the terms, the timeline, and the approach. The investigations section and some members of the Ministry of Finance—anxious about Kenya's credit rating and its ability to secure future loans—prioritized expeditious repayment, while settlement officers were more concerned with advancing agricultural development on the ground. Kenyatta—beholden to international lenders *and* citizens—worked to protect the nation's financial security, but while preserving his popularity and authority. In attempting to balance these two priorities, Kenyatta's inconsistent pronouncements about loan repayments created confusion among citizens.

The state remained more consistent in its reliance on cooperatives rhetorically. Policymakers continued to emphasize the importance of cooperatives for drawing on an indigenous past to create a better future, and to promote cooperatives as a solution to the problems of rural development. In a 1975 letter, the permanent secretary of Foreign Affairs wrote to the commissioner of Cooperative Development: "There is in Kenya wide participation by *wananchi* in all spheres of our economic development. The role played by your co-operatives in distributing the fruits of *Uhuru* [independence] to the small farmers and businessmen is a great contribution."[163] *Wananchi* [citizens] certainly sought to participate in economic development, especially their own. They often did not want to do so through cooperatives, and they contested state conceptualizations of proper economic citizenship. Ironically, while the state proclaimed how cooperative development represented a great equalizer, cooperatives contributed to rising debt and inequality.

The Kenyan state entrusted cooperatives—community organizations—with governance and credit brokerage. Cooperatives thus conducted some of the work usually attributed to an interventionist state, but they did so at an arm's length from state institutions. Despite the authority this position afforded these organizations and their officers, farmers made autonomous economic decisions on how to engage with or disengage from their cooperatives based on local factors, their interests, and their experiences. The eventual decline of cooperative development had vast implications for the indebted Kenyan state, which could not wholly control civic life, could not assign economic duties to citizens unchallenged, and could not chart a clear path for the political economy. The collapse of cooperative societies also made deep imprints on the lives of rural farmers, who were often further indebted as a result.[164]

Through cooperatives, nonstate actors mediated the policies and interventions of the Kenyan state and transnational organizations. These policies became transformed yet again, when rural citizens made quotidian economic decisions that reverberated in macrosettings. In putting forth conflicting ideas of suitable economic behavior, rural Kenyans, civic actors, and state officials—three imbricated and fluid groups—negotiated and elaborated upon ideas of authority and citizenship, and they carved out a contested trajectory for Kenya's economy. The economic policies of the new state certainly impacted smallholders, but rural Kenyans always reworked these policies on the ground. The next chapter carries this thread forward, focusing on how Kenyans contested state marketing policies and famine relief efforts.

5 "A Hungry Nation Cannot Be Contented"

The Political Economy of Famine

On 5 May 1965, the minister for Cooperative Development and Marketing, Paul Ngei, joined in vigorous legislative debate over African socialism in Kenya. Ngei declared on the parliamentary floor that applying African socialism in Kenya would ensure an "equitable distribution of national wealth," which would "not concentrate in the hands of the unscrupulous few while the less endowed millions starve."[1] As Ngei made his pronouncements, a maize shortage ravaged the nation. Some Kenyans went hungry while others enriched themselves, inflating maize prices and selling famine relief rather than distributing it to those in need. In other words, the exact situation Ngei railed against in Parliament was occurring at the precise moment he spoke. To make matters worse, Ngei would become implicated as one of the unscrupulous individuals personally profiting from the crisis.

From 1964 to 1966, drought, crop failure, and a subsequent maize shortage contributed to famine conditions in parts of Kenya. While the drought triggered the initial shortage, breakdowns in production and marketing and, later, failures in famine relief distribution, intensified and prolonged the food crisis.[2] Early on, reports emerged of Kenyans selling their maize on the black market rather than the state-regulated market, and of Kenyan traders smuggling maize into Uganda and Tanzania for better prices. The extensive circumvention of the state market exacerbated the shortage, as much-needed Kenyan-produced maize moved out of the country. Then relief efforts became marred by scandal. Despite forecasts of a shortage, policymakers postponed importing food aid, and, once it arrived, accounts surfaced of politicians selling American famine relief illegally to their business partners.

Various actors undermined state institutions in order to control how agricultural commodities were produced, processed, sold, and distributed both inside and outside Kenyan borders. State monopolistic control over the movement of resources never existed. Kenya's most valuable resources came out of the center of the country—agricultural produce, mostly from the highlands—and the state was unable to monitor or direct these resources, their producers, or their distribution. Instead, in the 1960s, the early postcolonial state relied a great deal upon the labor and cooperation of rural farmers, who made up 90 percent of the population.

Historians have long debated if the relationship between African producers and markets was one of integration, disconnection, or something in between.[3] The more important question is *why* African producers' relationships to the market varied so much over the years. When Kenyan farmers sold their maize on an unregulated nonstate market that channeled produce to Uganda and Tanzania, they remained "uncaptured" by the state's formal market mechanisms, but integrated into an international economy.[4] At other times and with other crops, if the conditions were favorable, Kenyans happily engaged with state markets intended solely for national distribution. Kenyan producers cultivated shifting ties to multiple markets simultaneously. Certainly, factors outside rural control—particularly the changing global marketplace and Kenya's national economic policy—made deep imprints on their livelihoods. Yet it was partially because of the constraints these forces could bring that farmers created imaginative outlets into multiple marketplaces and protected their ability to decide whether, how, and to whom to sell their produce.

State actors fashioned ideas about citizenship to prescribe particular forms of economic behavior. Not only did they envision Kenyan citizens as responsible borrowers, but as reliable and loyal producers who would sell exclusively to state-regulated markets. However, Kenyan smallholders contested the limits this citizenship placed on their economic autonomy and their agricultural profitability. Kenyans had long freely made decisions to engage with multiple markets in spite of stringent colonial controls, and they imagined independence would deliver more political and economic opportunities, not fewer. Significantly, in this case, liberty and livelihood converged. These sought-after liberties offered farmers not just more commercial choice, but better profits. Though many Kenyans abjured a form of citizenship characterized by economic restrictions, they imagined and enacted a form of citizenly duty that entailed building the nation by feeding it. The pursuit of continued individual capitalistic liberties may have driven smallholder rationalities, but these did not prohibit Kenyans from also embracing ideologies of social welfare.

With maize, prolonged economic dispute played a part in producing a food shortage and also became subject to popular debate. The maize shortage garnered daily newspaper coverage and eventually resulted in a commission of inquiry, bringing questions about state obligation to the foreground of public deliberation. When Kenyans participated in these debates, they drew upon multilayered experiences of famine and famine relief to refashion moral economies.[5] They blended precolonial norms, in which clients could expect patrons to provide protection from starvation, with colonial experiences, in which state institutions provided famine relief during times of great deprivation. Though specific expectations for independence were few, at their "most powerless and vulnerable," Kenyans anticipated some state assistance.[6] Many rural Kenyans articulated a political philosophy with limited state intervention, but that obligated the government to protect citizens from mortal insecurities. That a group of politicians and government officials enriched themselves while citizens starved produced distrust. For some, this distrust partially severed the incipient, and tenuous, moral contract between citizens and the state. It also generated a cycle where in times of need, Kenyans turned to individual patrons, who challenged formal institutional mechanisms of food relief by providing resources personally to clients.

Famines have long reordered social and political relationships in Africa.[7] The maize crisis was a constitutive moment for independent Kenya, as those affected drew on their experience to construct new political ideologies and affinities. The first section of this chapter provides a short background on the rise of maize production and consumption in Kenya, while the second section turns to changing postwar agricultural policy. The state had long been unable to control maize marketing, in large part because farmers had frequently evaded its constrictions. The third part examines the 1964–66 crisis as well as its aftermath. This section details how state officials undermined their own agencies and highlights the public outrage their actions engendered.[8] The last section explores how the government's mishandling of food distribution eroded citizens' trust in a state they had expected would ably take on the obligations of famine relief. Thus, the maize crisis propelled a return to clientage for certain protections.

In Uasin Gishu, maize delineates visible and tactile temporalities. Maize determines the seasonal labors of agriculturalists, and its annual harvesting marks another passing year. In January, farmers plow once, then a second time, followed by harrowing. They plant in March, when the rains should come. As seedlings germinate, farmers weed. In good years, the rains peak in May and August, continuing into September, when reaping begins. Farmers then spread maize in the sun to dry, and pack it in gunnysacks to sell. What they keep for their families to eat, they often pound by hand into maize meal. Rural residents chart their labors and lives through these cycles, and they also chart the years, particularly through periods of shortage. Kenyans remember famines vividly, and they often recount events as occurring before, after, or during years of hardship.[9]

Maize determines not only the cyclical labors of farmers, but also the sensory geography. It shapes the sights, sounds, and smells of Kenya's landscape. Just before harvest, rural spatiality is at its most divided and proximate, with visibility diminished as tall stalks of maize cover and partition the land, hundreds, thousands of times over. After harvesting, the landscape is transformed, vast and open yet again. Maize kernels dry over every spare inch of land adjacent to homesteads, and men and women pound the dried maize, penetrating the quiet. These interventions into temporality and spatiality extend beyond the village. The crop takes on new lives as it becomes a commodity, passing through the state, across borders, into the hands of millers and traders, then into other households for consumption.

This was not always the case; maize was not always so central. For about the past century, Uasin Gishu has been a part of Kenya's breadbasket, its farmers producing much of the maize on which the populace has subsisted.[10] Colonial authorities encouraged maize production, and the complete dominance of this foodstuff in Kenyan diets is a relatively recent phenomenon. Maize has a short growing season and higher yields per unit of land and labor than any other grain.[11] British officials made maize seeds available and offered inexpensive maize flour for consumption. By the 1920s and 1930s, the colonial state had successfully converted many African finger millet and sorghum producers into maize producers. In turn, Kenyans began using maize meal, or *posho*, in the preparation of their staple food, *ugali*.[12] By 1960, Kenyan smallholders planted maize on 44 percent of their land, and a decade later, on over 50 percent of small farmlands.[13] The quick adoption of maize increased food insecurity. Not only are many of Kenya's drier regions poorly suited to maize, but the outsized focus on maize production ignored centuries of risk-aversion practices founded upon scattered plots and polycropping.[14]

The introduction of maize and market economies heralded profound changes for Kenyan society—in agrarian practice, labor, gender relations, and capital accumulation. For many communities, agricultural labor had long been organized by gender, with men usually responsible for clearing the bush and herding cattle, and much else falling to women (though men were obligated to provide assistance).[15] While women's responsibilities centered on agricultural labor, and particularly on providing food, their rights to the products of their labor were often ambiguous.[16] Maize altered gendered labor divisions, and it also changed the social and economic significance of the product. Similar to past practices, in most Nandi families, harvested maize continued to be divided between husband and wife. As before, the wife's share of the grain was used for family consumption. Prior to maize production, the husband's grain share had gone toward beer brewing, and thus toward the performance of social obligations. When Nandi began producing maize as a cash crop, men often separated their maize fields from their wives'. Men then sold their maize shares, gaining sole control over the income, weakening women's economic position.[17] Maize also increased inequality among the Luyia. With railway extensions and growing demand, in the 1920s and 1930s, many Luyia became integrated into the wider capitalist system, producing more maize and selling it farther afield. Those with more land made greater profits, and elites began operating mills, contributing to additional stratification.[18]

As the state's efforts to convert African farmers into maize producers proved increasingly successful, colonial officials created regulations. Broadly speaking, the Kenyan colonial administration was characterized by its dual legal frameworks. Two main sets of policies—one for European cash-crop farmers and one for African subsistence farmers—governed agricultural production and marketing.[19] Considered both cash crop and subsistence crop, maize held an indeterminate position in colonial administrative ontology. In years of plenty, African maize farmers might both consume the "subsistence" maize they had grown and sell their surplus. With an average harvest, they might not sell any maize at all. In years of scarcity, maize growers might also become market consumers.

The goals of colonial administrators conflicted more for maize than for other crops. Though they aimed to protect European farmers from African competition, colonial officials also needed to protect African subsistence production and ensure tax payments.[20] Starting in the 1930s, the state began encouraging greater African agricultural production to respond to the economic setbacks of the depression. Africans also took initiative at this time, expanding their acreage and output dramatically for local market demands.[21] Even so, state actors still attempted to use legislation to keep production tightly controlled.

For white settlers, the colonial state initially promoted maize as an export crop. However, beginning in the 1940s, with a few exceptions, Europeans mostly grew maize for the domestic market.[22] The export market for cereals had declined during the depression, and Kenya experienced two droughts and two attendant maize shortages in the early 1940s. In response, the colonial government assembled a commission on food shortage. The commission advised the state to deter maize exports, recommending that Kenya should produce maize only for its self-sufficiency.[23] While maize had not been profitable to export during the depression, it had remained costly to store and import (and, it remained one of a few crops that poorer European settlers could afford to produce), justifying its continued domestic production. Yet, already by this point, some previously self-sufficient areas of Kenya, like Maragoliland—faced with rising population densities and growing land shortages—could no longer produce the necessary food to nourish their residents.[24]

WAR AND POSTWAR POLICY CHANGES

The rapid succession of depression and drought pushed officials to reform agricultural policy. In 1942, the colonial state established a cereals control statutory board to advise the Ministry of Agriculture and help regulate production and marketing.[25] With the advent of the cereals board, the Kenyan state centralized control over the marketing of maize and other cereals, and the minister of Agriculture required producers to sell their crops to appointed agents.[26] The agents for African maize growers in the reserves were licensed buyers set up under a 1935 ordinance. By and large, African maize producers were not allowed to sell or transport their surplus maize over reserve borders without a permit.[27] African growers in the highlands could legally sell their excess maize, but only to their European employers.[28]

The state also began offering guaranteed minimum returns for European-grown maize. In effect, this policy taxed African producers and consumers to subsidize price increases for European producers. Previously, Africans could sell a bag of maize for six or seven shillings. After the implementation of the Defence (Control of Maize) Regulations of 1942 Act, they received only 4/90 shillings per bag, yet consumer prices for maize meal rose by 80 percent. European farmers, on the other hand, were guaranteed 8/50 shillings for a bag of maize, close to twice the price offered to Africans.[29]

Metropolitan commercial needs and greater global demands for Kenya's produce during the war set in motion other changes. Though national self-sufficiency would be the long-term policy, from late 1942 through 1945, export production was renewed. Wartime demand and high commodity prices drove European settlers to once again plant maize for international markets.[30] With the guaranteed minimum returns offered by the colonial state, European farmers also continued selling maize on the national market.

As the international economy flourished and domestic demand heightened under the drought, African producers, like European settlers, took advantage of the higher prices offered for maize. Unlike white settlers, they found higher prices on the domestic black market, not the state-regulated market.[31] David Anderson and David Throup have shown, for example, that between 1942 and 1945, only 1,400 of an estimated 30,000 bags of maize surplus from Murang'a entered the state market.[32] Kenyans throughout the colony refused to heed the strict agricultural regulations that circumscribed their economic opportunities, and they moved and sold maize in contravention of colonial laws.[33]

During this same period, the government began repealing racialized restrictions that had previously prohibited African farmers from growing and selling produce the state defined as cash crops.[34] Starting in the postwar era, Africans could more easily enter state-sanctioned commodity production, though under tight regulation. Control over agricultural production—which statutory boards and cooperative societies theoretically delivered—was closely connected to state efforts to increase revenue by taxing commercial agriculture.[35]

Despite putting in place greater monitoring facilities for the maize market in the 1940s and 1950s, the distinctive characteristics of maize created challenges for its control. First, as marketing opportunities opened, an enormous number of producers began to sell maize in the state-controlled market.[36] Unlike other cash crops, almost every Kenyan farmer grew maize, and the sheer quantity of production and producers was nearly impossible to track. These farmers moved between subsistence and cash-crop production, depending upon the season, their output, the price offered, and their own circumstances. Second, because maize had become Kenya's staple food, the government was tasked with ensuring that maize production met local needs, particularly since it was so expensive to import.

The purpose of the Maize Marketing Board (MMB), the statutory board that ultimately came into being, was to assist the state with these issues. The government established the board "to regulate, control and improve the collection, storage, marketing and distribution and supply of maize and maize

FIGURE 5.1. Harvesting the maize crop, 1945. Photo courtesy of the British National Archives, CO 1069/173 (73).

products."[37] To do so, the Maize Marketing Board required Kenyan maize growers to sell their maize to the board or one of its agents. In 1960, that accounted for 1,659,051 bags of maize and £3.12 million in sales.[38] Yet this number represented a negligible proportion of Kenya's total maize production. Close to an estimated 90 percent of maize never entered the market, and thus did not come under the jurisdiction of the MMB.[39]

Despite these laws, many African maize growers continued selling their produce outside the state-regulated market, a practice the colonial state was highly aware of but unable to halt.[40] The chairman of the Uasin Gishu agricultural committee complained to the CEO of the Board of Agriculture in February 1959, "We are faced today with a position where hundreds of bags of maize are being moved into urban areas from rural areas on bicycles without a valid permit."[41] In the same period, the Soy-Turbo District Council demanded "the Police to take action regarding the increasing illegal movement of small quantities of maize."[42] The police responded to these entreaties by noting that during the first three months of 1959, sixteen "offenders" had been "apprehended" for illegally moving maize.[43] Arrests did little to deter farmers. Kenyans would continue selling maize outside the state market throughout the colonial period, and they would carry these practices over into the postcolonial era as well.

Because maize regulation was intended to generate revenue and guarantee the colony's sustenance, the government provided particular incentives for its production. The state published guaranteed prices to ensure the colony's self-sufficiency, prevent overproduction, and avoid the weak export market.[44] The government also offered credit facilities to maize farmers ahead of planting, and continued offering a guaranteed minimum return for "essential crops," including maize.[45] Government regulation extended to the milling process and sales, since most Kenyan consumers purchased *posho*—ground maize meal—rather than unprocessed maize. The maize marketing act decreed that only government-certified millers could buy maize from the Maize Marketing Board or its agents, and they had to do so at state-specified prices.[46] The government also fixed the retail price for maize meal, and the margins of profits for millers and traders were subject to statutory control.

This stringent regulatory program produced a large differential between the guaranteed price paid to farmers and the price at which posho sold to consumers. During the 1960 growing season, the producer's guaranteed price was 35/30 shillings per a two-hundred-pound bag of maize. This price represented 74 percent of the overall cost of posho to the consumer. The MMB added 2/47 shillings for the cost of the gunnysack, storage, and distribution; 4/03 for internal marketing costs; 3/50 for the milling costs; and 2/35 for the traders' sales commission, all of which added up to a cost of 47/65 shillings for posho.[47]

The differential represented one of the most unpopular aspects of the maize marketing regulations, and Kenyans complained a great deal about the discrepancy between producer payments and consumer costs. Minister of Agriculture Bruce McKenzie admitted to participating in this criticism in 1959, noting, "Maize and Produce Control has been an 'Aunt Sally' for members of the Legislative Council and the general public since its inception. I have myself on occasion hurled the odd brickbat at it!"[48] The Aunt Sally idiom—a reference to an English game where players throw sticks at a model of an old woman's head—gives a sense of the public vitriol directed at the maize board. Indeed, politicians and the public complained so much that the general manager of the MMB was frequently compelled to publish explanations and rationalizations of maize pricing in the *East African Standard*. In spite of these efforts, the MMB came under attack throughout the mid-twentieth century. Consumers believed controls unnecessarily inflated maize prices, while producers believed it cut into their profits.

Though the price differential engendered critiques, it constituted an important part of the risk-management system for years of shortfall. This system was put to the test in 1961, one of the poorest farming years in Kenya's recorded history, and the first time the MMB imported maize.[49] In Rift Valley Province alone, four different districts received food aid.[50] Though the cost of imported maize was substantially higher than locally grown maize, the board was able to maintain the price of posho. The 1961 drought, in effect, confirmed for policymakers one of the essential purposes of maize regulation and price fixing—to ensure against underproduction. The connection between the price differential and cheap import costs seems not to have been clarified to the public. Further, the policy basically taxed maize farmers to pay for famine relief and remained broadly disfavored.

Even so, late colonial famine relief did make an impression. Kenyans vividly recalled receiving food aid in 1961, especially because American yellow corn differed so much from the white maize they had become accustomed to.[51] The importation of such curious maize indicated its foreign origins. Just as Kenya received this aid, media access was improving, and average Kenyans were more poised than ever before to learn about its provenance. Western highlands residents recounted how they gathered around radios with family, friends, and neighbors, and they relayed the excitement of listening to world news, "even from America," in the early 1960s.[52] Improved media at a moment of growing international assistance from a widening set of partners fostered global connections. Better media access shaped more expansive ideas of authority and contributed to expectations for Kenyan leaders to ably procure and distribute foreign aid.

Various Kenyans showed their gratitude for the 1961 famine relief provided by the United States. A Kamba chief gave President Kennedy a walking stick in appreciation, as mentioned in the introduction to this book, and Duruma chiefs sent "hearty congratulations" to the president, noting that he had "saved many lives . . . during the time of famine which still haunts our people."[53] In a letter to the editor of the *East African Standard*, Nairobi resident Kabiru Deen wrote, "The US and its people have been most generous and kind towards this country in every way. They provided us with free food when it was so badly needed here."[54] While the imported food was not truly free, many recipients recognized American relief efforts. They also recognized the role the colonial government played in obtaining and distributing aid, and the 1961 experience generated expectations for future governments to take similar actions. The colonial state was by no means a welfare state, given its policy that "only in the severest conditions" should food aid "be a Government responsibility as distinct from a family, clan or tribal responsibility." Nonetheless, colonial officials did consider famine aid, and the maintenance of life, an "obligation."[55] Many rural Kenyans grasped that obligation and came to anticipate that the postcolonial state would also protect citizens' lives in this same way.[56]

In future years, Kenyan citizens and postcolonial state actors would engage in intense deliberations over government obligations. Ultimately, these obligations would come to look quite different from those the colonial state took on, representing a semi-abdication of institutional protections. While the postcolonial state continued to garner and import food relief, individual political leaders distributed food aid to their associates and constituents. Thus, they created a modern version of an older system of food security. This arrangement harkened back to that precolonial patrons had offered their clients, though it differed in its form of expected reciprocities and the marked inequalities underpinning these relationships.[57]

Much of the established colonial maize policy persisted in the postcolonial period, notwithstanding state promotion of hybrid and synthetic maize seeds after scientific breakthroughs.[58] As with many of the agricultural policies that independent Kenya would inherit, the policy on maize production and marketing remained largely unchanged from the early postwar years. The postcolonial state continued to try to strictly control the movement of maize, and farmers were still legally required to sell their maize to the MMB or one of its agents. With independence, though, the number of MMB agents proliferated, a by-product of assertions of regional autonomy.[59] The burgeoning number of MMB agents was part of a broader struggle over the control of Kenya's resources, its land and agricultural commodities. Each of the various agents to the MMB maintained subagents, often marketing cooperatives or registered traders, who purchased maize directly from farmers. For example, the Kenya Agriculture and Produce Marketing Board, the largest agent in Central, Coast, and Eastern Provinces, managed about six hundred subagents in 1966, one hundred of which were cooperative societies and unions.[60] The profusion of agents and subagents made this system of maize marketing an increasingly cumbersome one. Consequently, it became more difficult to control, though the system existed for regulatory purposes. Government motivations for supervision in the postcolonial era remained much the same as those before. Agricultural officials saw maize regulation as a way to generate revenue, channeling taxable produce into the state-controlled market.

State officials were particularly concerned with controlling the agricultural revenue on settlement schemes, because this revenue would go toward loan repayments and because settlement schemes sat on some of the most fertile and agriculturally lucrative land in Kenya. The state thus exerted greater pressure on African settlers to sell through the formal marketing channels by building in more stringent forms of regulation, usually through cooperative societies. Similar to government efforts to mold Kenyans into a particular brand of economic citizens through cooperatives, state officials added to the qualities of good economic citizenship with market regulation, hoping to make Kenyans into not only responsible borrowers but also patriotic producers. In one instance, when Kenyans from West Pokot wrote a complaint about local politicians, officials from the Ministry of Agriculture intervened: "In these Independent days, the emphasis should and must be on greater and better agricultural production. The elders, the women and the youth wings in West Pokot must channel all their efforts towards agriculture and enter fully into the spirit of Harambee [pulling together]."[61] In other words, Kenyans should put politics aside and focus on producing for the nation.

State officials never controlled maize production or marketing, in large part because they did not succeed in convincing settlers to sell maize through the cooperative societies that channeled produce to the marketing board, and because maize farmers on the whole disliked the policies and procedures of the MMB. The high deductions for fees, taxes, and loan repayments were especially loathed. On settlement schemes "the substantial burden of debt" basically meant "the denial of hard cash" for maize farmers.[62]

The 1966 accounts of one high-density scheme in Western Province serve to illustrate this point. After numerous deductions, farmers on this scheme received only four shillings per bag of maize, rather than the thirty-seven shillings the marketing board offered. A deduction of 20 percent was made for cooperative expenses, 50 percent for loan repayments, and ten shillings for the minimum financial return.[63]

Outside settlement schemes, the bureaucratic presence lessened, and there were fewer regulatory mechanisms directly incorporated. In turn, the new state came up against greater difficulties in regulating maize production and marketing within those spaces. While controlling the maize industry in the former reserves did not have major significance for loan repayments, it did have implications for Kenya's revenue stream, for its capacity to remain self-sufficient in food production, and for the state's ability to accurately forecast food shortages. However, without either policy incentives or bureaucratic pressure, the government had less success convincing Kenyan smallholders outside settlement to create and use marketing cooperatives, and thus to create a clear avenue for selling maize to the MMB.

Nandi farmer Kiptoo arap Maina recounted that the government-set maize price was very low in the 1960s, and that he blamed the officers of the cereals board. He chose to sell to private traders instead, because they offered cash on the spot, and there were no deductions. In explaining his marketing decisions, Maina declared, "We were free to do as we liked, because it was our property." An emphasis on economic liberties also permeated Maina's ideas about development, which he defined in terms of individual economic freedoms: "When nobody is restricting you for any job, you can plow as much as you want, can keep as many cattle as you want, and provide for your family."[64] In this statement Maina implicitly alluded to colonialism, an experienced marked by economic controls such as cattle and crop restrictions. Similar to other rural Kenyans, Maina expected that independence would deliver greater economic autonomy to citizens.

Many of the same problems with maize regulation that plagued the colonial state also plagued the postcolonial state, with the added challenges of political transition. Politicians and journalists continued to criticize the board and its policies. Farmers, too, persistently protested maize policies.[65] Alfred Machayo, a Maragoli farmer in Chekalini who served as a district agricultural officer in the mid-1960s, described the many deterrents: "You send maize to cereals board; they want to ask if it is dry, if it is dirty. So many questions, then so many deductions, and you don't know how long you will wait, and they don't want to pay on the spot. That sort of arrangement can't make me sell maize."[66] In spite of his position in the agricultural bureaucracy,

Machayo understood why maize farmers chose not to sell to the marketing board agents that channeled the maize into the state-regulated market. On the whole, maize growers were disappointed that the postcolonial government maintained a system they had long despised because they believed it was unfair and limited economic freedoms.

In response, many Kenyan maize farmers violated state policy, never allowing themselves to be inhibited by Kenya's marketing regulations, which were highly controlled only in theory. For decades, farmers had decided to sell their maize beyond the state-regulated market when they found government controls unfavorable, and as they continued to do so, they asserted their economic liberties and their rights to more advantageous marketing conditions. They also enacted a different vision of Kenya's political economy.

It is unclear how much maize Kenyans produced or consumed at this time, but very little of what state actors thought farmers were producing ever went through MMB agents or into the state-regulated market. The Kenyan government had long estimated that the country produced fifteen million bags of maize each year but sold only two million bags.[67] Maize growers' decisions about whether to enter the state market might not have made a deep impact in years of plenty, but they would in years of dearth.

THE CRISIS AND ITS AFTERMATH

Independence wrought both continuity and change in most government policies and spheres of economic life, and maize production and marketing were no different. A number of factors diminished maize harvests in the first half of the 1960s, particularly in the highlands. Droughts aside, maize production during this period was fairly atypical, a product of decolonizing transitions and rapid transfers of farmland. Land settlement programs created gaps between harvests. This had been expected, and the Kenyan state provided new African settlers with posho as they cleared and plowed their land, planted, and then harvested usually a full year after settling. In addition to a year or more without production, African settlers often recounted that it took time for them to adjust to the new land. Many said that a few years passed before they reaped decent harvests. Settlement schemes rarely met anticipated production outputs in their earliest years, which also directly coincided with the drought.[68]

Additionally, in 1963, the government lowered the set prices for maize, and, in response, many farmers—both African and European—planted less maize.[69] In Uasin Gishu and Trans Nzoia, especially, many cultivators began planting wheat instead of maize, principally because wheat pricing was so much more consistent.[70] European maize output declined precipitously, not only because of the low and irregular prices, but also because many fled the country at independence. Others stopped growing anything but the most essential crops to avoid taking out new loans for production or development. Between 1963 and 1964, maize acreage dropped 34 percent on large farms in Kenya.[71] All these factors played a role in the crisis.

Beginning in July 1964, the Maize Marketing Board counseled the Ministry of Agriculture to import twenty to thirty thousand tons of maize to fill a small crop shortage before the harvest.[72] Just eight months prior, Kenya had exported four hundred thousand bags of maize to Japan—thought to be "the largest consignment of white maize ever to leave an African port."[73] Ultimately, the decision to export this maize, rather than store it, would force Kenya to import more food aid in the coming year and a half. On 12 August 1964, the Ministry of Agriculture formally authorized the importation of 150,000 bags from Tanzania and Uganda. On 5 October, the MMB requested permission to use the Nairobi emergency maize reserve, noting that the 1964 planted crop was likely to be better than expected. The government granted permission the next day, and on 10 October, the MMB made a similar request about the Mombasa reserve, which the Kenyan government granted the same day.[74]

A month later, on 12 November, the chairman of the Maize Marketing Board issued a press statement warning about a possible shortage in 1965. Then, on 9 December, the MMB advised the Ministry of Agriculture that they would need to import a further 662,000 bags. At the end of December, officials in the Ministry of Finance wrote a letter to the US ambassador requesting five hundred thousand bags of maize.[75] The two governments signed an agreement a few months later, at the end of February 1965, but its fulfillment was slowed. Three months later, the maize still had not left US shores and became further delayed when the shipping agents were indicted under conspiracy to defraud charges.[76]

At this point, the Ministry of Agriculture rationed the country from an estimated consumption of 150,000 bags to 80,000 bags for May and June. In Nairobi, "long queues of women" waited outside the Kenya Farmers Association offices on Haile Selassie Avenue, desperate to purchase maize.[77] By 5 June 1965, the shipment from the US still had not arrived and the permanent secretary of Agriculture advised the MMB of the potential need for a second shipment, since the rains had failed in parts of the country. Two weeks later, on 17 June, the first part of the maize shipment from the United States—about 13,000 tons or 130,000 bags—finally arrived, over six months after Kenyan government officials agreed on the necessity for the shipment and almost a full year after the MMB noted an impending shortage.

The second and third shipments from the US arrived on 3 August and 26 August, respectively, completing the 500,000-bag order. Between the arrival of these two shipments, the board recommended importing a further 250,000 bags. The Kenyan government negotiated and signed a new agreement with the United States on 31 August, allowing for the supply of up to 500,000 additional bags of maize. A few days later, the board reviewed the position again and advised that Kenya now required the full amount. The first of this new set of shipments arrived on 15 November.[78]

The numerous misestimates about maize production and the missteps with maize importation make clear that despite the almost autocratic powers of the MMB, officials had little idea how much maize Kenyan growers actually produced, or how much of that maize would enter the state market. James Cooper, a bureaucrat in the Ministry of Cooperatives and Marketing, testified to this in 1966: "It has been estimated for years that the total production of maize in Kenya is fifteen million bags of maize per year, yet no one has ever seen or handled thirteen million of them, two million only go through the hands of the Board and no one ever knows whether the thirteen million is accurate within one million, or accurate within five million. It could be much more or much less."[79] Agricultural officials, in other words, were well aware of just how little they knew about maize production and sales.

Indeed, as the shipments of American maize arrived at Mombasa, other shipments of Kenyan maize exited different ports. In November 1965, local government officers wrote numerous reports about Kenyan farmers selling their maize on the "black market," often on to Kenya's neighbors, Uganda and Tanzania. In a 24 November 1965 "Safari Diary," an assistant commissioner for Cooperative Development remarked upon the growing number of "illegal" sales of maize, estimating that more than fifty-three thousand bags had been sold into Uganda.[80] Another cooperative development officer reported that "the unrealistic price paid by the Maize Marketing Board is causing the majority of settlers in Western Region Schemes to sell their maize in the Black Market for cash and for a comparatively higher price than that offered by the Maize Marketing Board."[81] Clearly, many maize farmers had managed to produce a surplus in spite of the poor rains, but they chose to sell their crops outside the state-controlled market, which meant those crops often made their way outside Kenya's national borders.

Even the arrival of American corn—which some MPs complained was pig feed—would not solve the crisis.[82] The situation was more dire than officials realized. Many regions of the country had shortfalls and needed aid. At the same time, much of the maize produced in-country was being moved out of Kenya. Uasin Gishu rainfall was down by about two-thirds compared to its long-term mean, and the drought produced a "partial failure" of the maize crop there. Compared with "previous drought years on record, 1965 was by far the worst for maize growing" in Uasin Gishu and its neighboring districts.[83] While many maize producers saw their outputs diminish, some could still meet subsistence needs. Even so, both Mautuma and Lumakanda required food aid.[84] Other areas of the country fared even worse. At the time, Nandi farmer Theresa Ngososei lived farther east in the Rift Valley in Laikipia, and she preserved vivid memories of the drought. She described how the "trees got so dry, a visitor would think the place was burnt." Ngososei recounted receiving yellow maize and, "because we had no other choice, we just accepted it."[85]

Not every Kenyan who needed relief received it promptly, as some government officials used famine aid indiscriminately. Bureaucrats in the provincial administration complained that E. A. Andere, the general manager of the MMB, made false promises about the arrival of maize rations.[86] Various government officials did not follow the famine relief distribution protocol. District committees were supposed to submit their requirements to the board, specify which certified traders should receive maize shipments, and then supervise the distribution. However, district officials often spurned practiced traders for inexperienced ones. They also overstated their needs and even duplicated applications for aid, fraudulently ordering emergency supplies for areas with already full rations. Distribution occurred largely unsupervised, and the exorbitant amounts charged to consumers—despite government price controls—often went unchecked.[87]

In other instances, politicians and elites bypassed district committees to obtain maize directly from MMB officials. Some members of Parliament approached General Manager Andere personally for maize handouts, which they sold on to traders with whom they had business connections.[88] Reports also circulated that some of the imported famine relief was being smuggled over the border into Uganda and Tanzania, similar to the route taken by much of the maize produced in-country.[89] More embarrassing for the government, allegations surfaced that the general manager of the West Kenya Marketing Board (an agent of the MMB), the general manager of the Maize Marketing Board, and the minister of Cooperatives and Marketing—three of the most senior officials involved in maize regulation—were involved in the smuggling.[90] Later, B. C. W. Lutta, former permanent secretary of the Ministry of Cooperatives and Marketing, would attest to this. "It is my opinion that the ultimate food shortage was caused more by maladministration of and malpractices in distribution than by the delay in arranging the importation," he wrote in a memorandum.[91]

The malpractices of Minister Ngei drew special public ire. Numerous officials alleged that the minister channeled maize directly to his wife's trading and milling companies—Emma Stores and Uhuru Millers—giving her about two thousand bags a week, while other traders received no maize at all. Multiple county councillors contended that Emma Ngei then refused to distribute the maize to subagents and, instead, sold it privately at inflated prices.[92] A Machakos county councillor said that "Mr. Ngei's elder brother, Mr. William K. Ngei, who operated a *pombe* [alcohol] club, was allocated 15 bags of maize daily, though not on the list of sub-agents, while traders received only five bags for each 200 people."[93] The *East African Standard* reported that traders who complained were told that "even the District Commissioner could not change the instructions of Mr. Ngei."[94] A councillor made similar charges, recounting that when he approached the district commissioner to complain, he was reminded of the "difficulty in dealing with a store belonging to a Minister."[95]

By the end of October, the Kenyan public showed signs of impatience and anger. On 27 October 1965, the *Daily Nation* published an editorial criticizing the government for its mishandling of the crisis, concluding that there was "something wrong somewhere" in the maize distribution system.[96] On the same day, the Kenya National Farmers Union (KNFU)—a union that originally represented European farmers to the colonial government—attacked the gross negligence of the MMB and the government.[97] The KNFU statement and the increasingly alarmist tone of newspaper reports catalyzed belligerent responses from various government officials, but particularly from the general manager of the Maize Marketing Board, E. A. Andere, who accused European farmers of trying to sabotage Kenyan agricultural production and the KNFU of being a racist organization.[98]

For the next two months, the maize crisis received regular coverage in the *Daily Nation* and the *East African Standard*. As more facts came to light, the newspaper editorial boards accused the government of the misuse of authority, of bribery and corruption, of unnecessary delay in ordering maize imports, and of a defective distribution system. Both papers demanded a commission of inquiry. Ngei, exhibiting both his brashness and insensitivity, responded that he did not take orders from newspapers.[99] In reply, one *Nation* editorial opined, "How much more is this country going to take? Nearly two million bags of maize will have been imported into Kenya by early next year in the space of 15 months and at a cost of not less than

£4½ million." The editorial concluded with a rhetorical question: "Why has the Minister responsible for feeding the nation not acted decisively?"[100]

Kenyan citizens also wondered about government responsibility and culpability. They wrote eloquent letters to the editor almost daily, detailing the position in their communities, revealing their hardships, and echoing journalists' calls for the government to better address the shortage. Many Kenyans emphasized that traders had no posho to sell and consumers could find no posho to buy. An anonymous Naivasha resident wrote in to the *Daily Nation* on 1 November 1965, "Several traders I have talked to say that every day hundreds of people come to ask for *posho*. They start from one end of the street, asking only one question. Have you any *posho*? The simple answer is NO."[101] James D. Gathuri of Kiambu wrote a similar letter to the *Daily Nation* on 4 November 1965, stating, "Though there are people in Kenya today starving because they do not have money to buy food with, hundreds of thousands of others are starving because they do not have something to buy."[102]

Other Kenyans expressed disappointment with the government, hinting that there might be ramifications for the unresponsive state. Manoah Kisame of Nakuru wrote to the *Daily Nation*, "Many an innocent person is experiencing difficulty due to the maize shortage and yet Mr. Andere dares tell a Press conference that the situation is being exaggerated! God have mercy on him."[103] In another letter to the *Daily Nation*, Gabriel Ndula wrote that average people had been "denied a voice in the maize issue." Ndula criticized Kenya's maize policy, noting that Uasin Gishu had maize "still in the fields untouched," but farmers could not transport maize "to their families in the reserves or in the towns because the cooperative's hand is well stretched out to arrest them." The letter concluded with a warning to government officials: "A hungry nation is not a contented nation."[104] Letters to the editor broadcast the difficult circumstances of Kenyans in various regions. In emphasizing Kenyan dissatisfaction with the Maize Marketing Board and the government, the letters implied that neither had met citizens' expectations. When Kenyans conveyed their discontent, they also articulated their ideas of government responsibility for famine relief.

The crisis had reached a fever pitch. Both Minister Ngei and MMB manager Andere continued answering public demands for an investigation abrasively. Finally, almost a year and a half into the shortage, in November 1965, Minister Ngei was pressured into agreeing to a commission of inquiry.[105] Even so, he continued to argue in Parliament that it was "wrong to assume that there has been any corruption." As he tried to make his case, a few angry MPs interrupted and heckled him.[106] Prior to the start of the commission, the state responded to public grievances in other ways. In December 1965, the Ministry of Agriculture took over the West Kenya Marketing Board—an MMB agent incriminated in the mismanagement allegations—and suspended five senior officers from the board.[107] Kenyatta also formed a committee to examine statutory boards and reshuffled the cabinet.[108]

Shortly after, on 10 January 1966, the commission of inquiry into Kenyan maize marketing began. Four and a half months, seventy-five witnesses, and five hundred interviews later, the commission published its findings. The commissioners did not make suggestions for sweeping changes. They recommended self-sufficiency in maize production within Kenya and the continuation of the fixed price system, though they emphasized that the government should announce prices as far ahead of the planting season as possible. They advised the government to encourage cooperative societies—already in place on the settlement schemes and in many nonsettlement maize-producing areas—to collect maize from small producers. The commission counseled the government to continue to build a price stabilization fund by adding fees to maize prices, thus perpetuating the high differential between the price paid to growers and the purchase price. They also recommended the continuation of the policy that prohibited the free buying and selling of maize between private individuals without the mediation of a statutory organization.[109]

Though its recommendations were conservative, the commission did lay blame for the crisis, concluding that the MMB and the Ministry of Cooperatives and Marketing were both partially at fault for the delay in obtaining maize shipments. The commission also published its conclusions on the state of the shortage and its causes, determining that the shortage of maize was around 10 percent, and that a considerable amount of maize was smuggled into Uganda, though the remainder of the shortage was due to drought.[110] The members of the commission found a number of the charges against the MMB, the West Kenya Marketing Board, district commissioners, members of Parliament, and Minister Ngei to be true. In fact, they dedicated an entire chapter of their report to the allegations against Ngei. The commissioners censured Ngei for allowing his personal interests in a milling company, a maize store, and an MMB-appointed agent "to come into conflict with his duty to a statutory Board to the certain detriment of the latter."[111] The commission of inquiry could only make recommendations, however, and their findings had no legal bearings.

The report did propose a few amendments to maize policy. It recommended that retailers' profits on sifted flour be reduced. The most substantial suggested modification was a repeal of the provision in the Maize

Marketing Act that compelled the board to work exclusively through agents unless otherwise authorized by the minister.[112] In spite of the commission's moderate findings, public pressure provoked other changes. Just after the start of the commission, Kenyatta replaced the Maize Marketing Board with the Maize and Produce Marketing Board, and on 23 February 1966, he suspended Paul Ngei from his new position as minister of Housing and Social Services. These adjustments proved to be largely cosmetic. By the end of May, Ngei had his ministerial position back, just three months following his suspension.[113] Further, despite the newspaper coverage, the national outcry, and the well-publicized commission of inquiry, the Kenyan maize industry remained beset by the same problems that first contributed to the crisis.

The testimonies to the commission of inquiry demonstrated that the high differential between the set price paid to maize growers and the cost to consumers continued to be not only wildly unpopular but broadly misunderstood, and farmers' dissatisfaction with the pricing system drove their black market sales. The purchase of American famine aid, however, put the reduction of this high differential out of the question. The Kenyan government had taken out large loans to pay for the importation of American famine relief, and Kenyan maize farmers bore the brunt of this cost in order to maintain consumer prices and avoid overburdening the Kenyan Treasury.[114]

The minor reforms did little to provide better regulatory mechanisms, or to keep the "black market" from undercutting the state-controlled market. For example, in 1966, seven settlement cooperative societies in the northwestern region of the Rift Valley did not pay back their loan advances for maize planting, largely because the farmers had not sold harvested maize to their cooperatives. State officers forced the offending societies to sign irrevocable orders to pay the full amount as soon as they harvested the next crop. When the harvest came in, only two paid.[115] The Maize and Produce Board wrote to the director of Settlement, calling the region a "complete mess," as farmers continued to refuse to sell their maize to cooperative societies they alleged did not pay them properly.[116] Instead, maize farmers acted as they always had when state marketing conditions were disadvantageous. "They are therefore finding out-lets in the markets or trading centres outside the settlement schemes. . . . Instead of co-operatives getting the loan repayments, some maize may be finding its way into the black market," Maize and Produce Board officials wrote.[117] In placing blame on smallholders, agricultural officials avoided scrutinizing *why* farmers continued to make these marketing decisions.

These actions fed into a vicious cycle, which ultimately benefited neither farmers nor the Kenyan state, as the loans of each accrued. In some cases, loan-granting institutions began withholding payments for maize products even for those individuals without debts, which only encouraged farmers to avoid selling to co-ops.[118] In 1967, the Agricultural Finance Corporation (AFC) seized Mautuma maize harvests to service cooperative debts, regardless of whether the individual farmers supplying the maize had outstanding loans.[119] Such actions had major repercussions, and, by 1969, Mautuma farmers sold an estimated 60 percent of their maize privately.[120] Kenyan farmers not only continued to sell maize outside their cooperatives, but they continued to do so with impunity, as the government was unable to stop them.

Despite the few reforms, many aspects of maize marketing remained the same, or even reverted back to previously eradicated practices. The Kenyan government rejected various proposals to raise maize prices, though prices in Uganda were, at times, twice as much as that offered by the MMB.[121] Indeed, in 1966, the government again reduced the price of maize, effectively discouraging maize planting and encouraging black market maize sales.[122] Ngei's second appointment made clear that the findings of the commission of inquiry held dubious importance.[123] His reappointment contributed to growing distrust of the state as an institution, which appeared not to prioritize the public good. This distrust encouraged various actors to circumvent the state. Kenyans not only continued to sell their produce outside state-controlled markets, but in times of need, they also increasingly turned to individual patrons rather than to a state that refused to take on important obligations.

STATE OBLIGATION, CITIZEN DISTRUST

Through their engagements in public debate during the maize crisis, Kenyans reflected on government obligation. When they crafted expectations of state obligation, rural Kenyans drew on a diverse set of experiences. They employed earlier expectations of security from food shortage under precolonial patrons. They used experiences of receiving state famine aid and communal assistance during the late colonial era. They drew from their engagements with other citizens and from public discourse.

Postcolonial politicians and political elites also contributed to this discourse. Paul Ngei proclaimed on the parliamentary floor, as this chapter opened, that independent Kenya should forge a redistributive state where citizens never starved. Other politicians made similar promises about safeguarding citizens from hunger. Tom Mboya argued that it was the government's obligation "to ensure the availability of free maize to any person in genuine need of famine relief."[124] With layered experiences in which the colonial state declared and demonstrated that food relief was a government obligation, and in which postcolonial Kenyan politicians promised to take on the same obligations, a broadly established conception of government responsibility for famine relief formed.

Citizens began to expect that the new state would meet those obligations. Many Uasin Gishu residents recounted that in times of need, particularly during a food shortage, it was the government's responsibility to take care of the people.[125] A chasm separated ideology from practice, though, and the disjuncture between expectations, promises, and realities produced disappointment. Such was the case for Nandi squatter Mary Kitur. In chapter 3, we first met Kitur, whose political ideologies were shaped by land insecurity. Her ideologies were also marked by other vulnerabilities. She noted, "After independence, some people were starving. The government was there, but there was no response. I expected a lot more."[126] Indeed, one of the ways in which Kitur said she had assessed Kenya's *maendeleo*, or development, was by whether or not people had enough food to eat.[127]

Landowners and Kenyans from other ethnic communities held similar beliefs. Maragoli settler James Sabatia recounted how inaction during the maize shortage shaped his opinions of the government. "The government only assisted us a little bit during the crisis, though people were having a very tough time. The minister [Ngei] was so corrupt. Because the minister was part of the government, I thought the whole government was corrupt," he recounted.[128] As the owner of fifteen acres of land, Sabatia was generally better protected from food shortages than other Kenyans. However, Sabatia lived in Lumakanda—one of the settlements that required food aid—and the inadequacy of state assistance made an impression on him. The maize crisis reveals how fundamental political philosophies came to be defined through experiences of development and aid in the early postcolonial era. It also shows how citizen distrust emerged when an unpredictable state did not keep its promises to provide the most basic protections, and in circumstances when broad ideological agreement diverged so sharply from material experience.

Through the maize crisis, Kenyans negotiated questions about the role of the state, but also about their duties as citizens. Kenyan disappointment in the government deepened in a context where the state already asked a great deal of its citizens, and where many Kenyans felt they made important contributions to nation-building. In fact, many farmers fashioned ideas about nation-building founded specifically upon producing food for "needy people" and "those living in arid places."[129] Nandi farmer Susan Rono now lives in Leseru, Uasin Gishu, but in the 1960s, she lived on a forty-acre farm in Nandi District, where she and her family produced maize, millet, and dairy. Rono emphasized how her agricultural work supported the nation and the destitute, in particular. "I assisted the nation through the supply of milk and maize," she said, continuing, "Because, after sending my products, they were being transported to far places to assist the needy who didn't have food."[130] Many Kenyan farmers took pride in their self-sufficiency, as well as in their ability to help feed those who were less prosperous. They also extended assistance to the needy within their local communities. Kenyans recounted donating money to poor families for their children's school fees, and giving maize to their church or to widows.[131]

Though rural producers willingly took on some duties, they contested others. Many Kenyan maize producers refused to accept any duties that infringed upon their economic autonomy. Politicians were well aware that farmers claimed rights to control their own produce and to make a greater profit. In the National Assembly in July 1965, MP George Oprong Oduya put forward a measure to remedy the maize shortage. While defending his motion, Oduya, whose Elgon West constituency bordered Uganda, discussed the issue of producer autonomy: "On the question of *tumbo*—that means on the question of produce—a law will have little effect, if the public opinion is ignored." He explained, "We have told the people not to send their maize to Uganda, and they say that the maize is theirs and they will look for the highest price for it."[132] Kenyan citizens asserted their rights to economic liberties, and they also claimed rights to famine relief. In an opinion piece for the *Daily Nation* in 1969, political activist Jael Mbogo—then head of Maendeleo ya Wanawake and secretary-general of the Freedom from Hunger council—asserted that "freedom from hunger" was "one of mankind's most basic rights."[133] In a context where the state did not always protect these rights and inconsistently performed obligations, Kenyan dissatisfaction grew.

Rural Kenyans recognized that certain forms of assistance went beyond the abilities of a small community.[134] In absence of adequate farm production, Kenyans expected the state to provide food to the hungry. Though Rift Valley residents believed their farmwork was central to developing and building Kenya, during a famine, they could no longer be responsible for feeding the nation. In such instances many Kenyans had expected the government would provide basic protections. With institutional actors intentionally undermining the provision of aid, the state could not dependably offer those protections, though individual patrons could. When patrons gave out famine relief, they offered state resources subsidized by citizens' taxes, often to clients from their particular region and ethnic group. In the process, they ultimately strengthened ethnonationalisms.

Throughout its short history in Kenya, maize has proved amorphous in the face of rigid state controls. Colonial state officials encountered difficulties determining whether maize constituted a subsistence crop or a cash crop, and they possessed ambivalence about whether maize should be exported or limited to national markets. Even when colonial administrators created strict legislation on maize production and marketing, they never managed to control how Africans grew, moved, processed, or sold maize.

Postcolonial state officials would face similar problems, since they made few amendments to colonial postwar maize policies. With aims to generate revenue and provide subsistence without overproducing, and with little idea just how much maize innumerable Kenyan farmers grew, bureaucrats confronted challenges to enacting state regulations. Kenyan refusal to abide by state policy was part and parcel of a dispute about the economic liberties of citizens. Kenyan producers had long asserted their rights to greater profits and to pursue integration into multiple markets. They continued to do so in the postcolonial era.

Decolonizing transitions and the unpredictability of the weather further complicated this setting. The conjuncture of black market sales, diminished production during land transfers, and a drought contributed to postcolonial Kenya's first maize shortage, beginning just a year after independence. The Kenyan state's inability to ensure the availability of the most basic foodstuff and, subsequently, its inability to effectively distribute famine aid had implications for the still-developing contract between citizens and the state. Though expectations at independence were few, with famine relief, Kenyans made use of layered precolonial and colonial experiences of protection, along with politicians' promises for safeguards, and they anticipated state assistance during famines.

The state eventually imported and distributed food aid, though some state actors undercut these efforts. In circumventing state channels to give out famine relief directly to their supporters, patrons proved themselves more reliable than state institutions. The maize scandal delegitimized state authority and created distrust as Kenyans realized the state would not take on expected obligations. Settings of insecurity constituted new political relationships when Kenyans turned to patrons instead of the state. Both the power of these patrons and their relationships with their clients transformed in this postcolonial setting. Not only did fewer patrons administer national food distribution, but poorer ethnic clients now paid for their protections.

The next chapter continues to explore how development shaped Kenyan ideas on state obligation and citizens' rights and duties. Kenyans asserted their rights to determine local development priorities through their community projects and, increasingly, came to expect state assistance for these programs.

6 "Those Poor People Who Sweated Themselves to Help Themselves"

Self-Help and the Contradictions of Citizenship and Development

ON 1 JUNE 1963—the day Kenya attained internal self-government—Jomo Kenyatta declared, "We must work harder to fight our enemies—ignorance, sickness and poverty. I therefore give you the call: HARAMBEE! Let us all work hard together for our country, Kenya."[1] *Harambee* (Swahili word meaning "pull together") became both a rallying cry and the maxim of Kenyatta's presidency. It would also become synonymous with self-help. Like Kenyatta's speech, self-help encouraged Kenyan citizens to contribute to nation-building, specifically by initiating local development projects. State actors promised Kenyans that after they did their part building roads, schools, and hospitals, the government would provide them with additional funding and materials and, if needed, technical experts and staff.[2] Implicit, then, in harambee was the notion that citizens had to fulfill their duties in local development before they could make claims to state assistance.

Through harambee, ordinary Kenyans could take control over their own development and gain access to services they had long desired. Community projects contributed to national development and self-help reduced state responsibility in the provision of services. Similar to cooperative programs, harambee relied on local communities and a form of incipient civic life in order to create development. While this program placed a heavy burden on citizens, the sheer number of self-help projects carried out after independence suggests that local groups accepted the work. Ultimately, harambee came to occupy an ambiguous arena—often government orchestrated, but just as often, largely absent of government support and dependent on citizens' initiative, capital, and labor.

A few years after independence, the landscape throughout much of Kenya had transformed as new, locally initiated schools and hospitals suddenly dotted the countryside. Though communities built schools and hospitals at a frenetic pace, these buildings often sat silent and empty for years, without teachers or nurses, desks or medications—expenses that fell to the government. The empty schools and hospitals revealed disputes between local self-help groups and state actors about the government's responsibilities, and about the rights and duties of citizens. The premise of harambee—that it would be locally led but nationally coordinated—had proved untenable. State officials began refusing to fund recurrent expenditures, because the government could not afford to continually hire nurses and teachers. Increasingly, the state intervened not to offer assistance or funding, but to regulate community efforts or to induce local groups to take up projects that advanced national development. Self-help groups contested state development priorities and state infringements on local sovereignty by moving forward with their projects. In undertaking these schemes, self-help groups put forth alternative visions of Kenya's development, they asserted local autonomy, and they claimed rights to state assistance. Though state actors had vowed that the government would help those who helped themselves, the government inconsistently offered aid to harambee projects. Many Kenyans saw this as another instance of state unreliability and another neglected state obligation.

Officials from competing arms of the state often disagreed on development priorities, but a bureaucratic consensus formed on harambee's efficacy in providing economical, nationwide community development. There was less agreement among these same actors on how to equitably and justly allocate the limited funding. By requiring local communities to raise their own capital, self-help compounded inequalities. Wealthier regions and communities could collect larger donations and initiate more expensive projects. They could rely on their better-educated and more well-connected populace to bring complicated projects to fruition. Though politicians and bureaucrats recognized that harambee could intensify regional and ethnic disparities, the state never introduced reparative policies, serving to intensify discourse on postcolonial injustices.

In the process of creating self-help projects, Kenyans negotiated development priorities, and they deliberated the labor and financial obligations of individuals to their communities. Ultimately, many people were excluded from fully participating in these discussions. Only a small set of community members—usually, wealthy, elite, educated men—could join the self-help committees, which exercised preeminent power in community-development decision making. Self-help, in turn, played a part in delineating communal boundaries and reifying social hierarchies. At times, those excluded from leadership positions within self-help and other community organizations, such as women and the poor, formed separate groups in an attempt to improve their lives and meet their own needs. They often looked beyond the state—especially to church missions and NGOs—to achieve their goals.

Self-help projects engendered debates about development, citizenship, and belonging in the nation and in local communities. The first section of this chapter provides background on the role of self-help in British colonial policy. The second section examines how Jomo Kenyatta built upon colonial models, but reframed self-help to emphasize the duties of citizens in nation-building. The third part explores conflict between rural Kenyans and state officials over self-help planning, implementation, and funding. The final section examines how reliance on self-help—rather than a centralized, redistributive policy—perpetuated and intensified existing forms of regional, communal, and gendered inequalities, though it also illustrates how some groups responded to their marginalization by forming their own mechanisms of support.

A LABOR OF LOVE? THE RISE OF SELF-HELP

At the turn of the twentieth century, Western states and mission societies increasingly embraced self-help programs.[3] Later, in the 1930s and 1940s, the British colonial government began focusing on African welfare, a shift borne in part from the launch of the British welfare state.[4] Despite the different conditions, metropolitan actors extended the idea of voluntarism and the practice of community development through self-help to colonial spaces. By the mid-twentieth century, there was a growing consensus among a wide range of Western actors that self-help could provide new social services that states with inadequate tax revenues could not.

As part of British postwar concessions to African nationalists, the Kenyan colonial state altered its administrative structure. In 1950, the colonial government passed an ordinance replacing Local Native Councils (LNCs) with African District Councils (ADCs) and introducing elections for African councillors. The modifications provided Kenyans with limited representative governance but also signified an attempt to resolve the growing problem of financing and administering local development. While British indirect rule had long decentralized and localized governance in Kenya, with the creation of African District Councils, for the first time Kenyans would tax themselves for community development.

Though self-help had promised to provide social services on a shoestring, it soon proved inadequate. As local development projects increased, local government spending grew exponentially, vastly outpacing tax returns. G. M. Bebb, district commissioner of Tambach, described the situation in the mid-1950s: "To sum it up the cry is improved services all round but of increased revenue to meet the cost, I see little sign."[5] In addition, the colonial government began compelling some ADCs to carry out expensive land reforms, causing program costs to skyrocket and further exceed local revenue. In 1955, the colonial state forced African District Councils in Rift Valley Province to implement the Swynnerton Plan—a massive program to privatize landownership for African smallholders.[6] The program's emphasis on surveying and agricultural planning required expensive technical equipment and expertise. Rift Valley ADCs took out large loans to fund this program. Samburu District, for instance, spent just £4,500 in 1951, but by 1955, the district spent £73,000 annually. Samburu's expenditures had grown by sixteen times in a matter of four years.[7]

Kenyan yearnings for development resonated little with the aims of the Swynnerton Plan. British administrators imposed these land reform measures in response to the Mau Mau State of Emergency. This was a particularly formative moment for Kenyan community development, as the Emergency provided openings for a policy overhaul, and colonial architects coupled agricultural reforms with social ones. As such, the Emergency allowed colonialists not only to justify the complete restructuring of rural landholdings, but also the "rehabilitation" of Mau Mau detainees. Detainee rehabilitation accelerated community development outside the camps, which focused on women, delinquents, and the destitute.[8] As part of this new focus, the colonial government created the Department of Community Development. In this same period, upper-class colonial women established the Maendeleo ya Wanawake (Progress for Women) organization.[9] Both the department and the organization took a welfare-oriented stance, which paralleled rehabilitation programs in detention, and both would remain fundamental to self-help in the postcolonial period.

State actors envisioned an expansive form of community development intended to remedy the moral ills of the colony through mandatory African participation. These development programs targeted supposedly atavistic Kenyans as well as the broader population. They aimed to rehabilitate social and economic pathologies simultaneously. Though social reforms seemingly held little in common with land and agricultural reforms, both were the coercive brainchild of colonial administrators rather than the ideas of African communities. Land reform programs had required African District Councils to take on loans and residents to pay taxes to programs they did not want. Rehabilitation forced detainees, delinquents, and the destitute to reform in order to rejoin society.

Colonial community development not only entailed coercion and forced Kenyans to shoulder a greater tax burden, but it also forced Kenyans to take on a greater labor burden.[10] In this context, "self-help" became a euphemistic term for repurposing colonial labor practices. The colonial state used self-help to complete community development programs British policymakers created, such as irrigation and soil erosion schemes. Kenyans contested these imposed programs and their reliance on forced, not voluntary, labor.[11] African District Councils also regularly depended on compulsory communal labor. A 1962 memo noted that ADC bylaws on "minor communal services" could remain in place, so long as they were "not used to exact compulsory labour for works which amount to economic development."[12] With these ambiguous guidelines, colonial administrators suggested ADCs use communal labor mostly for maintenance work. The imposition of these programs while Kenyans demanded different types of development foreshadowed future contention over the form, function, and financing of community development.

Not all colonial development entailed government coercion and forced labor. Some programs depended on voluntary labor and investment. A 1953–54 colonial report on education contrasted ADC practices of levying taxes on residents with emerging practices in which local communities voluntarily supplied labor and materials for school buildings.[13] Unlike government-dictated programs, many Kenyans wanted to improve access to education in their communities, and they willingly contributed to self-help schools. This practice evolved in response to the financial and administrative inadequacies of the colonial state and broadly followed the self-help model of the British welfare state. These programs established a precedent for communities to take on school construction. They shaped expectations about the labor responsibilities of local communities for their own development.

Notions of self-help were not only transferred from metropole to colony, but in the late 1950s and early 1960s, international actors of various ideological persuasions increasingly championed self-help. China's 1958–60 Great Leap Forward campaign—though of greater inspiration to Kenya's southern neighbor, Tanganyika—emphasized rural collectivization and self-reliance.[14] Bilateral donors, transnational institutions, and nongovernmental organizations placed increasing weight on the mobilization of self-help as a prerequisite for grants and loans. The Rockefeller Foundation trained communities to "help themselves" and "championed a model of human capital."[15] The US government also promoted self-help. In March 1963, "The Committee to Strengthen the Security of the Free World"—commonly known as the Clay Committee—proposed that "stringent self-reliance and self-help should be demanded of the recipients" of American aid.[16] The United States was particularly influential for Kenya's self-help programming. *This Is Community Development in Kenya*—a 1964 government pamphlet—was based on a booklet published by the United States Agency for International Development (USAID) in 1962.[17]

As independence approached, rural Kenyans were already familiar with the practice of self-help. Communities had long mobilized to provide new services in the absence of state assistance, and Kenyans had often been forced to labor for or pay taxes to the state in the name of community development. The decolonizing state increasingly depended on, encouraged, and coerced self-help labor as a way of garnering aid and recusing the government from providing development. While Kenyans desired some of the services borne of these programs, many also sought greater local control over the course of their own development. Incompatible ideas about development priorities, state obligation, and citizens' rights and duties made future conflict over these issues ineluctable.

FROM SELF-HELP TO HARAMBEE

When Kenyans celebrated independence, they did so in a setting of political and economic possibility, but also of paucity. While the fertile land of the Rift Valley highlands provided potential for a more prosperous future, European settlers had developed the area for their families and for estate farming. During the colonial period, the health and educational services made available to African laborers living in European areas had "lagged seriously behind" those in African areas.[18] As the independent state divided this land for Kenyan families, the inadequacy of schools, hospitals, and roads for the larger African population became clear.[19] Charles Murgor, MP for Eldoret South, spoke about this issue in Parliament, noting: "The population has doubled but services such as education and health do not exist there. . . . Today, you have hundreds, thousands of Africans in these areas with no schools."[20] Services in the Rift Valley became increasingly inadequate as the African population there grew.

The new, independent government was fiscally limited and did not have the resources to provide the desired developments quickly to the entire population. State actors in Kenya, and across the continent, drew inspiration from colonial policy, relying on self-help for community development.[21] A few months after independence, the Kenyan government announced a national plan for community development, emphasizing the role of citizens. The Kenyatta administration attempted to remake self-help by positioning everyday Kenyans as responsible for their own development and for nation-building. According to the official *This Is Community Development* pamphlet, Kenyatta said, "The actual business of Community Development is the concern of every Government Department, every voluntary organization, and in fact every citizen of Kenya. Community Development in Kenya means the democratic process of including people, as well as Government, in planning and working for the type of society we wish for ourselves."[22] Self-help, Kenyatta argued, would create development, and it would contribute to Kenya's burgeoning democracy. In articulating the role of average Kenyans in these processes, state actors advanced an idea of postcolonial citizenship that stressed duties over rights and made citizens "responsible for the work of Government."[23]

Postindependence self-help included a new, imaginative element, an additional responsibility for citizens. Not only were Kenyans to labor physically to develop themselves, but mentally to become stakeholders in decision-making processes. The postcolonial rhetoric on self-help suggested greater local control over development. Unlike colonial self-help, postcolonial self-help was to be "conceived and executed by the people."[24] Communities—not colonial bureaucrats—would imagine their own development and enact it.[25] As the community development officer of Western Province noted in a 1965 message to residents, "I am satisfied that during the passing year, many of you, if not all, accepted community development as your own concern and not an imposed idea as it was the case in the colonial days."[26] Local ownership of self-help was crucial to the idea of harambee, since it signified a departure from colonial imposition and the use of corvée labor.

The Kenyatta administration purposefully distanced itself from the colonial state to legitimize its rule and popularize development policy. State actors instead linked self-help to a deeper, utopian past. As with many other policies, the government emphasized the precolonial roots of harambee, arguing that it was "a development philosophy well embedded in [African] traditions."[27] Harambee harkened back to precolonial communal cooperation. Simultaneously, it evoked a present moment of Kenyans pulling together, and elicited visions of a better future. The discourse conflated temporalities and moved seamlessly across space. Harambee signified local communities coming together to improve their own lives. The term suggested broader development extending to the scale of the nation. Harambee's expansiveness was essential to its wide appeal, allowing Kenyans to draw from it what they liked.

Government discourse on harambee empowered citizens to guide their own development and to participate in nation-building. Even so, state actors divided self-help programs into two categories, "social and domestic facilities" and "economy developing."[28] In the 1960s and 1970s, communities most commonly undertook the former, focusing on schools, hospitals, and community centers, and participating in adult education, sports programming, and cultural affairs. The economy-developing category mainly consisted of infrastructure projects and agricultural ventures. On occasion, communities attempted some of these more technically challenging programs, such as building cattle dips or milk coolers. Despite the enthusiasm for education and health care, the government provided greater support to technical projects, concluding that these programs generated direct economic development for the nation, revealing, at the same time, the conflicting development priorities of local communities and the state.

To gloss over these tensions and encourage Kenyan groups to advance state priorities, the community development plan highlighted local autonomy while stressing the importance of government orchestration. The Ministry of Community Development and Social Services reasoned that self-help entailed cooperation between Kenyans and their government: "The flow of information concerning the people's needs is channeled upwards to assist in formulation of the overall development planning. In turn, the overall plans are fed back into the community development committee structure, in order that local plans be in tune with the larger picture. In this way, government plans truly reflect the needs and wishes of the people; objectives of the people and the government are one!"[29] This framing implied that simply through communication, the aims of Kenyans and their government could be reconciled.

To facilitate cooperation, the Kenyan state created a pyramid organization of community development staff. A 1964 circular outlined the structure, which provided "a framework for directing" community development and "the channel for financial and material assistance to Community Self-Help Schemes."[30] This framework comprised national, regional, local authority, location, and sublocation development committees, and the higher-level committees allocated funds and provided assistance to the committees below.[31] A 1966 document further elaborated how this framework would provide support at the local level: "Where local resources are insufficient to meet expressed community needs, the village or local Community

Development committee will detail the assistance required in terms of skilled labour or materials not available locally and submit an application."[32] In practice, Kenyan communities often contributed much of the money, materials, and labor for self-help, while government ministries, international sources, private individuals, and businesses supplemented self-help funding.

Official publications suggested that community development would blossom through conversations about local needs and national development plans, through voluntary labor and donations, and through the provision of small government grants. Uncertainty about the division of governmental powers complicated matters. At independence, county councils largely replaced the provincial administration. Even so, both county councils—which, during the colonial era, served only European populations in the white highlands—and the provincial administration—which had previously governed only African populations in the native reserves—continued to operate simultaneously. The existence of two different local government bodies created confusion. The new constitution also empowered the Regional Assemblies, rather than the Ministry of Local Government, to exercise control over local authorities.[33] In theory, *majimboism* (regionalism) instituted devolution.

However, KANU and President Kenyatta had never been in favor of a federal government. Soon after independence, Kenyatta gave a series of presidential directives that defunded local governments, purposefully withholding much-needed financing. Ultimately, this action helped drive KADU to dissolve, creating a de facto one-party state. The absence of an opposition party, in turn, paved the way for constitutional amendment.[34] Financial control over all local authorities was returned back to the Ministry of Local Government, centralizing state power.

The central government then delegated new responsibilities—particularly, the administration of financially onerous social services—to underfunded local authorities. In 1964, municipal and county councils became largely responsible for primary education. Later that year, the central government made councils responsible for the maintenance of roads and government buildings, while reducing grants to local authorities. Also in 1964, the state-sponsored Pratt Report called for higher salaries for government employees, another burden that fell on local authorities. As the state compelled county councils to provide facilities they could not afford, local authorities had to reduce services. In Uasin Gishu at the end of 1964, the County Council recommended the closure of a number of schools and public health units, as well as the discharge of teachers and staff, because they were unable to finance such services.[35]

In 1965, President Kenyatta announced the introduction of free outpatient health care for all Kenyans and free inpatient treatment for children in government hospitals and health centers. Within a year, this policy increased patient numbers at government hospitals by three to six times. In a 1966 memorandum, the provincial commissioner of Western Province, S. O. Josiah, wrote, "Quite a number of Health Centres in several districts have been closed down due to the fact that the Councils have not got adequate funds to run them. Since the Govt. has set itself to provide free medical services, I think it fitting that the burden now shouldered by local authorities should be taken over."[36]

Local authorities across the country struggled to provide health services. The clerk to the Sirikwa County Council, which included Uasin Gishu, wrote to the Ministry of Local Government in July 1965:

> Councillors found it extremely difficult to explain to the public that they had to recommend that these already inadequate health facilities, should be cut when the Central Government was at the same time promising free health services. It is hoped that the Central Government, appreciating the difficulties faced by the Council will find additional grants to raise the standards of Health Services at least to their former level. The local authority is otherwise placed in the position of having to shoulder the blame over commitments imposed on it by the Central Government without due regard to its financial resources.[37]

Attempts to provide free health services not only led to the closing of health centers, but also to the deterioration of services. By 1967, care at the Eldoret District hospital had become so poor that expectant mothers preferred to stay home.[38] Similarly, the Rift Valley Province annual report of 1969 stated that mission hospitals were more popular than government hospitals, because they were "more adequately staffed."[39]

Central-local government tensions diminished the efficacy of local authorities and led to a decline in the quality of services. In 1966, a national commission of inquiry investigated the organization of local government due to a growing "crisis of confidence."[40] In a statement to the commission, D. C. MacDonald, a lecturer at the Kenya Institute of Administration (KIA), outlined the problems with the division of responsibilities, asking: "But in the case of health and education, which account between them for nearly ¾ of the County Council's gross expenditure, all I question is—is it a good system, whereby we say the county council is responsible in law for running and financing the service, and yet they have to have a Government officer to run it for them?"[41] Though these debates centered on policy questions—the provision of social services in local settings, the financing of local bodies, and the division of responsibilities—they were also about the structures of power and authority in Kenya. As self-help groups became embroiled in the disagreements over financing and managerial power, additional questions came to the fore—about Kenya's developmental trajectory, and about the obligations of both citizens and the state in nation-building.

NEGOTIATING SELF-HELP

The Kenyan administration's community development plan proffered a citizen-state relationship heavy on citizenly duties and light on government obligations and citizens' rights. Many Kenyans willingly took on duties in local development and nation-building. However, the postcolonial government, in other settings, had made promises to provide education, medical care, and social security to all citizens.[42] Kenyan expectations coalesced, then, in a setting murky with conflicting assertions about citizens' responsibilities and government obligations, and further complicated by vague state promises and Kenyan ambitions.

In this context, self-help was initially "well-received," according to Rift Valley agricultural official Alfred Machayo.[43] While rural Kenyans expected improvements to health and educational facilities, they were also prepared to provide some of the labor and financing for these projects, just as they had done in the colonial era. Despite adopting some precedents established under colonial rule, many residents of the western highlands also trusted postcolonial government assurances that communities would head harambee projects. This idea appealed especially to Kenyans who had loathed colonial coercion. Western highlands residents spoke of how harambee taught them that the government no longer controlled everything, and any development created through self-help belonged to the community.[44] Harambee's promise of local control contrasted with colonial policy. Rural Kenyans valued having a greater voice in fashioning the collective future.

Mobilized by their belief that they had the right to choose local development priorities, Kenyans enthusiastically created self-help projects. Soon, however, some government actors decided that communities were too eager to start harambee programs. While officials publicly lauded the importance of self-help in Kenya's development, bureaucratic records disclose increasing concern about the government's inability to control local groups. The 1966 minutes of a Rift Valley district commissioners meeting, for example, mention that the demand for harambee schools had become "chronic," and local groups were building schools without following the correct procedure.[45] Likewise, in 1967, the Rift Valley Province annual report noted that "the problem of controlling 'mushrooming' self help projects continued."[46] Throughout Kenya, officials encountered, and bemoaned, similar issues.

In response to the explosion of self-help programs, Kenyan officials asserted in increasingly dogmatic terms that self-help required active supervision and national planning. In a 1967 letter, the personal secretary for the Ministry of Cooperatives and Social Services noted, "Haphazard projects can hinder rather than help."[47] He continued in the same vein, "Development can be viewed as a jigsaw puzzle where every piece must fit into its own place. Consequences must be taken into account."[48] Tensions between local charge and national coordination had started to emerge.

State officials designed policies to regulate self-help, but local enthusiasm often prevailed as communities skirted state regulatory mechanisms in their haste to complete projects.[49] This trend continued throughout Kenyatta's tenure and even after Daniel arap Moi took office in 1978. A 1979 Rift Valley Province annual report noted that Kenyans initiated projects without proper planning when their "zeal was misdirected and Community Development machinery namely the staff and committees not fully utilized."[50] Along with the provincial administration, relevant ministries attempted to control local groups. The Ministry of Health insisted in 1966, "No hospital, health centre or maternity hospital is built which does not conform to the Ministry's plans."[51] Unwilling to wait for government authorization, however, citizens continued to create self-help projects. When they moved forward without official approval, self-help groups contested restrictions on their local autonomy, and they put forth alternate development priorities.

In fact, many Kenyans initially did not want the government to take part in their projects. Hoseah arap Keter, a Nandi man who purchased a plot in Sosiani after independence, emphasized the importance of harambee in settlement schemes where new residents arrived to "find nothing." Because residents purchased land in Sosiani, they invested in the community and undertook a series of self-help projects: roads, a primary school, a nursery school, a dispensary, a health center, a secondary school, and water tanks. Keter recalled of these projects: "We didn't want the *serikali* [government] to be involved. . . . We thought that if the serikali was given the responsibility to build, they will take the premises. We were asking ourselves, 'What is our responsibility after owning the land?' It is our responsibility to head the institutions. The serikali was only to employ the teachers and nurses, and other people. We wanted to own the buildings."[52] Keter's ideas parallel other

Kenyan sentiments about ownership of harambee, underscoring the importance of localized systems of authority and governance. Placing significance on building ownership suggests that notions of possession, likely originally centered on land, were extended to development generally. Other interlocutors also used the language of ownership and proprietorship when discussing self-help and development. This emphasis speaks to desires to own land and control local development, and to a general distrust of the central government. While not everyone disavowed government assistance, Uasin Gishu residents tended to hold few expectations for government support and articulated a limited state role in community development.[53]

Rural confidence in community rights to control harambee helps explain disregard for state prescriptions. In Chekalini—a settlement village on the eastern edge of Western Province—a self-help group continued running a health center despite official efforts to suspend their operations. The provincial medical officer wrote in 1966 that the self-help group had not sought the medical statutory board's permission to open the health center and, without board approval, the center was operating illegally.[54] The medical officer's orders to close the health center "and to see that the premises are demolished" achieved little.[55] The Chekalini group carried on with their work despite the officer's directive, only later agreeing to modify the project.

Some local groups did coordinate with state bureaucrats on their projects, but it was not always to their benefit. In 1967, for example, a district officer wrote to his district commissioner in Kakamega about a self-help cattle dip in Kambiri. The officer recounted how people spoke with frustration about "the miscalculation and wrong advices rendered by the then Veterinary Assistant."[56] He added that the project had cost the community about three thousand shillings, "a big loss to those poor people who sweated themselves to help themselves and achieve nothing in the end."[57] The district commissioner responded to the appeal for redress without sympathy: "Advise them to regard the loss as the baby that dies, and a couple tries to get another."[58] With an overextended and often undertrained bureaucracy, such errors occurred throughout Kenya. With such little compassion for communities thwarted by government blunder and with little advantage to following government procedure, local self-help groups increasingly avoided state regulatory mechanisms.

The inability to control community development programs stemmed at least in part from the absence of state officials at self-help sites, the result of a skeletal bureaucratic staff. In the 1964 minutes of the national community development committee meeting, Daniel arap Moi, then MP, said "he was disappointed that no officers could be appointed for more than half the

Districts of the [Rift Valley] Region."[59] The representatives from Western Region made a similar complaint. Adding to the problem, community development staff were often the first to be let go during budget crises. A cabinet memo noted, "It is understandable that when money is not available staff has to be cut down. What we consider as most unsatisfactory is the fact that . . . the first to be axed are invariably Community Development workers."[60] The dearth of community development staff on the ground made regulating self-help nearly impossible and, for rural Kenyans, it highlighted that government priorities diverged from their own.

For a government that hoped communities would take on vast development responsibilities but also follow guidelines with little oversight, growing local defiance signaled trouble. In an October 1964 speech, Kenyatta opined: "Self-help schemes must not be regarded as being in competition with what the Government is trying to do. The people of this country must accept the guidance and advice given by officials of the Ministry of Education. Unless this is done, then the country's education might be in jeopardy."[61] Unable to convince Kenyans to voluntarily take government direction, the Kenyan state began withholding resources.[62] The December 1964 minutes of the national committee for community development makes clear that this strategy of control had been a possibility early on. At this meeting, a representative for the minister of Local Government suggested that "self-help projects which would involve subsequent recurrent expenditure by Councils, should be avoided. This included schools, health centres, youth centres, and nursery centres."[63] Yet, aside from land, Kenyans most wanted schools and health facilities. To propose that local communities would willingly discontinue these projects implied an abject misunderstanding of, or disregard for, how rural Kenyans imagined better futures.

Indeed, Kenyan groups tirelessly carried out their self-help projects, especially school construction, though the Kenyan state increasingly denied them financial support. By 1965, some members of Parliament joined their constituents in calling for the government to step in and fund schools. Carey Stanley Imbanga Godia, MP of Hamisi, put forth a motion calling for expanded access to education, lamenting how the Ministry of Education had "deliberately ignored the public pressure for the demand by the people of the Republic of Kenya to take up all of the established Harambee Secondary Schools opened on Self Help initiative spirit by the people."[64] In spite of the lack of state support, local groups kept working to create educational institutions in their communities. In a 1968 memorandum on self-help, Ronald Ngala, minister of Cooperatives and Social Services, and G. J. Njenga, director of the Department of Community Development and

Social Services, reported: "The number of schools undertaken continues to grow substantially. The thirst for education for the children of Kenya is apparently unquenchable, despite the increasing problem of meeting the recurrent costs of such schools."[65] In building schools and health centers without definite assurance of funding, Kenyan communities asserted their visions of development and made claims for these services.

Rather than fund schools and hospitals, officials tried to press state development priorities onto recalcitrant communities. State officials were especially keen to use harambee for the creation of new road networks. Road construction entailed little government investment, minimal technical expertise, and few recurrent expenses. Roads connected farmers to state-regulated markets and might increase tax revenue. A 1969 monthly report by a senior settlement officer reveals one strategy to correct what the government perceived as citizens' misguided development priorities. The officer advised that internal road access could be improved only through self-help and suggested that "at least monthly there should be meetings in various areas attended by heads of department of the area to institute the idea."[66] This strategy—where local government officials tried to persuade communities to execute specific projects—seems to have produced few results, since officials continued complaining about indiscipline in self-help groups.

State actors also attempted to exert control over self-help. In the period after majimbo, the central government assumed greater power over the budgets of local authorities, particularly in the provisioning of state grants to selected self-help projects. In many instances, national politicians recommended projects for funding without input from county councils, the community development bureaucracy, or local groups. The director of Community Development and Social Services wrote in 1968 that most applications for government aid to self-help "emanated from individuals like politicians."[67] The government selection process itself was cloaked in mystery. Speaking in 1973, Nandi MP Jean-Marie Seroney criticized the lack of transparency on government grants. "It is not good enough to see that £150,000 is given to aid self-help projects," he said. "We would like to know how this amount of money is divided."[68] Undeterred by Seroney's criticism, state officials continued to actively shape local programs through discretionary funding.

Despite administrative and fiscal stringency, at times the state intervened more forcefully, compelling citizens to provide donations, material, and labor for self-help. According to a 1966 Ministry of Labour and Social Services document: "Inevitably in any country there will be communities who see no reason to change their attitudes and whose philosophy of life will be based on traditional thinking. In these circumstances, the projection of ideas is necessary in order to stimulate social change."[69] The document then elaborated that accepted political leaders—such as cabinet members—should "spearhead the social revolution necessary in these communities."[70] The alternative plan for "backwards communities" controverted the local ownership self-help allegedly fostered. At the same time, the oblique phrasing on the imposition of ideas possessed unnerving parallels to colonial rhetoric and policy.

Compulsion and intervention were borne from the state's quest to control development, and officials pressured local groups throughout Kenya to conform to national planning. The minutes from a 1969 district commissioners meeting in Western Province reflect this practice: "A decision was made that in 1970 some force should be used in the collection of self-help funds with quotas say shs. 5,000/- being given to sub-locations as a target for the whole year."[71] The compulsory characteristics of this type of government directive had repercussions in local settings. A Kenyan farmer complained to his district officer:

> I am surprised that people just come at my home during my absence and take my things. . . . Firstly, a group of people came at my house and took my Iron box during my absence and my wife's absence. I tried to find out whom they were, and was told that they did that because they wanted me to pay for the school building. Secondly, they came again and caught 2 cocks and 2 hens during my children's presence and said the same. Thirdly, they came and found my wife sick in the home. They asked her to pay some money because she does not go and make the roads.[72]

Such property seizures belied the administration's early descriptions of harambee as a program reliant on individual and communal volition.

Masinde Muliro, the MP representing Kitale East, spoke out on the issue of compulsory self-help in Parliament in 1979: "We have seen, Mr. Speaker, that the district commissioners actually overstep their limits when it comes to contributions to the various self-help projects. Self-help projects are done voluntarily in the interests of the people in a given area and, therefore, if the people do not want to contribute it is their own fate. Therefore, the chiefs should not harass anybody if he has not paid the contributions."[73] In the decades after independence, bureaucrats pressured Kenyans to make monetary and labor donations to self-help. If Kenyan citizens did not comply, local officials often seized their belongings.

Selena Chelimo Barno, a Nandi settler in Sosiani, recounted that cows and hens were taken from people's homes, and that local leaders once took a chicken from her family's property. She said of this incident, "We were afraid that maybe it was the order of the *serikali* [government] to do such, so we were afraid that if one raises an alarm or complains, the same person could be arrested."[74] Barno's recollections reveal fears of state violence, a product of colonial experiences. When she spoke of colonialism, she focused on its various circumscriptions: of mobility, labor, property, and agricultural production. Even so, her interpretation of the incident was also reflective of the postcolonial context, since state-ordered quotas catalyzed local compulsory donations. Other Uasin Gishu residents also recounted that assistant chiefs or self-help leaders went to their houses asking for a precise amount of cash, and, in the absence of a contribution, they confiscated valuable goods.[75] Still, many rural Kenyans noted that they readily donated cash, materials, and labor to self-help projects. Differing experiences were a product of the variability of local government operations, and of disputes about the labor obligations and financial responsibilities of citizens and the state in local development.

State actors attempted to impose their visions of development when they regulated harambee, required the creation of specific self-help projects, and mandated donation quotas. The state reversal on, and intrusion into, a program that had once been championed as community-led did not go unnoticed or unchallenged. The 1968 minutes of a Rift Valley district commissioners meeting noted, "Concern was expressed because it is thought that certain ministries carry out development projects which are not regarded by the local people as priorities. District Commissioners felt that local people should be consulted before any project is started by a Ministry and use should be made of the Development Committees."[76] Kenyans recognized that their visions of development were at odds with those of the government.

Rural Kenyans were especially resentful of state actors' attempts to exert influence in local spaces while refusing to provide financial assistance to community-initiated projects. Samuel Kimeli Kiplagat, a Nandi man who squatted in the forest before purchasing land in Uasin Gishu, recalled, "We were overburdened . . . education you have to bring, hospitals you have to pay. Things which the government should have taken, because it was heavy for the people. The government returned that burden to the people."[77] In withdrawing funding from *harambee* (self-help) projects, the state broke its earlier promises to help those who first helped themselves, contributing to popular perceptions of the government as unreliable. Kiplagat exemplified this impression, noting: "We used to contribute [to harambee] because we didn't want to depend on the government. If you could depend on the government, they would not have been there. . . . When you depend on the government, you don't know whether they will give you some money or not."[78] Kiplagat's experience living as a forest squatter—where the state intervened more inconsistently and tended to invest less—profoundly shaped his ideas. Even so, other Rift Valley residents—some squatters, some landowners—echoed his account.[79]

Incompatible ideas about development, the state, and citizenship collided at self-help sites. Through self-help, Kenyans came to define more specific responsibilities for themselves and for the state. Deina Iboso, a Maragoli settler in Lumakanda, recounted that she used to contribute money to self-help. Through her participation in harambee projects, Iboso came to anticipate certain assistance from the government. "It was our responsibility to build schools, because it was our kids," she said, continuing, "But it was the responsibility of the government to build health centers, because we were new and didn't know where to get such services."[80] A number of interlocutors made similar distinctions between school and health center construction, though others believed local groups were responsible for building all facilities, while the government was responsible for staff and supplies. Many Kenyans came to conceptualize government obligation based on a combination of their aspirations, their financial and technical abilities, and state promises. A consensus seems to have formed on the state's responsibility for providing aid to projects that offered security, or to projects that local people deeply desired but could not complete on their own.

Such expectations often went unmet. Though hospitals were conceptualized as a government responsibility, local groups frequently constructed them, and though the government was responsible for teachers' salaries, parents often paid them.[81] The 1969 Rift Valley Province annual report described "the spirit of Harambee sweeping every corner of the Republic," with communities constructing an increasing number of self-help health centers. The report continued, "The people build these centres in good faith with the hope that after completion they would get the necessary staff and drugs. But one finds that is not the case."[82] In Uasin Gishu District in 1974, eight day-care center instructors were laid off, in what District Commissioner Charles Murage characterized as the "greatest blow to community development during the year." Subsequently, Murage noted, "parents were advised to employ their own nursery school teachers."[83] For those Kenyans who had come to expect that the government would take on these responsibilities, such experiences symbolized the state's broken promises.

Increasingly, local groups contested how the government defined its obligations. A Kakamega District community development officer had to encourage a group of local self-help leaders to finish their projects "without very rigidly dwelling on the Government aid, which will be for the coming according to the suitability of time, basing it of course on the PRIORITIES. Since you are aware that the planning is being done by the people, it will be unhealthy if any groups fall prey to the propagandist that our Government is not helping as it promised."[84] In some cases, according to the minutes of a 1967 self-help coordinating committee meeting, groups began projects "not out of their own need but with a false hope that by doing so they will be able to secure government aid."[85] By 1969, a provincial community development officer commented on the "ill conceived ideas that the people have done so much and the Government so little."[86] In refusing to complete their self-help projects, communities asserted visions of more robust government assistance. The conceptual rift on government obligation and citizens' duties continued to grow.[87]

Kenyans made claims to state aid with half-finished projects, but they also sought assistance from nonstate actors to help bring their development projects to fruition. Theresa Ngososei—a Nandi woman who lived east of Uasin Gishu in Laikipia during the late colonial and early postcolonial era—said that "*wazungu* [European] missionaries" from the Catholic Church and the Africa Inland Church built schools in her village after independence. She recounted that the community did not initiate many harambee projects where she lived, but local people worked with the missionaries to build schools.[88] Similarly, James Matunda, a Maragoli farmer, noted that in Lumakanda, local groups organized harambee for schools and dispensaries, and the Catholic Mission also contributed to their efforts.[89]

As the 1960s and 1970s wore on, a different set of nonstate actors helped to deliver social services. The independent Kenyan government attempted to overcome its financial and administrative limitations by seeking aid from foreign governments and transnational institutions. UNICEF provided aid to self-help projects as early as 1961, and CARE, the Freedom from Hunger Campaign, and the Ebert Foundation—along with other newly established nongovernmental organizations—also furnished assistance.[90] The majority of external aid for self-help projects in the early independent era came from other nations. This aid included both financial and technical support. By 1964, Kenya had received bilateral offers of assistance for self-help from more than twenty nations around the world.[91] The United States was one of the most active external funders, and USAID had a special self-help fund to assist in sectors where the agency did not have programming. This fund would not cover recurring expenses and was essentially meant "for roofs, not walls or labor," according to Carroll Hinman, the director of the USAID mission to Kenya.[92] Though the US channeled its financing largely through Kenya's central state, it earmarked some grants for specific projects, and some individual Kenyan actors sought to control the distribution of this money.

The presence of these new actors did not go unnoticed as Kenyan communities became aware of the growing role that external donors played in self-help. The chairman of the Lumakanda community development coordinating committee wrote to the district commissioner of Kakamega in 1966, "Your assistance will prove that Lumakanda can help and develop itself with the Assistance from Central Government in kind (including foreign aid)."[93] A school headmaster illustrated a similar knowledge of external funding for self-help, writing in 1967 that he used a USAID grant of seven thousand shillings to purchase blocks, roofing material, wood, and cement.[94] An editorial in a Kenyan student newspaper praised the US, observing that regional progress was "largely due to the United States Government, the Kenyan Government, and to the citizens of the surrounding area."[95]

A report by a USAID adviser included extensive remarks on Kenyan knowledge of American aid. In the report, the adviser recounted a conversation with a Kenyan health inspector who said the US had helped "stamp out typhoid fever as a disease in this area and you're the first American I've had a chance to tell."[96] The report then described a similar conversation with a schoolteacher, who wanted to show off "the shiney corrugated iron roof" purchased with American development funds. The US development practitioner concluded: "Our contribution has rarely been big, often amounting to no more than the tools in a community-built Youth Centre to teach vocational skills to boys who had not a chance to go beyond fourth grade. But these were known as the American tools, the American water pipe and the American cement."[97] The development worker may have embellished these stories to prove the value of US programs. Even so, collectively, the evidence illustrates that Kenyans—ranging from students to bureaucrats to national politicians—were well informed about the specific sources of external funding.

Encounters with international officials occurred episodically and unevenly. But those Kenyans who benefited from foreign aid could contrast international donations with Kenyan government refusals to finance projects. Despite their promises otherwise, officials pushed state development priorities onto self-help groups while withholding funding for locally initiated projects. Many rural Kenyans contested the state at self-help sites, and, in doing so, they proffered different developmental visions, asserted their local autonomy, made claims to desired services, and pressed the state to take on certain obligations.

Self-help did not just provoke contestations between citizens and the state. As the instances of property seizure indicate, self-help also engendered debates about labor and financial obligations, and about who had the right to determine local development priorities. The resolution of such disagreements makes clear that certain members of national and subnational polities occupied privileged positions. Yet even those excluded from state resources, or from positions of power within local communities, could sometimes achieve their developmental dreams.

PULLING TOGETHER OR PULLING APART?

The institutionalization of a community development system requiring local responsibility and state assistance had vast implications for inequality.[98] J. H. O. Omino, the permanent secretary of Natural Resources, wrote about this issue in 1978: "But for *harambee* spirit to be sustained, *wananchi* [citizens] are presumed to have the means. Left on its own, as is the case, self-help could result in undesirable imbalance in development." Omino was especially worried about pastoralists in poorer regions, continuing, "Concerned efforts must be made to take them along in the self-help and development tempo in which the country is marching."[99] For many marginalized groups, however, the development march often carried on without them.[100]

Despite its origins in the British welfare state, harambee contributed to widening inequality, since the privileged were better equipped to bring self-help projects to completion.[101] The reliance on contributions made "it easier to initiate *Harambee* projects in the economically more advanced areas."[102] These communities could not only raise greater amounts of money, but they could draw on the skills of their better-educated population, and they were more likely to possess connections to government actors. Self-help perpetuated existing regional inequalities, and it also heightened intracommunity inequality, as local elites often sidelined women, the poor, and ethnic minorities.[103]

Even so, state actors were aware of the need to appear mindful of uneven development. A cabinet development committee memorandum noted that the government was "committed to assisting the less developed areas."[104] This rhetorical commitment never translated into a reparative policy. The same memorandum continued, "Consequently, the North Eastern Province got a share equal to that of the other Provinces."[105] An equal share of grant money would not undo years of unequal development. Simultaneously, officials justified aiding more developed communities with euphemistic, financial language. In 1967, the permanent secretary of Cooperatives and Social Services wrote that the ministry had a duty to use self-help funds "to ensure the greatest value to the greatest number of both projects and people."[106] The ambiguity of "greatest value" accorded the government the liberty to award grants to already developed areas on the basis that they might offer a better return on investment. In combination with the government's aversion to redistributive policies, residents of historically neglected areas were less educated, presenting challenges for accessing aid. Communities with fewer educated residents encountered greater obstacles in submitting self-help applications.[107] The educated elite with close ties to the state also understood government priorities and government functioning, which were integral to obtaining aid.

A 1971 note from the permanent secretary to the Treasury illustrates how the application process could privilege certain regions: "It is intended to distribute these grants, as equitably as possible to the Provinces. . . . Initially, the allocation to each Province will be up to the maximum of K£14,000. It is expected that each Province will be able to formulate sound proposals within this ceiling. However, if any Province is unable to do so, its allocation will be diverted to other Provinces from whom supplementary proposals will be invited."[108] The explanation of this practice lays bare the process through which a purportedly unbiased system could benefit better-educated regions with greater political knowledge and cultural capital. Already privileged provinces were more capable of making successful initial and supplementary applications, while less advantaged provinces had greater difficulty formulating initial proposals, ultimately compounding regional and ethnic inequality. Within provinces, uneven allocations at the district or locational level contributed to additional disparities.

Self-help also extended inequalities between squatter communities and landholding communities. In 1968, the Rift Valley provincial commissioner described squatters' reaction to self-help as "strained," because they saw "no permanent utility in improving a place where they may be asked to vacate at any time."[109] Oral histories confirm that squatter communities were reluctant to create self-help projects. Squatters recounted that they wanted to build schools and health centers, but the government prohibited them from initiating projects on land they did not own.[110] Ultimately, this meant squatters had few services available in their villages.

Self-help also intensified local economic and social inequalities. Harambee played a role in defining and reaffirming communal boundaries and social hierarchies. Wealthy, educated men exercised disproportionate influence in choosing local development priorities.[111] Officials in the provincial administration often assumed formal or semiformal positions of authority in harambee projects. A 1965 letter from H. M. Stanley Njeru, provincial community development officer, to the Western provincial commissioner, makes clear how regularly bureaucrats inserted themselves into local self-help groups. Njeru wrote of self-help coordinating committees, "Most heads of Administration including yourself were popularly elected to positions of Chairmen and/or Presidential-Chairmen. Those heads of Administration who missed the chance, probably because they have not been long with the people in their areas of operation have assumed Presidency over the committees by virtue of their official status and are, in addition, serving in advisory capacities to the committees."[112] A 1966 Rift Valley Province annual report described similar practices, noting that chiefs and subchiefs "helped to organize and participated in self-help groups."[113] Alongside local officials, only a small set of community members—usually, men with some education and greater economic assets—served on these committees.[114]

Conversely, less prominent community members—women and ethnic minorities, the poor and the uneducated—were often excluded from harambee decision-making processes. If they participated, their ideas did not carry the same weight. In Uasin Gishu's Nandi communities, for example, there was some opportunity for deliberation, but community leaders would eventually appeal for unanimity. Many Nandi interlocutors used the word *kibagenge* (togetherness) to describe self-help, noting that community members would frequently disagree until a leader stood up and said, "Kibagenge."[115] The expectation for unity undercut alternative visions of local development that addressed the needs of the marginalized. Prevailing moral economies still required poorer families to donate money or material equally, or have their property confiscated.[116] Such actions broadened material inequalities and hardened class lines.

Harambee also further entrenched the gendered inequalities of development. It did so first in its division of labor. Elite men primarily became the trustees of local development, the "conceivers" of change that Kenyatta had so emphasized. They attended the meetings (*baraza*) to discuss and plan self-help projects, and men often made decisions about monetary donations on behalf of their households. While the mental work of self-help was inequitable, the physical work was more even, though there remained a gendered division of labor. Women were commonly expected to contribute by collecting natural building materials—sand, bushstone, and mud—for projects. They also participated in road-building. Men often drove tractors, made bricks, and completed construction work.

Men and women generally described the baraza as a way to "meet" the government through a representative—usually the chief or district commissioner—and as a space for men exclusively. The baraza served not only as a site for the government to relay messages to its citizens, but also as a site where citizens could articulate grievances and make claims, often to assistance on a self-help project. Many Kenyans noted that women could communicate with the government through their husbands, or that men would bring back news to their daughters, sisters, or wives from the meetings.[117]

Women's attendance at, participation in, and knowledge of baraza differed by household and community. Theresa Ngososei, a Nandi woman who lived in Uasin Gishu during the colonial and postcolonial periods, recalled of women's exclusion from these meetings, "Women were reluctant to attend baraza because we weren't given the opportunity to share our views. We thought we had no responsibility."[118] Ngososei—who generally described her marriage in positive terms—relied on her husband to speak for their household, and to give her a report about baraza.[119] In various western highlands communities, women recounted that they did not attend baraza. Maragoli farmer Karen Misavo asserted, "The baraza were meant for men. Women we used to ask ourselves 'Why should we go to baraza?' We never went to baraza. We used to say it belongs to men. . . . We used to see that men had a lot of time and women were very busy. So they had to attend baraza while we stayed at home."[120] Misavo moved from Vihiga to the Lumakanda settlement with her family in 1963, but her husband worked off the scheme. She is outgoing and confident, and it is hard to imagine Misavo submitting to familial or social pressure excluding women from baraza. She thrived during her husband's absences, managing their farm and deciding how to spend its profits. Her description of baraza suggests she believed she could have attended, but realized the futility, given that men did not take women's perspectives seriously. Instead, Misavo threw herself into the Quaker Friends Church and the local chapter of Maendeleo ya Wanawake, both of which offered women access to development assistance. Other women were even more fully excluded from community development discussions, particularly when their husbands or male relatives were unwilling to discuss these issues with them.[121]

Communities frequently excluded women's issues from the village-wide support leveraged for mainstream harambee projects. A memorandum from a Chepkorio (Rift Valley Province) self-help group to the minister of Health in 1967 illustrates the hardships women faced raising funds in the absence of broad community support:

> We have collected money towards the extension of the ward amounting to 3,600/- only after a period of eight months. Mr. Minister Sir, we have estimated the ward is to be extended will be 15,000/- and we have tried to collect the above figure and we are ready to do most of the labour by hand and still work hard to obtain accessible materials like stones, bricks, etc. Therefore Sir, we look upon you and request you to take our case to your ministry and consider assisting us in materials like iron sheets and bags of cement. . . . Sir, we hope that you can help to remind our husbands all over to help us too. . . . Mr. Minister, Sir, every mother donated 5/- and still continue till we see in reality the problem solved having enough space with health conditions thus create healthy people in a healthy nation.[122]

Even when women drew on state-favored gendered tropes about mothering the nation, they encountered difficulties in completing their self-help projects. Because rural women often had little control over household incomes, financing self-help posed major challenges in the absence of community or state support.[123]

Women reported, generally, that they felt ill informed about the channels to state funding. Some women said that they had expected government assistance, but "did not know who to follow, or who to go to."[124] Other women said that they never saw improvement or development unless someone in their community possessed knowledge of how to garner aid.[125] State unpredictability and state marginalization were mutually constitutive, expanding the responsibilities of the excluded for their own development.

At times, the lack of state support propelled marginalized groups to seek other means to complete self-help projects, turning to churches, local organizations, or international NGOs for assistance. Exclusion from state resources galvanized women's associations especially. In Sosiani village, residents recounted the activeness of the women's organization called Kogilgei. The majority of women remarked how Kogilgei empowered them economically, through microfinancing and collective entrepreneurial ventures.[126] Women emphasized especially their success in building a harambee health clinic. The women's group raised money to build the clinic, and they collected materials, while men helped only with driving tractors.[127] Priscilla Boit—wife of provincial commissioner Paul Kipkorir Boit, and a resident of Sosiani—played an important part in leading this women's group.

Throughout Kenya, women focused on improving access to maternal and child health care. In the 1961 Legislative Council elections, Jean-Marie Seroney chose a motorcar as his ballot symbol. At one rally and to the crowd's cheers, he noted that with a car, a man could take his pregnant wife to the hospital.[128] Seroney had tapped into popular desires for social services and maternal health care, but these services remained inadequate after independence. A 1964 letter from the assistant commissioner for Cooperative Development described how "there are frequent occasions when wives of members of Co-operative Societies suffer miscarriage or mal-presentations which can only be treated by hospital facilities not available on settlement schemes. Recently, a settler who was stony broke, applied to the Local Dispensary who recommended that his wife be taken to hospital immediately, and that they would supply transport for shs. 30/= cash, which he was unable to beg or borrow or otherwise obtain."[129] The distance of hospitals from rural areas, and the lack of available transportation, meant these facilities were critical to community health.

In the early 1970s, the Sosiani women's group began devising a project to construct the first clinic in their area. At the beginning of 1968, the only maternity clinic and health center in all of Uasin Gishu was located in the district's capital, Eldoret. Self-help groups had just completed building clinics in Soy and Moiben, but the Sirikwa County Council could not afford to pay the recurrent expenditures necessary for running the clinics at the time.[130] Zipora Ketera, a Nandi farmer who had settled on the Sosiani scheme with her husband and four children, actively participated in the women's self-help group. She emphasized women's collective imagination, recounting that because women "were mothers" and "were going far for clinics," they decided to construct the health center.[131] Many of those involved in the project emphasized local women's resourcefulness, as well as their labor and monetary contributions.[132]

As the clinic progressed, the women involved the local administration, the national government, and external funders. Here, Priscilla Boit's leadership, knowledge, and political connections became especially useful. The 1976 Uasin Gishu annual report described the Sosiani health center as "the most outstanding project in the District," and noted that "His Excellency the Vice-President Mr. D. Arap Moi presided over a Harambee meeting which realized K.Shs. 219,000/= in cash and material."[133] Many women recounted Moi's attendance at this meeting, noting how they had felt so "empowered" by their achievements that they invited the vice president.[134] The Sosiani health center was also recommended to nongovernmental organization CARE International as a project deserving of additional aid.[135]

All over Kenya, women actively participated in building schools and clinics. Women in the Mosop division of Keiyo, for example, decided the health accommodations in their region were insufficient, and they organized themselves to collect funds for a maternity wing.[136] A delegation of women from Cheptarit, Nandi, attended a Sirikwa County Council meeting in 1966 to seek advice on planning a maternity ward. They had already bought a plot of land, collected building materials, and solicited donations from government ministers. The women attended the meeting because they wanted "to be given a plan so that they will know exactly how much they have to do to get the project accomplished." The council agreed to the women's request, but only if it "would not commit the Council to incur capital and recurrent expenditure."[137] Self-help groups, broadly, encountered difficulties garnering government funding. County councils rarely possessed the financial capacity to support recurrent expenditures, and the central government had become progressively unwilling to do so.

In these circumstances, Kenyans drew on their political knowledge and networks. Marginalized groups often did not possess the ability to directly access state aid, making the presence of elite actors important. As the educated wife of a state official, Priscilla Boit understood the process for creating and executing a self-help project, she attended baraza to ask for community support, and she communicated with the district commissioner about state aid.[138] After the clinic's completion, it took the government a couple of years to send nurses and medicine.[139] Even so, many women recounted how the health center helped their families; to this day, it is the only one in the area.

In spite of the strength of state exclusion, small openings did exist. Local factors—in the case of Sosiani, a well-connected individual and unified determination—provided the potential for women to experience state and developmental inclusion. Other excluded groups took advantage of similar opportunities when they arose, though their ability to do so was undoubtedly limited in comparison to more privileged Kenyans. Sosiani women articulated a fleeting moment of political belonging when Vice President Moi and the state recognized their contributions to nation-building. Women, then, could at times achieve national political membership through harambee, but only after overcoming the countless marginalizing forces in place under local and institutional structures.

Despite the possibilities these moments afforded, and perhaps due to their infrequency, self-help played a part in demarcating the boundaries of national and subnational citizenships. Kenyatta had proclaimed that through harambee, all Kenyan citizens would participate in the work of government. Many Kenyans fulfilled their duties through self-help, but the state did not keep its promise to help all those who helped themselves. Not only did the state increasingly withhold recurrent expenditures and regulate community development planning, but not all Kenyans were endowed with rights to equivalent state support.

Some Kenyans—especially, women, squatters, marginalized ethnic groups, and the poor—thus came to define the government by its exclusiveness. Eunice Tele Maiyo, a Nandi farmer who lived on various cooperative farms in Uasin Gishu, tellingly recounted, "The *serikali* [government] during those days was somebody else, but not us. It was *Mzee* [Kenyatta] and others." She continued, "When Kenyatta was in power it was as if we were outsiders from another country."[140] In describing these feelings of exclusion, Maiyo specifically referenced the services most frequently initiated under self-help, noting the inadequacy of education, and that she was "very disappointed because one could go far to seek medication." She had believed it was the government's responsibility to help provide those services and "to give us knowledge on what to do and how to develop the nation together with other Kenyans."[141] Maiyo's exclusion from social services thus shaped her assessment of postcolonial governance.

Harambee did not provide a path for all Kenyans to access the services they had been promised. The unequal material realities of the early postcolonial era deeply shaped how Kenyans conceived of the nation, of the government, and of their inclusion in various forms of political membership. Rural Kenyans became increasingly disenchanted with the state for its refusal to meet its obligations, for its tone-deaf development priorities, for its unwanted interventions, and for its withdrawal of aid from local projects. Through self-help, Kenyan citizens contested the state, asserted local autonomy, and made claims to services. They also negotiated their relationships with international and local institutions, increasingly looking beyond the state to seek development assistance. While harambee did not function as government officials had promised, Kenyan communities still produced many successes—sometimes with assistance, sometimes without—building roads, schools, health centers, cattle dips, and bridges. Their achievements are testament to their aspirations for a better future.

The next chapter continues to examine mobilization from the margins of early postcolonial society and continues to explore how the rural poor shaped development outcomes. Chapter 7 focuses on a single international development program, a World Bank–funded forestry project that squatters contested, ultimately winning the support of President Kenyatta.

7 "Are You Planting Trees or Are You Planting People?"

Local Resistance, International Development, and the Making of Kenya

BETWEEN 1963 AND 1978, Nandi squatters resisted government attempts to start a paper factory. Squatters refused to move, they uprooted trees intended as raw materials for the factory, and they sent multiple delegations to President Kenyatta, demanding of him, "Are you planting trees or are you planting people?"[1] Squatters were asking Kenyatta whether he supported a forest and paper industry program *or* a settlement program, since the two projects had been planned on the same land.

Contending visions of development created a deadlock in Turbo, Kenya—the site planned for a sixty-thousand-acre afforestation program. The Kenyan government initially purchased land in Turbo from European farmers and promised it to squatters under a land settlement program. In November 1964, however, the Kenyan cabinet agreed on the "Turbo Afforestation Scheme" to establish softwood plantations on the very same land in order to provide timber for the planned paper factory.[2] Once lauded by officials as "the biggest single project ever undertaken," the paper factory symbolized some of the promises of independence.[3] The factory characterized the new government's lofty development goals to generate economic growth and employment, and the World Bank's involvement demonstrated the growing importance of transnational development institutions.

For many rural Kenyans, the promises of independence entailed greater access to agricultural land, and Turbo squatters contested the project from its start. Turbo residents clashed with and obstructed local government bureaucrats, cabinet members, and World Bank officials trying to implement the afforestation program. By 1966, largely as a result of effective squatter resistance, the Ministry of Economic Planning and Development described the program as a "political liability" and the progress as "depressing."[4] After meeting multiple delegations of squatters, President Kenyatta intervened in 1968, ordering that a portion of the planned Turbo forest be moved, and that a crash settlement scheme be carried out.[5] Kenyatta's directive did not resolve the crisis, as new squatters refused to leave new forest sites, government officials continued to argue over whether resettlement or industrial development was more important to the national interest, and the World Bank pressured the Kenyan government to meet project deadlines.

At rural development sites, citizens, state representatives, and transnational actors negotiated questions about Kenya's economic and political path. In Turbo, squatters played a decisive role in deciding whether and where the state-sponsored and World Bank–funded forestry project would be implemented. Nandi squatters physically contested national government attempts to create forests, but they also took advantage of the multiple nodes of power within their postcolonial world, drawing on political relationships that extended all the way up to the president. Through their resistance at Turbo, squatters helped resolve how development resources would be controlled and distributed. They played a part in negotiating new forms of political patronage and in defining the extent of presidential authority.

This chapter examines the planning and implementation of the Turbo afforestation program, focusing in particular on the fifteen years after independence (1963–78) when the turmoil surrounding the program peaked. It begins with background on the planning of the paper project. The second section offers a narrative of squatters' mounting resistance. The third section explores the context in which squatters—with support from political elites—contested and undermined the program. The fourth section examines how these issues were worked out on the ground with a focus on the role that President Kenyatta played, while the fifth section explores the longer outcomes. This chapter's analysis of a locally grounded episode provides insight into how the rural poor engaged as political actors in spaces that were simultaneously populated with local, national, and international agents and politics.

THE SHORT HISTORY OF A LENGTHY PLANNING EXERCISE

The history of the paper factory originates in 1945 with the colonial state, but longer histories of agrarian practice and colonial rule deeply shaped squatter contestation of this paper program. After experiencing forced removal to a native reserve during conquest, the Nandi community had long held on to hopes of land restitution, which mobilized their resistance.

Turbo sits on a strip of Uasin Gishu District and Rift Valley Province that juts out into Western Province (see map A.1). The Uganda highway, which closely follows the colonially constructed railway line, goes directly through Turbo. For the fifteen-mile stretch where this road runs through the Uasin Gishu strip, it serves as a geopolitical boundary. It separates Rift Valley Province in the south from Western Province in the north and, broadly, the Nandi from the Luyia.[6] This border was drawn during decolonization, when the district commissioners of North Nyanza, Nandi, and Uasin Gishu agreed that the road should serve as "the dividing line between the sphere of influence of the Nandi and the Abaluhya," declaring "that no Nandi Settlement should take place North of this road and that no Abaluhya Settlement should take place South of it."[7] Despite this pronouncement, the area remained hotly contested. Both Nandi and Luyia communities made competing claims to territory beyond these boundaries.

Webuye—formerly Broderick Falls and the site of the paper factory—is situated more firmly in recognized Luyia territory. Webuye lies only about twenty miles to the west of Turbo, a short distance, almost identical to the distance between Turbo and Eldoret, the capital of Uasin Gishu to the east. The orientation of Turbo residents has long been to the east or south, where they maintain social ties and political networks.

Beginning in 1945, the colonial government started planting pine and cypress trees in the western Rift Valley. When Kenyan colonial officials first examined the prospect of a paper industry in the 1950s, a consulting firm selected Broderick Falls—later called Webuye—in Western Province as the ideal location. The firm chose the site for its proximity to water, fertile forest areas, and cheap transportation routes. Investment companies refused to finance the project at the time, because of the Mau Mau Emergency and the increasing calls for self-government. Despite this setback, the Kenyan administration continued to plant trees, and, by 1961, the colony had established 192,000 acres of forest plantations, mostly quick-growing exotic softwoods in Rift Valley and Central Provinces.[8]

State actors returned to this development plan during decolonization. In 1963, the Kenyan government solicited a new survey on the feasibility of establishing a paper mill.[9] The Sandwell Report, published in September of that year, again concluded that Broderick Falls was the most suitable site and that an "unbleached, kraft pulp and paper mill producing industrial paper from Government owned softwood plantations would be a viable proposition."[10] With the optimistic report, government actors began assessing financing and approaching international firms. These discussions persuaded government actors that they were unlikely to partner with a commercial firm for a small-scale mill.[11] Throughout the negotiations with European firms, the Kenyan government and its consultants debated the best size for the mill, with some economic forecasting suggesting they should build a bigger mill—"four times as large" as initially planned[12]—and others questioning the general profitability of the industry. Uganda and Tanzania had also begun investigating the prospect of establishing their own paper mills, raising the question of whether there would be regional competition. In fact, the first firm to show interest in the project required that the mill have access to the whole East African market, and that Tanzania and Uganda support a common tariff for the industry.[13]

Within a year, Kenyan officials agreed to plan for an expanded paper industry. The larger mill required more softwood, and government actors reevaluated their ability to provide raw materials cheaply. Reducing the cost of transporting timber to the Broderick Falls factory was essential, and, consequently, the sites for afforestation became limited to the region around the mill. In 1964, the Kenyan cabinet concluded that "to overcome these problems, there is only one satisfactory solution and that is to acquire about 60,000 acres of land as near as possible to Broderick Falls."[14] The closest appropriate location, they argued, was Turbo.

When the cabinet published its first paper on the Turbo Scheme, three separate groups owned the land planned for afforestation. The Ministry of Settlement owned 29,000 acres, the East African Tanning and Extract Corporation (EATEC) owned 25,000 acres,[15] and "assisted owners"[16]—rural Kenyan farmers who received loans to buy land—possessed 5,000 acres. In total, this land was worth approximately £640,000, a sum greater than the Kenyan Treasury had available at the time.[17] The Settlement Fund Trustees agreed to allow the Ministry of Natural Resources to purchase 20,000 of those acres for about £200,000.[18] Settlement later released an additional area to the Ministry of Natural Resources, originally planned for the Osorongai settlement scheme, so the total area for sale to the Ministry of Natural Resources equaled about 33,000 acres.[19]

These early negotiations "dragged on" for three months as state actors struggled to compromise.[20] From the beginning, the project was slowed by the number of government officials involved. Four different ministries—Natural Resources, Treasury, Lands and Settlement, and Commerce and Industry—were required to cooperate. Ministerial officials disagreed both about fundamental aspects of the program and about the best economic path for Kenya. As Kenya sought funding, the project brought in additional actors, including officials from the World Bank, numerous other international financial institutions, and private firms.

Given the prohibitive cost of both the land and factory construction, the Kenyan state earnestly sought investors. This was particularly important by the mid-1960s, when the government found its financial position increasingly constrained. The British—who provided the bulk of initial aid and loans for land resettlement and agricultural development—were unwilling to make funds available on the same terms after the close of the Million Acre Scheme in 1967.[21] The Kenyan government also sought a financial partnership with a private firm to manage the paper mill. After numerous delays and ambivalent investors, in 1966, Kenya signed a memorandum of understanding with Orient Paper Mills—an Indian company associated with the Birla Group—to carry out the pulp and paper project with production of approximately 50,000 tons per annum.[22] The Birla Group formed the subsidiary company Pan African Paper Mills to run the Webuye factory. According to the agreement, Birla would take 80 percent of the equity and would arrange for the loan finance required, while the Kenyan government was responsible for 20 percent of the equity, to be invested by one of its financial agencies. The Kenyan government also agreed to reserve the Kenyan market for the factory's output and to restrict imports.[23]

Despite the memorandum of understanding, the Birla Group soon tried to change the terms of the agreement. Ultimately, nine financial institutions contributed both equity and loan funds for the project, including the International Finance Corporation (IFC) of the World Bank Group, the African Development Bank, the East African Development Bank, and the Development Finance Company of Kenya. National and Grindlays Finance and Development Corporation, Barclays Bank DCO and its subsidiary Barclays Overseas Development Corporation Ltd., the First National City Bank of New York, and the Arab African Bank participated in the IFC commitment. Local contributions represented about 10 percent of the financing.[24] Garnering World Bank funding in 1968 was particularly important, as the program relied heavily on this capital. From 1970 to 1975, a World Bank loan funded 65 percent of the project cost of £454,600.[25]

FIGURE 7.1. Signing a World Bank loan to the East African Development Bank, June 1972. Photo courtesy of G. Franchini for the World Bank. Country Photographs—Eastern Africa, Loan 843, Photograph, 1720760, Records of Office of External Affairs, WBGA.

In spite of international financing, other challenges emerged. Tanzania and Uganda—both determined to start their own independent industries—each planned paper mills. Uganda intended to complete a paper plant by late 1968 or early 1969, and Tanzania was considering manufacturing pulp and paper from sisal.[26] If such plans came to fruition, Kenya's neighbors would become industry competitors, and they would substantially reduce Kenya's target market.[27] Making matters worse, during this same period, the Lonrho Corporation built a domestic plant in Thika to produce eighteen tons of newsprint a day using imported pulp.[28]

Price competition from foreign sources outside Africa was another concern, as many of the major producing countries had significant surplus. This resulted in considerable price fluctuations and "periodic dumping of large consignments of pulp and paper products in East Africa at marginal costs of production, or even below."[29] The Kenyan government estimated that in order to achieve its price structure, a minimum import tariff of 40 percent would be necessary to prevent competition from cheap foreign sources.[30] The high interest on borrowed capital made it necessary to raise the domestic price to balance the budget. Despite these financial impediments, the Birla Brothers estimated the project would begin making profits in the fourth year of production.[31]

Global inflation added further uncertainty to this venture, as it became more difficult to project future pulp and paper prices. Between 1970 and 1974, the cost of growing trees increased dramatically, by 25 percent.[32] At that point, Kenya had already made a massive investment in afforestation and the paper industry. In 1968, the national forests contributed £6 million to the gross domestic product, and the construction of the Pan African Paper Mills (E.A.) Limited at Webuye was estimated to cost some £17 million. Between 1970 and 1974, the Kenyan government planned to spend close to 5 percent of its annual budget on forestry.[33]

MOUNTING OPPOSITION

Other obstacles would plague the forest-paper scheme—particularly, squatter resistance and interministerial fighting about whether the program was vital enough to implement at the expense of land resettlement. Nevertheless, the government began construction of the Turbo forest nursery in 1965 with the goal of planting three million seedlings by March 1966.[34] At the end of July 1965, an estimated three to four hundred families resided in the planned forest area.[35] In August 1965, a group of Nandi elders, led by Daniel arap Moi, approached the minister for Lands and Settlement about Turbo.[36] Following this meeting, Minister Angaine wrote: "It would be worthwhile reviewing intended land purchase in this area and possibly excluding it altogether and allowing the tenants to take up these farms, for it must be appreciated that the Nandi will be foregoing a considerable acreage which they anticipated and indeed know was coming to them for settlement purposes."[37] Moi's support of squatters and Angaine's unease hinted at latent official resistance to, and division over, the program. In February 1966, the divisional forest officer wrote that 552 families of an average size of five were living on the land demarcated for forest.[38] By August of the same year, government officials noted a new total of 639 families in the area—or, about 3,195 people.[39]

Turbo squatters not only refused to leave the land, but they actively disrupted afforestation efforts. A. F. Achieng, permanent secretary for the Ministry of Natural Resources and Tourism, noted in 1966 that the squatters "were cutting down trees, building huts and in general making a mess of the whole scheme."[40] Officials became increasingly concerned as they realized the challenges of settling squatters elsewhere. At the same time, more people flooded into Turbo to protest the seizure of Nandi territory and to make land claims for their families. In 1968, Kenyatta directed that a settlement scheme be carried out in Turbo, but the president's order did little to sate widespread land hunger. Despite the settlement, by 1969, the government estimated that 1,000 families—approximately 5,000 people—were squatting on land in Turbo intended for forests.[41]

By this time, the Nandi protest had reached a fever pitch. In July 1969, Nandi squatters published a memorandum declaring their grievances about broken promises for land. The memorandum explicitly alleged government wrongdoing and argued that planting trees had "hurt the Nandi people terrible because they had been promised settlement."[42] In the memo, the squatters also recounted their direct and aggressive confrontation with the government, describing how "the Nandi people turned out in the morning with spears arrows etc. to resist the planting of trees and protest for settlement."[43] It was clear that some members of the Nandi community were prepared for a long fight.

With World Bank funding, the problems in Turbo intensified as loan conditions and strict deadlines created further hurdles. The World Bank required that the Kenyan government set aside 65,000 acres for afforestation, and that at least 50 percent of the timber come from within a twenty-five-mile radius of the factory. The Bank insisted on these stipulations with profitability in mind, to ensure the production of an ideal amount of raw materials and lower transportation costs. World Bank conditions gave Kenyan policymakers few options for where to establish softwood plantations.

These options became further limited as squatters achieved greater victories through their resistance. The government converted more and more planned afforestation areas back into settlement schemes. The Ministry of Natural Resources continually sought new land for forest but encountered the same problems everywhere. The ministry's permanent secretary complained in a 1970 letter: "By losing 22,000 acres [to settlement] the land available has now been reduced to some 25,000 acres. We were asked to find alternative suitable land to be bought for the [forest] scheme, but each time we have met with difficulties. We lost two farms to squatters last year (1969) plus the National Farm. . . . The local people simply moved into the farms and refused to leave. The National Farm was invaded by armed men and we were forced out."[44] A sense of resignation following these repeated defeats is evident later in the same correspondence:

> Now we are at the point of being confronted at another farm i.e. Cooper's Farm. . . . People have moved in illegally and started ploughing the land. The Provincial Commissioner, Rift Valley

Province, was requested to remove the men out and he has ordered the DC [district commissioner] Eldoret to take action. Court action has been initiated, but already representations are being made. Allegations of mistreating *wananchi* [citizens] are being made. If Cooper's farm is lost to the scheme then we might abandon the whole idea of the pulp mill. The World Bank is financing the Turbo Afforestation Scheme for the next 6 years, and we plan to plant some 3,000 acres per year, but there seems to be calculated resistance to what we are trying to do.[45]

By April 1971, the World Bank forestry project manager noted that only 15,230 hectares of the required 30,300 hectares had been purchased. The manager added that Kenya's Ministry of Natural Resources had tried to acquire additional land, "but with very heavy pressures from other interests it is anticipated that great difficulty will be found in achieving the target."[46]

Despite these difficulties, the Kenyan government did eventually manage to build the factory. At the beginning of November 1972, Jomo Kenyatta attended the foundation stone laying ceremony. Two years later, on 24 November 1974, the factory produced its first roll of paper.[47] The factory opening did not, however, signify an end to the problems in the forestry portion of the project. A year after the factory's inception, the permanent secretary to the Ministry of Natural Resources penned a letter to the permanent secretary of Lands and Settlement expressing concern over negotiations for a new World Bank loan, since the project had not met the original conditions. He wrote, "One of those conditions relates to the question of land for afforestation and it is obvious that if some of the land acquired for this purpose has squatters, the project can be deemed unsuccessful. Concomitantly therefore, my chances of securing a second loan and a much bigger one, if I may add, are remote."[48]

LAND, DEVELOPMENT, AND INDEPENDENCE

Land overshadowed most other political issues in Kenya during decolonization, and continued to do so even after the transfer of more than one million acres from Europeans to Africans. Most Kenyan policymakers were skeptical of the economic benefits of giving small plots of land to Kenyans. They believed in the importance of economies of scale and assumed that rural Kenyans had little agricultural knowledge and would make unproductive farmers.[49] Poor, landless Kenyans became chief recipients of settlement land nonetheless, mostly out of concern that they "constituted a security risk."[50]

The state redistributed land to the rural poor as a preemptive strategy for defusing unrest, not as a means to achieving major economic development.

Despite these programs, the new Kenyan nation remained beset by landlessness, and also by unemployment. By 30 June 1961, reported employment levels had fallen by over 5 percent from just the year before, and this number was expected to continue decreasing.[51] In February 1964, the Kenyan government tried to address the problem by signing a labor agreement with the Federation of Kenya Employers and the Kenya Federation of Labour. The agreement required the government and public service sector to increase its employees by 15 percent and the private sector to increase its employees by 10 percent, and it stipulated that farmers could neither fire nor evict laborers from farms for a full year without government permission.[52] The tripartite agreement represented only a provisional attempt to increase employment, since inflated local governments could not maintain excess staff, especially without grants from the central government. For the longer term, many government and development officials believed that they could combat unemployment only by creating jobs through business and industry.

In spite of the 1964 labor agreement, job growth remained virtually stagnant from 1954 to 1970, even with a rapidly increasing population.[53] In the absence of adequate land to employ Kenyan farmers, the state turned to job creation. A 1968 rural development report noted: "The critical problem is to provide these rural people an opportunity to make a livelihood, and a better livelihood. Unemployment . . . is the central problem of the Kenya economy, and one of growing urgency and scale. Unless this problem can be solved, land-holdings will be sub-divided into smaller and smaller pieces, unemployed will go in even greater numbers to towns which cannot employ them."[54] Kenyan government bureaucrats and international financial institutions generally supported industrial development programs over squatter settlement, because they saw industry as a more sustainable solution.

The Pan African Paper Mills represented one such solution. A Treasury memorandum on the forest and paper industry program forecast, "In terms of employment alone 1,000 men would be employed permanently on the forestry operations with an additional 4,000 men employed as seasonal labour. This compares with 1,550 families (25 acres per settler) who would be provided for on the planned settlement schemes."[55] The government estimated that the establishment of the mill would create up to fifteen thousand jobs in total in forestry, logging, transport, factory operations, and industries connected to pulp and paper.[56]

The proponents of afforestation characterized the decision to prioritize industry over settlement as a more sophisticated approach to development that would lead to progress for the *entire* country, as opposed to benefiting a small number of settlers. In a 1966 meeting with a group of Kalenjin politicians, the minister for Natural Resources, Wildlife and Tourism, S. O. Ayodo, said, "Although the Government of the past might have promised that after the Europeans' departure, the land in question would be handed back to the Nandi, the present Government is thinking of developing the area in a way that will benefit the Nation as a whole, and the local people with employment."[57] This emphasis signified a fundamental amendment of policy priorities, one that downplayed the importance of settlement and agricultural development in favor of industry and job creation. Ayodo gestured to the new post-majimbo order as well, asserting that ethnic claims were no longer legitimate, especially when they undermined the national interest.

Rural imaginaries of the postcolonial order diverged from this vision of industrial development as panacea. Paul Kipkorir Boit, then provincial commissioner of Western Province, summed up the government's difficult position in a 1970 letter, noting that as long as there were squatters, "the public just do not understand why certain portions of land should be afforested."[58] As a provincial commissioner, Boit reported to the Office of the President but served a local, rural population, and he was well aware of the incongruous visions of development. As a Nandi farmer who had lived in both Nandi and Uasin Gishu Districts, Boit understood popular sentiments.[59] In the same letter, Boit wrote, "Economically of course provision of employment has to rank fairly high as well in our priorities but the prevalent sensitivity on land will always make any proposals to expand plantations of forests to be viewed with indignation."[60] Squatter resistance to the implementation of the forestry program grew out of popular postcolonial ideologies in which independence, land, citizenship, and development were intertwined. Land became a lens Kenyans used to gauge the successes and failures of decolonization, and some of those who did not receive land recounted that "it was as if there was no independence."[61] Not only did many Kenyans conceptualize independence through land access, but they connected citizenship and *maendeleo* (development) to property ownership and good farming.[62]

Rural aspirations were tied to land, but rural anxieties were tied to ethnic competition.[63] The inception of the forest and paper program occurred in a setting already rife with feelings of regional antagonism, and Turbo afforestation magnified Kalenjin concerns about marginalization.[64] Squatters did not believe the paper industry signified development because the factory was located outside the Rift Valley. Kiptoo arap Maina, a Nandi farmer who has lived near Turbo division since independence, articulated this sentiment: "Something like Pan [African] Paper in Webuye benefits those people in

Webuye alone, so how do I take it as a development if it's not of direct benefit to me?"[65] During the colonial period, Maina had moved between multiple locations in Uasin Gishu and Nandi, and then to eastern Uganda. His greatest desire, at independence, was to purchase land and remain settled.[66] Maina is lively and outgoing, and he is forthcoming and unequivocal with his opinions. Even so, other Turbo interlocutors also said they believed the paper industry would benefit only the Luyia in Western Province. Both Nandi and Luyia worried, in addition, that land resettlement would favor the Kikuyu because of their political dominance.[67] Kalenjin and Luyia farmers complained that those in government "brought their own people."[68] Many expressed the prevailing opinion that settlement disproportionately benefited the Kikuyu at the expense of the already marginalized. The long-standing competition for land in the northwest Rift Valley highlands—between Kikuyu, Kalenjin, and Luyia, and then, later, between forest and settlement—created an atmosphere of anxiety and vulnerability that buttressed squatter mobilization against government attempts to seize land.

Landlessness, regional competition, and inequality represented major issues in Turbo and throughout the nation. Many Kenyans questioned the government's commitment to addressing inequality. The "Citizens of Naivasha" wrote to the KANU district chairman in 1967, "How many types of policies has the Government? We want to know if there is policy for rich people Ministers and for poor citizens."[69] Rhetoric about the visible presence of rich and poor classes was common, and Kenyans tended to trace the creation of these polarized economic classes to land settlement. This type of public frustration created disquiet in government circles about the rural protests it might portend. Especially in the second half of the 1960s, officials became concerned about threats to the Kenyatta administration's hegemony. The populist Kenya People's Union (KPU) party formed in 1966, promising to settle more landless Kenyans, and intolerance heightened as ethnic communities contended for limited land and jobs.[70]

Events in Turbo proved the government's fears were well founded. Turbo squatters' discontent over landlessness and ethnic inequalities propelled a united resistance to the afforestation program. Squatters protested by sabotaging the tree planting and by seeking the support of local and national politicians. In resisting the physical planting of trees and in building partnerships with political elites, the squatters spurred intense government debate. Not only did word of squatter resilience and resistance circulate among government officials, but politicians lobbied on behalf of squatters in Nairobi. Central government actors became intensely divided over the program. Kalenjin politicians and officials in the Ministry of Lands and Settlement supported the squatters in the name of a welfare-oriented, redistributive, and just state, while the Ministry of Commerce and Industry and the Ministry of Natural Resources supported the forestry program, arguing that it was in the new nation's interest to develop sustainable, growth-oriented industries.

Beginning to crack under the pressure from Nandi squatters and their elite representatives, the ministers of Natural Resources and Lands and Settlement vowed on 11 February 1966 that alternative land would be found for squatters residing in Turbo. Pro-industry officials had come to realize that they lacked the political capital to drive the squatters off the land without promises of resettlement. After this announcement, however, V. E. M. Burke, deputy director of Settlement, noted, "It is quite clear that we cannot guarantee to accommodate all the . . . squatters elsewhere in normal settlement."[71]

"WE JUST REFUSED": RESISTANCE AND POSTCOLONIAL AUTHORITY

Conflicting visions of Kenya's economic and political future often translated into conflict at development sites.[72] Nandi squatters in Turbo contested national policy on land and resource distribution by undermining government attempts to create new forests. In response, the central state—vulnerable to public outrage over land inequality and to fractures among government ministries—made shrewd but largely superficial compromises. The assurance of alternative settlement represented the first of these compromises. A longer series of negotiations with local, national, and international actors would follow. The state coupled such negotiations with efforts to police squatter sabotage. These encounters became integral to affirming and consolidating political authority. The Turbo conflict, and other development conflicts like it, reordered political relationships among rural groups, politicians, government bodies, and international institutions.

Concern over rural mobilization played a part in government willingness to negotiate with squatters. Peter Shiyukah, the permanent secretary to the Ministry of Lands and Settlement, illustrated this government anxiety when he laid out the potential repercussions of promising squatters land elsewhere: "The trouble makers might wish to attack the Government on the grounds that perhaps the land they have been offered is poor agriculturally and also is far away from area 'B' of Turbo, and therefore would say NO! to the suggestion."[73] Jackson Angaine, minister of Lands and Settlement, showed similar concern: "Squatters have also refused to move off the land; to attempt to clear these people from the land by force might well create a considerable security problem."[74]

The director of Settlement had become progressively more anxious that there were no alternative settlements for those displaced by the scheme. In February 1966, he wrote: "In order to contain the feelings of the Nandi people we have, all the time, suggested that we would buy alternative land for them. This we thought we could easily accommodate within our proposed Land Settlement programme but as everybody knows this was greatly cut down in the London talks and we cannot now continue to make any more empty promises to the Nandi people."[75] Whether or not the director's angst was prompted by genuine concern for Nandi welfare or by worry about continued Nandi resistance is not clear. More apparent, though, is that—despite the director's pleas—the government would keep making empty promises to Nandi squatters.

The Ministry of Lands and Settlement did seek creative ways to find space for a new settlement scheme, investigating the possibility of resettling Turbo squatters in a portion of forest reserve.[76] Permanent Secretary Shiyukah wrote to the clerk of the Sirikwa County Council in October 1966 requesting the council's agreement to provide land from the Nandi forest for 550 squatter families from Turbo. He wrote: "This Ministry has explored every avenue to find land for these squatters, but it is now apparent that any farms that we might buy up for the Area B squatters would be already occupied by other squatters, largely ex-labourers on the farms, and as it is the Government's policy to give priority for settlement to ex-legal labour, there would be little or no land left for the Nandi on any farms we might buy."[77] Shiyukah did not come to this decision lightly and noted his own reluctance to recommend a reduction in protected indigenous forest. He believed, though, that it was necessary to find land for the Turbo squatters; otherwise, "it will not be possible to go ahead with the wood-pulp scheme, which would be a great loss to Sirikwa County and to the economy of the whole of Kenya."[78]

The long-standing apprehension about landlessness fueling rural protest kept government actors from employing force, which they worried might incite greater rebellion. Government plans to redress the situation instead depended on the compliance of squatters, an improbable expectation. The Turbo Afforestation advisory committee noted as late as 1973 the complete ineffectiveness of squatter evictions.[79] Squatters simply did not leave voluntarily after being evicted. Other government solutions to the squatter problem ranged from guarding the trees to raiding livestock to compel people to move away from the area. Some officials suggested less aggressive solutions, such as holding *baraza* (public meetings) to explain the situation and gain squatters' cooperation.[80] Eventually, the government decided on a mostly litigious strategy—fining, jailing, or serving court orders. This proved to be largely unsuccessful and required a great deal of time and money.[81] Despite the difficulties and inefficiencies of this system, the government continued serving eviction notices to squatters all the way into 1977.[82]

On occasion, government actors did hold meetings in an effort to gain squatter cooperation, but squatters also contested the government in these spaces. Turbo squatter Daniel Kebeney Bitok recounted, "Baraza were called, and we were asked why we were uprooting the trees, and we complained that it was another way of making the government realize that it wasn't fair to plant trees and evict people who were squatting on the land. We thought that after the *wazungu* [Europeans] left, the land would be for us. And, the government was planting trees. Where were we going to live?"[83] Bitok's political ideologies were deeply influenced by his experiences of landlessness and feelings of exclusion. He spoke of the various ways the independent state marginalized him, but also of the strategies he employed to make himself visible to government actors, whether that entailed paying taxes, visiting an agricultural extension officer, or uprooting trees.[84]

Former squatters described the ineffectiveness of other government tactics as well. Wilson Cheruyot Boit had been living in Nandi District for over a decade when he decided to move to the Turbo region in the mid 1960s to claim land. He had anticipated getting a "big *shamba* [farm], like an *mzungu* [European]" after independence, and this expectation propelled his migration. Boit recalled his encounters with officials on the land he farmed in Turbo: "I was planting maize, but when they [government officers] came, they started planting trees inside my maize by force. Some government officers spent days at my place supervising the tree planting. They had armed guards with them. . . . I did not bother despite the armed guards being around. So, when they planted trees in one area, I shifted to another region and planted my maize there. They then would follow me and plant trees there, and I would in turn go to another area and plant my maize."[85] He added that after the government planted trees, people would "spoil them."[86] Others recounted similar stories of evading government officers and disrupting the tree planting.

Landlessness represented a major issue throughout the new nation. In Turbo, squatting produced a more acute crisis, because World Bank funding depended upon the successful creation of a softwoods forest plantation, and because the government had planned for the pulp and paper factory to be one of the largest national development programs. J. H. O. Omino, permanent secretary to the Ministry of Natural Resources, wrote in 1973: "We are soon coming to the end of our first World Bank Forestry Project

Loan and are preparing details for the second phase. In the absence of land for sustained afforestation our plans in this direction will obviously come up against stiff opposition. The up-shot of all these obstacles is that Webuye Pulp and Paper Mill, the biggest single project ever undertaken in this country, will be frustrated into inevitable collapse."[87] The protracted impasse between squatters and the government risked international funding and the industrial development program as a whole.

While land and ethnic competition were the broad fault lines along which squatter resistance ran, the particularities of the program also inspired squatter contestation. Most squatters recalled feeling disbelief that trees could ever be more important than people. Wilson Boit, who earlier described his confrontation with officers and armed guards, articulated a clear choice between the welfare of people versus trees: "People continued to make noise by saying that they were dying of hunger and yet the government was busy planting trees instead of giving them land."[88] Squatters tended to characterize the government as a sinister body for allowing its citizens to starve for the sake of planting trees. The presence of World Bank officials managing the project further galvanized squatter resistance. Some Nandi squatters believed that these officials represented a return to colonial rule. Boit recounted, "We thought the wazungu were coming back."[89]

Turbo squatters noted, additionally, that they had no alternative but to contest the project, because its execution would lead to their homelessness and landlessness. Many wondered where they would live.[90] Similar to others, Priscilla Murei gave a straightforward reasoning for squatter activism: "People had courage, because they were many, and they were in need of the *shamba* [farm]."[91] Murei had migrated with her family to Turbo in the mid-1960s when a Nandi chief informed her husband about the available land. Murei's family was part of a group of squatters who did not make claims to Turbo based on prior residency or labor history, but had been encouraged by ethnic elites to defend communal claims to the region. Unlike Murei, Christina Cherotich had lived on land in Turbo division before independence. Cherotich's husband worked on a European farm in the area. She recounted her surprise when she saw the government planting trees close to her home and noted she had no idea what purpose the tree plantations served. Cherotich summed up the general attitude, pithily explaining communal reaction to the project: "We just refused."[92] Nandi contested the program by uprooting trees, intentionally squatting on planned forestry land, and by allying with politicians.

Local and national leaders bolstered the Turbo resistance, supporting squatters on the ground. Politicians' involvement reveals how jockeying for power in a one-party state shaped the exercise of authority in local settings. Politicians built up popular support and political legitimacy not from their party affiliations, but from their personal—and visible—distribution of resources to citizens. When national figures entered into local development politics, it was often to the mutual benefit of politicians and local groups. Politicians gained new clients by disbursing development aid; local communities gained access to resources. This was a context marked by a predominantly rural population, intense ethnic competition for scarce resources, interministerial disagreement about development, and networks that connected Nairobi-based politicians, local officials, rural Kenyans, and transnational representatives. Politics became defined by the formation of new, multitiered relationships, upending the notion that the state imposed its will on a quiescent citizenry.

Through these relationships—often forged at development sites—various actors redefined political authority and political practice. Members of Parliament easily took control from low-level officers on the ground, regardless of whether national policy supported their actions. A Turbo forest officer, C. B. Looman, recounted how MP and assistant minister for Foreign Affairs, Burudi Nabwera, met with about fifty "trespassers":

> He [Nabwera] enquired about their welfare and was told that I am trying to remove them from this Estate and stop them cultivating *shambas*. He was also told that I am pulling down their houses. As a matter of fact, I had taken the majority of the men present to court charged with illegal cultivation in July, 1970. The Court Magistrate fined some of the men and ruled that all should leave the Estate as soon as they had finished harvesting their crops. Mr. Nabwera then visited a house which had been pulled down by my headman, after the inhabitants . . . had moved away to the Settlement Scheme.[93]

Looman's letter reveals how Nabwera asserted his authority during their public encounter: "Mr. Nabwera instructed me to stop trying to move these people and allow them to cultivate on this estate. I told Mr. Nabwera that I was only carrying out my orders, but did not try to argue the point, as by this time a lot of people had collected . . . and I was feeling rather embarrassed."[94] Nabwera reprimanded the officer publicly to display his support for the Nandi squatters. While Nabwera was a Luyia politician, he was also a KANU dissident, often advocating for redistribution and allying himself with Nandi populists.

Physical meetings of this sort—between political leaders and the rural poor—shaped notions of political authority, particularly with regard to Jomo Kenyatta. In describing the story of their resistance, former Turbo squatters stressed the importance of traveling to see Kenyatta. In opposition to a sinister government, Kenyatta played a benevolent role in squatter imaginations for ultimately redressing government wrongdoing by creating a settlement scheme. Each interlocutor recounted asking Kenyatta, "Are you planting trees or are you planting people?" Their rhetoric was both literal and metaphorical and was deeply shaped by the independent context. These farmers wholeheartedly believed that they—not trees—were supposed to be the seeds of the new nation, which would grow and bring prosperity.

A tenor of intimacy suffused many retellings of the story. Some former Turbo squatters recounted coming "face-to-face" with Kenyatta and singing with him.[95] Michael Keter imbued his version of the story with a sense of familiarity. Keter moved to Turbo in the mid-1960s after he heard about the available land. He began squatting on land designated for forest and was among the group who visited Kenyatta to lobby their case.[96] Keter recounted that during this trip, he overheard a conversation between Kenyatta and the minister of Settlement, J. H. Angaine. As Keter retold it: "Kenyatta said to him [Angaine], 'These people who are coming here, where are the shambas they are complaining of?' Angaine replied, 'The shambas are between Ndalat, Sergoit, and Sosiani.' The president asked, 'Are we going to plant trees or are we going to plant people?' Angaine replied that it was better to plant people."[97] In these intimate retellings, squatters narrated the importance of Kenyatta's personal support.

Rural Kenyans imagined Kenyatta as the ultimate symbol of the nation, known familiarly as *baba taifa* (father of the nation) and *mzee* (a respectful name for an elder). Many Kenyans credited Kenyatta with bringing independence and giving out land. Some rural Kenyans recounted, for example, that Kenyatta led Mau Mau and fought for freedom.[98] More commonly, western Rift Valley residents credited Kenyatta with carrying out resettlement. Kenyan settlers, especially, thought of Kenyatta as equivalent to the government, and they tended to see him as a successful and caring president.[99] Given the outsized role Kenyatta played in Kenyan imaginaries, Turbo residents recounted that the president's intervention signified a turning point in their fight. Many described how, once Kenyatta agreed, settlement occured.[100]

Kenyans throughout the country believed in and often experienced the power of bringing a grievance directly to Kenyatta.[101] The Kenya National Archives hold countless petitions penned to the president, requesting assistance from the "Father of the Nation."[102] These petitioners, like many others, came to think of Kenyatta as the embodiment of the nation. Even some Kenyans from areas of the Rift Valley once dominated by KADU came to imagine Kenyatta as the singular leader, describing him as "active," and a person with a "vision."[103]

Kenyatta's emblematic role in the minds of the rural poor allowed him concrete presidential powers. In the Turbo case, he altered a World Bank–funded national development plan by making promises to squatter delegations. Kenyatta's ability to pledge land to Kenyans without consulting the government illustrates his personalized authority. The president did not just support the squatters, though. He avidly backed the squatters *and* the paper mill. His actions there, too, illustrate the nature of his early presidency. A 1966 memorandum on the paper factory noted that "years ago at Broderick Falls he [Kenyatta] pointed at the site and told the people that they would have the factory."[104] Kenyatta's power lay largely in his ability to make personal promises, to physically show a group of people where their factory would be located, where their development would come from. It was this very mode of governance that further endowed Kenyatta with authority.

The people of Webuye, too, remember the role the president played. They recall how Kenyatta liked to climb the concrete steps to a platform overlooking the Webuye falls, where he would gaze at the water and contemplate nature.[105] Joab Siundu Macheso has lived in Webuye all his life, long before the paper industry arrived, when Webuye was "very small, just a market, not even a town."[106] As chairman of the local council, Macheso was actively involved in town plans to inaugurate the paper mill. He recounted that when they began building the factory, residents invited President Kenyatta to come for the foundation-laying ceremony. Macheso said, "When he [Kenyatta] came to put the foundation, he found the area was still called Broderick Falls. Now when he came . . . he said, 'I cannot put the foundation when the area is still under colonialism. . . . I cannot put the foundation until we get the right name, the African name.'"[107] In this account, Kenyatta not only demonstrated his ability to distribute the resources of the state and to bring development, but he also brought symbolic decolonization by giving the town its rightful indigenous name.[108]

The events at Turbo reveal much about Kenyatta's style of government, but they also reveal the ways that citizens accessed the state through Kenyatta or through intermediaries that reached Kenyatta. The rural poor created connections with the Office of the President and, in doing so, they shaped government decision making and excluded mid-level state bureaucrats who frustrated their goals. Local communities came together to reshape national development plans, very often through their resistance and their willingness to enter into patronage relationships with elites. Rural Kenyans proved themselves astute political actors, both in negotiating for development and in their perspicacity of the workings of the postcolonial state.

Kenyatta's pronouncements could change the course of policymaking but did not always coincide with or lead to smooth and quick execution. After the president promised land to Turbo squatters, the government had difficulty bringing the proposed settlement to fruition, since it was unclear which squatters were most deserving, and where they could be settled once chosen. The last-minute land settlements were not included in the development estimates, and no financial provisions were available to purchase or prepare land for settlement.[109] Kenyatta's vague promises left officials and policymakers scrambling to find a solution.

For Kenyatta, though, his promises to the squatters were more important than their execution. Kenyatta maintained his authority by inculcating an image of himself as the "giver of land." So long as he could appease squatters by promising settlement, and he could perpetuate his own cult of personality without wholly disrupting the forest and paper program, then he had achieved his goal. The president benefited from the ad hoc governance he institutionalized.

"WE NEVER FOUGHT THE GOVERNMENT AGAIN": TURBO'S RESOLUTION?

The earliest crash settlement scheme in Turbo comprised 20,572 acres, subdivided into 734 plots, each about 27 acres. Most of these plots were settled by the end of April 1969.[110] This was the first—and by far the most quickly executed—of a series of settlements created after the president vowed land to squatters.[111] As with his personal promises, Kenyatta used the opening ceremonies of settlement schemes to impress upon Kenyans his role in land distribution. The minister of Lands and Settlement wrote to Kenyatta after the establishment of the first Turbo settlement scheme: "My officers and I, and indeed the settlers . . . will be extremely grateful to see Your Excellency visit these schemes and personally present certificates to a few settlers. It will indicate to them the determination of your Government to press ahead with the urgent task of tackling landlessness."[112] Settlement ceremonies represented another arena to augment the carefully curated image of Kenyatta as personal granter of land.

These schemes may have confirmed Kenyatta's authority for new settlers, but they did not resolve the Turbo squatter problem. Nor, therefore, did they convert those who remained landless to Kenyatta's personality cult.

There had long been more squatters than land in Turbo and nationwide. While some Turbo squatters received land, many did not, and many continue to squat to this day. The effective consolidation of Kenyatta's power, then, also revealed vulnerabilities to his rule. One way the Kenyatta state attempted to protect itself was by distributing resources to clients—both rural Kenyans and political elites—to maintain authority and silence dissent.[113] That the possibilities of the early postcolonial era came to fruition only for some Kenyans had profound implications, though.[114] The unequal distribution of resources and political voice affected how marginalized Kenyans understood independence and engaged, or disengaged, as political actors in the future. It also had implications for the coalescing of a political order revolving around patronage and clientelism.

Settler selection for squatter programs was marked by greater malfeasance than ordinary schemes. Countless new families had moved into Turbo by the time settlement began, and it was impossible to discern "real" squatters from those who had arrived later, or from the politically well-connected who had successfully jostled for handouts. Alfred Machayo, a former agriculture official, noted that squatter settlement programs gave government officials license to settle whomever they wanted. The government definition of a squatter was vague, and it was difficult to prove whether alleged "squatters" owned land elsewhere or how long they had lived in the area.[115] Squatter settlement thus provided an easy opening for disbursement to the clients of the state.

Turbo residents confirmed this account. Though Wilson Cheruyot Boit was able to purchase land in Turbo, he asserted that settlement there was done unfairly. Boit recounted, "Many people on the ground did not get land. But soon afterwards, the government brought people to take over the land. Those were *watu wakubwa* [big people], well connected to the government." Boit added that some of the "big people" who came to Turbo for the squatter settlement schemes "sold their land and left. Yet, others were farming and going back to Nairobi."[116] The wealthy and absentee landowners settled as squatters visibly epitomized the production of new inequality and injustice, and the workings of a patrimonial state.

Still, many former squatters did receive Turbo settlement plots, and their lives generally improved. The new settlers, government officials, and politicians who had contested afforestation often overlooked the conditions of squatters who were not as fortunate. The government had made a symbolic effort to conciliate the opposition to Turbo afforestation. Those who received land wanted little more. Jemosbei Kirwa Kili received land settlement in Turbo and recounted, "There were no other times we fought the government. We feared the government. There were men who were courageous enough to face the government, because they wanted to settle."[117] Priscilla Murei, another successful Turbo settler, echoed Kili, noting that Turbo settlers never fought the government again.[118] The Turbo settlement schemes both deflated the momentum of the organized resistance and protected Kenyatta from culpability for residual landlessness.

Those who remained squatters formed a different relationship to the state. Squatters' continued position of illegality fostered feelings of insecurity and fears of eviction. Because of these fears, many squatters—without the backing of an organized movement—felt they could not contest the state or make claims to rights and resources. Squatter communities often lacked government services such as schools and hospitals. Squatter livelihoods were continually at stake because they lacked property rights, nor did they have access to services that would give them greater security in the absence of land. Thus, squatters—similar to other marginalized groups—responded by forming alternative institutions to provide their own community safety nets. Because of their liminal and precarious position partially outside the nation-state, squatters took up strong rhetoric on early postcolonial disappointment, which they almost always connected to the injustices of unequal resource distribution.

The Turbo case paralleled Kenyan postcolonial politics more broadly. In 1978, J. H. O. Omino, permanent secretary to the Ministry of Natural Resources, who had been involved in Turbo afforestation, responded tellingly to a government survey: "Grabbing by a few individuals continues unabated with concomitant conspicuous consumption much to the frustration of the silent majority. Efforts must not only be made but must also be seen to be made by Government to make financial resources more easily and widely available as a necessary prerequisite for redressing the obvious imbalance that has been created."[119] The government largely disregarded Omino's advice. Rather, Turbo afforestation—and the consequent production of inequality and purchasing of political loyalties—makes clear that the Kenyatta state preferred to make shallow, expedient concessions. These concessions allowed the elite to continue to benefit disproportionately while suppressing the rural unrest catalyzed by economic injustices.

Land settlement and development often brought equivocal outcomes. Across the provincial border in Webuye, residents also spoke about the paper factory in ambivalent terms. They remembered the excitement of the factory's opening in the 1970s, and the positive changes—the growth of the town, and the creation of employment, business, and economic prosperity. However, residents also recounted the trade-offs they made in exchange for development. Despite promises that the mill would not cause environmental damage, newspaper articles, environmental reports, and Webuye residents' accounts suggest that the mill caused significant degradation. Both World Bank and Kenyan government officials were concerned that the factory would pollute the Nzoia River. Following a halfhearted review of a UNESCO ecological survey and reassurance from the management company, government ministries agreed that there was "no time for waiting" and "we have no choice but to proceed."[120]

Webuye residents spoke in detail about how the factory's pollution negatively affected their lives and their health. People spoke of the factory's chemical-laden fumes, which damaged plants, trees, and buildings, and they recounted how some workers became sick.[121] Fred Machasio, a Webuye native with roots going back multiple generations, described the changes wrought by the factory. Machasio noted that the paper industry first brought jobs, population growth, and economic development, but he also spoke in detail about the community's declining health. "The chemicals," he said. "We had a very big problem. Chemicals used to destroy the houses of residents. . . . People were sick, especially their eyes. Doctors said that the chemicals affected male functioning."[122] Both former workers and residents recounted taking the company to court over the pollution.

Webuye inhabitants not only recounted the impact of industrial pollution, but also how the management mistreated African factory workers. Former workers described a series of labor strikes between the 1970s and the 1990s. Workers often went on strike over their low wages and poor working conditions, and, in the 1997 strike, more than four hundred employees lost their jobs. Broadly speaking, the mostly African laborers had a contentious relationship with the Indian management. Machasio recalled, "People didn't like the Indians because they paid little money; they used to neglect us, abuse us. They [the Indian management] were not on good terms with the people."[123] Kenyatta might have emphasized the "Africanness" of the Webuye name, but development programs fostered international connections, many of which lay outside the continent. Such encounters often produced conflict, even when they involved other postcolonial nations such as India.

These examples indicate the types of sacrifices communities made for development. Most Webuye residents still thought the factory—on the whole—represented a positive change. They believed the industry had brought employment and growth, and that it benefited Kenya. When asked if he thought that the paper factory helped to build the nation, Webuye kiosk owner James Karanja said succinctly and emphatically, "Sana [Very much]."[124] Karanja moved to Webuye in 1975, just after the factory opened, to start a business and take advantage of the town's growing population and improving economic fortunes. Other Webuye residents spoke proudly of the spatial breadth of the paper industry—that the Rift Valley provided the timber, Western Province produced the paper, and the finished products might eventually travel through Mombasa for export. Similar to farmers who took pride in supplying the nation with food, industrial workers conceptualized development through interconnectedness and by the distances their products traveled. Indeed, cosmopolitan imaginaries characterized both the ways Kenyans sought development from multitiered actors and the ways they aspired to produce developmental goods that would travel beyond their local borders.

By the time the contention over the Turbo forestry program and the Pan African Paper Mills factory peaked, the politics of decolonization, development, and postcolonial state-making had long been entangled. This development program—like others—raised questions about Kenya's economic trajectory, and about how resources would be distributed in the new nation. Many Kenyan politicians supported industrialization programs, an approach with plenty of international backing, and one they characterized as sustainable and economically beneficial to the whole nation. Yet populist ethnic leaders, KANU dissidents, and some officials in the Ministry of Lands and Settlement recognized that the Nandi expected land. Indeed, many Kenyans envisioned a postcolony in which the landless were given the opportunity to purchase farms. Making matters worse—given that this was a context of ethnic antagonism and resource competition—the program optics were bad. The Nandi found it particularly egregious that the government reneged on a promise to give them land at Turbo to create a development program that offered jobs to the Luyia.

In the end, the debate among bureaucrats, politicians, and transnational development workers mattered little. Squatter intransigence compelled state actors to change a World Bank–funded program. Nandi squatters refused to move, and they uprooted trees. They also leveraged political support, making shrewd alliances with national politicians and ethnic elites who lobbied on their behalf. The government's inability to deal with squatters, and its concern about the political implications of removing them, gave squatters—more peripheral actors in other circumstances—the ability to force alterations on an international development program.

The resistance and its resolution had broader implications. State disunity helped empower Kenyatta as the face of the nation and allowed him to make personal promises to the public in the absence of broader clarity. These state divisions, however, slowed the implementation of the president's promises. The ad hoc mode of governance that emerged provided openings and incentives for patronage-based political practice. The rural poor came to see both the extent and the limitations of their power to resist a development program. They recognized that they needed to cultivate relationships to access development resources, producing new political loyalties and conceptions of authority. Rural actors at Turbo also came to realize that though such relationships could be fruitful, they might not always produce just results, and not all deserving Kenyans would get land or development. While Turbo is just one episode, it represents a microcosm of a larger set of processes through which postcolonial political culture materialized.

Conclusion

In Kenya, *maendeleo* is widely used to mean "development." It is a Swahili word that literally translates to moving forward toward a goal, derived from the verbs *kuenda*, "to go," and *kuendelea*, "to go on or continue." Along with this implicit temporal reference to the future, Kenya's nationalist development discourse conveyed divergent chronological orientations: national leaders continually referenced a romanticized precolonial "African past" in order to imagine the postcolonial future. Connecting an idyllic past to a prosperous future indicated that all Kenyans would be better cared for, while also helping to gloss over ethnic tensions and distancing the independent government from the colonial state. Though national actors drew on newly reworked moral economies of the past, ultimately, such political grammars would not coincide with the realities of the Kenyan political economy. For many rural Kenyans, decolonization signified minimal material change, and their political ideologies became marked by their experiences of continued economic marginalization.

Unlike government actors, when ethnic leaders drew on the past to imagine the future, they often invoked historical injustices. Over a century after the establishment of colonial rule and a half-century after independence, many Nandi elders continue to pass down oral traditions of anticolonial struggle to younger generations. Popular narrations of conquest and land loss during colonialism have played an important part in molding Nandi

FIGURE B.1. Koitalel calendar, 2015. Photo by the author.

ethnonationalism, founded upon a shared sense of historical injustice and an autochthonous assertion to restitution.[1] In retelling the killing of Koitalel—the leader who spearheaded the resistance to conquest—Nandi elders recount the trauma of their ancestors being forcibly moved, leaving their land behind. Kiptoo arap Maina, a gregarious and theatrical Nandi farmer living in Uasin Gishu, orated the tradition in great detail, performing parts of the plot while using props. At one point, Maina disappeared into

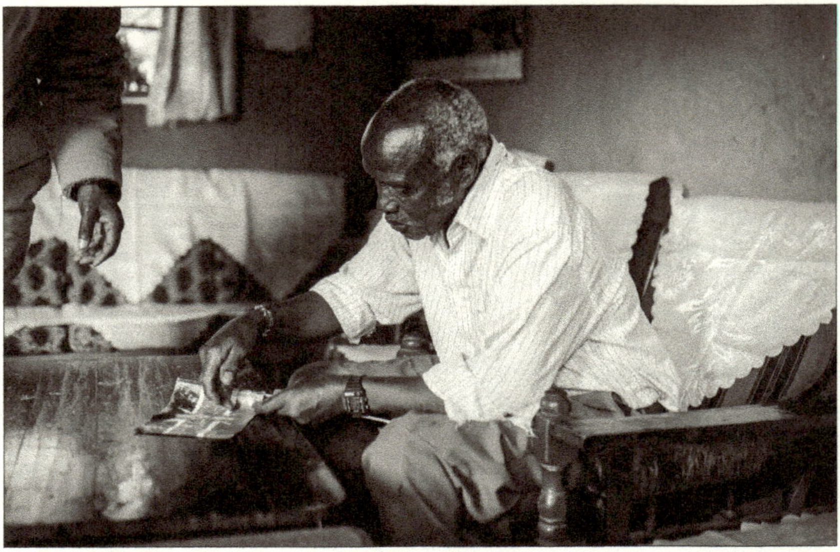

FIGURE B.2. Kaptulus shows the Kenyan flag, 2018. Photo courtesy of Joe Martinez.

his bedroom to search for a calendar of Nandi heroes, which included the independence leader Jean-Marie Seroney, and the current vice president, William Ruto. Tellingly, both leaders had been subordinated to Koitalel, whose image—thrice as large as any other Nandi hero depicted—was placed prominently in the center.[2]

These engagements with history serve as one animation of Nandi identity, and they resonated and continue to resonate with some members of the Nandi community. The coherence and unity they seem to exhibit are a representation, though. Indeed, the omissions from the calendar might be just as significant as Koitalel's dominant image. The calendar contains no picture of Daniel arap Moi, the former president and most significant Kalenjin politician in modern Kenyan history. In emphasizing territoriality and in making exclusive claims to land, Nandi citizenship could serve as an insular framework. Engagements in wider collectivities—the corporate Kalenjin ethnic group, the KADU party, the nation, and the world—were always premised on fragile alliances and shared political projects, often incompatible with local priorities, which were vulnerable to being further divided by the politics of class, gender, and religion. In other words, postcolonial citizens have long felt attachments to multiple, irreconcilable political subjectivities. There are, and always have been, tensions between "being" and "belonging," and each identity has been prone to contestation and reinvention.

For Kenyans throughout the nation, land conjures emotion while also serving as a public record of the outcomes of colonialism and decolonization. Kenya's independence negotiations centered on the structure of the government as Kenyan nationalists, European settlers, and British politicians debated who should control the distribution of land and development resources. The British colonial government directed a great deal of land transfer from European to African ownership ahead of independence. Though the independence constitution established a federal government with regional autonomy, ultimately Jomo Kenyatta's centralized vision would triumph as land administration returned to the national government, stoking anger about ethnic favoritism.

Since the 1960s, when the majority of land resettlement took place, the appearance of Kenya's highlands has changed dramatically. The population, and population density, has risen steeply. Where once large tracts of land remained uncleared and African smallholders maintained farms of fifteen to fifty acres, now the land has been divided into much smaller plots, sometimes of just one or two acres, with new homes springing up all the time and new footpaths to match. Partially as a result of declining field sizes, ordinary Kenyans have found it increasingly difficult to make a living on farming alone.

Population growth contributed to the reduction of landholdings, as some Kenyans chose to divide their farms among multiple heirs, but other factors played a part as well. Prior to 1980, few Kenyan settlers sold portions of their land, largely because stringent regulations inhibited the subdividing of settlement plots. However, as the government eased those restrictions, and as the financial position of farmers worsened, private land sales skyrocketed. Many farmers began selling off pieces of their *shamba* [farm] to pay the debts they first incurred at independence. Earlier, when farmers had quit their cooperatives or sold their maize to black market traders, they had asserted their economic autonomy but, in the process, accumulated debt. After Daniel arap Moi became Kenya's second president, indebtedness continued to pose a financial problem, and Moi—like his predecessor—threatened farmers with eviction and repossession.[3] Many settlers in the western Rift differentiated between Kenyatta's and Moi's debt policies. Most believed Kenyatta acted fairly, giving landowners time to pay, while they perceived Moi to be harsh. Some settlers who had fallen behind with their loan repayments recounted how the Moi administration threatened to sell people's land or confiscate their stock.[4] The looming foreclosures rapidly accelerated land sales.

Subdivision also stemmed from declining producer prices and the increasing cost of medical and educational services. In Lumakanda, Danson Esese found that households most commonly sold their land to pay for school tuition or medical expenses.[5] The deterioration of public social services drove land sales. As more and more smallholders were pushed into selling part of their land, they became dispossessed of their most valuable resource. In a way, they had to sacrifice one of the central promises of independence—land—to attain some of the other promises of independence—education and health care.

The outcomes of other development programs became observable soon after independence and are still visible to this day. The continued significance of "Harambee," the nation's first motto, remains readily apparent: in Kenya's coat of arms and in the name of its national football team. Yet the practice of harambee as self-help has changed considerably. While Kenyatta's maxim was "Pull together," Moi chose "Nyayo" (footsteps) as his slogan to signify that he would follow Kenyatta's lead. With harambee especially, Moi walked in Kenyatta's footsteps but quickly surpassed him. He made use of harambee as the site par excellence for the personal distribution of state resources and the consolidation of his political regime. In 1979, the year after he took office, Moi became the single largest individual harambee donor, contributing more than five times as much as the top donor from the previous year.[6]

The meaning and the form of harambee have changed to such an extent that, initially, when I asked Kenyans about early postindependence harambee programs, many said such programs did not exist back then.[7] Today, harambee rarely involves voluntary labor or community development but entails fund-raising money for specific personal needs. Kenyans might request donations for scholarships, funerals, or medical bills. Harambee, no longer equivalent to self-help, has become individualized and detached from communal development aspirations. Contemporary harambee reveals how much the form of development has changed in the past fifty years. Similar to land sales, it also makes clear the ramifications of the dearth of social services, as Kenyans must rely on family, friends, and neighbors in order to pay for school and health care.

In its earlier iteration, harambee represented a harbinger for later development paradigms. The initial harambee programs foreshadowed neoliberal reforms to come, quite possibly setting the footing for some of them. We might think of harambee, along with other development models instituted in the early independent era, as illustrative of what Gregory Mann calls the "years of neoliberal gnawing," which presaged the structural adjustment programs that so fully ushered in a new developmentalist era.[8] Like land resettlement, harambee required private capital investment and the engagement in market economies. Harambee—which made local communities responsible for the labor and fund-raising in their own development programs—initiated the privatization of development, minimized the role of the state, and increased inequality. Structural adjustment, and the other more explicitly neoliberal interventions of the 1980s and 1990s, undoubtedly broke from previous norms. Still, decolonizing programs in the Global South acted as antecedents to future neoliberal global practices.[9]

For the paper factory, the challenges of the planning period portended future problems to come. With the mill's opening new issues emerged, especially with the Indian management company. By 1986, Pan African Paper Mills (E.A.) Limited owed Kenya's Ministry of Environment and Natural Resources close to 14 million shillings, an amount the ministry described as "indeed colossal."[10] In fact, credit problems, underfunding, and unprofitability led to the closing of the factory in 2009 and 2010.[11]

Approaching the town from the main highway in western Kenya, the factory seems misplaced among the lush farm fields, where smallholders grow maize, sugarcane, beans, and vegetables. Even with the factory visible from the road, Webuye appears as an unexpected industrial center, juxtaposed with the extensive bucolic landscape in which it is ensconced. To turn off from the highway into the town is almost to retreat back to the decades in which many parts of the town were built. The architecture of the workers' housing blocks makes clear they were planned and constructed during the 1970s, and they appear not to have been updated or repaired since. The lodging remains sturdy and steadfast, but dilapidated, with paint peeling and signposts so fully corroded they are no longer legible. When I visited in 2013, Webuye—described by *Daily Nation* reporter Kenneth Lusaka as once "ever-full-of-life"—resembled a ghost town; it had a quietness about it, eerie for a place of its size.[12]

When the factory was shuttered, at least nine hundred people lost their jobs.[13] Many former workers left to seek employment or land elsewhere, and many small businesses suffered considerably. Residents recalled how, after the factor closed, "poverty *iliingia* [entered]."[14] Joseph Juma Lukorito moved to Webuye for a job at the paper factory in the mid-1970s. With his polytechnic training, he advanced quickly within the company. Similar to others, Lukorito was deeply affected by the factory's closing. He described the crisis: "We are IDPs [internally displaced persons] by way of the company and unattended by the government."[15] In this, Lukorito not only poignantly described feelings of state abandonment, but he also demonstrated the ways in which developmentalist and humanitarian discourse has come to pervade Kenyan vocabularies. The irony that an unsuccessful development project produced figurative humanitarian disaster was not lost on Lukorito or others.

FIGURE B.3. Webuye, July 2013. Photo by the author.

On 15 December 2016, the paper mill—newly branded as Rai Paper—reopened. This was only the latest attempt to revive the struggling factory.[16] News of the factory's resurrection once again ushered in fresh hopes for the town of Webuye. One *Daily Nation* article described the factory as "the Lazarus of Kenyan industry, repeatedly brought back to life long after its final rites have been concluded."[17] Despite the colorful description, the most recent opening probably feels cyclical to local residents who have perhaps resolved to temper their excitement. That the opening "triggered angry exchanges" between the two major political parties likely feels recurrent to all Kenyans. Politicians argued over the terms of recovery as they attempted to "leverage" the revival of this factory situated in a "vote-rich region" to garner support ahead of elections.[18] This clash to win voter favor through development parallels politics at so many other times, so many other places.

Infrastructural change is a part of the considerable transformations of the past fifty years and, similar to land, serves as a visible public archive of development projects. Where the railway once provided long-distance transport, now a highway has become the major thoroughfare transporting goods and people. It cuts through the Rift Valley escarpment connecting to Kampala in the west and Nairobi in the southeast. In Nairobi, the

FIGURE B.4. Pan African Paper factory sign, July 2013. Photo by the author.

Kenya-Uganda highway intersects with the Mombasa highway, which continues on to the port at the coast. Today in the western Rift Valley, eighteen-wheeler trucks are just as familiar a sight as overloaded *matatus*, the privately owned minibuses most commonly used by Kenyans for public transportation.[19] The trucks and matatus speed along the highway at a dizzying pace, dangerously overtaking one another. The highway itself acts as a record of the rapid infrastructural change. The innumerable dents that depress the road's surface showcase the dramatic increase in traffic over the years. The Chinese construction companies repairing the highway showcase not only how global capital continues to be injected into Kenya's countryside, but also the ways that international development relationships and models have shifted recently.

This road, the one that serves as a geopolitical boundary, now separates the mostly Kalenjin settlements from the mostly Luyia settlements. The ethnic makeup of this part of the highlands has been recently recast. Ethnic violence in the 1990s and 2000s served as a haunting epilogue to colonial histories of dispossession and to decolonizing histories of land resettlement. Indeed, competition over political power, and thus over land and development, motivated much of this violence. Most of the violence occurred at former land settlement sites in contested, ethnically heterogeneous regions like Uasin Gishu.[20] The violence has once again remade the ethnic landscape, as many Kikuyu fled. This conflict also forced Luyia and Kalenjin families on the "wrong" side of the border to trade places, to re-create the ethnically homogeneous niches colonial bureaucrats first carved into Kenya's countryside. The landscape thus evokes these historical episodes and their attendant displacements.

In the aftermath of the violence in 2007 and 2008, the opposing parties agreed to share power and permit a committee of international and national experts to draft a new constitution. This latest iteration of constitutional deliberation, like its forerunner at independence, centered on the degree of devolution to local authorities and the extent of presidential powers. Transnational actors, national politicians, and *wananchi* (citizens) revived debates over who would control the allocation of Kenya's development resources. In the end, not a great deal changed; power was only nominally decentralized to county councils, while a robust presidency prevailed. More than two-thirds of Kenyans ratified this constitution in a 2010 referendum.[21]

Since then, Uhuru Kenyatta, son of Jomo Kenyatta, has been twice elected president, most recently in 2017. The 2017 platforms of Kenyatta's Jubilee Party, and of Raila Odinga's opposition National Super Alliance (NASA), illustrate the continued relevance of the early postcolonial era to contemporary Kenya. Together, the manifestos of the two parties mention many of the development programs and political ideas at the heart of decolonizing processes: devolution, economic redistribution, land, farming cooperatives, strategic grain reserves, food security, and the Webuye paper factory.

Politics have not gone unchanged from independence until now, but many of the issues early independence-era development programs first brought to the foreground have endured, with powerful repercussions. At independence,

Kenyans assembled a citizenship toolkit to achieve their aspirations, pursue aid, define and protect their rights, and demand the state take on expected obligations. But the state acted erratically, and distributed development unequally, often to purchase rural political loyalties. Though many contested these injustices, sometimes quite successfully, state inconsistency pushed rural Kenyans to invest in other institutions, especially ethnic citizenships. It was not inevitable that ethnic ideologies would overshadow much else. In the mid- to late 1960s, some Kenyan politicians and citizens advocated effectively for a redistributive state, though their proposition conflicted with moral economies that emphasized individual, hard work. Ultimately, ethnonationalist ideologies dominated, localizing political dissent and frustrating discussions centered on class or economic inequality.

During decolonization, Kenyans throughout the new nation attempted to access aid, writing petitions, forming local development groups, and contesting or modifying programs. Rural Kenyans had been promised development, and they desired it as well. Many had come to imagine independence through service provision and resource access, and through improved standards of living. In actively engaging in development processes, rural Kenyans contributed to the experimentations of the transitional moment, helping to shape Kenya's political culture and political economy for years to come.

Ordinary Kenyans were able to participate in development processes, at least in part because the state had more limited reach than previous scholarship has suggested. Neither development funding nor implementation was ever channeled exclusively through state institutions, raising questions about the existence of the widely accepted gatekeeper state. Kenya's postcolonial state was neither a monolithic nor a monopolistic institution. Rather, it was composed of dissenting actors, who deliberated the merits of various economic development models, debated the meaning of development, and disagreed on how to order the nation's priorities. The state as an institution was marked by its many internal cleavages.

A whole array of new actors—Peace Corps volunteers, World Bank and IMF officials, Norwegian technocrats, Israeli economists, British politicians, and Western missionaries—played a growing role in Kenyan policymaking at this time, and each possessed distinctive ideas about development. Transnational institutions and actors became involved in the planning, funding, and execution of Kenyan development programs. The entrance and expanding influence of these actors further constricted the state's ability to determine Kenya's development path.

On the ground at the rural sites so central to Kenya's economy, both state actors and transnational practitioners exercised uneven control over development. The state often relied on local bureaucrats to serve as representative conduits and to implement development programs. Yet, in many cases, bureaucrats were inadequately trained, or inexperienced, or they lacked the resources to carry out their assigned tasks. With little oversight on the ground, some bureaucrats decided not to follow state directions, enacting nonconformist developmental visions. In other cases, when former colonial officials or white settlers took up bureaucratic posts, they symbolized the continuities of colonialism rather than the promises of independence. The state entered into rural lives irregularly, and many Kenyans felt there was a disjuncture between government discourse on development and their experiences of government intervention.

Kenyans contested, transformed, and initiated development in rural spaces. Residents of the western highlands petitioned for land, resources, and services. They sought the help of agricultural assistants and ignored technical advice they believed to be incorrect. They refused to send their produce through agricultural marketing cooperatives when they felt government prices were too low or their cooperative leaders were corrupt. They built schools and hospitals at unprecedented rates, regardless of state procedures or development plans. And they sabotaged a state-led, internationally financed industrialization program that appropriated land they felt should go to settlement. Though not always successful, rural Kenyans sought to improve their own lives through imaginative strategies. In the course of such efforts, they affected modes of development practice, the outcomes of development interventions, and the direction of national planning. They helped determine who set the policy priorities of the nation and how citizens accessed resources. In turn, rural actors formed new political philosophies and forged new political identities, helping to define the relationships between citizens, the state, and other institutional bodies.

Citizenship connotes legal status, a balance of individual rights and duties, and a sense of identity. In early postcolonial Kenya, debates over the rights of citizens and the obligations of the state overshadowed much else and also shaped ideas of belonging. Citizenship's balance of rights and duties was never clearly conferred but debated and differentiated in Kenya. Through negotiations over development, citizens, state actors, and transnational development practitioners charted a range of citizenly rights and duties. Development experiences, likewise, molded ideas about state obligations.

Not all citizens gained equal rights and not all citizens were burdened with equivalent duties. In such a setting—further confounded by the unreliability of the state, and by the existence of multiple institutions distributing amenities, social protections, and development assistance—plural, coexisting citizenships emerged.[22] Those excluded from reliably accessing citizenship rights often turned to other institutions, or drew on multiple institutions—multiple citizenships—simultaneously. A shifting, unequal set of citizens' rights and duties became vested in several relationships—between citizens and the state, citizens and ethnic communities, citizens and religious bodies, and citizens and nongovernmental organizations. National citizenship thus coexisted with other types of citizenship, which charted different sets of norms about the relationships between individuals and institutional bodies.

Where local elites and state actors might be seen as forces of marginalization, and where international bodies constituted known sources of funding, some Kenyans looked outward to international actors for leadership or assistance. Others created alternative political communities, or links to similarly marginalized actors, to acquire resources and construct local safety nets. Global institutions expected Kenyans to conform to their economic models in order to access aid, and they represented undemocratic bodies with few legal obligations to those they assisted. Ethnic communities often offered few inherent individual rights, instead, investing in the progression of the group. Still, seeing like a citizen makes clear that the heads of institutions did not determine the nature of these relationships, and that citizenship was a product of compromise.

Kenyans drew on their multiple citizenships to negotiate with the international, national, and local authorities responsible for land policy, the outcomes of which deeply colored notions of belonging. Those who remained landless or land-insecure after independence recounted feeling excluded and disappointed that the government did not distribute land more equitably. The experience of land insecurity often propelled squatters and women to look to NGOs, churches, and ethnic communities for greater protection. In Uasin Gishu—a site of intense land competition and historically layered claims-making—ethnic ideologies, especially, carved out conflicting threads of thought on land rights. Rural Kenyans from diverse communities were familiar with such ethnic thinking, and they drew on and reworked these ideas, along with many others, to make sense of their lived experiences and to make claims for more just policies.

Kenyan state actors and international donors proffered ideas of citizenly duty that revolved around rational economic conduct. For national and international policymakers, this often entailed being a devoted cooperative member, a loyal supplier of agricultural produce to state markets, and a responsible borrower. Rural Kenyans contested this vision of citizenship by withdrawing from cooperatives, selling agricultural goods on the black market, and paying back loans at a rate that accommodated their specific needs and visions of prosperity. In the process, they claimed rights to economic freedoms. Though rural Kenyans often contested citizenly duties that restricted economic autonomy, many willingly took on other expected duties, including feeding the nation and contributing to local development.

During the country's first postcolonial food shortage, many Kenyans demanded that the state take on the obligation of providing famine relief. Self-help programming also raised questions about state responsibility, particularly whether the performance of citizenly duties obligated the state to deliver assistance. Citizens and community groups shouldered enormous burdens in local development. When they built schools, roads, and hospitals, Kenyan self-help groups asserted their rights to local sovereignty, but increasingly, they called upon the state to aid their projects. With the government often unable to provide help, and widely perceived to be offering limited assistance inequitably, many Uasin Gishu residents came to believe that the state had not kept its promises to help those who first helped themselves. Similar to the maize crisis, self-help shaped expectations for more limited state obligations and pushed rural Kenyans to strengthen subnational affinities that could provide protection and assistance.

Residents of the western highlands perceived a disjuncture between state promises and practices, they contested and reworked notions of developmentalist citizenship, and some felt excluded from state resources and protections. Still, the state remained an option for assistance, as individual actors represented inconsistent channels to state aid. Rural Kenyans worked to exploit the different nodes of power in postcolonial Kenya, both within and without the state, extending from neighborhood elders to the Office of the President, and even, occasionally, all the way up to foreign leaders. Attempting to form partnerships with powerful, multitiered actors tended to produce patronage-based political practices, as Turbo afforestation exemplified. Simultaneously, rural Kenyans shored up local attachments and built, or participated in, nonstate institutions, always recognizing the multiple avenues to development that existed.

When they evaluated the independence proffered to them, residents of the western highlands took into account many overlapping factors—land access, local politics, material realities, government promises, bureaucratic effectiveness, ethnic ideologies, global economies, familial relationships, personal histories, and much more. Centering on rural Kenyan perspectives reveals the texture of political debate, and the differentiated understandings of independence, development, citizenship, and governance that emerged during this period.

Rural development has been at the heart of this book, because Kenya was profoundly rural. These development programs shaped the construction of new political ideologies, they deeply affected the nation's economy, and they altered the quotidian realities of ordinary people. Ultimately, the uneven distribution of development resources and social services produced new material existences, preserving—and in some cases, expanding—the unprecedented inequalities colonialism had first introduced. Growing disparities perpetuated and evolved long-standing debates within Kenyan society about justice and egalitarianism in their communities and in their nation. Since independence, such inequalities have remained largely unaddressed, though they have continually threatened the postcolonial order, creating discontentment and catalyzing resistance.

Archival Source Abbreviations and Labels Used in Notes

ABGC (ARCHIVES OF THE BILLY GRAHAM CENTER, WHEATON, ILLINOIS)

Collection 81	Africa Inland Mission, International

AIMRO (AFRICA INLAND MISSION REGIONAL OFFICE ARCHIVES, NAIROBI)

Box 1	Correspondence, A.-Dal
Box 9	Literature and Language
Box 10	Tribes Areas Mission Stations
Box 16	Educational Program, Policy Reports, Etc.
Box 24	Medical

CAC (UNIVERSITY OF CAMBRIDGE, CHURCHILL ARCHIVES CENTRE, CAMBRIDGE)

DOHP 118	Transcript of Interview—Buist, John
GBR/0014/AMEJ	Papers of Julian Amery
GBR/0115/RCMS 161	Papers of A. T. Matson
GBR/0115/RCMS 175	Kenya Days

JFKL (JOHN F. KENNEDY PRESIDENTIAL LIBRARY, BOSTON, MASSACHUSETTS)

NSF	Presidential Papers, National Security Files
WHCSF	Presidential Papers, White House Central Subject Files

KNA (KENYA NATIONAL ARCHIVES, NAIROBI)

The file names below reflect the classification system used from 2010 through 2018.

AB	Ministry of Community Development
ACW	Ministry of Finance

AE	Ministry of Economic Planning and Development
AVS	Department of Land Adjudication (Ministry of Lands and Settlement)
BA	Ministry of Environment and Natural Resources
BN	Lands Office (Ministry of Lands and Settlement)
BV	Ministry of Agriculture
BY	Ministry of Health
CAB	Central Agricultural Board
DC/ELD	District Commissioner, Eldoret
DC/KMG	District Commissioner, Kakamega
DC/KPT	District Commissioner, Kapsabet
DC/TAMB	District Commissioner, Tambach
DC/UG	District Commissioner, Uasin Gishu
DX	Ministry of Lands and Settlement
HB	Provincial Commissioner, Western Province
JA	Ministry of Local Government
KA	Office of the President
KY	Housing Development Department (Ministry of Works)
MAA	Ministry of African Affairs
MOH	Ministry of Health
PC/NKU	Provincial Commissioner, Nakuru
PC/RVP	Provincial Commissioner, Rift Valley Province
TR	Ministry of Cooperative Development and Marketing
VF	Forestry Department (Ministry of Environment and Natural Resources)
XJ	Ministry of Education

NAUK (NATIONAL ARCHIVES OF THE UK, KEW)

CO 533	Colonial Office: Kenya Original Correspondence, 1905–51
CO 822	Colonial Office: East Africa Original Correspondence, 1927–64
CO 895	Kenya Constituencies Delimitation Commission Papers, 1962
CO 897	Colonial Office: Kenya Regional Boundaries Commission Papers, 1962
CO 1054	Colonial Office and Successors: Maps and Plans, Post-1940 Collection
DO 213	Commonwealth Relations Office and Commonwealth Office: East Africa Departments, 1963–67
DO 214	Commonwealth Relations Office and Commonwealth Office: East Africa Economic Department, 1964–66
FCO 31	Commonwealth Office and Foreign and Commonwealth Office: East Africa Departments, 1967–80
FCO 141	Foreign and Commonwealth Office and Predecessors: Records of Former Colonial Administrations, Migrated Archives, 1835–2012
FO 925	Foreign Office: Library, Maps and Plans
OD 16	Department of Technical Co-Operation and Successors: Personnel Services
OD 26	Department of Technical Co-Operation and Successors: East Africa Department, 1964–75
T 236	Treasury: Overseas Finance Division, 1919–79

RHL (UNIVERSITY OF OXFORD, BODLEIAN LIBRARY OF COMMONWEALTH AND AFRICAN STUDIES AT RHODES HOUSE, OXFORD)

MSS Afr s 746 Papers of Sir Michael Blundell
MSS Afr s 1669 Papers of William Crawford Heaney
MSS Afr s 1688 Papers of J. Michael Popkin, 1946–64
MSS Afr s 1843 Papers of Patrick Edward W. Williams
MSS Afr s 2229/1 Papers of W. F. P. Kelly
MSS Afr s 2234/1 Papers of T. G. Askwith

RVPRC (RIFT VALLEY PROVINCIAL RECORD CENTER, NAKURU)

ED Uasin Gishu District
ZL Land Disputes

SOAS (SCHOOL OF ORIENTAL AND AFRICAN STUDIES—UNIVERSITY OF LONDON, SPECIAL COLLECTIONS, LONDON)

CA Christian Aid, c. 1946–1990s
ICA Inter-Church Aid Constitutional Papers, 1949–60
PP MS 17 Huntingford, George Wynn Brereton, 1920s–1974
PP MS 46 Hake, Andrew, 1949–91

NACP (NATIONAL ARCHIVES AT COLLEGE PARK, MARYLAND)

286 Department of State

WBGA (WORLD BANK GROUP ARCHIVES, WASHINGTON, DC)

1082474 Correspondence with Ex Agriculture Development Service Staff, Vol. 5
1413176 Kenya: General—1972–74 Correspondence, Vol. 1
1413177 Kenya: General—1975–80 Correspondence, Vol. 1
1413805 Kenya: Agriculture Sector—1972–74 Correspondence, Vol. 1
1575763 East Africa: General—Correspondence, Vol. 1
1575861 East Africa: General—Technical Assistance, 1969–71 Correspondence, Vol. 1
1575864 East Africa: General—Treaty for Co-Operation, 1969–71 Correspondence, Vol. 1
1575878 East Africa: ADS—Admin, Correspondence, Vol. 2
1575882 East Africa: Agricultural Development Service—Reports, Vol. 1

1575904 East Africa: Agriculture—General, Correspondence, Vol. 1
1865536 Kenya: General—Technical Assistance, Correspondence, Vol. 1
1865537 Kenya: General—Technical Assistance. 1969–71 Correspondence, Vol. 1
1870259 Africa: General—Mission, Mr. Shoaib, Kenya, Correspondence, Vol. 1
30261245 Kenya: General—1975–80 Correspondence, Vol. 2

Notes

INTRODUCTION

1. KNA BV/1/538, Zebedeo T. Omwando to His Highness the President, United States of America, "Farming Loan," 15 July 1961.

2. KNA BV/1/538, Richard B. Freund, American Consul General, to Mr. Zebedeo T. Omwando, Catholic Mission, Kisii South Nyanza, 8 March 1962.

3. JFKL, Papers of John F. Kennedy, Presidential Papers, National Security Files, Series 01. Countries, Box 127, Folder Kenya: General, 1961, L. D. Battle, Executive Secretary, Memorandum for Mr. McGeorge Bundy, The White House, "Subject: Presentation to the President of a Carved Walking Stick from the Kamba Tribe of Kenya," 29 August 1961.

4. The British Parliament passed the Colonial Development and Welfare Act in 1940, while the French passed the Investment Fund for Economic and Social Development in 1946. Some scholars have questioned this chronology, arguing that colonial development, or its conceptualization, began earlier: David M. Anderson and David Throup, "Africans and Agricultural Production in Colonial Kenya: The Myth of the War as a Watershed," *Journal of African History* 26, no. 4 (1985): 327–45; Dorothy L. Hodgson, *Once Intrepid Warriors: Gender, Ethnicity, and the Cultural Politics of Maasai Development* (Bloomington: Indiana University Press, 2001); Monica Van Beusekom, *Negotiating Development: African Farmers and Colonial Experts at the Office Du Niger, 1920–1960* (Portsmouth, NH: Heinemann, 2002); Helen Tilley, *Africa as a Living Laboratory: Empire, Development, and the Problem of Scientific Knowledge, 1870–1950* (Chicago: University of Chicago Press, 2011).

5. For clarity, IBRD is generally referred to as the World Bank.

6. KNA KA/6/20, Kericho Township Residents to Jomo Kenyatta, 13 December 1972.

7. On the expansion of nongovernmental organizations during decolonization, see Matthew Hilton, "Charity and the End of Empire: British Non-Governmental Organizations, Africa, and International Development in the 1960s," *American Historical Review* 123, no. 2 (2018): 493–517.

8. Frederick Cooper's emphasis on the concurrent emergence of international development and independent African states has been influential, and other scholars have expanded his findings. Cooper, *Decolonization and African Society: The Labor Question in French and British Africa* (Cambridge: Cambridge University Press, 1996); Frederick Cooper and Randall M. Packard, eds., *International Development and the Social Sciences: Essays on the History and Politics of Knowledge* (Berkeley: University of California Press, 1997); Joanna Lewis, *Empire State-Building: War and Welfare in Kenya, 1925–52* (Athens: Ohio University Press, 2001); John Aerni-Flessner,

"Development, Politics, and the Centralization of State Power in Lesotho, 1960–75," *Journal of African History* 55, no. 3 (2014): 401–21; Giacomo Macola, "'It Means as If We Are Excluded from the Good Freedom': Thwarted Expectations of Independence in the Luapula Province of Zambia, 1964–6," *Journal of African History* 47, no. 1 (2004): 43–56; Kate Skinner, "Who Knew the Minds of the People? Specialist Knowledge and Developmentalist Authoritarianism in Postcolonial Ghana," *Journal of Imperial and Commonwealth History* 39, no. 2 (2011): 297–323; Michael Jennings, *Surrogates of the State: NGOs, Development, and Ujamaa in Tanzania* (Bloomfield, CT: Kumarian Press, 2008).

9. Bethwell A. Ogot and William R. Ochieng', eds., *Decolonization and Independence in Kenya, 1940–93* (London: James Currey, 1995).

10. Much of the literature has focused on urban and metropolitan actors: Cooper, *Decolonization and African Society*; Elizabeth Schmidt, *Cold War and Decolonization in Guinea, 1946–1958* (Athens: Ohio University Press, 2007); Todd Shepard, *The Invention of Decolonization: The Algerian War and the Remaking of France* (Ithaca, NY: Cornell University Press, 2006); John W. Harbeson, *Nation-Building in Kenya: The Role of Land Reform* (Evanston, IL: Northwestern University Press, 1973); Gary Wasserman, *Politics of Decolonization: Kenya, Europeans and the Land Issue, 1960–1965* (Cambridge: Cambridge University Press, 1976).

11. An emerging scholarship has highlighted the deliberations of a wider set of actors, and has provided new understandings of decolonization as a fraught historical process, marked by alternative political projects. Yet these works have centered on national leaders and party activists, or have relied on newspapers to understand non-elite ideologies. Frederick Cooper, *Citizenship between Empire and Nation: Remaking France and French Africa, 1945–1960* (Princeton, NJ: Princeton University Press, 2014); Kate Skinner, *The Fruits of Freedom in British Togoland: Literacy, Politics and Nationalism, 1914–2014* (New York: Cambridge University Press, 2015); Schmidt, *Cold War and Decolonization*; Emma Hunter, *Political Thought and the Public Sphere in Tanzania: Freedom, Democracy and Citizenship in the Era of Decolonization* (New York: Cambridge University Press, 2015).

12. Most famously, James C. Scott, *Seeing Like a State: How Certain Schemes to Improve the Human Condition Have Failed* (New Haven, CT: Yale University Press, 1998). For a critique: Daniel Immerwahr, *Thinking Small: The United States and the Lure of Community Development* (Cambridge, MA: Harvard University Press, 2015).

13. Arturo Escobar's work has influenced much of this discursive scholarship. See Escobar, *Encountering Development: The Making and Unmaking of the Third World* (Princeton, NJ: Princeton University Press, 1995). For a critique of Escobar: Peter D. Little and Michael Painter, "Discourse, Politics, and the Development Process: Reflections on Escobar's 'Anthropology and the Development Encounter,'" *American Ethnologist* 22, no. 3 (1995): 602.

14. Cooper, *Decolonization and African Society*; James Ferguson, *The Anti-Politics Machine: "Development," Depoliticization, and Bureaucratic Power in Lesotho* (Minneapolis: University of Minnesota Press, 1994); Leander Schneider, *Government of Development: Peasants and Politicians in Postcolonial Tanzania* (Bloomington: Indiana University Press, 2014); Benedetta Rossi, *From Slavery to Aid: Politics, Labour, and Ecology in the Nigerien Sahel, 1800–2000* (New York: Cambridge University Press, 2015), 22. For exceptions, see Van Beusekom, *Negotiating Development*; Priya Lal,

African Socialism in Postcolonial Tanzania: Between the Village and the World (New York: Cambridge University Press, 2015).

15. Colin Leys, *The Rise and Fall of Development Theory* (London: James Currey, 1996), vi, 7.

16. Such ideas can be found, for example, in Kenya People's Union, *KPU Manifesto* (Nairobi: Pan Africa Press, 1967); and in Republic of Kenya, *African Socialism and Its Application to Planning in Kenya* (Nairobi: Information Services of Kenya, 1965).

17. Ruth Malakwen Cheptekeny, interview by author, Leseru, 9 January 2013; Simon Limo, interview by author, Leseru, 27 November 2012; Kipkugat arap Ngososei, interview by author, Leseru, 27 November 2012; David Tororei, interview by author, Sosiani, 3 December 2012.

18. Cooper, *Decolonization and African Society*. See also Frederick Cooper, *Africa since 1940: The Past of the Present* (Cambridge: Cambridge University Press, 2002), chap. 7. James Ferguson and Akhil Gupta emphasize the need to approach analyses of the state with more complicated spatializations than simply "up there." Ferguson and Gupta, "Spatializing States: Toward an Ethnography of Neoliberal Governmentality," *American Ethnologist* 29, no. 4 (2002): 981–1002.

19. Tania Murray Li, "Beyond 'the State' and Failed Schemes," *American Anthropologist* 107, no. 3 (2005): 383–94; Matthew Connelly, "Seeing Beyond the State: The Population Control Movement and the Problem of Sovereignty," *Past and Present*, no. 193 (2006): 197–233.

20. Ferguson, *Anti-Politics Machine*, xiv. For an exception, see Achille Mbembe's notion of the "illicit cohabitation" between state and society: Mbembe, "Provisional Notes on the Postcolony," *Africa* 62, no. 1 (1992): 4.

21. There is a growing literature on cosmopolitanism in Africa: Harri Englund, "Cosmopolitanism and the Devil in Malawi," *Ethnos* 69, no. 3 (2004): 293–316; Kwame Anthony Appiah, *Cosmopolitanism: Ethics in a World of Strangers* (New York: W. W. Norton, 2006); Andrew Ivaska, *Cultured States: Youth, Gender, and Modern Style in 1960s Dar es* Salaam (Durham, NC: Duke University Press, 2011); Mike McGovern, *Unmasking the State: Making Guinea Modern* (Chicago: University of Chicago Press, 2013); Julie MacArthur, *Cartography and the Political Imagination: Mapping Community in Colonial Kenya* (Athens: Ohio University Press, 2016).

22. Scholars have largely focused on bilateral interactions—between citizens and the state, between rural actors and local elites, and between states and transnational institutions. Angelique Haugerud, *The Culture of Politics in Modern Kenya* (Cambridge: Cambridge University Press, 1995); Achille Mbembe, *On the Postcolony* (Berkeley: University of California Press, 2001); Sara Berry, *No Condition Is Permanent: The Social Dynamics of Agrarian Change in Sub-Saharan Africa* (Madison: University of Wisconsin Press, 1993). For exceptions, see Meredith Terretta, *Nation of Outlaws, State of Violence: Nationalism, Grassfields Tradition, and State Building in Cameroon* (Athens: Ohio University Press, 2014); Molly McCullers, "'The Time of the United Nations in South West Africa Is Near': Local Drama and Global Politics in Apartheid-Era Hereroland," *Journal of Southern African Studies* 39, no. 2 (2013): 371–89.

23. For works that question the accepted periodization, see Gregory Mann, *From Empires to NGOs in the West African Sahel: The Road to Nongovernmentality* (New York: Cambridge University Press, 2014); Jean Comaroff and John L. Comaroff, *Theory from the South: Or, How Euro-America Is Evolving toward Africa* (Boulder, CO:

Paradigm, 2012); Talbot C. Imlay, "International Socialism and Decolonization during the 1950s: Competing Rights and the Postcolonial Order," *American Historical Review* 118, no. 4 (2013): 1105–32.

24. James Ferguson, *Global Shadows: Africans in the Neoliberal World Order* (Durham, NC: Duke University Press, 2006), 5.

25. Mann calls this "nongovernmentality," though Ferguson and Gupta would call the same phenomenon, in a later period, "transnational governmentality." Mann, *From Empires to NGOs*; Ferguson and Gupta, "Spatializing States."

26. Kelly M. Askew, *Performing the Nation: Swahili Music and Cultural Politics in Tanzania* (Chicago: University of Chicago Press, 2002), 5.

27. Helen Kirua, interview by author, Leseru, 3 December 2012; Joseph Dugere Munge, interview by author, Mautuma, 11 November 2012.

28. *Baraza* were a long-standing political tradition in Kenya adapted from coastal Swahili society for use in the colonial and postcolonial periods: Haugerud, *Culture of Politics in Modern Kenya*.

29. For more on the ways in which a translocal institution "is made visible in localized practices," see Akhil Gupta, "Blurred Boundaries: The Discourse of Corruption, the Culture of Politics, and the Imagined State," in *The Anthropology of the State: A Reader*, ed. Aradhana Sharma and Akhil Gupta (Malden, MA: Blackwell, 2006), 212.

30. Frederick Kemboi arap Tum Kaptulus, interview by author, Leseru, 9 June 2015.

31. KNA JA/7/7, D. N. Ndegwa, PS, Office of the President, "Commission on Local Government. Memorandum by the Office of the President," July 1966.

32. William Serem, interview by author, Leseru, 3 December 2012.

33. WBGA, IBRD/IDA AFR, East Africa, 1082474, Correspondence with ex-Agriculture Development Service Staff-Vol. 5, L. J. C. Evans, "The ADS" [undated].

34. John Lonsdale, "Moral Ethnicity, Ethnic Nationalism and Political Tribalism: The Case of the Kikuyu," in *Staat und Gesellschaft in Afrika: Erosions und Reformprozesse*, ed. Peter Meyns (Hamburg: Lit Verlag, 1996), 93–106; Derek R. Peterson, *Ethnic Patriotism and the East African Revival: A History of Dissent, c. 1935–1972* (Cambridge: Cambridge University Press, 2012).

35. Derek Sayer suggests that state formation provides openings for citizens to reconfigure the political order: Sayer, "Everyday Forms of State Formation: Some Dissident Remarks on 'Hegemony,'" in *Everyday Forms of State Formation: Revolution and the Negotiation of Rule in Modern Mexico*, ed. Gilbert M. Joseph and Daniel Nugent (Durham, NC: Duke University Press, 1994), 369.

36. Sally Kogo, interview by author, Leseru, 23 November 2012.

37. KNA AVS/4/4, R. St. J. Matthews, Civil Secretary, Nyanza Region, to the Director of Settlement, SFT, "Roads and Health Services in Settlement Schemes," 18 April 1964.

38. Scott, *Seeing Like a State*, 5.

39. Scott, *Seeing Like a State*, 2.

40. Historical analysis of African political philosophies has focused principally on ethnic ideologies, but more recent scholarship has examined the construction of citizenship: Lahra Smith, *Making Citizens in Africa: Ethnicity, Gender, and National Identity in Ethiopia* (Cambridge: Cambridge University Press, 2013); Cooper, *Citizenship between Empire and Nation*; Jeffrey S. Ahlman, *Living with Nkrumahism: Nation, State, and Pan-Africanism in Ghana* (Athens: Ohio University Press, 2017).

41. MacArthur, *Cartography and the Political Imagination*; Stephen N. Ndegwa, "Citizenship and Ethnicity: An Examination of Two Transition Moments in Kenyan Politics," *American Political Science Review* 91, no. 3 (1997): 600.

42. Hannah Arendt, *The Origins of Totalitarianism* (New York: Harcourt, Brace, 1951), 177; Margaret R. Somers, *Genealogies of Citizenship: Markets, Statelessness, and the Right to Have Rights* (Cambridge: Cambridge University Press, 2008).

43. Niraja Gopal Jayal, *Citizenship and Its Discontents: An Indian History* (Cambridge, MA: Harvard University Press, 2013).

44. Charles Tilly, "Epilogue: Now Where?" in *State/Culture: State Formation after the Cultural Turn*, ed. George Steinmetz (Ithaca, NY: Cornell University Press, 1999).

45. Citizenly duties were important for nation-building in many parts of Africa. Priya Lal, "Self-Reliance and the State: The Multiple Meanings of Development in Early Post-Colonial Tanzania," *Africa* 82, no. 2 (2012): 212–34; Emma Hunter, "Voluntarism, Virtuous Citizenship, and Nation-Building in Late Colonial and Early Postcolonial Tanzania," *African Studies Review* 58, no. 2 (2015): 43–61.

46. Daniel Kebeney Bitok, interview by author, Leseru, 26 November 2012.

47. Eunice Tele Maiyo, interview by author, Leseru, 9 January 2013.

48. Daniel Kebeney Bitok, interview by author, Leseru, 26 November 2012.

49. Daniel Kebeney Bitok, interview by author, Leseru, 26 November 2012.

50. The Kenyan literature includes rich studies of ethnic identity and ethnic nationalism: Bruce J. Berman and John Lonsdale, *Unhappy Valley: Conflict in Kenya and Africa*, bk. 2, *Violence and Ethnicity* (Athens: Ohio University Press, 1992); Derek R. Peterson, *Creative Writing: Translation, Bookkeeping, and the Work of Imagination in Colonial Kenya* (Portsmouth, NH: Heinemann, 2004); David W. Cohen and E. S. Atieno Odhiambo, *Siaya: The Historical Anthropology of an African Landscape* (London: James Currey, 1989); Thomas Spear and Richard Waller, eds., *Being Maasai: Ethnicity and Identity in East Africa* (London: James Currey, 1993); Gabrielle Lynch, *I Say to You: Ethnic Politics and the Kalenjin in Kenya* (Chicago: University of Chicago Press, 2011); Bill Bravman, *Making Ethnic Ways: Communities and Their Transformations in Taita, Kenya, 1800–1950* (Portsmouth, NH: Heinemann, 1998); Justin Willis, *Mombasa, the Swahili, and the Making of the Mijikenda* (Oxford: Clarendon Press, 1993).

51. G. W. B. Huntingford, *The Nandi of Kenya: Tribal Control in a Pastoral Society* (London: Routledge, 1953), 23.

52. Rose Ruto-Korir, "The Faint Voice in Academia, Including the Excluded: An Analysis of the Psychology of Nandi Proverbs and Its place in Critical Psychology," *Annual Review of Critical* Psychology 5 (2006): 333; Richard Kemboi, email conversation with author, 28 December 2017.

53. CAC, RCMS 161/2/2/1-2, A. T. Matson, "The Nandi Election, 1961."

54. Godfrey K. Sang, *Just for Today: The Life and Times of Jean-Marie Seroney* (Coventry: Dolman Scott, 2015), 195–96.

55. Ben E. Kipkorir, *People of the Rift Valley: Kalenjin* (London: Evans Brothers, 1978), 3–4.

56. Karuti Kanyinga, "The Land Question in Kenya: Struggles, Accumulation and Changing Politics" (PhD diss., Roskilde University, 1998), 226.

57. Lynch, *I Say to You*, 39, 47, 96.

58. Ainea Alulu, interview by author, Lumakanda, 20 July 2016; Frederick Kemboi arap Tum Kaptulus, interview by author, Leseru, 21 July 2016; Pauline Tum, interview by author, Leseru, 21 July 2016.

59. See, for example, JFKL, WHCSF, Series 17, Gifts (GI), Box 269; NAUK FCO 141/7141.

60. Fay Gadsden, "The African Press in Kenya, 1945–1952," *Journal of African History* 21, no. 4 (1980): 532; Graham Mytton, *Mass Communication in Africa* (London: Edward Arnold, 1983), 3; Steven Feierman, *Peasant Intellectuals: Anthropology and History in Tanzania* (Madison: University of Wisconsin Press, 1990), 251.

61. Kenya African National Union and Jomo Kenyatta, *The KANU Manifesto* (Cairo: Dar El-Hana Press, 1960), 13–14; Jomo Kenyatta, *Harambee! The Prime Minister of Kenya's Speeches, 1963–1964: From the Attainment of Internal Self-Government to the Threshold of the Kenya Republic* (Nairobi: Oxford University Press, 1964), chap. 3–4.

62. See Bruce J. Berman and John Lonsdale, *Unhappy Valley: Conflict in Kenya and Africa*, bk. 1, *State and Class*; and bk. 2, *Violence and Ethnicity* (Athens: Ohio University Press, 1992); Tabitha Kanogo, *Squatters and the Roots of Mau Mau, 1905–63* (Athens: Ohio University Press, 1987); David M. Anderson, *Eroding the Commons: The Politics of Ecology in Baringo, Kenya, 1890s–1963* (Athens: Ohio University Press, 2002); Peterson, *Creative Writing*; Kenda Mutongi, *Worries of the Heart: Widows, Family, and Community in Kenya* (Chicago: University of Chicago Press, 2007); Fiona Mackenzie, *Land, Ecology and Resistance in Kenya, 1880–1952* (Edinburgh: Edinburgh University Press, 1998); MacArthur, *Cartography and the Political Imagination*.

63. Colin Leys, *Underdevelopment in Kenya: The Political Economy of Neo-Colonialism, 1964–1971* (Berkeley: University of California Press, 1975); Geoff B. Lamb, *Peasant Politics: Conflict and Development in Murang'a* (New York: St. Martin's Press, 1974); Gavin N. Kitching, *Class and Economic Change in Kenya: The Making of an African Petite-Bourgeoisie, 1905–1970* (New Haven, CT: Yale University Press, 1980); Joel D. Barkan and Frank Holmquist, "Peasant-State Relations and the Social Base of Self-Help in Kenya," *World Politics* 41, no. 3 (1989): 359–80; Wasserman, *Politics of Decolonization*; Harbeson, *Nation-Building in Kenya*.

64. Daniel Branch, *Kenya: Between Hope and Despair, 1963–2011* (New Haven, CT: Yale University Press, 2011); David M. Anderson, "'Yours in Struggle for Majimbo': Nationalism and the Party Politics of Decolonization in Kenya, 1955–64," *Journal of Contemporary History* 40, no. 3 (2005): 547–64.

65. For recent works that move beyond the ethnic paradigm, see Keren Weitzberg, *We Do Not Have Borders: Greater Somalia and the Predicaments of Belonging in Kenya* (Athens: Ohio University Press, 2017), 5; Paul Ocobock, *An Uncertain Age: The Politics of Manhood in Kenya* (Athens: Ohio University Press, 2017), 6–7.

66. MacArthur, *Cartography and the Political Imagination*.

67. Kanyinga, "Land Question in Kenya," 168–69.

68. Christopher P. Youe, "Settler Capital and the Assault on the Squatter Peasantry in Kenya's Uasin Gishu District, 1942–63," *African Affairs* 87, no. 348 (1988): 393.

69. The place-name Uasin Gishu is derived from the Uas Nkishu Maasai.

70. The 2010 constitution reformed Kenya's electoral constituencies. The forty-seven districts of Kenya in 1992—which had ballooned in the two decades that followed—became forty-seven counties in 2010. Uasin Gishu, a former colonial and independent district, is one of these counties.

71. John E. G. Sutton, "The Kalenjin," in *Kenya before 1900*, ed. Bethwell A. Ogot (Nairobi: East African Publishing House, 1976).

72. Christopher Ehret, "Aspects of Social and Economic Change in Western Kenya, c. A.D. 500–1800," in Ogot, *Kenya before 1900*, 1.

73. This section relies largely on secondary sources, along with some oral traditions collected by the author. This deeper ethnohistory is helpful for interpreting the modern historical period. Richard Reid, "Past and Presentism: The 'Precolonial' and the Foreshortening of African History," *Journal of African History* 52, no. 2 (2011): 135–55.

74. Ehret, "Aspects of Social and Economic Change in Western Kenya," 4; Alice E. Gold, "The Nandi in Transition: Background to the Nandi Resistance to the British, 1895–1906," *Kenya Historical Review* 6, nos. 1–2 (1978): 91. To use Nandi here is anachronistic.

75. A. T. Matson, *Nandi Resistance to British Rule, 1890–1906* (Nairobi: East African Publishing House, 1972), 11; Matson, "Nandi Traditions on Raiding," in *Hadith 2: Proceedings of the Annual Conference of the Historical Association of Kenya*, ed. Bethwell A. Ogot (Nairobi: East African Publishing House, 1970), 73–74; John Lonsdale, "The Conquest State of Kenya, 1895–1905," in Berman and Lonsdale, *Unhappy Valley*, bk. 1, 20; Ehret, "Aspects of Social and Economic Change in Western Kenya," 12; Christopher Ehret, *The Civilizations of Africa: A History to 1800* (Charlottesville: University Press of Virginia, 2002), 394; Gold, "Nandi in Transition," 89; MacArthur, *Cartography and the Political Imagination*, 42–43.

76. Kimeli Korir, interview by author, Nairobi, 13 July 2018.

77. Sutton, "Kalenjin," 26.

78. Matson, *Nandi Resistance to British Rule*, 17.

79. Sutton, "Kalenjin"; Richard D. Waller, "Interaction and Identity on the Periphery: The Trans-Mara Maasai," *International Journal of African Historical Studies* 17, no. 2 (1984): 250.

80. Richard D. Waller, "The Maasai and the British, 1895–1905: The Origins of an Alliance," *Journal of African History* 17, no. 4 (1976): 532.

81. Waller, "Interaction and Identity on the Periphery," 250–51.

82. P. K. arap Magut, "The Rise and Fall of the Nandi Orkoiyot, c. 1850–1957," in *Ngano: Studies in Traditional and Modern East African History*, ed. Brian G. McIntosh (Nairobi: East African Publishing House, 1969), 95–109; Alfred C. Hollis, *The Nandi: Their Language and Folk-Lore* (Oxford: Clarendon Press, 1909).

83.While powers of the *orkoiik* (diviners) were hereditary among the Talai clan, only some members of the clan could use those powers. David M. Anderson, "Black Mischief: Crime, Protest and Resistance in Colonial Kenya," *Historical Journal* 36, no. 4 (1993): 855.

84. Gold, "Nandi in Transition," 92.

85. Luise White, *The Comforts of Home: Prostitution in Colonial Nairobi* (Chicago: University of Chicago Press, 1990), 21.

86. Lonsdale, "Conquest State," 18.

87. This is not to suggest that the precolonial past was an idyllic period in which there was no death, conflict, disease, violence, or drought. Rather, an equilibrium kept these environmental and human insecurities in check.

88. Richard D. Waller, "Emutai: Crisis and Response in Maasailand, 1883–1902," in *The Ecology of Survival: Case Studies from Northeast African History*, ed. Douglas H. Johnson and David M. Anderson (London: Lester Crook Academic, 1988), 73.

89. Waller, "Emutai," 73.

90. Lonsdale, "Conquest State," 23.

91. White, *Comforts of Home*, 29; Waller, "Emutai," 112.

92. Lonsdale, "Conquest State," 29; Hollis, *Nandi*, 50; Magut, "Rise and Fall of the Nandi Orkoiyot," 101; Gold, "Nandi in Transition," 95.

93. Gold, "Nandi in Transition," 96; Magut, "Rise and Fall of the Nandi Orkoiyot," 102.

94. In fact, Koitalel's importance supersedes his father's to such an extent that contemporary oral traditions diverge from the oral histories taken in the early twentieth century, with many Nandi today crediting Koitalel for prophesying the British arrival.

95. Gold, "Nandi in Transition," 96.

96. For the fullest account of the Nandi resistance at the end of the nineteenth century, see Matson, *Nandi Resistance to British Rule*.

97. Construction of the railway began in the port city of Mombasa in 1896 and ended in Kisumu in western Kenya in 1901.

98. Lonsdale, "Conquest State," 29.

99. Diana Ellis, "The Nandi Protest of 1923 in the Context of African Resistance to Colonial Rule in Kenya," *Journal of African History* 17, no. 4 (1976): 557.

100. Gold, "Nandi in Transition," 91.

101. Sutton, "Kalenjin," 24.

102. Waller, "Maasai and the British," 536.

103. Robert L. Tignor, "The Maasai Warriors: Pattern Maintenance and Violence in Colonial Kenya," *Journal of African History* 13, no. 2 (1972): 275; Lonsdale, "Conquest State," 28. Estimates of the Nandi population at the time vary. Ellis says the population was around 40,000 in 1905, while Matson puts it at 20–30,000. Ellis, "Nandi Protest of 1923," 557; Matson, *Nandi Resistance to British Rule*, 13.

104. Anderson, "Black Mischief," 858; Gold, "Nandi in Transition," 98; Magut, "Rise and Fall of the Nandi Orkoiyot," 103–4.

105. Anderson, "Black Mischief," 860. Conquest upset the social order regulating young men's acquisition of cattle, wives, and authority, which had formerly been almost wholly dependent on familial elders.

106. H. W. O. Okoth-Ogendo, *Tenants of the Crown: Evolution of Agrarian Law and Institutions in Kenya* (Nairobi: ACTS Press, 1991), 15.

107. Ben E. Kipkorir, *The Marakwet of Kenya: A Preliminary Study* (Nairobi: East African Literature Bureau, 1973); Geoffrey S. Snell, *Nandi Customary Law* (London: Macmillan, 1954), 47.

108. Ellis, "Nandi Protest of 1923," 558. The colonial government tried to "depasturize" the Nandi by taking large tracts of grazing land to encourage farming.

109. Berry, *No Condition Is Permanent*, 84.

110. Jacqueline Klopp, "Can Moral Ethnicity Trump Political Tribalism? The Struggle for Land and Nation in Kenya," *African Studies* 61, no. 2 (2002): 276–77.

111. While Kikuyu squatters made up the biggest group of resident laborers on settler estates in the white highlands during the colonial period, most worked east of Uasin Gishu. Kanogo, *Squatters and the Roots of Mau Mau*, 1.

112. Cooper, *Decolonization and African Society*; Timothy Parsons, *The African Rank-and-File: Social Implications of Colonial Military Service in the King's African Rifles, 1902–1964* (Portsmouth, NH: Heinemann, 1999), 94.

113. Gadsden, "African Press in Kenya," 515. A great deal of evidence from throughout the continent demonstrates that as Luise White has argued, "virtually all newspapers were read by more than one person, and many more were read aloud, translated, summarized, amended." White, *Speaking with Vampires: Rumor and*

History in Colonial Africa (Berkeley: University of California Press, 2000), 252. See also Jonathon Glassman, "Sorting out the Tribes: The Creation of Racial Identities in Colonial Zanzibar's Newspaper Wars," *Journal of African History* 41, no. 3 (2000): 395–428; Charles H. Ambler, "Mass Media and Leisure in Africa," *International Journal of African Historical Studies* 35, no. 1 (2002): 124.

114. Anderson, *Eroding the Commons*, 20.

115. Years-long efforts, and contestations, over how to standardize Kalenjin orthography preceded translation work. Stuart M. Bryson, *Light in Darkness: The Story of the Nandi Bible* (London: Parry Jackman Scripture Illustrations, 1959); AIMRO, Box 9, Literature and Language, Folder 2, Kalenjin Research and Folder 3, Kalenjin Correspondence; AIMRO, Box 1 Correspondence, Folders 3, 4, Stuart Bryson; ABGC, Kenya Folder 5, Box 34, Collection 81, Africa Inland Mission, International, Norman C. Thomas, Kenya Field Secretary, AIM, to Mr. David M. Gitari, the Bible Society of Kenya, 2 December 1971.

116. Monone Omosule, "Kalenjin: The Emergence of a Corporate Name for the 'Nandi-Speaking Tribes' of East Africa," *Geneve-Afrique* 27, no. 1 (1989): 79; Lynch, *I Say to You*, 38.

117. Gadsden, "African Press in Kenya," 515.

118. Mytton, *Mass Communication in Africa*, 3.

119. M. P. K. Sorrenson, *Land Reform in the Kikuyu Country: A Study in Government Policy* (Nairobi: Oxford University Press, 1967), 70, 117.

120. United Kingdom, Hansard Parliamentary Debates, "Written Answers," House of Commons, 29 April 1953, vol. 514: col 99.

121. Lynch, *I Say to You*, 38–39. See also Omosule, "Kalenjin," 75; Kipkorir, *People of the Rift Valley*, 2.

122. Lynch, *I Say to You*, 52.

123. Anderson, "'Yours in Struggle for Majimbo,'" 547.

124. Anderson, "'Yours in Struggle for Majimbo,'" 563.

125. Branch, *Kenya*, 9–10, 55–70. Most notably, the Kenya People's Union (KPU), a populist party, formed in 1966 and remained active until 1969, when the party was banned.

126. Ogot and Ochieng', *Decolonization and Independence in Kenya*, xii.

127. Shula Marks, *The Ambiguities of Dependence in South Africa: Class, Nationalism, and the State in Twentieth-Century Natal* (Baltimore, MD: Johns Hopkins Press, 1986); Lal, *African Socialism in Postcolonial Tanzania*, 17; James Ferguson, *Expectations of Modernity: Myths and Meanings of Urban Life on the Zambian Copperbelt* (Berkeley: University of California Press, 1999).

128. KNA BN/85/12, W. Wamalwa, PS Ministry of Economic Planning and Development, to all PSs, "Plan Implementation: Progress Reports," 9 July 1966.

129. I conducted archival and oral research during the summers of 2010 and 2011, from June 2012 to October 2013, and during the summers of 2015, 2016, and 2018.

130. In my oral historical methodology, I have been influenced by David W. Cohen, "Doing Social History from *Pim's* Doorway," in *Reliving the Past: The Worlds of Social History*, ed. Olivier Zunz (Chapel Hill: University of North Carolina Press, 1985); Steven Feierman, "Colonizers, Scholars, and the Creation of Invisible Histories," in *Beyond the Cultural Turn: New Directions in the Study of Society and Culture*, ed. Victoria E. Bonnell and Lynn Hunt (Berkeley: University of California Press, 1999); White, *Speaking with Vampires*; White, *Comforts of Home*; Luise White, Stephan F.

Miescher, and David W. Cohen, eds., *African Words, African Voices: Critical Practices in Oral History* (Bloomington: Indiana University Press, 2001).

131. I spoke with many Kenyans on multiple occasions and, in total, conducted 158 oral history sessions of around 155 hours altogether.

132. This area had historically been part of Uasin Gishu District, but became part of Kakamega District and Western Province during decolonization.

133. Feminist scholars, particularly those working in the Global South, have argued for the importance of women's life histories. Margaret Strobel, *Muslim Women in Mombasa, 1890–1975* (New Haven, CT: Yale University Press, 1979); Susan N. G. Geiger, "Women's Life Histories: Method and Content," *Signs* 11, no. 2 (1986): 334–51; Geiger, *TANU Women: Gender and Culture in the Making of Tanganyikan Nationalism, 1955–1965* (Portsmouth, NH: Heinemann, 1997).

134. The first set of oral histories took place in an uncertain political climate, ahead of the March 2013 elections. This contemporaneous political uncertainty, as well as longer histories of political violence in the Rift Valley, shaped recollections of the early postcolonial period.

135. Emma L. Jones, "Attitudes to Abortion in the Era of Reform: Evidence from the Abortion Law Reform Association Correspondence," *Women's History Review* 20, no. 2 (2011): 286.

CHAPTER 1: "CAN I BE ONE OF THEM?"

1. KNA DC/ELD/1/10/9, Ndugu Kariuki to the Ministry of Agriculture, the District Commissioner, Eldoret, 11 June 1960.

2. Many petitions were not written by the petitioners themselves, as evidenced by different applicants using identical language, or by typewritten letters using perfect English but then signed with a thumbprint. Here, it is helpful to draw on Peterson's ideas about how "writing scripts for people to follow" could "open up 'grooves of ideation' along which the political imagination could run." Derek R. Peterson, *Creative Writing: Translation, Bookkeeping, and the Work of Imagination in Colonial Kenya* (Portsmouth, NH: Heinemann, 2004), 3.

3. Colony and Protectorate of Kenya, *Legislative Council Debates, Official Report (Hansard)*, vol. 85, 20 July 1960.

4. Eugene R. Black, President of the World Bank Group, "Report and Recommendations of the President to the Executive Directors on a Proposed Loan to the Colony and Protectorate of Kenya," Washington, DC: World Bank Group, 20 November 1961, http://documents.worldbank.org/curated/en/356681468273331257/pdf/multiopage.pdf.

5. World Bank History Project, Brookings Institution, John Lewis, Richard Webb, Devesh Kapur, "Transcript of interview with Willi A. Wapenhans," Washington, DC, 6 September 1991.

6. International Bank for Reconstruction and Development, "Project for the Development and Settlement of Land in the Scheduled Areas, Kenya," 20 November 1961, http://documents.worldbank.org/curated/en/538671468091473751/pdf/multi-page.pdf.

7. The terms of the academic debate on land in Africa have remained narrow, with scholars largely focusing on rural class differentiation and ethnic conflict over land. In Kenya, historians have focused disproportionately on the Kikuyu. See

M. P. K. Sorrenson, *Land Reform in the Kikuyu Country: A Study in Government Policy* (Nairobi: Oxford University Press, 1967); Hans Ruthenberg, *African Agricultural Production Development Policy in Kenya, 1952–1965* (Berlin: Springer, 1966); Colin Leys, *Underdevelopment in Kenya: The Political Economy of Neo-Colonialism, 1964–1971* (Berkeley: University of California Press, 1975); Gavin N. Kitching, *Class and Economic Change in Kenya: The Making of an African Petite-Bourgeoisie, 1905–1970* (New Haven, CT: Yale University Press, 1980); Christopher Leo, *Land and Class in Kenya* (Toronto: University of Toronto Press, 1984); Sara Berry, *No Condition Is Permanent: The Social Dynamics of Agrarian Change in Sub-Saharan Africa* (Madison: University of Wisconsin Press, 1993); Pauline E. Peters, "Inequality and Social Conflict over Land in Africa, *Journal of Agrarian Change* 4, no. 3 (2004): 269–314.

8. The colonial administration referred to the European migrants who lived and farmed in Kenya as "settlers." During decolonization, Kenyans who purchased land through resettlement programs were also called "settlers." In order to distinguish between the two, European farmers in Kenya will always be referred to fully as "European settlers," "Europeans," or "white settlers."

9. *Report of the Kenya Land Commission* (London: His Majesty's Stationery Office, 1934).

10. H. W. O. Okoth-Ogendo, *Tenants of the Crown: Evolution of Agrarian Law and Institutions in Kenya* (Nairobi: ACTS Press, 1991), 59.

11. Berry, *No Condition Is Permanent*, 84.

12. David M. Anderson, *Histories of the Hanged: The Dirty War in Kenya and the End of Empire* (New York: W. W. Norton, 2005), 26.

13. Eunice Tele Maiyo, interview by author, Leseru, 9 January 2013; Kiptoo arap Maina, interview by author, Leseru, 23 November 2012; Helen Kirua, interview by author, Leseru, 3 December 2012.

14. Bruce J. Berman, "Bureaucracy and Incumbent Violence: Colonial Administration and the Origins of the 'Mau Mau' Emergency," in Bruce J. Berman and John Lonsdale, *Unhappy Valley: Conflict in Kenya and Africa*, bk. 2, *Violence and Ethnicity* (Athens: Ohio University Press, 1992), 254.

15. This represented a complete reversal of previous British colonial policy, which deemed Africans incapable of individual tenure or property rights. Martin Chanock, "Paradigms, Policies and Property: A Review of the Customary Law of Land Tenure," in *Law in Colonial Africa*, ed. Kristin Mann and Richard L. Roberts (Portsmouth, NH: Heinemann, 1991).

16. Sorrenson, *Land Reform in the Kikuyu Country*, 201.

17. KNA PC/RVP/2/3/6, Rift Valley Province Annual Report, 1950; KNA PC/RVP Rift Valley Province Annual Report, 1951.

18. Berry, *No Condition Is Permanent*. For analysis of how these processes aggravated gendered and generational tensions, see Fiona Mackenzie, "Gender and Land Rights in Murang'a District, Kenya," *Journal of Peasant Studies* 17, no. 4 (1990): 609–43; Julie MacArthur, *Cartography and the Political Imagination: Mapping Community in Colonial Kenya* (Athens: Ohio University Press, 2016), 196.

19. Leys, *Underdevelopment in Kenya*, 52.

20. Frederick Cooper, *Decolonization and African Society: The Labor Question in French and British Africa* (Cambridge: Cambridge University Press, 1996). Much of southern Africa represents an exception.

21. Peterson, *Creative Writing*, 11.

22. MacArthur, *Cartography and the Political Imagination*, 5–6.

23. Ian Spencer, "Settler Dominance, Agricultural Production and the Second World War in Kenya," *Journal of African History* 21, no. 4 (1980): 497–514.

24. KNA BN/81/144, Ministry of Agriculture, Animal Husbandry and Water Resources, "Confidential: Land Reform in the Scheduled Areas," 1959.

25. NAUK PREM 11/4979, "Note for the Prime Minister's Meeting on the 27th March with a Parliamentary Delegation led by Mr. Patrick Wall."

26. Daniel Branch, *Kenya: Between Hope and Despair, 1963–2011* (New Haven, CT: Yale University Press, 2011), 49–55.

27. Oginga Odinga, *Not Yet Uhuru: The Autobiography of Oginga Odinga* (New York: Hill and Wang, 1967), 257–59.

28. Leys, *Underdevelopment in Kenya*, 63.

29. Mahmood Mamdani, *Citizen and Subject: Contemporary Africa and the Legacy of Late Colonialism* (Princeton, NJ: Princeton University Press, 1996), 61.

30. Ruthenberg, *African Agricultural Production*, 72.

31. David M. Anderson and Emma Lochery, "Violence and Exodus in Kenya's Rift Valley, 2008: Predictable and Preventable?" *Journal of Eastern African Studies* 2, no. 2 (2008): 335. Policymakers gave "absolute priority to persons with four years service on farms bought by the Settlement Board." KNA DC/ELD/1/10/9, J. A. H. Wolff, PC Rift Valley Province, to the PC, Nyanza Province, "Settlement Schemes: Selection of Settlers," 7 March 1963.

32. P. D. Abrams, *Kenya's Land Re-settlement Story: How 66,000 African Families Were Settled on 1325 Large Scale European Owned Farms* (Nairobi: Challenge, 1979), 25. See also C. P. R. Nottidge, *The Million-Acre Settlement Scheme, 1962–1966* (Nairobi: Department of Settlement, 1966).

33. KNA JA/31/7, "A Project for Agricultural Settlement Schemes in Scheduled Areas of Kenya" [undated].

34. KNA DC/ELD/1/10/9, T. A. Watts, Chief Executive Officer, to DC, Nandi, "Smallholder Settlement Scheme—Lessos," 9 August 1961.

35. KNA JA/31/7, "A Project for Agricultural Settlement Schemes in Scheduled Areas of Kenya" [undated]. Though planners preferred those with greater assets, high-density settlers were ultimately required to provide only £5 to £7 up front. Gerald Holtham and Arthur Hazlewood, *Aid and Inequality in Kenya: British Development Assistance to Kenya* (London: Routledge, 2010), 79.

36. KNA JA/31/7, "A Project for Agricultural Settlement Schemes in Scheduled Areas of Kenya" [undated].

37. Christopher Leo, "The Failure of the 'Progressive Farmer' in Kenya's Million-Acre Settlement Scheme," *Journal of Modern African Studies* 16, no. 4 (1978): 621, 624; John W. Harbeson, *Nation-Building in Kenya: The Role of Land Reform* (Evanston, IL: Northwestern University Press, 1973), 78.

38. KNA DC/ELD/1/10/9, J. S. Rowlands for Director of Settlement to Senior Settlement Officers, "Selection of Smallholders," 23 January 1963.

39. KNA BN/81/168, Secretary to the Cabinet to the Permanent Secretary for Lands and the Permanent Secretary for Labour, "Selection of Settlers on High Density Schemes—Action Extract from the Minutes of the 4th Meeting," 3 July 1963.

40. KNA BN/81/168, T. W. Morgan, Acting Senior Agricultural Officer, "Selection of Settlers," 27 June 1963.

41. KNA DX/21/10/10, P. J. Gachati, PS Ministry of Lands and Settlement, to Civil Secretaries, Nyeri, Nakuru, Kakamega, Kisumu, Embu, "Selection of Settlers for Land Purchase for Settlement," 8 May 1964.

42. Richard Otieno Kisiara, "Labor Contracts in a Polyethnic Agricultural Resettlement in Western Kenya" (PhD diss., Washington University, 1998), 13.

43. More than one-third of the settlement schemes had more Kikuyu than other ethnic groups, and about 60 percent of the schemes in Central Province were located in areas excised from the Rift Valley. Karuti Kanyinga, "The Legacy of the White Highlands: Land Rights, Ethnicity and the Post- 2007 Election Violence in Kenya," *Journal of Contemporary African Studies* 27, no. 3 (2009): 336–37.

44. KNA DX/21/10/10, Regional Government Agent, Kakamega, to the Civil Secretary, Western Region, "Selection of Settlers—Land Purchased for Settlement," 16 June 1964.

45. KNA DX/21/10/10, Regional Government Agent, Kakamega, to the Civil Secretary, Western Region, "Selection of Settlers—Land Purchased for Settlement," 16 June 1964.

46. Kikuyu dominance in government only made matters worse. With Jomo Kenyatta as president, many Kenyans felt that their communities were underrepresented.

47. KNA DC/ELD/1/10/3, W. B. G. Raynor, DC Kiambu, to Mrs. Barrow, "Applications for Land," 15 August 1962.

48. Chepsiror arap Leleli, interview by author, Tapsagoi, 12 January 2013; Jemosbei Kirwa Kili, interview by author, Tapsagoi, 12 January 2013; Rev. Philomon Tanai, interview by author, Leseru, 9 January 2013; Aaron Juma Wechuli, interview by author, Lumakanda, 14 November 2012.

49. Selena Busianey, interview by author, Sosiani, 29 November 2012; Helen Chepkuto, interview by author, Sosiani, 30 November 2012.

50. KNA DC/ELD/1/10/9, "Applications for Plots in Settlement Schemes" [undated]. Oral histories broadly support this archival evidence.

51. KNA DC/ELD/1/10/9, R. H. Symes-Thompson, DC Nandi, "Lessos Settlement Scheme," 11 November 1961.

52. KNA JA/31/7, "A Project for Agricultural Settlement Schemes in the Scheduled Areas of Kenya" [undated].

53. KNA AVS/3/69, P. Shiyukah, PS Ministry of Lands and Settlement, to PCs, "Selection of Settlers," 2 February 1965.

54. KNA HB/27/9/9, Paul Kipkorir Boit, to the PS, Ministry of Lands and Settlement, "Selection of Settlers," 9 February 1965.

55. Republic of Kenya, *The National Assembly, House of Representatives Official Report (Hansard)*, vol. 5, 14 July 1965.

56. KNA DX/21/10/10, P. J. Gachati, PS Ministry of Lands and Settlement, to Civil Secretaries, Nyeri, Nakuru, Kakamega, Kisumu, Embu, "Selection of Settlers for Land Purchase for Settlement," 8 May 1964; KNA DX/21/10/10, Regional Government Agent, Kakamega, to the Civil Secretary Western Region, "Selection of Settlers—Land Purchased for Settlement," 16 June 1964.

57. KNA BN/81/168, Philip Ndegwa, for Permanent Secretary, to P. Shiyukah, Ministry of Land and Settlement, "Land Holdings of Settlement Farmers in their Former Areas," 6 January 1966.

58. KNA DX/21/10/10, P. Shiyukah, PS Ministry of Lands and Settlement, to PCs, "Selection of Farmers to Settlement Schemes," 4 February 1965.

59. KNA DX/21/10/10, S. K. Karimi, for PC Western, to the Chairman, Western Provincial Advisory Council, 12 May 1965.

60. KNA DX/21/10/10, DC Kakamega to PC Western, "Lugari Settlement Scheme," 26 July 1966.

61. NAUK OD 26/61, "Land Settlement: 100 Acre Plots," 16 December 1966.

62. Alfred Machayo, interview by author, Chekalini, 1 November 2012.

63. Peters, "Inequality and Social Conflict."

64. KNA AVS/1/15, E. J. M. Rabu, Assistant Director of Agriculture (S), "Extension Services in Settlement Schemes," October 1971.

65. Leys, *Underdevelopment in Kenya*, 81. By the end of 1968, the Department of Settlement had an operational cost of £7.1 million.

66. Leys, *Underdevelopment in Kenya*, 74.

67. On the failures of such high-modernist planning: James C. Scott, *Seeing Like a State: How Certain Schemes to Improve the Human Condition Have Failed* (New Haven, CT: Yale University Press, 1998); Michel de Certeau, *The Practice of Everyday Life*, trans. Steven F. Rendall (Berkeley: University of California Press, 2011); Stephan F. Miescher, "Building the City of the Future: Visions and Experiences of Modernity in Ghana's Akosombo Township," *Journal of African History* 53, no. 3 (2012): 367–90.

68. KNA BV/3/636, "Minutes of the 13th Meeting of the Planning Committee," Silo Park House, 4 March 1963.

69. KNA DC/ELD/1/10/9, M. A. Meager, for Acting Permanent Secretary for Lands, Survey, and Town Planning, to PCs, DCs, ADCs, and CCs, "Markets in Settlement Schemes Areas," 11 December 1962.

70. KNA DC/ELD/1/10/9, T. A. Watts to the Chairman of Provincial Agricultural Committees (Non Scheduled Areas), "Planning Smallholder Settlement Schemes," 29 August 1961.

71. KNA AVS/1/150, "Land Transfer and Land Settlement 1974–78."

72. KNA AVS/1/15, P. M. Vuyiya, Chief Technical Officer, to the PS, Ministry of Lands and Settlement, "Transfer of Settlement Schemes from the Ministry of Agriculture to the Ministry of Lands and Settlement," 3 December 1970.

73. KNA AVS/1/15, P. M. Vuyiya, Chief Technical Officer, to the PS, Ministry of Lands and Settlement, "Transfer of Settlement Schemes from the Ministry of Agriculture to the Ministry of Lands and Settlement," 3 December 1970.

74. KNA PC/RVP, Rift Valley Province Annual Report, 1961.

75. KNA PC/RVP, Rift Valley Province Annual Report, 1961.

76. KNA PC/RVP, Rift Valley Province Annual Report, 1965.

77. KNA PC/RVP, Rift Valley Province Annual Report, 1969.

78. Hanan Sabea, "Mastering the Landscape? Sisal Plantations, Land, and Labor in Tanga Region, 1893–1980s," *International Journal of African Historical Studies* 41, no. 3 (2008): 430.

79. Sally Kogo, interview by author, Leseru, 23 November 2012. James Musamusi Matunda, interview by author, Lumakanda, 2 November 2012; Veronica Masiza, interview by author, Lumakanda, 5 June 2015.

80. John E. Casida, ed., *Pyrethrum: The Natural Insecticide* (New York: Academic Press, 1973).

81. KNA BN/81/158, J. S. Mburu, Director of Settlement, to the PS, Ministry of Lands and Settlement, "Measures to Increase Employment," 22 May 1970. While

coffee quotas could benefit smallholders, Mburu argued, "with the restrictive quotas for such lucrative cash crops, as coffee, the African citizens who would have availed himself the benefits of growing this cash crop is now excluded." William G. Clarence-Smith and Steven Topik, eds., *The Global Coffee Economy in Africa, Asia, and Latin America, 1500–1989* (Cambridge: Cambridge University Press, 2003).

82. KNA AVS/13/21, Senior Settlement Officer Sotik area, "Re: Department of Settlement," February 1969.

83. KNA AVS/13/21, Senior Settlement Officer Sotik area, "Re: Department of Settlement," February 1969.

84. KNA BN 81/78, S. K. Mwendia, Area Settlement Controller (N), to the Director of Settlement, Ministry of Lands and Settlement, "Visit to Schemes," 28 June 1967. By 1966, Kenya had only 70 percent of its target amount of dairy cattle. Harbeson, *Nation-Building in Kenya*, 303.

85. KNA DC/ELD/1/10/9, T. A. Watts, Chief Executive Officer, to DC, Nandi, "Smallholder Settlement Scheme—Lessos," 9 August 1961.

86. KNA TR/17/11, L. V. Bhandari, CEO, Central Agricultural Board, "Costs of Agricultural Input," 4 July 1968.

87. Leys, *Underdevelopment in Kenya*, 79; KNA BN/81/34, C. Kahara, "Summary of Van Arkadie Report," 15 February 1967. Debt will be discussed in greater detail in chapter 4.

88. Republic of Kenya, *Development Plan for the Period, 1965/66 to 1969/70* (Nairobi: Ministry of Economic Planning and Development, 1966).

89. SOAS CA/CA2/01/117, Principal Warren Short, "Lugari Farmers' Training Centre Annual Report for 1966."

90. KNA AVS 1/15, W. E. Adero, for Director of Settlement, to the Settlement Officer I, "Extension Tour: Turbo Schemes," 15 May 1973.

91. Manasi Esipeya, interview by author, Chekalini, 11 January 2013.

92. Manasi Esipeya, interview by author, Chekalini, 11 January 2013.

93. Rev. Philomon Tanai, interview by author, Leseru, 9 January 2013.

94. Some evidence suggests that agricultural education programs might have reinforced gendered inequalities, contributing to women's sense of exclusion. SOAS CA/CA2/01/117, "Njabini Farmers Training Centre Annual Report," 1967.

95. Joseph Dugere Munge, interview by author, Mautuma, 11 November 2012; Florence Konyonyi, interview by author, Lumakanda, 7 November 2012.

96. KNA AVS/1/15, H. M. Bridgman, Deputy Area Settlement Controller, North Division, "S.A.A.O.'s and A.A.O.'s Agricultural Policy," 18 October 1965.

97. Alfred Machayo, interview by author, Chekalini, 1 November 2012; Ainea Alulu, interview by author, Lumakanda, 5 November 2012.

98. Aaron Masista, interview by author, Lumakanda, 2 November 2012; Alfred Machayo, interview by author, 1 November 2012.

99. KNA AVS 1/15, E. J. M. Rabu, Assistant Director of Agriculture (S), "Extension Services in Settlement Schemes," October 1971.

100. KNA TR/8/1826, R. C. Noble, Co-operative Officer, Eldoret, to the Assistant Commissioner for Co-operative Development (Settlement), "Application for Registration. Chekalini Farmers Co-operative Society," 26 March 1964.

101. Wilberforce Oyalo, interview by author, Chekalini, 11 January 2013.

102. KNA AVS/1/15, W. E. Adero, for Director of Settlement, to the Settlement Officer I, "Extension Tour: Turbo Schemes," 15 May 1973.

103. KNA AVS/1/18, G. R. Henderson, Deputy Director of Settlement, to the Ministry of Agriculture, "Peace Corps," 11 June 1964.

104. KNA AVS/3/22, A. Storrar, Director of Settlement, to the PS, 29 March 1965. Leys notes that farmers with more land received more "advice." Leys, *Underdevelopment in Kenya*, 101. David K. Leonard came to similar conclusions. Leonard, "The Social Structure of the Agricultural Extension Services in the Western Province of Kenya," in *Government and Rural Development in East Africa: Essays on Political Penetration*, ed. Lionel Cliffe, J. S. Coleman, and M. R. Doornbos (The Hague: Martinus Nijhoff, 1977).

105. Kiptoo arap Maina, interview by author, Leseru, 23 November 2012.

106. Karen Misavo, interview by author, Lumakanda, 31 October 2012.

107. Rebecca Aliviza Maneno, interview by author, Lumakanda, 6 November 2012; Selena Serem, interview by author, Leseru, 28 November 2012. Other research supports these oral histories: Regina Smith Oboler, *Women, Power, and Economic Change: The Nandi of Kenya* (Stanford, CA: Stanford University Press, 1985), 160; Kathleen Staudt, "The Effects of Government Agricultural Policy on Women Farmers: Preliminary Findings from Idakho Location, Kakamega District" (Working Paper No. 225, University of Nairobi Institute for Development Studies, 1975), 78.

108. Rastos Omamo, interview by author, Lumakanda, 9 November 2012; Phillip Metto, interview by author, Leseru, 15 January 2013; Steven Kiplemai Ngetich, interview by author, Sosiani, 4 December 2012; Chebagui Bwalei, interview by author, Leseru, 23 November 2012.

109. Hoseah arap Keter, interview by author, Sosiani, 21 November 2012.

110. Steven Kiplemai Ngetich, interview by author, Sosiani, 4 December 2012.

111. KNA TR/8/1826, Chekalini Co-operative to Senior Settlement Officer, Turbo, "We Don't Want Settlement Officer of Chekalini Mr. T. M. Esipeya," 16 March 1965.

112. James Musamusi Matunda, interview by author, Lumakanda, 14 November 2012.

113. KNA AVS/3/41, J. H. Hickman, Admin. Officer, SSO Nakuru, Minutes of the Settlement Officers, "Staff Meeting Held by Senior Settlement Officer Mr. P. G. A. Smith," Eldoret, 14 October 1965.

114. KNA TR/1/351, The Treasury, "Application to HM Government for Assistance towards Extending the Period of Supervision on Settlement Schemes," 21 July 1965.

115. KNA BN/81/24, British High Commission to Mr. J. N. Michuki, PS, Ministry of Finance, 14 February 1966.

116. KNA DC/ELD/1/10/9, Settlement Officer to DCs—Eldoret and Nandi, "Monthly Report on Lessos Peasant Resettlement Schemes," 2 July 1961.

117. KNA AVS/1/13, Ministry of Lands and Settlement, "Settlement Schemes Town Planning Standards" [undated].

118. KNA BN/81/35, "Review of Kenya's Five Year Progress and Achievement in the Tenure and Administration," 6 August 1968.

119. KNA JA/31/7, "A Project for Agricultural Settlement Schemes in the Scheduled Areas of Kenya" [undated].

120. KNA JA/27/52, T. A. Watts, Acting Director of Settlement, to the PS, Ministry of Health and Housing, "Public Health Services Smallholder Settlement Schemes," 17 May 1962.

121. KNA JA/31/29, T. A. Watts, Chief Executive Officer, LDSB, to the Uasin Gishu County Council Clerk, 23 May 1962.

122. KNA JA/27/52, Uasin Gishu County Council, Clerk to Council, to PS, Ministry of Local Government and Lands, "Smallholders Settlement Schemes," 7 March 1962.

123. KNA AVS/4/4, R. Tatton Brown PS, Ministry of Local Government, to the Clerk to the Council, All County Councils, "Local Government Services: Settlement Schemes," 27 November 1962.

124. KNA BY/21/212, M. A. Faxal, Medical Officer of Health, Sirikwa County Council, to Assistant Director of Medical Services, Ministry of Health, "Re: Settlement Schemes," 14 February 1968.

125. KNA DC/UG/2/3/16, S. M. N. Rattray, Health Visitor, Eldoret, "Uasin Gishu County Council, Health Visitor's Report for the Month of April 1963," 2 May 1963.

126. Republic of Kenya, *The National Assembly, "House of Representatives Official Report (Hansard)*, vol. 5, 1 June 1965.

127. KNA AVS/15/93, Gitu Nanga, Chairman South Kinangop Scheme, to the Prime Minister, 14 September 1963.

128. KNA AVS/15/93, Gitu Nanga, Chairman South Kinangop Scheme to the Prime Minister, 14 September 1963; KNA AVS/1/13, "Settlement Schemes Town Planning Standards" [undated].

129. Kibet arap Busianey, interview by author, Sosiani, 29 November 2012.

130. KNA BN/81/24, Statement by Rt. Hon. Barbara Castle, MP, Minister of Overseas Development, "For the Record," British Information Services, 19 November 1965.

131. KNA BN/81/24, Statement by Rt. Hon. Barbara Castle, MP, Minister of Overseas Development, "For the Record," British Information Services, 19 November 1965.

132. KNA BN/81/24, Statement by Rt. Hon. Barbara Castle, MP, Minister of Overseas Development, "For the Record," British Information Services, 19 November 1965. After the close of the Million Acre Scheme, the British funded the low-density Harambee settlement.

133. KNA BN/81/24, "Working Paper for Kenya Ministers and Officials, Discussions with British Government Concerning Aid for Kenya's Agricultural Development (July–August, 1965)."

134. Kanyinga, "Legacy of the White Highlands," 213.

CHAPTER 2: "WE MUST RETURN TO THE LAND THAT WE LOVE"

1. Jomo Kenyatta, "Back to the Land" speech, in *Harambee! The Prime Minister of Kenya's Speeches, 1963–1964: From the Attainment of Internal Self-Government to the Threshold of the Kenya Republic* (Nairobi: Oxford University Press, 1964), 62.

2. KNA DC/ELD/1/0/9, Kenya Government Information Services, *Teach Yourself Citizenship for Self-Government*, 1962.

3. KNA DC/ELD/1/0/9, Kenya Government Information Services, *Teach Yourself Citizenship for Self-Government*, 1962.

4. KNA DC/UG/2/2/8, Provincial Information Officer, Monthly Report, July 1962. I did not find the Kalenjin version, only correspondence about it.

5. On mapping and identity, see Julie MacArthur, *Cartography and the Political Imagination: Mapping Community in Colonial Kenya* (Athens: Ohio University Press, 2016).

6. Christopher P. Youe, "Settler Capital and the Assault on the Squatter Peasantry in Kenya's Uasin Gishu District, 1942–63," *African Affairs* 87, no. 348 (1988): 393, 395; Diana Ellis, "The Nandi Protest of 1923 in the Context of African Resistance to Colonial Rule in Kenya," *Journal of African History* 17, no. 4 (1976): 563.

7. See NAUK CO 895/1, CO 897/1.

8. Kenda Mutongi, *Worries of the Heart: Widows, Family, and Community in Kenya* (Chicago: University of Chicago Press, 2007), 87; Robert Maxon, *Going Their Separate Ways: Agrarian Transformation in Kenya, 1930–1950* (Madison, NJ: Farleigh Dickinson University Press, 2003), 29–30.

9. MacArthur, *Cartography and the Political Imagination*, 47.

10. MacArthur, *Cartography and the Political Imagination*, 49.

11. Mutongi, *Worries of the Heart*, 17; Joseph Thomson, *Through Masai Land: A Journey of Exploration among the Snowclad Volcanic Mountains and Strange Tribes of Eastern Equatorial Africa* (London: Sampson Low, Marston, Searle, and Rivington, 1887), 284.

12. Mutongi, *Worries of the Heart*, 18.

13. Mutongi, *Worries of the Heart*, 26–27, chap. 4.

14. Aidan W. Southall, "The Illusion of Tribe," in *The Passing of Tribal Man in Africa*, ed. Peter C. W. Gutkind (Leiden: Brill, 1970); MacArthur, *Cartography and the Political Imagination*.

15. On the Regional Boundaries Commission and claims to the western highlands, see NAUK CO 897/1, CO 897/4, CO 897/5; Kenya Regional Boundaries Commission, *Report of the Regional Boundaries Commission* (London: Her Majesty's Stationery Office, 1962).

16. MacArthur, *Cartography and the Political Imagination*, 207–9.

17. On the fractured politics of KADU, and its apogee over Kitale, Trans Nzoia, see David M. Anderson, "'Yours in Struggle for Majimbo': Nationalism and the Party Politics of Decolonization in Kenya, 1955–64," *Journal of Contemporary History* 40, no. 3 (2005): 560–62; and Gabrielle Lynch, *I Say to You: Ethnic Politics and the Kalenjin in Kenya* (Chicago: University of Chicago Press, 2011), 73–80.

18. Kenya Regional Boundaries Commission, *Report of the Regional Boundaries Commission* (London: Her Majesty's Stationery Office, 1962).

19. KNA DC/KMG/2/13/2, Al Naaz, for DC Kakamega, to the Secretary, Electoral Commission, "Review of Constituencies," 25 September 1965.

20. Mutongi, *Worries of the Heart*, 82.

21. Conversation with Muey Saeteurn; Western Provincial Archives, Kakamega, HB/9/18, C. H. Williams, "On the Subject of Over Population in the Maragoli and Bunyore Locations 1952"; KNA DC/KMG/2/12/11, North Nyanza African District Council, "Survey of Unemployment," 30 January 1960.

22. Alfred Machayo, interview by author, Chekalini, 1 November 2012.

23. Danson P. Lumumba Esese, "The Changing System of Land Ownership and Its Socio-Economic Effects in Lugari Division, Western Province of Kenya, c. 1880–2000" (PhD diss., Michigan State University, 2009), 278–79.

24. Jamin Maneno Kihinga, interview by author, Lumakanda, 8 November 2012.

25. KNA HB/27/9/9, J. G. Mackley, DC Uasin Gishu, to J. A. H. Wolff, PC RVP, "Lugari Settlement Scheme," 11 December 1962.

26. KNA HB/27/9/9, J. O. Okeyo, for District Officer, Lugari, to the DC Kakamega, "Masai and Nandis," 23 September 1965.

27. KNA HB/27/9/9, J. O. Okeyo, for District Officer, Lugari, to the DC Kakamega, "Masai and Nandis," 23 September 1965.

28. Wilberforce Oyalo, interview by author, Chekalini, 11 January 2013.

29. Machayo would go on to become Kenya's permanent representative to the Food and Agricultural Organization, and to be an ambassador to a number of countries.

30. Alfred Machayo, interview by author, Chekalini, 1 November 2012.

31. Alfred Machayo, interview by author, Chekalini, 1 November 2012.

32. Deina Iboso, interview by author, Lumakanda, 12 November 2012; Muzole Shioani, interview by author, Lumakanda, 13 November 2012; Ismael Kagode, interview by author, Lumakanda, 12 November 2012; Veronica Masiza, interview by author, Lumakanda, 12 November 2012; Fanike Chanzu, interview by author, Lumakanda, 9 November 2012; Florence Konyonyi, interview by author, Lumakanda, 7 November 2012.

33. KNA DC/UG, Uasin Gishu District Annual Report, 1962; KNA DC/ELD/1/10/9, Bevan, Settlement Officer, Lessos, to CEO LDSB, "Monthly Report for the Lessos Small Holders Settlement Schemes," 2 August 1961.

34. Wilberforce Oyalo, interview by author, Chekalini, 11 January 2013.

35. KNA DC/ELD/1/10/9, J. G. Mackley, DC, Uasin Gishu, to the Settlement Officer, "Tugen Settlers," 12 January 1963.

36. Respectability was tied to building a permanent house. Esese, "Changing System of Land Ownership," 350.

37. Solomon Ndeche Muriga, interview by author, Lumakanda, 9 November 2012.

38. Ainea Alulu, interview by author, Lumakanda, 5 November 2012.

39. Esese, "Changing System of Land Ownership," 346–47.

40. Regina Smith Oboler, *Women, Power and Economic Change: The Nandi of Kenya* (Stanford, CA: Stanford University Press, 1985), 7; G. W. B. Huntingford, *Nandi Work and Culture* (London: His Majesty's Stationery Office, 1950), 17.

41. Alfred C. Hollis, *The Nandi: Their Language and Folk-Lore* (Oxford: Clarendon Press, 1909).

42. For an excellent study on attachment to land containing "meaning-laden graves," see Parker Shipton, *Mortgaging the Ancestors: Ideologies of Attachment in Africa* (New Haven, CT: Yale University Press, 2009), xi.

43. Daniel Kebeney Bitok, interview by author, Leseru, 10 June 2015.

44. Kenya Land Commission, *Report of the Kenya Land Commission* (London: His Majesty's Stationery Office, 1934).

45. Kenya Land Commission, *Report of the Kenya Land Commission* (London: His Majesty's Stationery Office, 1934).

46. NAUK CO/895/1, The Kalenjin Chiefs and People of the Nandi District, "The Memorandum to the Constituencies Delimitation Commission," 22 August 1962.

47. The most famous example of this occurred with the 1969 Nandi Hills declaration, when Jean-Marie Seroney and Joseph arap Cheruiyot Mitei claimed all land in Nandi District and Tinderet for the Nandi. Lynch, *I Say to You*, 98–99; Daniel Branch, *Kenya: Between Hope and Despair, 1963–2011* (New Haven, CT: Yale University Press, 2011), 87.

48. The KADU coalition included additional ethnic groups—including the Turkana, Samburu, and coastal peoples—who did not vie for Uasin Gishu.

49. Karuti Kanyinga, "The Land Question in Kenya: Struggles, Accumulation and Changing Politics" (PhD diss., Roskilde University, 1998), 173.

50. Kanyinga, "Land Question in Kenya," 175–76.

51. E. S. Atieno Odhiambo, "Ethnic Cleansing and Civil Society in Kenya, 1969–1992," *Journal of Contemporary African Studies* 22, no. 1 (2004): 36.

52. Huntingford, *Nandi Work and Culture*, 76.

53. Odhiambo, "Ethnic Cleansing and Civil Society in Kenya," 36. G. W. B. Huntingford has slightly different numbers, writing that in 1931, about 13,346 Nandi squatters worked in the highlands, or around a quarter of the ethnic group. Colonial censuses were notoriously inaccurate, however, and Huntingford approached these numbers with skepticism. Huntingford, *Nandi Work and Culture*, 73; Huntingford, *The Nandi of Kenya: Tribal Control in a Pastoral Society* (London: Routledge, 1953), 3.

54. Youe, "Settler Capital," 400–401.

55. Youe, "Settler Capital," 402.

56. KNA AB/12/15, "Uasin Gishu County Council. Twenty-Eighth Annual Report of the Uasin Gishu District Council," 1957.

57. John Arusei, interview by author, Leseru, 15 January 2013. Cattle were "a source of wealth and status" for the Nandi. Youe, "Settler Capital," 401.

58. Eunice Tele Maiyo, interview by author, Leseru, 9 January 2013.

59. Oboler, *Women, Power, and Economic Change*, 26.

60. Priscilla J. Tanui, "A Gender Analysis of the Influence of Colonial Policies on Access to Land and Agricultural Technology among the Nandi in Kenya, 1895–1954," *International Journal of Humanities and Social Science* 5, no. 9 (2015): 226.

61. KNA PC/RVP/2/3/6, Rift Valley Province Annual Report, 1950; KNA PC/RVP, Rift Valley Province Annual Report, 1951.

62. Tanui, "Gender Analysis," 226.

63. KNA DC/ELD/1/10/9, Settlement officer to DCs—Eldoret and Nandi, "Monthly Report on Lessos Peasant Resettlement Schemes," 2 July 1961.

64. KNA DC/ELD/1/10/9, Symes-Thompson to the EO LDSB, "Lessos Settlement Selection Committee," 13 November 1961.

65. Colony and Protectorate of Kenya, *Legislative Council Debates Official Report (Hansard)*, vol. 89, 22 June 1962.

66. KNA AVS/15/93, Bongo Locational Committee to the Minister for Settlement Devt. Board, "Warning to the Settlement Officers S. Kinangop Scheme," 22 January 1964.

67. KNA DC/ELD/1/10/9, P. Shiyukah, DC Kitale, to PC RVP, "Settlement Schemes for Tribes other than Kikuyu," 22 February 1963.

68. KNA DC/ELD/1/10/9, DC, Uasin Gishu, to PC, Rift Valley Province, "Settlement Schemes—Selection," 1 March 1963.

69. KNA TR/8/698, "Sosiani Scheme Economic Appreciation," 28 June 1967.

70. KNA TR/8/1184, "Sosiani (Proposed) Farmers Co-operative Society Ltd. Economical Appreciation" [undated, likely 1967].

71. Joseph arap Bir'geng, interview by author, Sosiani, 20 November 2012.

72. ABGC, Box 13, Folder 12, Collection 81, Catherine S. Miller, "The Eldoret Advance: Africa Inland Mission" [undated].

73. Huntingford, *Nandi Work and Culture*, 118.

74. Joseph arap Bir'geng, interview by author, Sosiani, 20 November 2012.

75. Tabitha Kanogo, *Squatters and the Roots of Mau Mau, 1905–63* (Athens: Ohio University Press, 1987), 97.

76. KNA PC/NKU/2/16/29, Henry Gikonyo Mbui to PC RVP, "Application for Land Settlement Schemes," 9 September 1962.

77. For example, Kanogo, *Squatters and the Roots of Mau Mau*; Derek R. Peterson, *Creative Writing: Translation, Bookkeeping, and the Work of Imagination in Colonial Kenya* (Portsmouth, NH: Heinemann, 2004); Bruce J. Berman and John Lonsdale, *Unhappy Valley: Conflict in Kenya and Africa*, bk. 2, *Violence and Ethnicity* (Athens: Ohio University Press, 1992); David M. Anderson, *Histories of the Hanged: The Dirty War in Kenya and the End of Empire* (New York: W. W. Norton, 2005); David Throup, *Economic and Social Origins of Mau Mau, 1945–53* (London: James Currey, 1988).

78. Hans Ruthenberg, *African Agricultural Production Development Policy in Kenya, 1952–1965* (Berlin: Springer, 1966), 72.

79. KNA AVS/15/37, Provincial Commissioner, Central Province, to R. E. Wainwright, Chief Commissioner, Office of the Leader of the House, "The Kikuyu Problem," 2 February 1962; KNA AVS/15/37, "Record of a Meeting Held in the Chief Commissioner's Office on the 13 February 1962, to plan the settlement of 5,000 Kikuyu families."

80. KNA BN/85/16, J. H. Angaine, Minister for Lands and Settlement, to Hon. W. O. Omamo, MP, Minister for Natural Resources, "Forest Excisions for Settlement: Get Phase II," 9 July 1970.

81. KNA KA/6/31, Paul Mwangi Kimani, c/o Armstrong Farm, Ainabkoi, to Hon. PM Jomo Kenyatta, 24 November 1964.

82. KNA PC/NKU/2/16/29, Henry Magu Kahigu to PC RVP, "Kinangop Land Settlement Scheme" 1 August 1962; KNA PC/NKU/2/16/29, Mwangi Njoroge and Stanley Mwangi Maina to PC RVP, "Re-Application for Settlement Scheme Plots," 5 September 1962.

83. Peterson, *Creative Writing*, 142.

84. Joseph Dugere Munge, interview by author, Mautuma, 11 November 2012.

85. Joseph Dugere Munge, interview by author, Mautuma, 11 November 2012.

86. KNA BN/81/134, "Land Purchase Programme," November 1965.

87. Esese, "Changing System of Land Ownership," 270.

88. Joseph Dugere Munge, interview by author, Mautuma, 11 November 2012.

89. Wilberforce Oyalo, interview by author, Chekalini, 11 January 2013.

90. Phillip Metto, interview by author, Leseru, 15 January 2013.

91. KNA KA/6/19 Samwel Ngugi (for behave [*sic*] of Kikuyu), Turbo, to the Minister of Administration (Hon. Koinange), 18 July 1969.

92. Margaret Wanjiru Nyanya, interview by author, Mautuma, 11 November 2012; Joseph Dugere Munge, interview by author, 11 November 2012; Jotham Njau Mwangi, interview by author, Lumakanda, 5 November 2012.

93. Margaret Wanjiru Nyanya, interview by author, Mautuma, 11 November 2012.

CHAPTER 3: "THE LAND WAS OURS, BUT IT WAS NOT MINE"

1. KNA KA/6/20, James K. Sitieney, Eldoret, to the PS, Office of the President, "Re: Gen. 116/016/86 Plot No. 676 Kondoo Squatters Scheme," 21 February 1973.

2. KNA KA/6/32, Joseph C. Langat and David K. Koghe to the Kenya Prime Minister, "Harambee na Wamasikini," trans. Mwendwa Musyimi, 1 February 1964.

3. Kenya African National Union and Jomo Kenyatta, *The KANU Manifesto* (Cairo: Dar El-Hana Press, 1960).

4. The "Jet Scheme" excised the Kinangop area from Rift Valley to Central Province in June 1963, resettling landless Kikuyu to avoid a land grab. Gary Wasserman, *Politics of Decolonization: Kenya, Europeans and the Land Issue, 1960–1965* (Cambridge: Cambridge University Press, 1976), 149; Karuti Kanyinga, "The Legacy of the White Highlands: Land Rights, Ethnicity and the Post-2007 Election Violence in Kenya," *Journal of Contemporary African Studies* 27, no. 3 (2009): 331.

5. KNA BN/81/41, Office of the President to the permanent secretary, Ministry of Agriculture, permanent secretary, Ministry of Lands and Settlement, and all provincial commissioners, 2 March 1967.

6. KNA BN/81/35, Z. B. Shimechero, special commissioner, Squatters, "Squatter Rehabilitation," 30 July 1968.

7. KNA AVS/13/63, "A Covering Letter for the Report on the Special Commissioner's Visits to Provinces to Investigate the Squatter Problem," 12 July 1965.

8. KNA AVS/13/63, Z. B. Shimechero, special commissioner, Squatters, "Functions of Assistant Commissioners for Squatters," 20 July 1965.

9. KNA AVS/13/63, Z. B. Shimechero, special commissioner, Squatters, "Functions of Assistant Commissioners for Squatters," 20 July 1965.

10. KNA BN/81/41, Office of the President to the PS, Ministry of Agriculture, PS, Ministry of Lands and Settlement, and All PCs, 2 March 1967.

11. KNA DC/KMG/2/12/49, Z. B. Shimechero, special commissioner, Squatters, to the provincial commissioners Rift Valley, Central, Eastern, Nyanza, Western, Coast and North Eastern Provinces, "Investigation of Squatters," 6 January 1966.

12. KNA BN/97/3, J. H. Angaine, minister for Lands and Settlement, "Note on the Minister for Agriculture's Memorandum on Squatters," 2 February 1966.

13. KNA BN/85/16, S. Nyachae, provincial commissioner, Rift Valley Province, to the permanent secretary, Office of the President, "Turbo Settlement Scheme," 28 April 1969.

14. Robert H. Bates, *Beyond the Miracle of the Market: The Political Economy of Agrarian Development in Kenya* (New York: Cambridge University Press, 1992), 67–69.

15. KNA BN/81/35, Z. B. Shimechero, special commissioner, Squatters, "Squatter Rehabilitation," 30 July 1968.

16. KNA BN/97/3, Sub-committee of the cabinet on the squatter problem, "The Squatter Problem," 14 April 1966.

17. KNA BN/97/3, Ministry of Economic Planning and Development, "Comments on Ministry of Lands and Settlement's Paper on Squatters," April 1966.

18. KNA BN/85/14, "Record of Meeting Held at the Ministry of Overseas Development at 3 pm on Monday, 26th July, 1965, to discuss the Interim Stamp Report: 1st Meeting."

19. KNA BN/97/3, L. S. Sherriff, state counsel, to the PS, Ministry of Lands and Settlement, "Removal of Squatters from Land Occupied Illegally by Them," 15 April 1966.

20. KNA BN/81/41, Memorandum by the minister for Lands and Settlement, "The Final Paper of the Cabinet Sub-Committee on the Squatter Problem," 15 June 1966.

21. KNA BN/97/4, J. H. Angaine, minister for Lands and Settlement, and Bruce McKenzie, minister for Agriculture, "The Cabinet: Difficulties Experienced in Obtaining Land Purchase Money in Squatter Settlement Programme," 18 September 1968.

22. Western Province, for example, was listed as having only 715 squatter families.

23. KNA BN/97/4, Memorandum by the minister for Lands and Settlement, "The Final Paper of the Cabinet Sub-Committee on the Squatter Problem," 15 June 1966.

24. KNA BN/97/4, Memorandum by the minister for Lands and Settlement, "The Final Paper of the Cabinet Sub-Committee on the Squatter Problem," 15 June 1966.

25. KNA BN/85/15, Director of Settlement, "Land Purchase Programme and Turbo Afforestation Scheme," 2 February 1966.

26. KNA BN/97/4, Deputy secretary to the permanent secretary, Ministry of Lands and Settlement, "Squatter Settlement," 6 March 1969.

27. KNA BN/81/41, Z. B. Shimechero, special commissioner, Squatters, to the PS, Ministry of Lands and Settlement, "The Role of the Special Commissioner, Squatters," 21 June 1968.

28. KNA BN/85/16, S. D. Gathiuni to the permanent secretary, Office of the President, "Land for Squatters or Landless People," 11 March 1970.

29. KNA TR/29/5, Settlement Fund Trustees, "The Shirika Settlement Program" [undated].

30. Sylvester Barngetung Sing'ari, interview by author, Leseru, 19 November 2012.

31. Among others: Nora Kasigene, interview by author, Lumakanda, 30 October 2012; Coretta Visyafua, interview by author, Lumakanda, 7 November 2012; Solome Teregin, interview by author, Leseru, 26 November 2012.

32. Kimeli arap Chepkwony, interview by author, Sosiani, 30 November 2012; Sylvester Barngetung Sing'ari, interview by author, Leseru, 19 November 2012.

33. Kimeli arap Chepkwony, interview by author, Sosiani, 30 November 2012.

34. Land-purchase cooperatives represented the easiest route to corporate status—a necessity to engage with sellers and banks. Over time, limited liability companies, with fewer shareholders, became common. Partnerships tended to be composed of a few people. Colin Leys, *Underdevelopment in Kenya: The Political Economy of Neo-Colonialism, 1964–1971* (Berkeley: University of California Press, 1975), 90.

35. KNA TR/27/24, Nikolaus Newiger, "Co-operative Farming in the Former Scheduled Areas of Kenya," 14 October 1965.

36. KNA TR/27/24, Nikolaus Newiger, "Co-operative Farming in the Former Scheduled Areas of Kenya," 14 October 1965.

37. John Lonsdale, "The Moral Economy of Mau Mau: Wealth, Poverty, and Civic Virtue in Kikuyu Political Thought," in Bruce J. Berman and John Lonsdale, *Unhappy Valley: Conflict in Kenya and Africa*, bk. 2, *Violence and Ethnicity* (Athens: Ohio University Press, 1992), 460–63; Catherine Boone, "Land Conflict and Distributive Politics in Kenya," *African Studies Review* 55, no. 1 (2012): 81.

38. KNA TR/27/24, Nikolaus Newiger, "Co-operative Farming in the Former Scheduled Areas of Kenya," 14 October 1965; Leys, *Underdevelopment in Kenya*, 91.

39. KNA AVS/3/69, "CAB Paper No. 133: AFC Loan Deposits," 31 March 1970.

40. Alfred Machayo, interview by author, Chekalini, 1 November 2012.

41. KNA TR/27/15, Jopheth K. Tigoi (Chairman) and Tom K. Rotich (Secretary) to Tom Mboya, minister for Economic Planning and Development, "Problems of People without Land Title—Deeds" [undated, but 1965–66].

42. KNA TR/27/15, Jopheth K. Tigoi (Chairman) and Tom K. Rotich (Secretary) to Tom Mboya, minister for Economic Planning and Development, "Problems of People without Land Title—Deeds" [undated, but 1965–66].

43. KNA TR/1/100, Mwaniki Mwangi to the minister of Co-operative Societies, "Re: Yamumbi Uasin Gishu Farmer's Co-operative Society Ltd. Registration No.C.S./1339," 31 October 1966.

44. KNA TR/1/100, Mwaniki Mwangi to the minister of Co-operative Societies, "Re: Yamumbi Uasin Gishu Farmer's Co-operative Society Ltd. Registration No.C.S./1339," 31 October 1966.

45. KNA TR/1/351, D. Thiongo, for special commissioner, Squatters, to the deputy commissioner, Department of Cooperative Development, 22 May 1967; KNA DC/UG Uasin Gishu District Annual Report, 1967.

46. Helen Kirua, interview by author, Leseru, 3 December 2012; William Serem, interview by author, Leseru, 3 December 2012.

47. Sally Kogo, interview by author, Leseru, 23 November 2012.

48. Kiptoo arap Maina, interview by author, Leseru, 23 November 2012.

49. KNA BN/81/35, A. Davies, for director of Land Adjudication, "Five Year Development Review: Land Adjudication, Consolidation, and Registration," 27 May 1968.

50. KNA AVS/15/69, Chairman, Co-op Society Ltd. Lessos Settlement Scheme to the director of Settlement Scheme, 10 August 1964; KNA AVS/15/69, E. K. A. Barngetuny to Settlement Scheme Officer, Lessos, "Mr. Edwin Kiprotich Arap Barngetuny," 9 October 1964.

51. Kimeli arap Chepkwony, interview by author, Sosiani, 30 November 2012.

52. KNA TR/1/100, Uasin Gishu District co-operative societies, "The Shirika Settlement Programme" [undated].

53. KNA TR/1/201, J. R. Njenga, director of Settlement, "Land Transfer and Land Settlement 1974/78."

54. KNA AVS/1/16, L. N. Mucemi, acting director of Settlement to the PS, Ministry of Lands and Settlement, "Re: National Assembly Question No. 953," 2 October 1975.

55. Gerald Holtham and Arthur Hazlewood, *Aid and Inequality in Kenya: British Development Assistance to Kenya* (London: Routledge, 2010), 84–85.

56. Republic of Kenya, *The National Assembly Official Report (Hansard)*, vol. 34, 4 July 1974.

57. Republic of Kenya, *The National Assembly Official Report (Hansard)*, vol. 34, 4 July 1974.

58. Holtham and Hazlewood, *Aid and Inequality*, 85.

59. KNA DC/KPT/2/13/4, J. A. H. Wolff, PC RVP, to A. A. A. Ekirapa for DC, Nandi, February 1963.

60. Gavin N. Kitching, *Class and Economic Change in Kenya: The Making of an African Petite-Bourgeoisie, 1905–1970* (New Haven, CT: Yale University Press, 1980), 240; Fiona Mackenzie, *Land, Ecology and Resistance in Kenya, 1880–1952* (Edinburgh: Edinburgh University Press, 1998); Leigh Brownhill, *Land, Food, Freedom: Struggles for the Gendered Commons in Kenya, 1870 to 2007* (Trenton, NJ: Africa World Press, 2009). Both colonial officials and African men saw single women as a threat. Luise White, *The Comforts of Home: Prostitution in Colonial Nairobi* (Chicago: University of Chicago Press, 1990); KNA PC/NKU/3/1/7, "General Meeting of the Kalenjin Union held on the Grounds of the Native Location," 26 July 1950.

61. Regina Smith Oboler, *Women, Power, and Economic Change: The Nandi of Kenya* (Stanford, CA: Stanford University Press, 1985), 252.

62. Margaret Jean Hay, "Women as Owners, Occupants, and Managers of Property in Colonial Western Kenya," in *African Women and the Law: Historical Perspectives*, ed. Margaret Jean Hay and Marcia Wright (Boston, MA: Boston University, 1982), 110–12.

63. Mackenzie, *Land, Ecology and Resistance in Kenya.*

64. On Kenyan widows, see Kenda Mutongi, *Worries of the Heart: Widows, Family, and Community in Kenya* (Chicago: University of Chicago Press, 2007).

65. Republic of Kenya, *The National Assembly Official Report (Hansard)*, vol. 10, 13 October 1966.

66. KNA DC/ELD/1/10/3, Wambui w/o Muiruri, Ainabkoi to DC, Uasin Gishu, 12 January 1963. Though this chapter makes use of land petitions, these are complex sources. Many poor Kenyans were illiterate and unnamed intermediaries wrote their petitions. Thus, petitions were a product of collaboration between the named petitioner(s) and the unknown intermediary, and likely incorporated the ideas of both.

67. KNA DC/ELD/1/10/3, DC, Uasin Gishu, to Wambui, 18 January 1962.

68. The Kenya National Archives contain hundreds of petitions for land, and petitioners almost always included a biographical narrative.

69. KNA DC/ELD/1/10/9, Kuria s/o Kimani for the Adam's Employees (A. J. Van Rensburg, Ainabkoi) to DC, Eldoret, 10 February 1963.

70. KNA DC/ELD/1/10/9, DC, Uasin Gishu, to Kuria Kimani, 18 February 1963.

71. KNA DX/21/10/10, District Officer, Vihiga, to the DC, Kakamega, "Lugari Settlement Schemes," 18 May 1966.

72. KNA KA/6/19, KANU Women's Wing, Cherangani Scheme, Kitale, to the President's Office, "Request for Intervention," 15 November 1968.

73. Solome Teregin, interview by author, Leseru, 26 November 2012.

74. Rebecca Aliviza Maneno, interview by author, Lumakanda, 6 November 2012.

75. Kenyan women had long resisted land dispossession. Brownhill, *Land, Food, Freedom.*

76. Mutongi, *Worries of the Heart*, 4.

77. Florence Machayo, interview by author, Chekalini, 1 November 2012.

78. Florence Machayo, interview by author, Chekalini, 1 November 2012.

79. KNA AVS/3/22, "Draft Memorandum for Council of Ministers, Inheritance on Settlement Schemes," 1962.

80. KNA AVS/3/22, N. S. Carey Jones to R. I. Guthrie, Esq., Attorney-General's Chambers, "Inheritance on Settlement Schemes," 12 February 1963.

81. Mutongi, *Worries of the Heart*, 166–70.

82. Susan Rono, interview by author, Leseru, 22 November 2012.

83. KNA KA/6/31, Wambui w/o Gatungu to Kenyatta, 26 October 1964.

84. Pauline Tum, interview by author, Leseru, 22 November 2012.

85. Anna Chelimo Kipkalum, interview by author, Leseru, 28 November 2012.

86. Rael Serem, interview by author, Leseru, 3 December 2012; Karen Misavo, interview by author, Lumakanda, 31 October 2012.

87. Though women continue to be marginalized with respect to landownership in contemporary Kenya, their opportunities have expanded more recently.

88. Mutongi, *Worries of the Heart*, 7–8.

89. There is a rich literature on women, labor, and development: Ester Boserup, *Woman's Role in Economic Development* (New York: St. Martin's Press, 1970); Margaret Jean Hay, "Economic Change in Late Nineteenth Century Kowe, Western Kenya," in *Hadith 5: Economic and Social History of East Africa*, ed. Bethwell A. Ogot (Nairobi: East African Literature Bureau, 1976), 92–109; Jane I. Guyer, *Women's Work in the Food Economy of the Cocoa Belt: A Comparison* (Brookline, MA: African Studies Center, Boston University Press, 1978); Jean Davison, *Agriculture, Women, and Land:*

The African Experience (Boulder, CO: Westview Press, 1988); Miriam Goheen, *Men Own the Fields, Women Own the Crops: Gender and Power in the Cameroon Grassfields* (Madison: University of Wisconsin Press, 1996); Kathleen E. Sheldon, *Pounders of Grain: A History of Women, Work, and Politics in Mozambique* (Portsmouth, NH: Heinemann, 2002).

90. Pauline Ngetich, interview by author, Sosiani, 21 November 2012.

91. Regina Smith Oboler analyzes a similar phenomenon in spousal negotiations over cattle. Oboler, "Whose Cows Are They, Anyway? Ideology and Behavior in Nandi Cattle 'Ownership' and Control," *Human Ecology* 24, no. 2 (1996): 255–56.

92. Pauline Ngetich, interview by author, Sosiani, 21 November 2012.

93. Felistas Muriga Nasambu, interview by author, Lumakanda, 9 November 2012.

94. Karen Misavo, interview by author, Lumakanda, 31 October 2012.

95. Fanike Chanzu, interview by author, Lumakanda, 9 November 2012.

96. Rebecca Aliviza Maneno, interview by author, Lumakanda, 6 November 2012.

97. KNA KA/6/19, S. M. Kubai to Kenyatta, 25 February 1966.

98. On African women's contestations over household management and labor, see Jane I. Guyer, "Household and Community in African Studies," *African Studies Review* 24, nos. 2–3 (1981): 87–138.

99. Eunice Birir, interview by author, Leseru, 27 November 2012.

100. Eunice Birir, interview by author, Leseru, 27 November 2012.

101. Grace Nasimiyu, interview by author, Lumakanda, 12 November 2012.

102. Julie MacArthur, *Cartography and the Political Imagination: Mapping Community in Colonial Kenya* (Athens: Ohio University Press, 2016), 14; see also David W. Cohen, "Doing Social History from *Pim's* Doorway," in *Reliving the Past: The Worlds of Social History*, ed. Olivier Zunz (Chapel Hill: University of North Carolina Press, 1985).

103. Mutongi, *Worries of the Heart*, 151–54; Brett L. Shadle, "Bridewealth and Female Consent: Marriage Disputes in African Courts, Gusiiland, Kenya," *Journal of African History* 44, no. 2 (2003): 241–62. On divorce in colonial Asante, see Jean M. Allman and Victoria B. Tashjian, *"I Will Not Eat Stone": A Women's History of Colonial Asante* (Portsmouth, NH: Heinemann, 200), chap. 5.

104. Grace Nasimiyu, interview by author, Lumakanda, 12 November 2012.

105. Grace Nasimiyu, interview by author, Lumakanda, 12 November 2012.

106. Sylvester Barngetung Sing'ari, interview by author, Leseru, 19 November 2012.

107. This has been at the center of many of the nation's land debates. Karuti Kanyinga, "The Land Question in Kenya: Struggles, Accumulation and Changing Politics" (PhD diss., Roskilde University, 1998), 208.

108. Christopher Lelei Lilan, interview by author, Leseru, 26 November 2012.

109. Frederick Kemboi arap Tum Kaptulus, interview by author, Leseru, 22 November 2012.

110. Gabrielle Lynch, *I Say to You: Ethnic Politics and the Kalenjin in Kenya* (Chicago: University of Chicago Press, 2011), 63–72.

111. Godfrey K. Sang, *Just for Today: The Life and Times of Jean-Marie Seroney* (Coventry: Dolman Scott, 2015), 237, 343, 344.

112. Sang, *Just for Today*, 250; Titus Too, "Jean Marie Seroney: A Fearless Champion of Democracy," *East African Standard*, 11 July 2010.

113. Pauline Tum, interview by author, Leseru, 9 June 2015.

114. Aaron Juma Wechuli, interview by author, Lumakanda, 31 October 2012; Stanley arap Songok, interview by author, Sosiani, 20 November 2012.

115. Helen Kirua, interview by author, Leseru, 3 December 2012; Karen Misavo, interview by author, Lumakanda, 31 October 2012; Difina Agatha, interview by author, Lumakanda, 3 November 2012; Coretta Visyafua, interview by author, Lumakanda, 7 November 2012; Felistas Muriga Nasambu, interview by author, Lumakanda, 9 November 2012.

116. Jamin Maneno Kihinga, interview by author, Lumakanda, 8 November 2012; Florence Konyonyi, interview by author, Lumakanda, 7 November 2012; Jepkosgei Kirwa Kili, interview by author, Tapsagoi, 12 January 2013.

117. Pauline Tum, interview by author, Leseru, 22 November 2012.

118. Rael Serem, interview by author, Leseru, 3 December 2012.

119. Nora Kasigene, interview by author, Lumakanda, 18 July 2016.

120. Rael Serem, interview by author, Leseru, 3 December 2012.

121. KNA KA/6/20, Philip Musungu, Secretary Salande Squatters, to Mr. Kariithi, PS Office of the President, "Ref: The Complaint from a Group of Squatters Who Call Themselves as 'Salande Squatters,'" 26 February 1973.

122. Frederick Kemboi arap Tum Kaptulus, interview by author, Leseru, 22 November 2012.

123. Kenya's first elections in 1957 did not offer franchise to women, the landless, or the poor, and weighted votes. Even when these rights were amended as franchise was extended and votes were no longer weighted, gender and class continued to determine landownership and the spectrum of rights accessible to citizens.

124. Some communities experienced dramatic improvements to maternal and child health-care provision. However, such services became available unevenly. For squatters, access to clinics often remained limited.

125. Mary Kitur, interview by author, Leseru, 19 November 2012.

126. From the 1963 independence elections to the 1969 elections, Kenyan voter turnout dropped from 71.6 percent of registered voters to just 46.7 percent. David Throup, "Elections and Political Legitimacy in Kenya," *Africa* 63, no. 3 (1993): 375.

CHAPTER 4: "IF I WAS EVICTED, WHERE COULD I GO?"

1. KNA TR/27/24, "List of Farm Purchasing Co-operatives Which Have Purchased Farms as of 10/9/65."

2. KNA TR/27/24, Nikolaus Newiger, "Co-operative Farming in the Former Scheduled Areas of Kenya," 14 October 1965.

3. KNA TR/8/885, Turbo Munyaka Co-op Society to the commissioner for Cooperative Development, Nairobi, the co-operative officer, Eldoret, "Most Urgent, Re: Expulsion of Mr. Makumi Muiru," 30 April 1968.

4. KNA TR/8/885, Makumi Muiru to co-operative officer, Eldoret, May 1968.

5. KNA TR/8/885, Makumi Muiru to co-operative officer, Eldoret, May 1968.

6. See file KNA TR/8/885.

7. KNA AVS/3/45, "Minutes of Staff Meeting held in office of area settlement controller (West) on Tuesday, 27th April, 1965."

8. KNA BN/85/12, Settlement Fund Trustees to the PS, Ministry of Lands and Settlement, "Re: Implementation of Revised Development Plan 1966/70 Progress Report," January 1967.

9. KNA BN/84/20, T. K. Patel, senior investigations officer, "Yearly General Report on Progress Loan Repayments—Investigations and Legal Matters," 5 September 1967.

10. Many African nations promoted cooperative societies: Dwayne Woods, "The Politics of Organising the Countryside: Rural Cooperatives in Côte D'Ivoire," *Journal of Modern African Studies* 37, no. 3 (1999): 489–506; John H. Hamer, "Preconditions and Limits in the Formation of Associations: The Self-Help and Cooperative Movement in Subsaharan Africa," *African Studies Review* 24, no. 1 (1981): 113–32.

11. John W. Harbeson, *Nation-Building in Kenya: The Role of Land Reform* (Evanston, IL: Northwestern University Press, 1973), 287.

12. KNA BN/85/12, Settlement Fund Trustees to the PS, Ministry of Lands and Settlement, "Re: Implementation of Revised Development Plan 1966/70 Progress Report," January 1967.

13. The 1970 USAID-sponsored Tootell Mission on Agricultural Credit noted that no institution can "extend production-increasing credit in the near future to scores of thousands of Kenya small farmers." Cited from Colin Leys, *Underdevelopment in Kenya: The Political Economy of Neo-Colonialism, 1964–1971* (Berkeley: University of California Press, 1975), 98.

14. For works that focus on the state as development agent, see Colin Leys, *The Rise and Fall of Development Theory* (London: James Currey, 1996), vi, 7; James Ferguson, *The Anti-Politics Machine: "Development," Depoliticization, and Bureaucratic Power in Lesotho* (Minneapolis: University of Minnesota Press, 1990), xiv. Much of the scholarship that moves beyond the state centers on NGOs: Gregory Mann, *From Empires to NGOs in the West African Sahel: The Road to Nongovernmentality* (New York: Cambridge University Press, 2014); Michael Jennings, *Surrogates of the State: NGOs, Development, and Ujamaa in Tanzania* (Bloomfield, CT: Kumarian Press, 2008).

15. Here, Mamdani's notion of "decentralized despotisms" is useful for its state spatialization. Mahmood Mamdani, *Citizen and Subject: Contemporary Africa and the Legacy of Late Colonialism* (Princeton, NJ: Princeton University Press, 1996).

16. Jack Shaffer, *Historical Dictionary of the Cooperative Movement* (Lanham, MD: Scarecrow Press, 1999).

17. KNA TR/1/118, Michael Chege Kuria, Ministry of Cooperative Development, "Special Focus on Co-operative Movement in Independent Kenya" [undated, but likely 1983].

18. Paul Mosley, *The Settler Economies: Studies in the Economic History of Kenya and Southern Rhodesia, 1900–1963* (Cambridge: Cambridge University Press, 1983), 40.

19. KNA TR/1/118, Michael Chege Kuria, Ministry of Cooperative Development, "Special Focus on Co-operative Movement in Independent Kenya" [undated, but likely 1983].

20. KNA TR/1/118, Michael Chege Kuria, Ministry of Cooperative Development, "Special Focus on Co-operative Movement in Independent Kenya" [undated, but likely 1983].

21. Expensive inputs and licenses, administrative prohibitions, and exclusion from credit services made it nearly impossible for Africans to produce crops such as coffee, tea, or pyrethrum. Mosley, *Settler Economies*, 40.

22. Wattle production represents an exception and was encouraged among African smallholders earlier. Gavin N. Kitching, *Class and Economic Change in Kenya: The Making of an African Petite-Bourgeoisie, 1905–1970* (New Haven, CT: Yale University Press, 1980), 63–64.

23. Michael P. Cowen, "The Commercialization of Food Production in Kenya after 1945," in *Imperialism, Colonialism, and Hunger: East and Central Africa*, ed. Robert I. Rotberg (Lexington, MA: Lexington Books, 1983), 199.

24. KNA TR/1/118, Michael Chege Kuria, Ministry of Cooperative Development, "Special Focus on Co-operative Movement in Independent Kenya" [undated, but likely 1983].

25. KNA TR/10/114, Registrar of co-operative societies to the Hon. Chief Secretary, "Co-operation," 3 July 1947.

26. Steven Feierman has argued that cooperatives were "the economic equivalent of indirect rule's Native Authorities." Feierman, *Peasant Intellectuals: Anthropology and History in Tanzania* (Madison: University of Wisconsin Press, 1990), 233. See also Paul B. Rich, "Bernard Huss and the Experiment in African Cooperatives in South Africa, 1926–1948," *International Journal of African Historical Studies* 26, no. 2 (1993): 297.

27. KNA TR/1/118, Michael Chege Kuria, Ministry of Cooperative Development, "Special Focus on Co-operative Movement in Independent Kenya" [undated, but likely 1983].

28. KNA TR/1/118, Michael Chege Kuria, Ministry of Cooperative Development, "Special Focus on Co-operative Movement in Independent Kenya" [undated, but likely 1983].

29. KNA TR/10/114, Registrar of co-operative societies to the Hon. Chief Secretary, "Co-operation," 3 July 1947.

30. KNA TR/10/114, Registrar of co-operative Societies to the Hon. Chief Secretary, "Legislative Council: Communication from the Chair," 24 September 1947.

31. KNA TR/10/114, E. J. A. Leslie, registrar of cooperative societies, to the secretary for Agriculture, "The Co-operative Movement in Kenya," 29 May 1952.

32. KNA TR/10/114, E. J. A. Leslie, registrar of cooperative societies, to the secretary for Agriculture, "The Co-operative Movement in Kenya," 29 May 1952.

33. KNA TR/10/114, M. X. Rodrigues, for registrar of cooperative societies, "Co-operative Societies and Their Place in Economic and Social Development," 21 March 1955.

34. Mosley, *Settler Economies*, 40.

35. KNA TR/10/114, M. X. Rodrigues, for registrar of cooperative societies, "Co-operative Societies and Their Place in Economic and Social Development," 21 March 1955.

36. KNA TR/10/114, M. X. Rodrigues, for registrar of cooperative societies, "Co-operative Societies and Their Place in Economic and Social Development," 21 March 1955.

37. KNA TR/10/114, M. X. Rodrigues, for registrar of cooperative societies, "Co-operative Societies and Their Place in Economic and Social Development," 21 March 1955.

38. KNA TR/10/114, E. J. A. Leslie, registrar of cooperative societies, to the secretary for Agriculture, "The Co-operative Movement in Kenya," 29 May 1952.

39. KNA BN/81/165, P. M. Gordon, Ministry of Agriculture and Animal Husbandry, to Ministry of Commerce and Industry, Ministry of Labour, Ministry of Land Settlement and Water Development, Department of the Registrar-General, "Co-operative Development," 18 May 1962.

40. Hans Holmén, *State, Cooperatives and Development in Africa* (Uppsala: Scandinavian Institute of African Studies, 1990), 5.

41. Amy L. S. Staples, *The Birth of Development: How the World Bank, Food and Agriculture Organization, and World Health Organization Changed the World, 1945–1965* (Kent, OH: Kent State University Press, 2006), 10.

42. KNA BN/81/165, "Minutes of a Meeting held in the Office of the Minister for Land Settlement on 5/7/62 . . ."

43. The expansion of cooperatives was based on Israeli cooperatives. KNA BN/81/165, P. M. Gordon, Ministry of Agriculture and Animal Husbandry, to Ministry of Commerce and Industry, Ministry of Labour, Ministry of Land Settlement and Water Development, Department of the Registrar-General, "Co-operative Development," 18 May 1962.

44. KNA BN/81/165, Sandy Storrar, Deputy Director of Agriculture, "Preliminary Paper on Co-operative Farming Based on Observation Made during a Recent Visit to Israel," 6 March 1962; Tom Mboya, *Freedom and After* (London: Andre Deutsch, 1963), 172; David Samuelson, "A Citizen of Israel," *American Jewish Times Outlook*, September 1964, 90, https://archive.org/stream/americanjewishti1964unse/americanjewishti1964unse_djvu.txt. French Algeria also looked to Israel and sent technocrats there for training.

45. KNA BN/81/165, T. A. Watts, acting director of Settlement, to PS/SW, "Land Ownership and Management by Co-operative Societies" [undated, but likely 1962].

46. KNA BN/81/165, T. A. Watts, acting director of Settlement, to PS/SW, "Land Ownership and Management by Co-operative Societies" [undated, but likely 1962]. Tom Mboya, Masinde Muliro, and Bruce McKenzie all publicly advocated for the Israeli model.

47. KNA TR/1/118, Michael Chege Kuria, Ministry of Cooperative Development, "Special Focus on Co-operative Movement in Independent Kenya" [undated, but likely 1983]; Shaffer, *Historical Dictionary of the Cooperative Movement*, 280.

48. KNA TR/1/118, Michael Chege Kuria, Ministry of Cooperative Development, "Special Focus on Co-operative Movement in Independent Kenya" [undated, but likely 1983].

49. SOAS, Christian Aid (second deposit), Box CA2/A/9/4, Standing Conference of Voluntary Organisations Co-operating in Overseas Social Service, "Voluntary Service in Kenya," August 1967.

50. SOAS, Christian Aid (second deposit), Box CA2/A/9/5, "Annual Progress Report January 1973: Partnership for Productivity (PFP) and West Kenya Productivity Investments Ltd. (WKPI)."

51. KNA TR/27/24, "Co-operative Farming within the Context of African Socialism" [unauthored, undated].

52. KNA TR/1/350, "Report on Cooperative Development within Settlement for the Year ended 30th June, 1964."

53. Josephine H. Wanja, "Land on Loan: An Analysis of the Factors Affecting Loan Repayment on the Million Acre Schemes" (Working Paper No. 355, University of Nairobi, 1979), 55.

54. KNA TR/27/24, "Co-operative Farming within the Context of African Socialism," [unauthored, undated]; KNA AVS/3/45, "Minutes of the first staff meeting held in the Board's Offices, Kericho, at 10.30 A.M. on Tuesday, 30th October, 1962."

55. KNA TR/1/129, "Speech by the Permanent Secretary for Cooperatives and Social Services, Mr. J. N. Oluoch, at the Kenya Institute of Administration on 5th May, 1971."

56. Cooperative membership in settlement was "nearly universal," and administrators "gave high priority to gaining 100 percent membership." Harbeson, *Nation-Building in Kenya*, 286.

57. Rastos Omamo, interview by author, Lumakanda, 9 November 2012.

58. KNA TR/27/24, "Cooperative Farming within the Context of African Socialism [unathored, undated].

59. Patrick Zieze, interview by author, Lumakanda, 7 November 2012.

60. KNA TR/1/350, "Report on Cooperative Development within Settlement for the Year ended 30th June, 1964."

61. KNA TR/1/350, "Report on Cooperative Development within Settlement for the Year ended 30th June, 1964."

62. KNA TR/1/208, "Sessional Paper No. 8 of 1970: Co-operative Development Policy for Kenya."

63. Shaffer, *Historical Dictionary of the Cooperative Movement*, 280.

64. KNA BN/81/165, Acting commissioner for Co-operative Development, "Memorandum: An Appreciation of Settlement Problems and the Role of Co-operative Societies" [undated, but likely 1962].

65. KNA TR/1/208, "Sessional Paper No. 8 of 1970: Co-operative Development Policy for Kenya." Another report on cooperatives uses different numbers, recording 1,632 cooperatives in 1973. KNA TR/1/208, "A Brief Report on the Kenya Co-operative Movement in the Last Decade: Progress, Achievement, and Problems," 1973 [unauthored].

66. KNA TR/1/75, J. M. Wanyoike, executive officer of Kenya Dairy Board, to all dairy farmers co-operative societies, 14 July 1967.

67. KNA TR/11/168, G. Waithaka, cooperative assistant education (Settlement), to the assistant commissioner for Cooperative Development (Settlement), "Education and Training Participation Problems," 8 February 1971.

68. KNA TR/1/210, "Record of Meeting of the Committee set up by the Minister to Consider the Half Million Acre Scheme on the 25th October, 1963."

69. KNA TR/11/168, M. Teravainen, Nordic adviser (Ed)(S), for assistant commissioner for Cooperative Development (S), to the principal, Dairy Training School, Naivasha, 1 September 1970.

70. KNA TR/1/75, J. M. Wanyoike, executive officer of Kenya Dairy Board, to all dairy farmers co-operative societies, 14 July 1967.

71. KNA TR/1/75, J. M. Wanyoike, executive officer of Kenya Dairy Board, "The Dairy Industry in Kenya" [undated].

72. The Dairy Board tended to protect the KCC by refusing to license smallholders for direct deliveries, and Kenyan farmers accused the KCC of racial discrimination, neocolonialism, and regionalism. Robert H. Bates, *Beyond the Miracle of the Market: The Political Economy of Agrarian Development in Kenya* (New York: Cambridge University Press, 1992), 83.

73. KNA TR/1/208, Ministry of Co-operative Development, "Sessional Paper No. 14 of 1975, Co-operative Development Policy for Kenya," January 1975.

74. KNA TR/8/1184, Sosiani Farmers Co-op Society Ltd., to the commissioner for Co-operative Development, "Application for Purchase of Tractor 1972," 21 July 1972.

75. Alfred Machayo, interview by author, Chekalini, 1 November 2012.

76. Kiptoo arap Maina, interview by author, Leseru, 23 November 2012.

77. KNA DC/UG, B. A. Osundwa, senior district commissioner, Uasin Gishu District Annual Report, 1970.

78. Ainea Alulu, interview by author, Lumakanda, 5 November 2012.

79. Jairo Murunga Libapu, interview by author, Lumakanda, 3 November 2012.

80. KNA TR/1/75, J. M. Wanyoike, executive officer of Kenya Dairy Board, to all dairy farmers co-operative societies, 14 July 1967.

81. KNA TR/8/1617, H. E. Agimba, assistant commissioner for Co-operative Development (S) to co-operative officer (s), Turbo, "Milk Delivery to KCC," 11 July 1973.

82. KNA TR/8/1617, Members of Lumakanda extension Block D to the commissioner of Co-operatives, 14 June 1974.

83. Wanja, "Land on Loan," 29–30.

84. KNA TR/8/885, P. A. Gwada, for commissioner for Co-operative Development, to the district co-operative officer, Kitale, 1 April 1971.

85. See all of KNA TR/8/885, Turbo Munyaka Coop Society Ltd.

86. KNA TR/8/885, Turbo Munyaka Farmer Co-op Society (signed by "Chairman") to the commissioner for Co-operative Development, "Re: Removal of the Society's Officers," 19 March 1973.

87. KNA TR/8/885, Turbo Munyaka Farmer Co-op Society (signed by "Chairman") to the commissioner for Co-operative Development, "Re: Removal of the Society's Officers," 19 March 1973.

88. KNA TR/8/885, William M. Njoroge, district cooperative officer, Kitale, to the acting assistant commissioner for Co-operative Development, Rift Valley Province, 6 March 1973.

89. KNA TR/8/885, William M. Njoroge, district cooperative officer, Kitale, to the commissioner for Co-operative Development, 23 July 1973.

90. KNA TR/1/118, Michael Chege Kuria, Ministry of Cooperative Development, "Special Focus on Co-operative Movement in Independent Kenya" [undated, but likely 1983].

91. Many of these programs took place at farmer's training centers, first established in the 1950s and 1960s by the colonial state to educate Africans about high-modernist agriculture. KNA TR/11/168, Harry Pederson, Nordic adviser, to the commissioner for Co-operative Development (S), "Education and Training Within Settlement," August 1968; KNA TR/11/168, Harry Pederson, Nordic adviser, "Summary and Evaluation of Education Activities within the Department of Settlement in the Last Half of 1968—from 1st July to 31st December, 1968."

92. KNA TR/27/24, Nikolaus Newiger, "Co-operative Farming in the Former Scheduled Areas of Kenya," 14 October 1965.

93. KNA TR/1/231, Per Tau Strand, Nordic education adviser, to the commissioner for Co-operative Development, "Notes on Uasin Gishu/Trans Nzoya [*sic*]. Mainly Large Scale Co-operative Farms," 16 October 1972.

94. KNA AVS/3/45, "Minutes of the staff meeting held in the office of the Area Settlement Controller (West) on Wednesday, 24th February, 1965."

95. KNA TR/1/201, H. E. Agimba, acting assistant commissioner for Co-operative Development, to the commissioner for Co-operative Development, "Cooperative Organisation in Settlement Schemes," 6 November 1971.

96. Jomo Kenyatta, "Speech at the Opening of Gatanga Coffee Co-operative Factory," 10 October 1964, in *Harambee! The Prime Minister of Kenya's Speeches*,

1963–1964: *From the Attainment of Internal Self-Government to the Threshold of the Kenya Republic* (Nairobi: Oxford University Press, 1964), 71.

97. KNA TR/8/1849, D. Onyango Arende, for acting assistant commissioner for Coop. Development (S), to the area settlement controller (N), "Sosiani Farmers Co-operative Society Ltd (Proposed)," 16 November 1967. The original Ndalat cooperative spanned Nandi and Uasin Gishu Districts; the cooperatives split along the district boundary.

98. Steven Kiplemai Ngetich, interview by author, Sosiani, 4 December 2012; Selena Chelimo Barno, interview by author, Leseru, 28 November 2012.

99. KNA TR/8/1849, D. Onyango Arende, for acting assistant commissioner for Coop. Development (South), to the area settlement controller (North), "Sosiani Farmers Co-operative Society Ltd (Proposed)," 16 November 1967. This could have been a coded term for clan or neighborhood differences, but it might have regarded the split in the Nandi community between those in reserve and those in the former scheduled areas.

100. Margaret Wanjiru Nyanya, interview by author, Mautuma, 11 November 2012; Joseph Dugere Munge, interview by author, Mautuma, 11 November 2012.

101. Muzole Shioani, interview by author, Lumakanda, 13 November 2012.

102. Alfred Machayo, interview by author, Chekalini, 1 November 2012. See also Leys, *Underdevelopment in Kenya*, 98.

103. Mary Kitur, interview by author, Leseru, 19 November 2012.

104. Muzole Shioani, interview by author, Lumakanda, 13 November 2012.

105. Tiengik arap Sawe, interview by author, Tapsagoi, 12 January 2013.

106. KNA TR/1/100, David Ndegwa Karanja, Ngene Nganga, and Mwangi Maina to the PS, Co-op Society, "Ref: Claims," 6 August 1967.

107. KNA TR/1/100, David Ndegwa Karanja, Ngene Nganga, and Mwangi Maina to the PS, Co-op Society, "Ref: Claims," 6 August 1967.

108. Rastos Omamo, interview by author, Lumakanda, 16 November 2012.

109. Alfred Machayo, interview by author, Chekalini, 1 November 2012.

110. Joseph arap Bir'geng, interview by author, Sosiani, 20 November 2012.

111. Joseph arap Bir'geng, interview by author, Sosiani, 20 November 2012.

112. KNA TR/8/779, A. K. Ndeti, acting assistant commissioner for Co-operative Development (S), to the commissioner for Co-operative Development (S), "Lugari Farmers Cooperative Society Ltd," 14 June 1965.

113. KNA TR/8/779, A. K. Ndeti, acting assistant commissioner for Co-operative Development (S), to the commissioner for Co-operative Development (S), "Lugari Farmers Cooperative Society Ltd," 14 June 1965.

114. KNA TR/8/77, Roop Lal Chadha, inquiry officer of SFT, to commissioner for Co-operative Development, 2 July 1965.

115. KNA TR/8/77, Roop Lal Chadha, inquiry officer of SFT, to commissioner for Co-operative Development, 2 July 1965.

116. KNA TR/8/77, Roop Lal Chadha, inquiry officer of SFT, to commissioner for Co-operative Development, 2 July 1965.

117. Patrick Zieze, interview by author, Lumakanda, 7 November 2012; Aaron Juma Wechuli, interview by author, Lumakanda, 31 October 2012; Mareb Noyi, interview by author, Lumakanda, 8 November 2012; Solome Teregin, interview by author, Leseru, 26 November 2012.

118. KNA BN/81/35, A. Davies, director of Land Adjudication, "Five Year Development Progress Review. Land Adjudication, Consolidation and Registration," 27 May 1968. Land loans only represented the largest of the agricultural loans farmers gained access to on settlement schemes.

119. Kenya's dependence on agriculture also contributed to close state regulation.

120. KNA TR/8/779, E. V. Powell, assistant commissioner for Co-operative Development (S), to commissioner for Co-operative Development, Ministry of Commerce and Industry, "Application for Registration: Lugari Farmers Cooperative Society Limited," 6 September 1963.

121. KNA AVS/3/45, "Minutes of the staff meeting held in the office of the Area Settlement Controller (West)," 24 February 1965.

122. KNA BV/6/877, B. B. F. Russell, acting chief executive officer, to all members of the CAB, "Information to all Farmers," 11 June 1964.

123. KNA BV/6/877, Memorandum by Minister McKenzie of Agriculture and Animal Husbandry, "Draft: The Cabinet: The Wheat Industry" [undated, but 1963].

124. KNA BN/81/34, C. Kahara, "Summary of Van Arkadie Report," 15 February 1967.

125. Republic of Kenya, *The National Assembly, House of Representatives Official Report (Hansard)*, vol. 5, 14 July 1965.

126. By the 1970s, policymakers realized settlers' loan burden was unmanageable. J. R. Njenga, director of Settlement, noted that "the level of production on small plots in the Million Acre programme cannot service the high rate of interest, namely 6½% so far charged on land and development loans. It is, therefore, proposed to discontinue charging interest on arrears." KNA TR/1/201, J. R. Njenga, director of Settlement, "Land Transfer and Land Settlement 1974/78." See also KNA AVS/1/150, Department of Co-operative Development (Settlement), "Land Transfer and Land Settlement 1974/78."

127. Wanja, "Land on Loan," 56.

128. KNA AVS/13/20, Senior settlement officer Sirikwa (Standa), to the director of Settlement, "Monthly Report for January 1970. Sirikwa Area," 31 March 1970.

129. Alfred Machayo, interview by author, Chekalini, 1 November 2012.

130. KNA BV/1/538, J. M. B. Butter for G. M. Bebb, executive officer, to chief agriculturalist, "Loan to African Farmers—Legco Question No. 229 (Hon. J. L. Porter MLC), Loans to African Farmers," 19 April 1962.

131. KNA TR/1/201, J. R. Njenga, director of Settlement, "Land Transfer and Land Settlement 1974/78." Settlers had paid £4.07 million out of the £7.50 million due by that time.

132. Certainly, it was not the only cause. The impossible loan terms, changing global market, and misinformed planning also played a part.

133. Rastos Omamo, interview by author, Lumakanda, 9 November 2012.

134. Wanja, "Land on Loan," 57.

135. Wanja, "Land on Loan," 56–57.

136. KNA BN/84/20, T. K. Patel, senior investigations officer, "Yearly General Report on Progress Loan Repayments—Investigations and Legal Matters," 5 September 1967.

137. KNA AVS/3/22, G. R. H. to director of Settlement, "Re: Agricultural Amendment Bill," 29 January 1965.

138. KNA BN/81/34, C. Kahara, "Summary of Van Arkadie Report," 15 February 1967; Leys, *Underdevelopment in Kenya*, 79–80.

139. KNA BN/84/20, T. K. Patel, senior investigations officer, "Yearly General Report on Progress Loan Repayments—Investigations and Legal Matters," 5 September 1967.

140. KNA BN/84/20, T. K. Patel, senior investigations officer, "Yearly General Report on Progress Loan Repayments—Investigations and Legal Matters," 5 September 1967.

141. KNA BN/84/8, J. S. Mburu, director of Settlement, to PCs Nyeri, Western, Rift Valley, Eastern, Nyanza, "Eviction of Settlers from Settlement Scheme Plots and Selection of Replacement of Settlers," 4 May 1967.

142. KNA BN/84/20, "Record of Meeting . . . on Friday 4th August, 1967 to discuss a Two Year Moratorium for Settlers."

143. KNA BN/84/20, T. K. Patel, senior investigations officer, "Yearly General Report on Progress Loan Repayments—Investigations and Legal Matters," 5 September 1967. See also NAUK FCO 141/18961.

144. KNA AVS/3/41, J. H. Hickman, Admin. Officer, Senior Settlement Officer, Nakuru, "Staff Meeting Held by Senior Settlement Officer Mr. P. G. A. Smith," Eldoret, 14 October 1965.

145. KNA BN/84/20, T. K. Patel, senior investigations officer, "Yearly General Report on Progress Loan Repayments—Investigations and Legal Matters," 5 September 1967. After Jomo Kenyatta's statement about the moratorium, the rate of repayment dropped by 50 percent.

146. KNA BN/84/20, J. N. Michuki, PS the Treasury, to G. K. Kariithi, PS, Office of the President, and P. Shiyukah, PS Ministry of Land and Settlement, "Moratorium to Settlers," 30 May 1967.

147. KNA BN/84/20, J. N. Michuki, PS the Treasury, to G. K. Kariithi, PS, Office of the President, and P. Shiyukah, PS Ministry of Land and Settlement, "Moratorium to Settlers," 30 May 1967.

148. KNA BN/84/20, P. Shiyukah, PS Ministry of Land and Settlement, to G. K. Kariithi, PS, Office of the President, "Moratorium to Settlers," 5 May 1967.

149. KNA BN/84/20, P. Shiyukah, PS Ministry of Land and Settlement, to all Area Settlement Controllers, "Re: Evictions of Settlers v/s Two Year Moratorium," 6 June 1967.

150. KNA BN/84/20, M. A. Collings, financial secretary (Settlement), to the Officer Administering the Settlement Funds, 24 May 1967.

151. KNA BN/84/20, M. A. Collings, financial secretary (Settlement), to the Officer Administering the Settlement Funds, 24 May 1967.

152. KNA BN/84/20, "Land Settlement: Loan Repayments: Overall financial effect of a moratorium for new settlers and for cases of hardship among existing settlers," 10 July 1967.

153. Warengai is one of the few members of Parliament depicted in a positive light. More often, interlocutors recalled that politicians came around only ahead of elections when they wanted votes.

154. KNA BN/84/20, P. Shiyukah, PS Ministry of Land and Settlement, to G. K. Kariithi, PS Office of the President, "Moratorium to Settlers," 5 May 1967.

155. Patrick Zieze, interview by author, Lumakanda, 7 November 2012.

156. Patrick Zieze, interview by author, Lumakanda, 7 November 2012.

157. Joseph arap Bir'geng, interview by author, Sosiani, 20 November 2012.

158. On loans and indebtedness in Western Kenya, see Parker Shipton, *Mortgaging the Ancestors: Ideologies of Attachment in Africa* (New Haven, CT: Yale University Press, 2009).

159. Patrick Zieze, interview by author, Lumakanda, 7 November 2012.

160. Wanja, "Land on Loan," 18–20.

161. Patrick Zieze, interview by author, Lumakanda, 7 November 2012.

162. KNA BN/81/35, "Review of Kenya's Five Year Progress and Achievement in Land Tenure and Administration," 6 August 1968.

163. KNA TR/1/208, L. O. Kibinge, PS Ministry of Foreign Affairs, to Mr. Joshua Muthami, commissioner of Co-operatives, "Heads of Missions of Meeting," 19 July 1975.

164. Even for those who were not evicted, their indebtedness often meant they would eventually sell a portion of their land. This will be discussed in the conclusion.

CHAPTER 5: "A HUNGRY NATION CANNOT BE CONTENTED"

1. KNA TR/1/333, Paul Ngei, "The Application of African Socialism to Co-operative Marketing in Kenya," 5 May 1965.

2. Famines occur not because of shortages, but because of distribution mechanisms at both macro- and microlevels. Amartya Sen, *Poverty and Famines: An Essay on Entitlement and Deprivation* (Oxford: Clarendon Press, 1981).

3. Among scholars of Kenya, this debate has been particularly robust and has focused on indigenous capitalist accumulation and development. Gavin N. Kitching, *Class and Economic Change in Kenya: The Making of an African Petite-Bourgeoisie, 1905–1970* (New Haven, CT: Yale University Press, 1980); Colin Leys, *Underdevelopment in Kenya: The Political Economy of Neo-Colonialism, 1964–1971* (Berkeley: University of California Press, 1975); Michael P. Cowen, "Wattle Production in the Central Province: Capital and Household Commodity Production, 1903–1964" (Miscellaneous Paper 104, University of Nairobi Institute of Development Studies, 1975); Colin Leys, "Capital Accumulation, Class Formation and Dependency: The Significance of the Kenyan Case," *Socialist Register* 15 (1978): 241–66; Raphael Kaplinsky, "Capitalist Accumulation in the Periphery: The Kenyan Case Re-Examined," *Review of African Political Economy* 7, no. 17 (1980): 83–105; Steven Langdon, "Industry and Capitalism in Kenya: Contributions to a Debate," in *The African Bourgeoisie: Capitalist Development in Nigeria, Kenya, and the Ivory Coast*, ed. Paul M. Lubeck (Boulder, CO: Lynne Rienner, 1987). More generally, see A. G. Hopkins, *An Economic History of West Africa* (New York: Columbia University Press, 1973); Edward A. Alpers, *Ivory and Slaves: Changing Pattern of International Trade in East Central Africa to the Later Nineteenth Century* (Berkeley: University of California Press, 1975); Frederick Cooper, "Africa and the World Economy," *African Studies Review* 24, nos. 2–3 (1981): 8.

4. Goran Hyden, *Beyond Ujamaa in Tanzania: Underdevelopment and an Uncaptured Peasantry* (Berkeley: University of California Press, 1980).

5. On moral economies, see John Lonsdale, "Moral Ethnicity, Ethnic Nationalism and Political Tribalism: The Case of the Kikuyu," in *Staat und Gesellschaft in Afrika: Erosions und Reformprozesse*, ed. Peter Meyns (Hamburg: Lit Verlag, 1996), 93–106; Derek R. Peterson, *Creative Writing: Translation, Bookkeeping, and the Work of Imagination in Colonial Kenya* (Portsmouth, NH: Heinemann, 2004).

6. Clifton Crais, *Poverty, War, and Violence in South Africa* (Cambridge: Cambridge University Press, 2011), 1.

7. Gregory Maddox, "*Mtunya*: Famine in Central Tanzania, 1917–20," *Journal of African History* 31, no. 2 (1990): 188–89; James L. Giblin, *The Politics of Environmental Control in Northeastern Tanzania, 1840–1940* (Philadelphia: University of Pennsylvania Press, 1992), 122; Charles H. Ambler, *Kenyan Communities in the Age of Imperialism: The Central Region in the Late Nineteenth Century* (New Haven, CT: Yale University Press, 1988), 123.

8. Joel S. Migdal. *State in Society: Studying How States and Societies Transform and Constitute One Another* (Cambridge: Cambridge University Press, 2001), 36.

9. Many African societies used famine to make sense of historical transformations: Maddox, "*Mtunya*," 182; Ambler, *Kenyan Communities*, 3.

10. The district has historically produced over 10 percent of the nation's maize and about a quarter of its wheat. Karuti Kanyinga, "The Land Question in Kenya: Struggles, Accumulation and Changing Politics" (PhD diss., Roskilde University, 1998), 169.

11. James C. McCann, *Maize and Grace: Africa's Encounter with a New World Crop, 1500–2000* (Cambridge, MA: Harvard University Press, 2005), 6. See also Peter D. Little, *The Elusive Granary: Herder, Farmer, and State in Northern Kenya* (New York: Cambridge University Press, 1992).

12. Steven Kiplemai Ngetich, interview by author, Sosiani, 3 December 2012; Joseph arap Bir'geng, interview by author, Sosiani, 20 November 2012; Stanley arap Songok, interview by author, Sosiani, 20 November 2012; Little, *Elusive Granary*; McCann, *Maize and Grace*, 170; Cynthia Brantley, *The Giriama and Colonial Resistance in Kenya, 1800–1920* (Berkeley: University of California Press, 1981), 21.

13. McCann, *Maize and Grace*, 173.

14. Little, *Elusive Granary*, 37. The adoption of maize might have contributed to nutritional deficiencies and disease outbreaks, as it did elsewhere. Crais, *Poverty, War, and Violence*, 21–22.

15. Alfred C. Hollis, *The Nandi: Their Language and Folk-Lore* (Oxford: Clarendon Press, 1909), 19; Martin S. Shanguhyia, *Population, Tradition, and Environmental Control in Colonial Kenya* (Rochester, NY: University of Rochester Press, 2015), 63–64.

16. Claire C. Robertson, *Trouble Showed the Way: Women, Men, and Trade in the Nairobi Area, 1890–1990* (Bloomington: Indiana University Press, 1997), 65.

17. Regina Smith Oboler, *Women, Power, and Economic Change: The Nandi of Kenya* (Stanford, CA: Stanford University Press, 1985), 259. In 1940s Nyeri, Kikuyu men worried about their wives' control over cash and the implications for the household. Peterson, *Creative Writing*, 169.

18. Shanguhyia, *Population, Tradition, and Environmental Control*, 66.

19. The laws governing African maize production were also differentiated by location.

20. Paul Mosley, *The Settler Economies: Studies in the Economic History of Kenya and Southern Rhodesia, 1900–1963* (Cambridge: Cambridge University Press, 1983), 41.

21. David M. Anderson, "Depression, Dust Bowl, Demography, and Drought: The Colonial State and Soil Conservation in East Africa during the 1930s," *African Affairs* 83, no. 332 (1984): 322; Kitching, *Class and Economic Change in Kenya*; Mosley, *Settler Economies*.

22. Leys, *Underdevelopment in Kenya*, 106.

23. Government of Kenya, *Report of the Maize Commission of Inquiry* (Nairobi: Republic of Kenya, 1966), 3.

24. Robert Maxon, *Going Their Separate Ways: Agrarian Transformation in Kenya, 1930–1950* (Madison, NJ: Farleigh Dickinson University Press, 2003), 173–75, 219.

25. Much of the literature on African marketing boards focuses on cocoa in British West Africa: Rod Alence, "Colonial Government, Social Conflict and State Involvement in Africa's Open Economies: The Origins of the Ghana Cocoa Marketing Board, 1939–46," *Journal of African History* 42, no. 3 (2001): 397–416; David Meredith, "The Colonial Office, British Business Interests and the Reform of Cocoa Marketing in West Africa, 1937–1945," *Journal of African History* 29, no. 2 (1988): 285–300.

26. KNA TR/27/1, "Mr. Blundell's Speech on 'The Foundation of Kenya's Prosperity'" [undated]; KNA TR/3/96, "Minutes of the 110th Meeting of the Interim Management Committee of the Joint Maize and Produce Controls, 10th July, 1959."

27. KNA DC/ELD/1/24/21, E. Chapman, divisional forest officer, Eldoret, to senior foresters, Nabkoi, Kaptagat, Timboroa, and Foresters, Nandi, Kipkabus, "Export of Maize," 7 February 1961. Africans in the reserves could barter their maize.

28. KNA DC/ELD/1/24/21, P. G. Tait, district commissioner, Uasin Gishu, to Mrs. L. A. Cooke, "Re: Posho Prices," 5 May 1959.

29. Mosley, *Settler Economies*, 50–52.

30. David M. Anderson and David Throup, "Africans and Agricultural Production in Colonial Kenya: The Myth of the War as a Watershed," *Journal of African History* 26, no. 4 (1985): 335.

31. Anderson and Throup, "Africans and Agricultural Production," 345.

32. Anderson and Throup, "Africans and Agricultural Production," 338.

33. See also Maxon, *Going Their Separate Ways*, 169.

34. Michael P. Cowen, "The Commercialization of Food Production in Kenya after 1945," in *Imperialism, Colonialism, and Hunger: East and Central Africa*, ed. Robert I. Rotberg (Lexington, MA: Lexington Books, 1983), 199.

35. Anderson and Throup, "Africans and Agricultural Production."

36. KNA TR/17/7, "Maize Commission of Inquiry 21st Day: 9th February, 1966."

37. KNA TR/17/4, "Draft: Maize Distribution," 1965.

38. KNA BV/1/368, "The Agricultural Economy of Kenya," 1961–62. Bags of maize are two hundred pounds.

39. Kenya, *Report of the Maize Commission of Inquiry*, 6.

40. Anderson and Throup, "Africans and Agricultural Production," 345.

41. KNA DC/ELD/1/24/20, (Sgd) J. P. Barnard, chairman of Uasin Gishu agricultural committee, to the CEO, Board of Agriculture, "Illegal Movement of Maize," 3 February 1959.

42. KNA DC/ELD/1/24/21, "Uasin Gishu County Council: Finance and General Purposes Committee," 24 February 1959.

43. KNA DC/ELD/1/24/21, Kenya Police to the district commissioner, Eldoret, 7 May 1959.

44. KNA BV/6/837, M. L. Dunlap, acting legal draftsman, to the PS Ministry of Agriculture, Animal Husbandry and Water Resources, "The Agricultural Ordinance, 1955 Payment of Fixed Prices for Scheduled Crops," 24 June 1959. The agricultural ordinance of 1955 required the minister to pay fixed prices to farmers.

45. KNA BV/1/368, Council of Ministers, "The Agricultural Economy of Kenya," 1961–1962.

46. Kenya, *Report of the Maize Commission of Inquiry*, chap. 1.

47. KNA TR/17/9, A. A. Haller, "Factors in Maize Prices," *East African Standard*, 29 October 1960.

48. KNA TR/3/96, Bruce McKenzie, minister for Agriculture, "Minister's Address," at the Inaugural Meeting of the Maize Marketing Board, 10 July 1959.

49. KNA DC/UG, Uasin Gishu District Annual Report, 1961.

50. KNA PC/RVP, Rift Valley Province Annual Report, 1961.

51. Frederick Kemboi arap Tum Kaptulus, interview by author, Leseru, 22 November 2012; Theresa Ngososei, interview by author, Leseru, 27 November 2012.

52. Aaron Masista, interview by author, Lumakanda, 20 July 2016.

53. JFKL, Papers of John F. Kennedy, Presidential Papers, White House Central Subject Files, Series 07. Countries, Box 63, Folder: Kenya, District Officer, Hinterland, on behalf of the Hinterland Chiefs, to JFK, 12 September 1962. Tanganyika also received American food aid in 1961, a year Tanzanians today mark as their independence anniversary, but also as the year of "Merika" or "Kenedi." Kristin D. Phillips, *An Ethnography of Hunger: Politics, Subsistence, and the Unpredictable Grace of the Sun* (Bloomington: Indiana University Press, 2018), 65.

54. Kabiru Deen, Nairobi, "Letters to the Editor: President Kennedy," *East African Standard*, 26 November 1963.

55. KNA DC/KPT/2/3/2, T. Neil, PS Office of the Minister of State for Constitutional Affairs and Administration, to all provincial commissioners, "Note on the Provision of Famine Relief," 1 August 1962.

56. Kristin Phillips has come to a similar conclusion in central Tanganyika. Following a few decades of British rule, a "minimalistic sense of entitlement to relief from famine" existed. Phillips, *Ethnography of Hunger*, 64.

57. Giblin, *Politics of Environmental Control*.

58. McCann, *Maize and Grace*, 171–72. McCann notes that the new hybrid synthetic seed H611 had a 40 percent better yield than the nonhybrid, and, after 1965, well-capitalized farms began using it.

59. In the mid-1960s, a number of different agents bought maize for the Maize Marketing Board: the MMB, the Kenya Agriculture and Produce Marketing Board (KAPMB), the Kenya Farmers Association (KFA), and the West Kenya Marketing Board.

60. KNA TR/27/1, "Evidence Submitted by the Kenya Agricultural Produce Marketing Board to the Maize Commission of Inquiry," 13 January 1966.

61. KNA BV/1/372, Bruce McKenzie to J. P. Lorema, MP, the Hon. Senator J. K. arap Chemjor, the Hon. Senator E. K. Poriott, 17 January 1964.

62. John W. Harbeson, *Nation-Building in Kenya: The Role of Land Reform* (Evanston, IL: Northwestern University Press, 1973), 311.

63. Harbeson, *Nation-Building in Kenya*, 311.

64. Kiptoo arap Maina, interview by author, Leseru, 23 November 2012.

65. KNA TR/27/1, "Evidence Submitted by the Kenya Agricultural Produce Marketing Board to the Maize Commission of Inquiry," 13 January 1966.

66. Alfred Machayo, interview by author, Chekalini, 1 November 2012. Machayo later went on to become the chief agriculturalist of Kenya and the Kenyan representative to the Food and Agriculture Organization of the United Nations. See also NAUK FCO/141/18966, T. A. Phillips, "Kenya Land Development and Settlement: Report on the Visit of July 1965."

67. KNA TR/17/5, "We Say: Look at the Great Maize Muddle," *Sunday Daily Nation*, 7 November 1965.

68. Deina Iboso, interview by author, Lumakanda, 12 November 2012; Muzole Shioani, interview by author, Lumakanda, 13 November 2012.

69. "Big Cut in Price of Kenya Posho," *Daily Nation*, 2 December 1963.

70. KNA TR/17/6, "Maize Shortage Due to 'Enormity of Export Cess,'" *East African Standard*, 5 February 1966.

71. KNA TR/17/6, "Form a Cabinet Body on Food—Mboya Proposes to Inquiry," *Daily Nation*, 21 January 1966.

72. One ton of maize is equivalent to ten bags (of two hundred pounds each).

73. KNA TR/17/6, "Marketing Board Alleged to Have Flouted Directive," 13 January 1966; "Cargo of Maize 'Largest Ever,'" *Daily Nation*, 23 November 1963.

74. KNA TR/17/4, Ministry of Cooperatives and Marketing, "Imports: Maize Commission of Inquiry" [undated, but 1966].

75. This request fell under the US Agricultural Trade Development and Assistance Act, more commonly known as PL-480 or Food for Peace.

76. KNA TR/17/4, B. C. W. Lutta, Ministry of Housing and Social Services (formerly of Ministry of Cooperatives and Marketing), "Memorandum to the Commission of Inquiry—Maize," 31 March 1966.

77. KNA TR/17/7, "Maize Commission of Inquiry Friday, 24th Day," 18 February 1966.

78. KNA TR/17/4, Ministry of Cooperatives and Marketing, the Commission of Inquiry Maize, "Imports" [undated, but 1966].

79. KNA TR/17/7, James Cooper, Ministry of Cooperatives and Marketing, "Maize Commission of Inquiry 21st Day," 9 February 1966.

80. KNA TR/1/350, Acting assistant commissioner for Cooperative Development (S), "Safari Diary," 24 November 1965.

81. KNA TR/1/350, T. W. Morgan, for acting assistant commissioner for Cooperative Development (S), to the commissioner for Cooperative Development, "Black Market in Maize in the Western Region, Upkeep of Roads in Cooperative Society Areas," 25 November 1964.

82. Republic of Kenya, *The National Assembly Official Report (Hansard)*, vol. 4, 6 May 1965.

83. Kenya, *Report of the Maize Commission of Inquiry*. See also KNA PC/RVP, Rift Valley Province Annual Report, 1965.

84. KNA TR/1/350, "Safari Diary, Ag. Asst. Commissioner for Cooperative Development (S)," 24 November 1965.

85. Theresa Ngososei, interview by author, Leseru, 27 November 2012.

86. KNA TR/17/4, B. C. W. Lutta, Ministry of Housing and Social Services (formerly of Ministry of Cooperatives and Marketing), "Memorandum to the Commission of Inquiry—Maize," 31 March 1966.

87. KNA TR/17/4, J. Cooper (SAS), "Cabinet Committee—Food Shortage," 12 July 1965.

88. KNA TR/17/4, Provincial commissioner, Western Province, to Mr. Andere, G.M., Kenya Marketing Board, 27 July 1965.

89. KNA TR/17/4, J. Cooper to PS, "Maize Distribution" [undated].

90. KNA TR/17/4, B. C. W. Lutta to D. N. Ndegwa, PS Office of the President, "Maize Distribution," 29 October 1965.

91. KNA TR/17/4, B. C. W. Lutta, Ministry of Housing and Social Services (formerly of Ministry of Cooperatives and Marketing), "Memorandum to the Commission of Inquiry—Maize," 31 March 1966.

92. KNA TR/17/6, "'Unappointed Minister': Ngei Never Signed Letter, Maize Inquiry Told," *Daily Nation*, 23 February 1966; "'Agents Probably Sold Maize Privately,'" *Daily Nation*, 15 March 1966; "Emma Stores Now Closed Inquiry Told," *East African Standard*, 16 March 1966.

93. KNA TR/17/6, "Emma Stores Now Closed Inquiry Told," *East African Standard*, 16 March 1966.

94. KNA TR/17/6, "Emma Stores Now Closed Inquiry Told," *East African Standard*, 16 March 1966.

95. KNA TR/17/6, "'Agents Probably Sold Maize Privately,'" *Daily Nation*, 15 March 1966.

96. KNA TR/17/5, "Maize Probe Urged: Farmers' Union President Hits out at Marketing Board," *Daily Nation*, 27 October 1965.

97. KNA TR/17/5, "KNFU Attacks Maize Board on Famine Attitude," *East African Standard*, 27 October 1965.

98. KNA TR/17/5, "'Full Maize Quotes for Millers,' Posho should be available—Ngei," *Daily Nation*, 3 November 1965.

99. KNA TR/17/5, "We Say: Look at the Great Maize Muddle," *Sunday Nation*, 7 November 1965.

100. KNA TR/17/5, "We Say: Look at the Great Maize Muddle," *Sunday Nation*, 7 November 1965.

101. KNA TR/17/5, Non-Posho Eater and Seller, Naivasha, "Face the Facts, Mr. Andere," *Daily Nation*, 1 November 1965.

102. KNA TR/17/5, James. D. Gathuri, Kiambu, "Letters to the Editor: Call for Inquiry," *Daily Nation*, 4 November 1965.

103. KNA TR/17/5, Manoah Kisame, Nakuru, "A 'Thank You' on Maize Shortage," *Daily Nation*, 6 November 1965.

104. KNA TR/17/5, Gabriel Ndula, Nairobi, "Letters to the Editor: Hungry Nation Cannot Be Contented," *Daily Nation*, 4 November 1965.

105. KNA TR/17/4, "Statement by the minister for Co-operatives and Marketing, the Hon. P. J. Ngei, MP, on the Maize Situation: Commission of Inquiry to be Set Up," 1 November 1965.

106. Republic of Kenya, *The National Assembly, House of Representatives Official Report (Hansard)*, vol. 7, 9 November 1965.

107. KNA BV/6/903, "Minutes of a Special Meeting of the Board [WKMB]," 21 December 1965.

108. KNA TR/17/6, "£100,000 Loss by Board in a Year," *East African Standard*, 21 January 1966.

109. Kenya, *Report of the Maize Commission of Inquiry*, 160.

110. Kenya, *Report of the Maize Commission of Inquiry*, 42.

111. Kenya, *Report of the Maize Commission of Inquiry*, 166.

112. Kenya, *Report of the Maize Commission of Inquiry*, chap. 7.

113. Myles Osborne, "'The Cat with Nine Lives': Paul Ngei and the Making of Modern Kenya," *Journal of Eastern African Studies* 6, no. 2 (2012): 204.

114. KNA TR/1/351, "Minutes of the 18th Meeting of the Central Agricultural Board," Conference Room of the Ministry of Agriculture Rhodes House, 4 October 1966.

115. KNA TR/17/13, "MFR and Maize Marketing in Area (N)" [undated, but a report from 1971–72].

116. KNA TR/17/11, Maize and Produce Board to the director of Settlement, "Marketing of Maize—Northern Settlement Areas," 22 May 1968.

117. KNA TR/17/11, Maize and Produce Board to the director of Settlement, "Marketing of Maize—Northern Settlement Areas," 22 May 1968.

118. KNA TR/17/11, Pius Odhiambo, acting assistant commissioner for Cooperative Development (S), to the general manager Maize and Produce Board, "Marketing of Maize—Northern Settlement Areas," 30 May 1968.

119. Josephine H. Wanja, "Land on Loan: An Analysis of the Factors Affecting Loan Repayment on the Million Acre Schemes" (Working Paper No. 355, University of Nairobi, 1979), 26.

120. Danson P. Lumumba Esese, "The Changing System of Land Ownership and Its Socio-Economic Effects in Lugari Division, Western Province of Kenya, c. 1880–2000" (PhD diss., Michigan State University, 2009), 332.

121. Republic of Kenya, *The National Assembly, House of Representatives Official Report (Hansard)*, vol. 5, 23 July 1965.

122. Republic of Kenya, *The National Assembly, House of Representatives Official Report (Hansard)*, vol. 6, 6 October 1966.

123. Ngei's reappointment was undoubtedly a product of his alliance with Kenyatta, newly threatened by the formation of the Kenya People's Union.

124. KNA TR/17/6, "Single Body to Control Maize Suggested," *East African Standard*, 21 January 1966.

125. Tororei arap Rongei, interview by author, Leseru, 15 January 2013; Rael Serem, interview by author, Leseru, 3 December 2012.

126. Mary Kitur, interview by author, Leseru, 19 November 2012.

127. Mary Kitur, interview by author, Leseru, 19 November 2012.

128. James Sabatia, interview by author, Lumakanda, 31 October 2012.

129. Daniel Kebeney Bitok, interview by author, Leseru, 26 November 2012.

130. Susan Rono, interview by author, Leseru, 22 November 2012.

131. Rev. Philomon Tanai, interview by author, Leseru, 9 January 2013.

132. Republic of Kenya, *The National Assembly, House of Representatives Official Report (Hansard)*, vol. 5, 23 July 1965.

133. Jael Mbogo, "Freedom From Hunger—A Basic Right," *Daily Nation*, 9 May 1969.

134. Selena Serem, interview by author, Leseru, 28 November 2012.

CHAPTER 6: "THOSE POOR PEOPLE WHO SWEATED THEMSELVES TO HELP THEMSELVES"

1. Jomo Kenyatta, *Harambee! The Prime Minister of Kenya's Speeches, 1963–1964: From the Attainment of Internal Self-Government to the Threshold of the Kenya Republic* (Nairobi: Oxford University Press, 1964), 7.

2. There is a rich academic literature on self-help in Africa, but little historical scholarship: Immanuel M. Wallerstein, *Africa: The Politics of Independence* (New York: Vintage Books, 1961); Joel D. Barkan, "Development through Self-Help: The Forgotten Alternative," *Rural Africana* 19–20 (1984): 115–29; Barbara P. Thomas-Slayter, *Politics,*

Participation, and Poverty: Development through Self-Help in Kenya (Boulder, CO: Westview Press, 1985); Joel D. Barkan and Frank Holmquist, "Peasant-State Relations and the Social Base of Self-Help in Kenya," *World Politics* 41, no. 3 (1989): 359–80; Priya Lal, "Self-Reliance and the State: The Multiple Meanings of Development in Early Post-Colonial Tanzania," *Africa* 82, no. 2 (2012): 212–34; Michael Jennings, "'A Very Real War': Popular Participation in Development in Tanzania during the 1950s and 1960s," *International Journal of African Historical Studies* 40, no. 1 (2007): 71–95.

3. Jennings, "Very Real War," 76.

4. Joanna Lewis, *Empire State-Building: War and Welfare in Kenya, 1925–52* (Athens: Ohio University Press, 2001), 1.

5. KNA JA/12/225, G. M. Bebb, DC Tambach, "ADC Finance," 7 September 1957.

6. M. P. K. Sorrenson, *Land Reform in the Kikuyu Country: A Study in Government Policy* (Nairobi: Oxford University Press, 1967); Angelique Haugerud, "Land Tenure and Agrarian Change in Kenya," *Africa* 59, no. 1 (1989): 61–90.

7. KNA PC/RVP, Rift Valley Province Annual Report, 1955.

8. Luise White, "Separating the Men from the Boys: Constructions of Gender, Sexuality, and Terrorism in Central Kenya, 1939–1959," *International Journal of African Historical Studies* 23, no. 1 (1990): 24.

9. Audrey Wipper, "The Maendeleo ya Wanawake Organization: The Co-Optation of Leadership," *African Studies Review* 18, no. 3 (1975): 99–120; Alexandra Tibbetts, "Mamas Fighting for Freedom in Kenya," *Africa Today* 41, no. 4 (1994): 27–48.

10. Benedetta Rossi, "What 'Development' Does to Work," *International Labor and Working-Class History* 92 (2017): 15.

11. Opolot Okia tracks how, after the International Labor Organization's (ILO) Forced Labour Convention in 1930, the Kenyan colonial state continued to legally rely on compulsory labor, because the ILO definition "excluded many coercive labor practices, including communal labor." Okia, *Communal Labor in Colonial Kenya: The Legitimization of Coercion, 1912–30* (New York: Palgrave Macmillan, 2012), 4–5. See also Alice Wiemers, "'It Is All He Can Do to Cope with the Roads in His Own District': Labor, Community, and Development in Northern Ghana, 1919–1936," *International Labor and Working-Class History* 92 (2017): 89–113.

12. KNA DC/UG/2/3/50, Commissioner for Local Government to all PCs, "Minor Communal Services," 29 October 1956.

13. KNA JA/12/224, "Report of the 1953/54 Committee on Financial Relations between the Kenya Government and African District Councils."

14. Priya Lal, *African Socialism in Postcolonial Tanzania: Between the Village and the World* (New York: Cambridge University Press, 2015), 53, 59.

15. David Nally and Stephen Taylor, "The Politics of Self-Help: The Rockefeller Foundation, Philanthropy and the 'Long' Green Revolution," *Political Geography* 49 (2015): 51.

16. Usha Mahajani, "Kennedy and the Strategy of Aid: The Clay Report and After," *Political Research Quarterly* 18, no. 3 (1965): 657, 659; Jacob Viner, George Meany, Fowler Hamilton, Otto Passman, and Paul Hoffman, "The Report of the Clay Committee on Foreign Aid: A Symposium," *Political Science Quarterly* 78, no. 3 (1963): 344–45. See also "Report to the President of the United States from The Committee to Strengthen the Security of the Free World: The Scope and Distribution of United States Military and Economic Assistance Programs," Washington, DC, 20 March

1962, USAID Mission to Kenya Program Division, P 573 Subject Files: 1961–1980, Box 2, PRM 4 Program Evaluation FY 63, Department of State, Record Group 286; NACP. The American embrace of self-help impacted domestic policy as well. Alyosha Goldstein, *Poverty in Common: The Politics of Community Action during the American Century* (Durham, NC: Duke University Press, 2012).

17. KNA JA/31/19, *This Is Community Development in Kenya* (Nairobi: East African Literature Bureau, 1964).

18. KNA BY/4/159, Director of Medical Services, "Relative Responsibility of Central and Local Government Authorities for African Health Services," 5 June 1952. Interviews in former European settlement areas confirm that these services remained poor for years into independence and often remained behind those in the former native reserves.

19. These inadequacies were equally striking in other parts of the country, particularly areas where there had been few missionaries, where the colonial state had not attempted to invest in social services, and in poorer, pastoral regions.

20. Republic of Kenya, *The National Assembly Official Report (Hansard)*, vol. 19, 3 March 1970.

21. John H. Hamer, "Preconditions and Limits in the Formation of Associations: The Self-Help and Cooperative Movement in Sub-Saharan Africa," *African Studies Review* 24, no. 1 (1981): 114.

22. KNA JA/31/19, *This Is Community Development in Kenya* (Nairobi: East African Literature Bureau, 1964).

23. KNA JA/31/19, *This Is Community Development in Kenya* (Nairobi: East African Literature Bureau, 1964).

24. KNA JA/7/9, Local Government Commission of Inquiry Memoranda, "A National Policy of Community Development Submitted by the Ministry of Labour and Social Services," 1966.

25. This differs from Emma Hunter's findings in early postcolonial Tanzania. Emma Hunter, "Voluntarism, Virtuous Citizenship, and Nation-Building in Late Colonial and Early Postcolonial Tanzania," *African Studies Review* 58, no. 2 (2015): 54–57.

26. KNA DC/KMG/2/4/32, H. M. Stanley Njeru, provincial community development officer, Western Province, "Good-bye 1965 and Welcome 1966" [undated, but early 1966].

27. KNA ACW/1/425, Kefa Onyoni, for PS Ministry of Housing and Social Services, to PS Ministry of Finance and Planning, "Comments on Sessional Paper No. 10 of 1965 on African Socialism," 1978.

28. KNA BY/54/1, Ministry of Co-operatives and Social Services, Ronald Ngala, Minister, Department of Community Development and Social Services, G. J. Njenga, Director, "The Self-Help Movement, Kenya, 1968."

29. KNA BY/54/1, Ministry of Co-operatives and Social Services, Ronald Ngala, Minister, Department of Community Development and Social Services, G. J. Njenga, Director, "The Self-Help Movement, Kenya, 1968."

30. KNA JA/31/19, "Draft Circular: National Development Committees," 16 October 1964.

31. KNA JA/31/19, "Draft Circular: National Development Committees," 16 October 1964.

32. KNA JA/7/9, Local Government Commission of Inquiry Memoranda, "A National Policy of Community Development Submitted by the Ministry of Labour and Social Services," 1966.

33. KNA JA/37/3, A. Altorfer, for PS Ministry of Local Government, to the Principal, LF Training Centre, Mzumbe, Morogoro, 28 May 1964.

34. Daniel Branch, *Kenya: Between Hope and Despair, 1963–2011* (New Haven, CT: Yale University Press, 2011), 15.

35. KNA BY/21/211, N. Charlton, Sirikwa county treasurer, to chief education officer, district education officers, school managers, chief officers of the Council, "Proposed Closure of Schools and Public Health Units," 29 December 1964.

36. KNA JA/7/9, S. O. Josiah, Esq., provincial commissioner, Western Province, "The Memorandum on Commission of Inquiry into Local Government," 24 May 1966.

37. KNA BY/21/211, Sgd. B. K. arap Tanui, acting clerk to Sirikwa County Council, to PS Ministry of Local Government, "Re: Health Services in Sirikwa," 5 July 1965.

38. KNA BY/21/212, "Sirikwa County Council Minutes of the 17th Meeting of the Full Council," 23 June 1967.

39. KNA PC/RVP, Rift Valley Province Annual Report, 1969.

40. KNA JA/7/7, D. N. Ndegwa, Office of the President, "Commission on Local Government. Memorandum by the Office of the President," July 1966.

41. KNA JA/7/6, Mr. D. C. MacDonald, KIA Lecturer, "Local Government Commission of Inquiry, Nairobi Hearings," 7 June 1966.

42. Kenda Mutongi, *Worries of the Heart: Widows, Family, and Community in Kenya* (Chicago: University of Chicago Press, 2007), 165.

43. Alfred Machayo, interview by author, Chekalini, 1 November 2012.

44. Frederick Kemboi arap Tum Kaptulus, interview by author, Leseru, 22 November 2012.

45. KNA HB/27/8/6, "Minutes of the Meeting of the District Commissioners held at Provincial Headquarters, Rift Valley Province Nakuru—on Friday, 25th February, 1966."

46. KNA PC/RVP, Rift Valley Province Annual Report, 1967.

47. KNA DC/KMG/2/4/32, G. S. K. Boit, PS Ministry of Cooperatives and Social Services, to provincial community development officers, "Finance for Self-Help Projects," 25 May 1967.

48. KNA DC/KMG/2/4/32, G. S. K. Boit, PS Ministry of Cooperatives and Social Services, to provincial community development officers, "Finance for Self-Help Projects," 25 May 1967.

49. KNA BY/54/1, J. G. Njenga, director of Community Development and Social Services, to all provincial community development officers, "Special Assistance to Self-Help Project," 25 July 1968.

50. KNA PC/RVP, Rift Valley Province Annual Report, 1979.

51. KNA MOH/8/157, Deputy director of medical services to the assistant secretary, "Re: Harambee Hospitals and Health Centres," 30 June 1966.

52. Hoseah arap Keter, interview by author, Sosiani, 21 November 2012.

53. Joseph arap Bir'geng, interview by author, Sosiani, 20 November 2012.

54. KNA MOH/8/157, S. N. Ngure, provincial medical officer, Western, to the DC, Kakamega, "Re: Chekalini Health Centre," 1 September 1966.

55. KNA MOH/8/157, S. N. Ngure, provincial medical officer, Western, to the DC, Kakamega, "Re: Chekalini Health Centre," 1 September 1966.

56. KNA DC/KMG/2/4/32, District officer, Central, to DC Kakamega, "Cattle Dip Kambiri Self-Help Project," 1 March 1967.

57. KNA DC/KMG/2/4/32, District officer, Central, to DC Kakamega, "Cattle Dip Kambiri Self-Help Project," 1 March 1967.

58. KNA DC/KMG/2/4/32, F. M. Nthenge, DC Kakamega, to the district officer, Central, "Kambiri Self-Help Cattle Dip Project," 3 March 1967.

59. KNA JA/31/19, "Minutes of the Inaugural Meeting of the National Committee for Community Development," 8 December 1964.

60. KNA JA/31/19, G. S. K. Boit, PS Ministry of Cooperatives and Social Services, to All PS's, "Cabinet: Development Committee: Plan Implementation: The Need for Positive Action" [undated, likely 1965–66].

61. Kenyatta, *Harambee!*, 84.

62. This was a favored tactic of the Kenyatta state to centralize power. Kara Moskowitz, "From Possibility to Postcolony: The Politics of Decolonization, Development, and Inequality in Kenya (*c.* 1950-1980)" (PhD diss., Emory University, 2014), chap. 2; Branch, *Kenya*, 15.

63. KNA JA/31/19, "Minutes of the Inaugural Meeting of the National Committee for Community Development," 8 December 1964.

64. Republic of Kenya, *National Assembly, House of Representatives Official Report (Hansard)*, vol. 7, 9 November 1965.

65. KNA BY/54/1, Ronald Ngala, minister of Co-operatives and Social Services, and G. J. Njenga, director, Department of Community Development and Social Services, "The Self-Help Movement, Kenya, 1968."

66. KNA AVS/13/21, Senior settlement officer, Sotik, "S.S.O.'s Sotik Area Monthly Report for July, 1969."

67. KNA BY/54/1, J. G. Njenga, director of Community Development and Social Services, to all provincial community development officers, "Special Assistance to Self-Help Project," 25 July 1968.

68. Republic of Kenya, *National Assembly Official Report (Hansard)*, vol. 30, 12 July 1973.

69. KNA JA/7/9, Ministry of Labour and Social Services, Local Government Commission of Inquiry Memoranda, "A National Policy of Community Development," 1966.

70. KNA JA/7/9, Ministry of Labour and Social Services, Local Government Commission of Inquiry Memoranda, "A National Policy of Community Development," 1966.

71. KNA HB/27/8/4, "Minutes of the District Commissioners' Meeting held at the Provincial Commissioner's Office on 19th December, 1969."

72. KNA DC/KMG/2/4/33, William A. Kigame, Kakamega, to the district officer Lugari, "Re: Self Help in Lugari," 20 June 1969.

73. Republic of Kenya, *National Assembly Official Report (Hansard)*, vol. 51, 25 July 1979.

74. Selena Chelimo Barno, interview by author, Leseru, 28 November 2012.

75. Chelimo Martha Keino, interview by author, Leseru, 19 November 2012; Christopher Lelei Lilan, interview by author, Leseru, 26 November 2012; Daniel Kebeney Bitok, interview by author, Leseru, 26 November 2012; Peter Muchai, interview by author, Lumakanda, 6 November 2012; Alan Maikuma, interview by author, Lumakanda, 3 November 2012; Fanike Chanzu, interview by author, Lumakanda, 9 November 2012.

76. KNA HB/27/8/6, "Minutes of the District Commissioners' Meeting held at the Provincial Headquarters, Rift Valley Province, Nakuru, on the 5th February, 1968."

77. Samuel Kimeli Kiplagat, interview by author, Sugoi, 10 January 2013.

78. Samuel Kimeli Kiplagat, interview by author, Sugoi, 10 January 2013.

79. Jotham Njau Mwangi, interview by author, Lumakanda, 5 November 2012; Karen Misavo, interview by author, 14 November 2012.

80. Deina Iboso, interview by author, Lumakanda, 12 November 2012.

81. Ainea Alulu, interview by author, Lumakanda, 14 November 2012; James Musamusi Matunda, interview by author, Lumakanda, 2 November 2012.

82. KNA PC/RVP, Rift Valley Province Annual Report, 1969.

83. KNA DC/UG, Uasin Gishu District Annual Report, 1974.

84. KNA DC/KMG/2/4/33, E. Mugo, district community development officer, Kakamega, to the group self-help leaders, Kakamega District, "Massage [*sic*] to the Self-Help Group Leaders Kakamega District," 23 May 1968.

85. KNA DC/KMG/2/4/32, "Western Province Self-Help Co-ordinating Committee Meeting: Minutes of a Meeting held in the PC's Conference Room," 16 January 1967.

86. KNA HB/27/8/4, "Minutes of Administrative Officers' Meeting held at the Provincial Commissioner's Conference Room on 16th July, 1969." Frank Holmquist found that self-help initiatives ultimately pushed the state to spend more on social services. Holmquist, "Self-Help: The State and Peasant Leverage in Kenya," *Africa* 54, no. 3 (1984): 78, 85.

87. KNA HB/27/8/6, "Minutes of the Administrative Officers' Meeting held in the Conference Room on the 22nd July, 1968 at 9.30 A.M."

88. Theresa Ngososei, interview by author, Leseru, 27 November 2012. This followed from a much longer history of missionary intervention to provide education and health care alongside salvation. Jean Comaroff and John L. Comaroff, *Of Revelation and Revolution*, vol. 1, *Christianity, Colonialism, and Consciousness in South Africa* (Chicago: University of Chicago Press, 1991); Mutongi, *Worries of the Heart*.

89. James Musamusi Matunda, interview by author, Lumakanda, 2 November 2012.

90. KNA JA/31/17, Assistant commissioner for Social Services, to the PS Ministry of Local Government and Lands, 12 July 1961; KNA BY/54/1, J. G. Njenga, director of Community Development and Social Services, to all provincial community development officers, "Special Assistance to Self-Help Project," 25 July 1968.

91. KNA JA/31/19, *This Is Community Development in Kenya* (Nairobi: East African Literature Bureau, 1964).

92. KNA MOH/8/157, Carroll S. Hinman, director of USAID, to Mr. G. S. K. Boit, PS Ministry of Cooperatives and Social Services, 29 December 1967.

93. KNA DC/KMG/2/4/32, Moses Kevogo Mudaki, chairman, Lumakanda community development coordinating committee, to the DC Kakamega, "Re: Health Problem," 27 October 1966.

94. KNA DC/KMG/2/4/33, Harry Nachtigall, headmaster, Emusire Secondary School, to the DC Kakamega, 24 August 1967.

95. "A Changing School in a Changing Land (North Nyanza Educational Development, 615-AB-65-AH-5)," Chavakali, 1963; USAID Mission to Kenya Program Division, P 573 Subject Files: 1961–1980, Box 2, PRM 4 Program Evaluation FY 63, Department of State, Record Group 286; NACP.

96. "People Remember (Report by the AID Community Development Advisor, Project 615-AD-81-AA-5)," USAID Mission to Kenya Program Division, P 573 Subject Files: 1961–1980, Box 2, PRM 4 Program Evaluation FY 63, Department of State, Record Group 286; NACP.

97. "People Remember (Report by the AID Community Development Advisor, Project 615-AD-81-AA-5)," USAID Mission to Kenya Program Division, P 573 Subject

Files: 1961–1980, Box 2, PRM 4 Program Evaluation FY 63, Department of State, Record Group 286; NACP.

98. For an analysis of how community participation divides "those who do the labor of development from the decision making that drives how it happens—ultimately reproducing many of the social and economic relationships," see Kristin D. Phillips, "Dividing the Labor of Development: Education and Participation in Rural Tanzania," *Comparative Education Review* 57, no. 4 (2013): 641.

99. KNA ACW/1/425, J. H. O. Omino, PS Ministry of Natural Resources, to Mr. L. O. Kibinge, PS Ministry of Finance and Planning, "African Socialism and Its Application to Planning in Kenya, Some Thoughts," 4 April 1978.

100. This sits in contrast to Jennings's work on early postcolonial Tanzania. He argues that self-help "was central to this attempt to refocus the orientation of people from subject, from tribal member, to 'Tanzanian.'" Jennings, "Very Real War," 76.

101. For a statistical analysis of regional differentiation in self-help, see Edgar V. Winans and Angelique Haugerud, "Rural Self-Help in Kenya: The *Harambee* Movement," *Human Organization* 36, no. 4 (1977): 334–51.

102. Arne Bigsten, *Regional Inequality and Development: A Case Study of Kenya* (Nairobi: Institute for Development Studies, University of Nairobi, 1977), 160.

103.Though this chapter does not focus on pastoralists, they were long marginalized by the colonial and postcolonial states. For some of the extensive literature on pastoralism and development in East Africa, see Thomas Spear and Richard Waller, eds., *Being Maasai: Ethnicity and Identity in East Africa* (London: James Currey, 1993); Peter D. Little, *The Elusive Granary: Herder, Farmer, and State in Northern Kenya* (New York: Cambridge University Press, 1992); Dorothy L. Hodgson, *Once Intrepid Warriors: Gender, Ethnicity, and the Cultural Politics of Maasai Development* (Bloomington: Indiana University Press, 2001).

104. KNA JA/31/19, G. S. K. Boit, PS Ministry of Cooperatives and Social Services, to all PS's, "Cabinet: Development Committee: Plan Implementation: The Need for Positive Action" [undated, but likely 1964–66].

105. KNA JA/31/19, G. S. K. Boit, PS Ministry of Cooperatives and Social Services, to all PS's, "Cabinet: Development Committee: Plan Implementation: The Need for Positive Action" [undated, but likely 1964–66].

106. KNA DC/KMG/2/4/32, G. S. K. Boit, PS Ministry of Cooperatives and Social Services, to provincial community development officers, "Finance for Self-Help Projects," 25 May 1967.

107. KNA MOH/8/157, Councillor Tim Mibei, adviser to the committee Roret Health Centre, 'Harambee,' Kericho, to the PS Ministry of Health, "Re: Financial Donation to the Above Harambee Health Centre," 7 November 1967.

108. KNA BN/87/19, P. Ndegwa, PS Treasury, to all PCs, all provincial planning officers, "Grants to District Development Committees," 3 November 1971.

109. KNA PC/RVP, Rift Valley Province Annual Report, 1968.

110. Daniel Kebeney Bitok, interview by author, Leseru, 26 November 2012; Kimeli arap Chepkwony, interview by author, Sosiani, 30 November 2012.

111. This occurred all over Kenya. In 1980, a farmer from Embu complained that the harambee committee members were "untrustworthy" and did not "consider the needs of ordinary people." Angelique Haugerud, *The Culture of Politics in Modern Kenya* (Cambridge: Cambridge University Press, 1995), 96–97.

112. KNA DC/KMG/2/4/32, H. M. Stanley Njeru, provincial community development officer, Western, to PC Western, "Chairmanship and Presidency of Self-Help Development Co-ordinating Committees," 2 February 1965.

113. KNA PC/RVP, Rift Valley Province Annual Report, 1966.

114. Karen Misavo, interview by author, Lumakanda, 18 July 2018; Pauline Tum, interview by author, Leseru, 17 July 2018.

115. William Serem, interview by author, Leseru, 17 July 2018.

116. Ainea Alulu, interview by author, Lumakanda, 18 July 2018.

117. Rev. Philomon Tanai, interview by author, Leseru, 9 January 2013.

118. Theresa Ngososei, interview by author, Leseru, 27 November 2012.

119. Theresa Ngososei, interview by author, Leseru, 27 November 2012; Kipkugat arap Ngososei, interview by author, Leseru, 27 November 2012.

120. Karen Misavo, interview by author, Lumakanda, 31 October 2012.

121. Ruth Malakwen Cheptekeny, interview by author, Leseru, 9 January 2013.

122. KNA MOH/8/157, Mrs. G. Ego, chairman Chepkorio Maternity Extension women's self-help group, "Memorandum to the Honourable Minister of Health Mr. J. Otiende," 23 March 1967.

123. Moskowitz, "From Possibility to Postcolony," chap. 7.

124. Dorcas Lagat, interview by author, Sugoi, 10 January 2013.

125. Helen Kirua, interview by author, Leseru, 3 December 2012.

126. Pauline Tum, interview by author, Leseru, 22 November 2012; Pauline Ngetich, interview by author, Sosiani, 21 November 2012.

127. Pauline Ngetich, interview by author, Sosiani, 21 November 2012; Pauline Tum, interview by author, Leseru, 22 November 2012; Selena Chelimo Barno, interview by author, Leseru, 28 November 2012.

128. Godfrey K. Sang, *Just for Today: The Life and Times of Jean-Marie Seroney* (Coventry: Dolman Scott, 2015), 196.

129. KNA TR/1/350, Joseph G. Ayugi, for assistant commissioner for Cooperative Development (S), to acting cooperative officers, "Maternity Cases," 31 July 1964.

130. KNA BY/21/212, M. A. Fazal, medical officer of Health, to the assistant director of Medical Services, "Re: Health Centres in Uasin Gishu," 14 February 1968.

131. Zipora Ketera, interview by author, Sosiani, 21 November 2012.

132. Chebagui Bwalei, interview by author, Leseru, 23 November 2012; Pauline Tum, interview by author, Leseru, 22 November 2012; Rael Serem, interview by author, Leseru, 3 December 2012.

133. KNA DC/UG, Uasin Gishu District Annual Report, 1976.

134. Theresa Ngososei, interview by author, Leseru, 27 November 2012.

135. KNA DC/UG, Uasin Gishu District Annual Report, 1976.

136. KNA BY/21/211, "Sirikwa County Council Public Health and Lands Committee Minutes of the 4th Meeting," 11 October 1966.

137. KNA BY/21/211, "Sirikwa County Council Public Health and Lands Committee Minutes of the 4th Meeting," 11 October 1966.

138. Kimeli Korir (son of Priscilla Boit), interview by author, Nairobi, 13 July 2018.

139. Pauline Tum, interview by author, Leseru, 22 November 2012.

140. Eunice Tele Maiyo, interview by author, Leseru, 9 January 2013.

141. Eunice Tele Maiyo, interview by author, Leseru, 9 January 2013.

CHAPTER 7: "ARE YOU PLANTING TREES OR ARE YOU PLANTING PEOPLE?"

1. The meaning of the term "squatter" has changed. The colonial state used "squatter" to mean resident farm laborer. The independent state made a distinction between those living on property to which they had no title and resident laborers. In this chapter, I use the term broadly to mean Kenyans living on land in the planned Turbo afforestation area.

2. KNA BN/85/14, The Cabinet, "Kenya Pulp and Paper Mill, Proposed Turbo Pulpwood Afforestation Scheme," 1964.

3. KNA BA/2/38, J. H. O. Omino, PS Ministry of Natural Resources, to the Minister, "Your Folio (107) Refers," 24 August 1973.

4. KNA AE/22/142, W. Wamalwa, PS Ministry of Economic Planning and Development, "Pulp and Paper Project," 9 June 1966.

5. KNA BN/85/16, J. K. arap Koitie to PS Ministry of Natural Resources, 14 March 1969.

6. The highway does not follow the geopolitical border exactly, but residents of the area use it as such.

7. KNA HB/27/9/9, DC North Nyanza to PC Nyanza, "Tribal Spheres of Influence Abaluhya Settlement Schemes in the Lugari Area," 19 February 1962.

8. KNA BN/96/4, Memorandum by the minister for Tourism, Forests, and Wildlife, "Secret Council of Ministers: Future Organisation of the Departments and Services in the Ministry of Tourism, Forests and Wild Life" [undated].

9. KNA AE/22/139, "Paper Mill Survey Starts this Week," *East African Standard*, 22 April 1963.

10. KNA AE/22/141, Joint Memorandum by Ministry of Natural Resources and Ministry of Commerce and Industry, "Kenya Government. Draft Cabinet Paper. Broderick Falls Pulp and Paper Project," 15 May 1964.

11. KNA BN/85/15, The Treasury, "Memorandum to Her Majesty's Government on the Turbo Afforestation Scheme," June 1966.

12. KNA BN/85/14, Memorandum by the Minister for Natural Resources, "The Cabinet. Kenya Pulp and Paper Mill. Proposed Turbo Pulpwood Afforestation Scheme," 1964.

13. KNA AE/22/141, Joint Memorandum by Ministry of Natural Resources and Ministry of Commerce and Industry, "Kenya Government. Draft Cabinet Paper. Broderick Falls Pulp and Paper Project," 15 May 1964.

14. KNA AE/22/141, Memorandum by the Minister for Natural Resources, "The Cabinet. Kenya Pulp and Paper Mill: Proposed Turbo Pulpwood Afforestation Scheme," 1964.

15. KNA AE/22/217, H. S. Fisher, general manager, to the Hon. Member for Agriculture and Natural Resources, "East African Tanning Extract Company, Limited—Application for Transfer of Factory Licences to Subsidiary Companies in Formation," 16 October 1953.

16. From 1961 to 1962, the government approved the purchase of farms by "assisted owners," who provided at least 30 percent of the total capital to qualify. P. D. Abrams, *Kenya's Land Re-Settlement Story: How 66,000 African Families Were Settled on 1325 Large Scale European Owned Farms* (Nairobi: Challenge, 1979), 31.

17. KNA AE/22/141, The Treasury, "Turbo Afforestation Project," 14 April 1965.

18. KNA BN/85/14, A. Davies, for PS, to PS Ministry of Natural Resources, "Broderick Falls Wood Pulp Factory," 26 January 1965.

19. KNA BN/85/14, J. W. Maina, acting deputy director of Settlement, 3 February 1965.

20. KNA BN/85/14, P. Shiyukah to A. P. Achieng, PS Ministry of Natural Resources, 18 March 1965.

21. KNA BN/81/34, C. Kahara, "Summary of Van Arkadie Report," 15 February 1967.

22. The Birla Group began their overseas expansion in the late 1950s with a textile plant in Ethiopia. By the 1960s, they were one of the largest Indian business groups. Prema-Chandra Athukorala, "Outward Foreign Direct Investment from India," *Asian Development Review* 26, no. 2 (2009): 147–48.

23. KNA AE/22/142, Mwai Kibaki, Minister for Commerce and Industry, to Birla Brothers, 30 August 1966.

24. KNA TR/13/2, "First Pulp and Paper Mill in East Africa," *East African Standard*, July 1970.

25. KNA BA/6/26, T. A. M. Gardner, project manager, World Bank forestry project, to the chief statistician, agriculture section, "Turbo Afforestation Scheme," 2 April 1971.

26. KNA AE/22/146, Memorandum by Kenya, "Draft: East African Industrial Promotion Advisory Committee Tariff Protection Pulp and Paper Industries," 1968.

27. The competition between Kenya, Tanzania, and Uganda to establish domestic paper industries paralleled tensions within the East African Community more broadly, with disagreements over customs policy and monopolies over the East African market.

28. KNA AE/22/145, O. S. Knowles to Mr. Kibe, "Pulp and Paper Project," 12 August 1968.

29. KNA AE/22/146, "Draft: East African Industrial Promotion Advisory Committee, Tariff Protection Pulp & Paper Industries—Memorandum by Kenya" [undated but 1968].

30. KNA AE/22/146, "Draft: East African Industrial Promotion Advisory Committee, Tariff Protection Pulp & Paper Industries—Memorandum by Kenya" [undated but 1968].

31. KNA AE/22/146, S. N. Bhandari, Birla Brothers, to the PS Ministry of Commerce and Industry, "Sale: Pulp & Paper Project Broderick Falls Protection Tariff," 28 August 1968.

32. KNA BA/2/27, J. H. O. Omino, PS Ministry of Natural Resources, to the PS, Ministry of Finance and Planning, PS, Ministry of Commerce and Industry, executive director, Industrial and Commercial Development Corporation, "Pan African Paper Mills (E.A.) Ltd.—Royalty Payment," 17 June 1974.

33. KNA VF/4/12, F. M. Kamau, project manager, and J. E. M. Kiilu, assistant project manager, "World Bank Forestry Loan Project Soft Wood Plantations Cost Analysis 1969 to 1970 and 1972 to 1973," January 1974.

34. KNA AE/22/142, "Pulp and Paper Company of East Africa, Limited: Working Committee Meeting," 20 December 1965.

35. KNA BN/85/14, J. S. Spears, conservator of forests, to the director of Settlement, 29 July 1965.

36. Moi was minister for Home Affairs at the time and the most prominent Kalenjin politician. He became vice president in 1967 and Kenya's second president from 1978 to 2002. The Nandi had hoped one of their leaders would head the Kalenjin confederacy,

creating tensions with Moi and his Tugen community, as some felt he betrayed the Kalenjin. Karuti Kanyinga, "The Land Question in Kenya: Struggles, Accumulation and Changing Politics" (PhD diss., Roskilde University, 1998), 175.

37. KNA BN/85/14, J. H. Angaine, minister for Lands and Settlement, to S. O. Ayodo, minister for Natural Resources and Wildlife, 19 August 1965.

38. KNA BN/85/15, "Turbo Project Afforestation Scheme: Notes on a Meeting," 11 February 1966.

39. KNA BN/85/15, PC Western Province, "Squatters: Turbo Afforestation Scheme," 30 August 1966.

40. KNA BN/85/15, P. Shiyukah, PS Ministry of Lands and Settlement, to A. F. Achieng, Esq., PS Ministry of Natural Resources and Tourism, 26 January 1966.

41. KNA BN/85/16, Z. B. Shimechero, special commissioner Squatters, to the minister of Lands and Settlement, "Re: Turbo—Kudler's Farm," 29 July 1969.

42. KNA BN/85/16, "Memorandum from Nandi Squatters (LR 6438/2 Turbo, National Farm)," 17 July 1969.

43. KNA BN/85/16, "Memorandum from Nandi Squatters (LR 6438/2 Turbo, National Farm)," 17 July 1969.

44. KNA BA/6/26, PS Ministry of Natural Resources, "Turbo Afforestation Scheme and Broderick Falls Paper Project," 14 May 1970.

45. KNA BA/6/26, PS Ministry of Natural Resources, "Turbo Afforestation Scheme and Broderick Falls Paper Project," 14 May 1970.

46. KNA BA/6/26, T. A. M. Gardner, project manager, World Bank forestry project, to the chief statistician, agriculture section, 2 April 1971.

47. KNA BA/2/27, F. C. Dhariwal, Pan African Paper Mills, to Mr. J. H. O. Omino, PS Ministry of Natural Resources, "Sub: Commissioning of the Mills at Webuye," 30 November 1974.

48. KNA BN/85/16, J. H. O. Omino, PS Ministry of Natural Resources, to Mr. N. S. Kungo, PS Ministry of Lands and Settlement, 31 May 1975.

49. Abrams, *Kenya's Land Resettlement Story*.

50. KNA BN/97/3, "Minutes of a Meeting of Officials on Squatters," 23 April 1966. See also chapter 3.

51. KNA BN/81/158, "Unemployment," 1961 [unauthored].

52. KNA BN/81/158, T. G. Lovering, secretary to the Central Land Board, to PS Lands and Settlement, 12 February 1964.

53. KNA BN/81/158, "Memorandum by the minister for Economic Planning and Development on Government's Unemployment Policies," 1970.

54. KNA TR/3/58, "Rural Development: Programme in Representative Areas," 29 November 1968.

55. KNA BN/85/14, "Memorandum to Her Majesty's Government on the Turbo Afforestation Scheme in Relation to the Expanded Settlement Scheme (Draft)," 27 October 1965.

56. KNA BN/85/15, The Treasury, "Memorandum to Her Majesty's Government on the Turbo Afforestation Scheme (Second Revision)," June 1966.

57. KNA BN/85/15, Ministry of Lands and Settlement, "Turbo Project Afforestation Scheme: Notes on a Meeting," 11 February 1966.

58. KNA BN/85/16, P. K. Boit, PC Western, to the PS Office of the President, "Land for Squatters or the Landless People," 18 March 1970.

59. Kimeli Korir, interview by author, Nairobi, 13 July 2018.

60. KNA BN/85/16, P. K. Boit, PC Western, to the PS Office of the President, "Land for Squatters or the Landless People," 18 March 1970.

61. Daniel Kebeney Bitok, interview by author, Leseru, 26 November 2012.

62. Numerous interlocutors defined citizenship as owning land and connected development to farming.

63. David M. Anderson, "'Yours in Struggle for Majimbo': Nationalism and the Party Politics of Decolonization in Kenya, 1955–64," *Journal of Contemporary History* 40, no. 3 (2005): 547.

64. Gabrielle Lynch, *I Say to You: Ethnic Politics and the Kalenjin in Kenya* (Chicago: University of Chicago Press, 2011), 6–7.

65. Kiptoo arap Maina, interview by author, Leseru, 23 November 2012.

66. Kiptoo arap Maina, interview by author, Leseru, 23 November 2012.

67. KNA KA/6/19, Senator Gerald Nathaniel Kalya, Kapsabet (Nandi), to President Kenyatta, 21 May 1966.

68. Simon Limo, interview by author, Leseru, 27 November 2012; Christopher Lelei Lilan, interview by author, Leseru, 26 November 2012.

69. KNA KA/6/19, Citizens of Naivasha to the KANU district chairman, 1967.

70. Daniel Branch, *Kenya: Between Hope and Despair, 1963–2011* (New Haven, CT: Yale University Press, 2011), 84–87.

71. KNA BN/85/15, V. E. M. Burke, deputy director of Settlement, "Turbo Forest Station Scheme," 25 March 1966.

72. For some of the literature on local contestations over development, see David M. Anderson, *Eroding the Commons: The Politics of Ecology in Baringo, Kenya, 1890s–1963* (Athens: Ohio University Press, 2002); Tania Murray Li, *The Will to Improve: Governmentality, Development, and the Practice of Politics* (Durham, NC: Duke University Press, 2007); Pauline E. Peters, *Dividing the Commons: Politics, Policy, and Culture in Botswana* (Charlottesville: University Press of Virginia, 1994); and Richard A. Schroeder, *Shady Practices: Agroforestry and Gender Politics in the Gambia* (Berkeley: University of California Press, 1999).

73. KNA BN/85/15, P. Shiyukah, "Re: Your Conf. 143/132," 1 April 1966.

74. KNA BN/85/15, Memorandum from J. H. Angaine, "Turbo Afforestation Scheme Area B: Settlement of Squatters," 25 October 1966.

75. KNA BN/85/15, Director of Settlement, "Land Purchase Programme and Turbo Afforestation Scheme," 2 February 1966.

76. Forest reserves differed from afforestation. Reserves were protected, indigenous forests.

77. KNA DX/21/10/8, P. Shiyukah, PS Ministry of Lands and Settlement, to the clerk to the Sirikwa County Council, "Squatters on Turbo Area B," 31 October 1966.

78. KNA DX/21/10/8, P. Shiyukah, PS Ministry of Lands and Settlement, to the clerk to the Sirikwa County Council, "Squatters on Turbo Area B," 31 October 1966.

79. KNA BA/6/29, "Turbo Afforestation Advisory Committee Minutes of the 9th Meeting," 2 March 1973.

80. KNA DX/21/10/8, "Joint Meeting of Nandi, Kakamega and Uasin Gishu District Commissioners held at Osorongai," 15 September 1966.

81. KNA DX/21/10/9, Divisional forest officer, Turbo, to the superintendent of Police, "Operational Orders: Coopers Farm and Manzini Farm," 15 February 1972.

82. KNA DX/21/10/9, J. M. Tiampati, DC Kakamega, to the PC Western, "Squatters—E.A. Tanning Co.," 9 February 1977. The 1977 evictees were mostly former employees

of East African Tanning and Extract Company, which sold its land to the government that year. The estimated number of employees displaced ranged between 152 and 600.

83. Daniel Kebeney Bitok, interview by author, Leseru, 26 November 2012.

84. Daniel Kebeney Bitok, interview by author, Leseru, 26 November 2012.

85. Wilson Cheruyot Boit, interview by author, Sugoi, 10 January 2013.

86. Wilson Cheruyot Boit, interview by author, Sugoi, 10 January 2013.

87. KNA BA/2/38, J. H. O. Omino, PS Ministry of Natural Resources, to the Minister, "Your Folio (107) Refers," 24 August 1973.

88. Wilson Cheruyot Boit, interview by author, Sugoi, 10 January 2013.

89. Wilson Cheruyot Boit, interview by author, Sugoi, 10 January 2013.

90. Simon Limo, interview by author, Leseru, 27 November 2012.

91. Priscilla Murei, interview by author, Sugoi, 14 January 2013.

92. Christina Cherotich, interview by author, Tapsagoi, 12 January 2013.

93. KNA BN/85/16, C. B. Looman, forestal lands estate, to the estates manager, Turbo, "Re: Trespassers on Forestal Lands," 12 January 1971.

94. KNA BN/85/16, C. B. Looman, forestal lands estate, to the estates manager, Turbo, "Re: Trespassers on Forestal Lands," 12 January 1971.

95. Chepsiror arap Leleli, interview by author, Tapsagoi, 12 January 2013.

96. There is some discrepancy in oral histories over whether this meeting took place in Nairobi or Nakuru.

97. Michael Keter, interview by author, Sugoi, 14 January 2013.

98. David Tororei, interview by author, Sosiani, 3 December 2012. This was a common conception, in spite of the complex relationship between both Mau Mau and independence, and Kenyatta and Mau Mau.

99. Jamin Maneno Kihinga, interview by author, Lumakanda, 8 November 2012; Simon Limo, interview by author, Leseru, 27 November 2012.

100. Ruth Jepng'eno Kipkurui, interview by author, Tapsagoi, 12 January 2013.

101. "Kenyatta's preferred highly personalized way of handling government business became the dominant model. Sitting in court in his private and official residences dotted around the country, the president hosted delegations from provinces and districts, listened to their grievances and issued decrees in response." Branch, *Kenya*, 72–73.

102. KNA KA 6/31, J. W. Gaithi and Others to the Rt. Hon. Father of Nation, "Re: Unoccupied Plot No. 136. Naru-Moru Settlement Scheme," 26 October 1964; KNA BN 81/8, Sons and Daughters of Kenya to the Prime Minister of Kenya, Father of Our Nation, 19 August 1963; KNA KA/6/20, James K. Sitieney, to the PS, Office of the President, "Re: Gen. 116/016/86 Plot No. 676 Kondoo Squatters Scheme," 21 February 1973.

103. Pauline Tum, interview by author, Leseru, 22 November 2012; Frederick Kemboi arap Tum Kaptulus, interview by author, Leseru, 22 November 2012.

104. KNA AE/22/142, K. S. N. Matiba, "The Pulp and Paper Project," 19 May 1966.

105. Dave Zarembka, interview by author, Lumakanda, 8 June 2015.

106. Joab Siundu Macheso, interview by author, Webuye, 11 July 2013.

107. Joab Siundu Macheso, interview by author, Webuye, 11 July 2013.

108. Joab Siundu Macheso, interview by author, Webuye, 11 July 2013. Macheso recounted that the name Webuye came from a local creek, but a *Daily Nation* article says the name came from a cobbler who repaired shoes for railway workers. David Misiko, "Webuye Lost Paper Mill but Not Its Chicken Soup," *Daily Nation*, 10 January 2014.

109. KNA BN/85/16, J. K. arap Koitie, PS Ministry of Lands and Settlement, to J. N. Michuki Esq., PS the Treasury, "New Settlement in the Turbo Area," 5 January 1970.

110. KNA BN/85/16, J. H. Angaine to Kenyatta, 22 April 1969.

111. Kenyatta's ad hoc promises and the piecemeal acquisition of land for settlement and forest schemes make it difficult to estimate how many squatters in total were settled on land once planned for afforestation, or to estimate how many remained landless.

112. KNA BN/85/16, J. H. Angaine to Kenyatta, 22 April 1969.

113. In other instances, particularly with the leaders of the political opposition, the Kenyatta state used repression, intimidation, imprisonment, and violence.

114. Frederick Cooper, "Possibility and Constraint: African Independence in Historical Perspective," *Journal of African History* 49, no. 2 (2008): 167–96.

115. Alfred Machayo, interview by author, Chekalini, 1 November 2012.

116. Wilson Cheruyot Boit, interview by author, Sugoi, 10 January 2013.

117. Jemosbei Kirwa Kili, interview by author, Tapsagoi, 12 January 2013.

118. Priscilla Murei, interview by author, Sugoi, 14 January 2013.

119. KNA ACW/1/425, J. H. O. Omino, PS Ministry of Natural Resources, to Mr. L. O. Kibinge, PS Ministry of Finance and Planning, "African Socialism and Its Application to Planning in Kenya, Some Thoughts," 4 April 1978.

120. KNA BA/2/27 O. M. Mburu, chief conservator of forests, to director, water development and chief health inspector, "Webuye Paper Factory," 12 July 1974.

121. Joab Siundu Macheso, interview by author, Webuye, 11 July 2013.

122. Fred Machasio, interview by author, Webuye, 12 July 2013.

123. Fred Machasio, interview by author, Webuye, 12 July 2013.

124. James Karanja, interview by author, Webuye, 11 July 2013.

CONCLUSION

1. Most famously, the 1969 Nandi Hills declaration, when Jean-Marie Seroney and Joseph arap Cheruiyot Mitei claimed all land in Nandi District and the Tinderet area for the Nandi. Gabrielle Lynch, *I Say to You: Ethnic Politics and the Kalenjin in Kenya* (Chicago: University of Chicago Press, 2011), 98–99; Daniel Branch, *Kenya: Between Hope and Despair, 1963–2011* (New Haven, CT: Yale University Press, 2011), 87.

2. Anderson suggests that the acceptance of Koitalel, and other *orkoiik*, as "simply heroes of resistance" obscures conflict between orkoiik and elders for authority. David M. Anderson, "Black Mischief: Crime, Protest and Resistance in Colonial Kenya," *Historical Journal* 36, no. 4 (1993): 876.

3. Settlers did not receive a freehold title until they paid off the entire land loan. John W. Harbeson, *Nation-Building in Kenya: The Role of Land Reform* (Evanston, IL: Northwestern University Press, 1973), 281.

4. Nora Kasigene, interview by author, Lumakanda, 18 July 2016.

5. Danson P. Lumumba Esese, "The Changing System of Land Ownership and Its Socio-Economic Effects in Lugari Division, Western Province of Kenya, c. 1880–2000" (PhD diss., Michigan State University, 2009), 389–90.

6. Lynch, *I Say to You*, 121. The Office of the President also donated funds to harambee on behalf of other politicians to manipulate elections. Jennifer A. Widner, *The Rise of a Party-State in Kenya: From "Harambee!" to "Nyayo!"* (Berkeley: University of California Press, 1992), 200.

7. After further discussion, almost everyone I spoke with had specific recollections of participating in self-help programs.

8. Gregory Mann, *From Empires to NGOs in the West African Sahel: The Road to Nongovernmentality* (New York: Cambridge University Press, 2014), 245.

9. Jean Comaroff and John L. Comaroff, *Theory from the South: Or, How Euro-America Is Evolving toward Africa* (Boulder, CO: Paradigm), 2012.

10. KNA VF/12/16, J. N. Kariuki, for PS Ministry of Environment and Natural Resources, to M/S Panafrican Sawmills, Webuye, "Outstanding Amount – KSHS. 13,936,431.75," 25 August 1986.

11. Erick Ngobilo, "Second Time Closure for Pan Paper," *Daily Nation*, 6 October 2010. The factory first closed in 2009 and then again in 2010, shortly after reopening.

12. Kenneth Lusaka, "Pan Paper's Revival a Boost for Bungoma," *East African Standard*, 3 August 2016.

13. Jackline Inyanji, "When Pan Paper Collapsed, Hopes of Webuye Town Died with It," *East African Standard*, 29 November 2015.

14. Joab Siundu Macheso, interview by author, Webuye, 11 July 2013.

15. Joseph Juma Lukorito, interview by author, Webuye, 12 July 2013.

16. Raphael Wanjala, "Uhuru to Commission Reopening of Pan Paper Mills in Webuye," *Daily Nation*, 15 December 2016.

17. Kwamchetsi Makokha, "Webuye Must Produce Paper or the Local Population Will Become Extinct," *Daily Nation*, 17 December 2016.

18. Alex Wakhisi, "CORD, Jubilee Battle over Webuye Pan Paper's Revival in Western Kenya," *East African Standard*, 7 May 2016.

19. Kenda Mutongi, *Matatu: A History of Popular Transportation in Nairobi* (Chicago: University of Chicago Press, 2017).

20. David M. Anderson and Emma Lochery, "Violence and Exodus in Kenya's Rift Valley, 2008: Predictable and Preventable?" *Journal of Eastern African Studies* 2, no. 2 (2008): 328–43.

21. Branch, *Kenya*, 281–83.

22. Stephen N. Ndegwa, "Citizenship and Ethnicity: An Examination of Two Transition Moments in Kenyan Politics," *American Political Science Review* 91, no. 3 (1997): 600.

Bibliography

ARCHIVAL SOURCES

Africa Inland Mission Regional Office Archives, Nairobi
Archives of the Billy Graham Center, Wheaton, Illinois
John F. Kennedy Presidential Library, Boston, Massachusetts
Kenya National Archives, Nairobi
National Archives at College Park, Maryland
National Archives of the UK, Kew
Rift Valley Provincial Record Center, Nakuru
School of Oriental and African Studies—University of London, Special Collections, London
University of Cambridge, Churchill Archives Centre, Cambridge
University of Oxford, Bodleian Library of Commonwealth and African Studies at Rhodes House, Oxford
World Bank Group Archives, Washington, DC

PUBLISHED PRIMARY SOURCES

Annual Reports

Nandi District Annual Reports
Rift Valley Province Annual Reports
Uasin Gishu District Annual Reports
Western Province Annual Reports

State, Official, and Party Publications

Colony and Protectorate of Kenya. *Legislative Council Debates Official Report* (Hansard), 1945–62.

Kenya African National Union and Jomo Kenyatta. *The KANU Manifesto*. Cairo: Dar El-Hana Press, 1960.

Kenya Land Commission. *Report of the Kenya Land Commission*. London: His Majesty's Stationery Office, 1934.

Kenya People's Union. *KPU Manifesto*. Nairobi: Pan Africa Press, 1967.

Kenya Regional Boundaries Commission. *Report of the Regional Boundaries Commission*. London: Her Majesty's Stationery Office, 1962.

Republic of Kenya. *African Socialism and Its Application to Planning in Kenya*. Nairobi: Information Services of Kenya, 1965.

——. *Development Plan for the Period, 1965/66 to 1969/70*. Nairobi: Ministry of Economic Planning and Development, 1966.
——. *The National Assembly Official Report (Hansard)*, 1963–79.
——. *Report of the Local Government Commission of Inquiry*. Nairobi: Government Printer, 1966.
——. *Report of the Maize Commission of Inquiry*. Nairobi: Government Printer, 1966.
United Kingdom. *Hansard Parliamentary Debates* (1950–80).

Books and Articles

Abrams, P. D. *Kenya's Land Re-settlement Story: How 66,000 African Families Were Settled on 1325 Large Scale European Owned Farms*. Nairobi: Challenge, 1979.
Aerni-Flessner, John. "Development, Politics, and the Centralization of State Power in Lesotho, 1960–75." *Journal of African History* 55, no. 3 (2014): 401–21.
Ahlman, Jeffrey S. *Living with Nkrumahism: Nation, State, and Pan-Africanism in Ghana*. Athens: Ohio University Press, 2017.
Alence, Rod. "Colonial Government, Social Conflict and State Involvement in Africa's Open Economies: The Origins of the Ghana Cocoa Marketing Board, 1939–46." *Journal of African History* 42, no. 3 (2001): 397–416.
Allman, Jean M., and Victoria B. Tashjian. *"I Will Not Eat Stone": A Women's History of Colonial Asante*. Portsmouth, NH: Heinemann, 2000.
Alpers, Edward A. *Ivory and Slaves: Changing Pattern of International Trade in East Central Africa to the Later Nineteenth Century*. Berkeley: University of California Press, 1975.
Ambler, Charles H. *Kenyan Communities in the Age of Imperialism: The Central Region in the Late Nineteenth Century*. New Haven, CT: Yale University Press, 1988.
——. "Mass Media and Leisure in Africa." *International Journal of African Historical Studies* 35, no. 1 (2002): 119–36.
Anderson, David M. "Black Mischief: Crime, Protest and Resistance in Colonial Kenya." *Historical Journal* 36, no. 4 (1993): 851–77.
——. "Depression, Dust Bowl, Demography, and Drought: The Colonial State and Soil Conservation in East Africa during the 1930s." *African Affairs* 83, no. 332 (1984): 321–43.
——. *Eroding the Commons: The Politics of Ecology in Baringo, Kenya, 1890s–1963*. Athens: Ohio University Press, 2002.
——. *Histories of the Hanged: The Dirty War in Kenya and the End of Empire*. New York: W. W. Norton, 2005.
——. "'Yours in Struggle for Majimbo': Nationalism and the Party Politics of Decolonization in Kenya, 1955–64." *Journal of Contemporary History* 40, no. 3 (2005): 547–64.
Anderson, David M., and Emma Lochery. "Violence and Exodus in Kenya's Rift Valley, 2008: Predictable and Preventable?" *Journal of Eastern African Studies* 2, no. 2 (2008): 328–43.
Anderson, David M., and David Throup. "Africans and Agricultural Production in Colonial Kenya: The Myth of the War as a Watershed." *Journal of African History* 26, no. 4 (1985): 327–45.
Appiah, Kwame Anthony. *Cosmopolitanism: Ethics in a World of Strangers*. New York: W. W. Norton, 2006.

Arendt, Hannah. *The Origins of Totalitarianism*. New York: Harcourt, Brace, 1951.

Ashforth, Adam. "Reckoning Schemes of Legitimation: On Commissions of Inquiry as Power/Knowledge Forms." *Journal of Historical Sociology* 3, no. 1 (1990): 1–22.

Askew, Kelly M. *Performing the Nation: Swahili Music and Cultural Politics in Tanzania*. Chicago: University of Chicago Press, 2002.

Athukorala, Prema-Chandra. "Outward Foreign Direct Investment from India." *Asian Development Review* 26, no. 2 (2009): 125–53.

Barkan, Joel D. "Development through Self-Help: The Forgotten Alternative." *Rural Africana* 19–20 (1984): 115–29.

Barkan, Joel D., and Frank Holmquist. "Peasant-State Relations and the Social Base of Self-Help in Kenya." *World Politics* 41, no. 3 (1989): 359–80.

Bates, Robert H. *Beyond the Miracle of the Market: The Political Economy of Agrarian Development in Kenya*. New York: Cambridge University Press, 1992.

Bayart, Jean-Francois. *The State in Africa: The Politics of the Belly*. London: Longman, 1993.

Berman, Bruce J. "Bureaucracy and Incumbent Violence: Colonial Administration and the Origins of the 'Mau Mau' Emergency." In Berman and Lonsdale, *Unhappy Valley*, bk. 2, 227–64.

——. *Control and Crisis in Colonial Kenya: The Dialectic of Domination*. Athens: Ohio University Press, 1990.

——. "Ethnicity, Patronage and the African State: The Politics of Uncivil Nationalism." *African Affairs* 97, no. 388 (1998): 305–41.

Berman, Bruce J., and John Lonsdale. *Unhappy Valley: Conflict in Kenya and Africa*. Bk. 1, *State and Class*. Bk. 2, *Violence and Ethnicity*. Athens: Ohio University Press, 1992.

Berry, Sara. *Fathers Work for Their Sons: Accumulation, Mobility, and Class Formation in an Extended Yoruba Community*. Berkeley: University of California Press, 1985.

——. *No Condition Is Permanent: The Social Dynamics of Agrarian Change in Sub-Saharan Africa*. Madison: University of Wisconsin Press, 1993.

Bigsten, Arne. *Regional Inequality and Development: A Case Study of Kenya*. Nairobi: Institute for Development Studies, University of Nairobi, 1977.

Boone, Catherine. "Land Conflict and Distributive Politics in Kenya." *African Studies Review* 55, no. 1 (2012): 75–103.

Boserup, Ester. *Woman's Role in Economic Development*. New York: St. Martin's Press, 1970.

Bourdieu, Pierre. "Rethinking the State: Genesis and Structure of the Bureaucratic Field." Translated by Loïc J. D. Wacquant and Samar Farage. *Sociological Theory* 12, no. 1 (1994): 1–18.

Bowman, Andrew. "Mass Production or Production by the Masses? Tractors, Cooperatives, and the Politics of Rural Development in Post-Independence Zambia." *Journal of African History* 52, no. 2 (2011): 201–21.

Branch, Daniel. *Kenya: Between Hope and Despair, 1963–2011*. New Haven, CT: Yale University Press, 2011.

Brantley, Cynthia. *The Giriama and Colonial Resistance in Kenya, 1800–1920*. Berkeley: University of California Press, 1981.

Bravman, Bill. *Making Ethnic Ways: Communities and Their Transformations in Taita, Kenya, 1800–1950*. Portsmouth, NH: Heinemann, 1998.

Brownhill, Leigh. *Land, Food, Freedom: Struggles for the Gendered Commons in Kenya, 1870 to 2007*. Trenton, NJ: Africa World Press, 2009.

Bryson, Stuart M. *Light in Darkness: The Story of the Nandi Bible*. London: Parry Jackman Scripture Illustrations, 1959.

Casida, John E., ed. *Pyrethrum: The Natural Insecticide*. New York: Academic Press, 1973.

Certeau, Michel de. *The Practice of Everyday Life*. Translated by Steven F. Rendall. Berkeley: University of California Press, 2011.

Chanock, Martin. "Paradigms, Policies and Property: A Review of the Customary Law of Land Tenure." In *Law in Colonial Africa*, edited by Kristin Mann and Richard L. Roberts, 61–84. Portsmouth, NH: Heinemann, 1991.

Clarence-Smith, William G., and Steven Topik, eds. *The Global Coffee Economy in Africa, Asia, and Latin America, 1500–1989*. Cambridge: Cambridge University Press, 2003.

Cohen, David W. "Doing Social History from *Pim's* Doorway." In *Reliving the Past: The Worlds of Social History*, edited by Olivier Zunz, 191–235. Chapel Hill: University of North Carolina Press, 1985.

Cohen, David W., and E. S. Atieno Odhiambo. *Siaya: The Historical Anthropology of an African Landscape*. London: James Currey, 1989.

Comaroff, Jean, and John L. Comaroff. *Of Revelation and Revolution*. Vol. 1, *Christianity, Colonialism, and Consciousness in South Africa*. Chicago: University of Chicago Press. 1991.

——. *Theory from the South: Or, How Euro-America Is Evolving toward Africa*. Boulder, CO: Paradigm, 2012.

Connelly, Matthew. "Seeing Beyond the State: The Population Control Movement and the Problem of Sovereignty." *Past and Present*, no. 193 (2006): 197–233.

Cooper, Frederick. "Africa and the World Economy." *African Studies Review* 24, nos. 2–3 (1981): 1–86.

——. *Africa since 1940: The Past of the Present*. Cambridge: Cambridge University Press, 2002.

——. *Citizenship between Empire and Nation: Remaking France and French Africa, 1945–1960*. Princeton, NJ: Princeton University Press, 2014.

——. *Colonialism in Question: Theory, Knowledge, History*. Berkeley: University of California Press, 2005.

——. *Decolonization and African Society: The Labor Question in French and British Africa*. Cambridge: Cambridge University Press, 1996.

——. "Possibility and Constraint: African Independence in Historical Perspective." *Journal of African History* 49, no. 2 (2008): 167–96.

Cooper, Frederick, and Randall M. Packard, eds. *International Development and the Social Sciences: Essays on the History and Politics of Knowledge*. Berkeley: University of California Press, 1997.

Corrigan, Philip, and Derek Sayer. *The Great Arch: English State Formation as Cultural Revolution*. Oxford: Blackwell, 1985.

Cowen, Michael P. "Change in State Power, International Conditions and Peasant Producers: The Case of Kenya." *Journal of Development Studies* 22, no. 2 (1986): 355–84.

——. "The Commercialization of Food Production in Kenya after 1945." In *Imperialism, Colonialism, and Hunger: East and Central Africa*, edited by Robert I. Rotberg, 199-223. Lexington, MA: Lexington Books, 1983.

———. "Wattle Production in the Central Province: Capital and Household Commodity Production, 1903–1964." Miscellaneous Paper 104, University of Nairobi Institute of Development Studies, 1975.
Crais, Clifton. *The Politics of Evil: Magic, State Power, and the Political Imagination in South Africa*. Cambridge: Cambridge University Press, 2002.
———. *Poverty, War, and Violence in South Africa*. Cambridge: Cambridge University Press, 2011.
Davison, Jean. *Agriculture, Women, and Land: The African Experience*. Boulder, CO: Westview Press, 1988.
Ehret, Christopher. "Aspects of Social and Economic Change in Western Kenya, c. A.D. 500–1800." In Ogot, *Kenya before 1900*, 1–20.
———. *The Civilizations of Africa: A History to 1800*. Charlottesville: University Press of Virginia, 2002.
Ellis, Diana. "The Nandi Protest of 1923 in the Context of African Resistance to Colonial Rule in Kenya." *Journal of African History* 17, no. 4 (1976): 555–75.
Englund, Harri. "Cosmopolitanism and the Devil in Malawi." *Ethnos* 69, no. 3 (2004): 293–316.
Escobar, Arturo. *Encountering Development: The Making and Unmaking of the Third World*. Princeton, NJ: Princeton University Press, 1995.
Esese, Danson P. Lumumba. "The Changing System of Land Ownership and Its Socio-Economic Effects in Lugari Division, Western Province of Kenya, c. 1880–2000." PhD diss., Michigan State University, 2009.
Feierman, Steven. "Colonizers, Scholars, and the Creation of Invisible Histories." In *Beyond the Cultural Turn: New Directions in the Study of Society and Culture*, edited by Victoria E. Bonnell and Lynn Hunt, 182–216. Berkeley: University of California Press, 1999.
———. *Peasant Intellectuals: Anthropology and History in Tanzania*. Madison: University of Wisconsin Press, 1990.
Ferguson, James. *The Anti-Politics Machine: "Development," Depoliticization, and Bureaucratic Power in Lesotho*. Minneapolis: University of Minnesota Press, 1990.
———. *Expectations of Modernity: Myths and Meanings of Urban Life on the Zambian Copperbelt*. Berkeley: University of California Press, 1999.
———. *Global Shadows: Africans in the Neoliberal World Order*. Durham, NC: Duke University Press, 2006.
Ferguson, James, and Akhil Gupta. "Spatializing States: Toward an Ethnography of Neoliberal Governmentality." *American Ethnologist* 29, no. 4 (2002): 981–1002.
Gadsden, Fay. "The African Press in Kenya, 1945–1952." *Journal of African History* 21, no. 4 (1980): 515–35.
Geiger, Susan N. G. *TANU Women: Gender and Culture in the Making of Tanganyikan Nationalism, 1955–1965*. Portsmouth, NH: Heinemann, 1997.
———. "Women's Life Histories: Method and Content." *Signs* 11, no. 2 (1986): 334–51.
Geschiere, Peter. *The Perils of Belonging: Autochthony, Citizenship, and Exclusion in Africa and Europe*. Chicago: University of Chicago Press, 2009.
Giblin, James L. *A History of the Excluded: Making Family a Refuge from State in Twentieth-Century Tanzania*. With Blandian Kaduma Giblin. Athens: Ohio University Press, 2006.

——. *The Politics of Environmental Control in Northeastern Tanzania, 1840–1940*. Philadelphia: University of Pennsylvania Press, 1992.

Glassman, Jonathon. "Sorting out the Tribes: The Creation of Racial Identities in Colonial Zanzibar's Newspaper Wars." *Journal of African History* 41, no. 3 (2000): 395–428.

Goheen, Miriam. *Men Own the Fields, Women Own the Crops: Gender and Power in the Cameroon Grassfields*. Madison: University of Wisconsin Press, 1996.

Gold, Alice E. "The Nandi in Transition: Background to the Nandi Resistance to the British, 1895– 1906." *Kenya Historical Review* 6, nos. 1–2 (1978): 84–104.

Goldstein, Alyosha. *Poverty in Common: The Politics of Community Action during the American Century*. Durham, NC: Duke University Press, 2012.

Gupta, Akhil. "Blurred Boundaries: The Discourse of Corruption, the Culture of Politics, and the Imagined State." In Sharma and Gupta, *Anthropology of the State*, 211–42.

Guyer, Jane I. "Household and Community in African Studies." *African Studies Review* 24, nos. 2–3 (1981): 87–138.

——. *Women's Work in the Food Economy of the Cocoa Belt: A Comparison*. Brookline, MA: African Studies Center, Boston University, 1978.

Hamer, John H. "Preconditions and Limits in the Formation of Associations: The Self-Help and Cooperative Movement in Sub-Saharan Africa." *African Studies Review* 24, no. 1 (1981): 113–32.

Harbeson, John W. *Nation-Building in Kenya: The Role of Land Reform*. Evanston, IL: Northwestern University Press, 1973.

Haugerud, Angelique. *The Culture of Politics in Modern Kenya*. Cambridge: Cambridge University Press, 1995.

——. "Land Tenure and Agrarian Change in Kenya." *Africa* 59, no. 1 (1989): 61–90.

Havinden, Michael, and David Meredith. *Colonialism and Development: Britain and Its Tropical Colonies, 1850–1960*. London: Routledge, 1993.

Hay, Margaret Jean. "Economic Change in Late Nineteenth Century Kowe, Western Kenya." In *Hadith 5: Economic and Social History of East Africa*, edited by Bethwell A. Ogot, 92–109. Nairobi: East African Literature Bureau, 1976.

——. "Women as Owners, Occupants, and Managers of Property in Colonial Western Kenya." In *African Women and the Law: Historical Perspectives*, edited by Margaret Jean Hay and Marcia Wright, 110–23. Boston, MA: Boston University Press, 1982.

Hilton, Matthew. "Charity and the End of Empire: British Non-Governmental Organizations, Africa, and International Development in the 1960s." *American Historical Review* 123, no. 2 (2018): 493–517.

Hodgson, Dorothy L. *Once Intrepid Warriors: Gender, Ethnicity, and the Cultural Politics of Maasai Development*. Bloomington: Indiana University Press, 2001.

Hollis, Alfred C. *The Nandi: Their Language and Folk-Lore*. Oxford: Clarendon Press, 1909.

Holmén, Hans. *State, Cooperatives and Development in Africa*. Uppsala: Scandinavian Institute of African Studies, 1990.

Holmquist, Frank. "Self-Help: The State and Peasant Leverage in Kenya." *Africa* 54, no. 3 (1984): 72–91.

Holtham, Gerald, and Arthur Hazlewood. *Aid and Inequality in Kenya: British Development Assistance to Kenya*. London: Routledge, 2010.

Hopkins, A. G. *An Economic History of West Africa*. New York: Columbia University Press, 1973.
Hunter, Emma. *Political Thought and the Public Sphere in Tanzania: Freedom, Democracy and Citizenship in the Era of Decolonization*. New York: Cambridge University Press, 2015.
———. "Voluntarism, Virtuous Citizenship, and Nation-Building in Late Colonial and Early Postcolonial Tanzania." *African Studies Review* 58, no. 2 (2015): 43–61.
Huntingford, G. W. B. *The Nandi of Kenya: Tribal Control in a Pastoral Society*. London: Routledge, 1953.
———. *Nandi Work and Culture*. London: His Majesty's Stationery Office, 1950.
Hyden, Goran. *Beyond Ujamaa in Tanzania: Underdevelopment and an Uncaptured Peasantry*. Berkeley: University of California Press, 1980.
Iliffe, John. *The African Poor: A History*. Cambridge: Cambridge University Press, 1987.
Imlay, Talbot C. "International Socialism and Decolonization during the 1950s: Competing Rights and the Postcolonial Order." *American Historical Review* 118, no. 4 (2013): 1105–32.
Immerwahr, Daniel. *Thinking Small: The United States and the Lure of Community Development*. Cambridge, MA: Harvard University Press, 2015.
Ivaska, Andrew. *Cultured States: Youth, Gender, and Modern Style in 1960s Dar es Salaam*. Durham, NC: Duke University Press, 2011.
Jayal, Niraja Gopal. *Citizenship and Its Discontents: An Indian History*. Cambridge, MA: Harvard University Press, 2013.
Jennings, Michael. *Surrogates of the State: NGOs, Development, and Ujamaa in Tanzania*. Bloomfield, CT: Kumarian Press, 2008.
———. "'A Very Real War': Popular Participation in Development in Tanzania during the 1950s and 1960s." *International Journal of African Historical Studies* 40, no. 1 (2007): 71–95.
———. "'We Must Run While Others Walk': Popular Participation and Development Crisis in Tanzania, 1961–9." *Journal of Modern African Studies* 41, no. 2 (2003): 163–87.
Jones, Emma L. "Attitudes to Abortion in the Era of Reform: Evidence from the Abortion Law Reform Association Correspondence." *Women's History Review* 20, no. 2 (2011): 283–98.
Kanogo, Tabitha. *Squatters and the Roots of Mau Mau, 1905–63*. Athens: Ohio University Press, 1987.
Kanyinga, Karuti. "The Land Question in Kenya: Struggles, Accumulation and Changing Politics." PhD diss., Roskilde University, 1998.
———. "The Legacy of the White Highlands: Land Rights, Ethnicity and the Post-2007 Election Violence in Kenya." *Journal of Contemporary African Studies* 27, no. 3 (2009): 325–44.
Kaplinsky, Raphael. "Capitalist Accumulation in the Periphery: The Kenyan Case Re-Examined." *Review of African Political Economy* 7, no. 17 (1980): 83–105.
Kenyatta, Jomo. *Harambee! The Prime Minister of Kenya's Speeches, 1963–1964: From the Attainment of Internal Self-Government to the Threshold of the Kenya Republic*. Nairobi: Oxford University Press, 1964.
———. *Suffering without Bitterness: The Founding of the Kenya Nation*. Nairobi: East African Publishing House, 1968.

Kipkorir, Ben E. *The Marakwet of Kenya: A Preliminary Study*. Nairobi: East African Literature Bureau, 1973.

———. *People of the Rift Valley: Kalenjin*. London: Evans Brothers, 1978.

Kisiara, Richard Otieno. "Labor Contracts in a Polyethnic Agricultural Resettlement in Western Kenya." PhD diss., Washington University, 1998.

Kitching, Gavin N. *Class and Economic Change in Kenya: The Making of an African Petite-Bourgeoisie, 1905–1970*. New Haven, CT: Yale University Press, 1980.

Klopp, Jacqueline. "Can Moral Ethnicity Trump Political Tribalism? The Struggle for Land and Nation in Kenya." *African Studies* 61, no. 2 (2002): 269–94.

Lal, Priya. *African Socialism in Postcolonial Tanzania: Between the Village and the World*. New York: Cambridge University Press, 2015.

———. "Militants, Mothers, and the National Family: *Ujamaa*, Gender, and Rural Development in Postcolonial Tanzania." *Journal of African History* 51, no. 1 (2010): 1–20.

———. "Self-Reliance and the State: The Multiple Meanings of Development in Early Post-Colonial Tanzania." *Africa* 82, no. 2 (2012): 212–34.

Lamb, Geoff B. *Peasant Politics: Conflict and Development in Murang'a*. New York: St. Martin's Press, 1974.

Langdon, Steven. "Industry and Capitalism in Kenya: Contributions to a Debate." In *The African Bourgeoisie: Capitalist Development in Nigeria, Kenya, and the Ivory Coast*, edited by Paul M. Lubeck, 343–82. Boulder, CO: Lynne Rienner, 1987.

Langley, Myrtle S. *The Nandi of Kenya: Life Crisis Rituals in a Period of Change*. New York: St. Martin's Press, 1979.

Leo, Christopher. "The Failure of the 'Progressive Farmer' in Kenya's Million-Acre Settlement Scheme." *Journal of Modern African Studies* 16, no. 4 (1978): 619–38.

———. *Land and Class in Kenya*. Toronto: University of Toronto Press, 1984.

Leonard, David K. *Reaching the Peasant Farmer: Organization Theory and Practice in Kenya*. Chicago: University of Chicago Press, 1985.

———. "The Social Structure of the Agricultural Extension Services in the Western Province of Kenya." In *Government and Rural Development in East Africa: Essays on Political Penetration*, edited by Lionel Cliffe, J. S. Coleman, and M. R. Doornbos, 251–71. The Hague: Martinus Nijhoff, 1977.

Lewis, Joanna. *Empire State-Building: War and Welfare in Kenya, 1925–52*. Athens: Ohio University Press, 2001.

Leys, Colin. "Capital Accumulation, Class Formation and Dependency: The Significance of the Kenyan Case." *Socialist Register* 15 (1978): 241–66.

———. *The Rise and Fall of Development Theory*. London: James Currey, 1996.

———. *Underdevelopment in Kenya: The Political Economy of Neo-Colonialism, 1964–1971*. Berkeley: University of California Press, 1975.

Li, Tania Murray. "Beyond 'the State' and Failed Schemes." *American Anthropologist* 107, no. 3 (2005): 383–94.

———. *The Will to Improve: Governmentality, Development, and the Practice of Politics*. Durham, NC: Duke University Press, 2007.

Little, Peter D. *The Elusive Granary: Herder, Farmer, and State in Northern Kenya*. New York: Cambridge University Press, 1992.

Little, Peter D., and Michael Painter. "Discourse, Politics, and the Development Process: Reflections on Escobar's 'Anthropology and the Development Encounter.'" *American Ethnologist* 22, no. 3 (1995): 602–9.

Lonsdale, John. "The Conquest State of Kenya, 1895–1905." In Berman and Lonsdale, *Unhappy Valley*, bk. 1, 13–44.

———. "The Moral Economy of Mau Mau: Wealth, Poverty, and Civic Virtue in Kikuyu Political Thought." In Berman and Lonsdale, *Unhappy Valley*, bk. 2, 315–504.

———. "Moral Ethnicity, Ethnic Nationalism and Political Tribalism: The Case of the Kikuyu." In *Staat und Gesellschaft in Afrika: Erosions und Reformprozesse*, edited by Peter Meyns, 93–106. Hamburg: Lit Verlag, 1996.

Lonsdale, John, and Bruce Berman. "Coping with the Contradictions: The Development of the Colonial State in Kenya, 1895–1914." *Journal of African History* 20, no. 4 (1979): 487–505.

Lynch, Gabrielle. *I Say to You: Ethnic Politics and the Kalenjin in Kenya*. Chicago: University of Chicago Press, 2011.

MacArthur, Julie. *Cartography and the Political Imagination: Mapping Community in Colonial Kenya*. Athens: Ohio University Press, 2016.

Mackenzie, Fiona. "Gender and Land Rights in Murang'a District, Kenya." *Journal of Peasant Studies* 17, no. 4 (1990): 609–43.

———. *Land, Ecology and Resistance in Kenya, 1880–1952*. Edinburgh: Edinburgh University Press, 1998.

Macola, Giacomo. "'It Means as If We Are Excluded from the Good Freedom': Thwarted Expectations of Independence in the Luapula Province of Zambia, 1964–6." *Journal of African History* 47, no. 1 (2006): 43–56.

Maddox, Gregory. "*Mtunya*: Famine in Central Tanzania, 1917–20." *Journal of African History* 31, no. 2 (1990): 181–97.

Magut, P. K. arap. "The Rise and Fall of the Nandi Orkoiyot, c. 1850–1957." In *Ngano: Studies in Traditional and Modern East African History*, edited by Brian G. McIntosh, 95–110. Nairobi: East African Publishing House, 1969.

Mahajani, Usha. "Kennedy and the Strategy of Aid: The Clay Report and After." *Political Research Quarterly* 18, no. 3 (1965): 656–68.

Mamdani, Mahmood. *Citizen and Subject: Contemporary Africa and the Legacy of Late Colonialism*. Princeton, NJ: Princeton University Press, 1996.

Mann, Gregory. *From Empires to NGOs in the West African Sahel: The Road to Nongovernmentality*. New York: Cambridge University Press, 2014.

Marks, Shula. *The Ambiguities of Dependence in South Africa: Class, Nationalism, and the State in Twentieth-Century Natal*. Baltimore, MD: Johns Hopkins University Press, 1986.

Matson, A. T. *Nandi Resistance to British Rule, 1890–1906*. Nairobi: East African Publishing House, 1972.

——— "Nandi Traditions on Raiding." In *Hadith 2: Proceedings of the Annual Conference of the Historical Association of Kenya*, edited by Bethwell A. Ogot, 61–78. Nairobi: East African Publishing House, 1970.

Maxon, Robert. *Going Their Separate Ways: Agrarian Transformation in Kenya, 1930–1950*. Madison, NJ: Farleigh Dickinson University Press, 2003.

Mbembe, Achille. *On the Postcolony*. Berkeley: University of California Press, 2001.

———. "Provisional Notes on the Postcolony." *Africa* 62, no. 1 (1992): 3–37.

Mboya, Tom. *The Challenge of Nationhood: A Collection of Speeches and Writings by Tom Mboya*. New York: Praeger, 1970.

———. *Freedom and After*. London: Andre Deutsch, 1963.

McCann, James C. *Maize and Grace: Africa's Encounter with a New World Crop, 1500–2000*. Cambridge, MA: Harvard University Press, 2005.

McCullers, Molly. "'The Time of the United Nations in South West Africa Is Near': Local Drama and Global Politics in Apartheid-Era Hereroland." *Journal of Southern African Studies* 39, no. 2 (2013): 371–89.

McGovern, Mike. *Unmasking the State: Making Guinea Modern*. Chicago: University of Chicago Press, 2013.

Meredith, David. "The Colonial Office, British Business Interests and the Reform of Cocoa Marketing in West Africa, 1937–1945." *Journal of African History* 29, no. 2 (1988): 285–300.

Miescher, Stephan F. "Building the City of the Future: Visions and Experiences of Modernity in Ghana's Akosombo Township." *Journal of African History* 53, no. 3 (2012): 367–90.

Migdal, Joel S. *State in Society: Studying How States and Societies Transform and Constitute One Another*. Cambridge: Cambridge University Press, 2001.

Mitchell, Timothy. "The Limits of the State: Beyond Statist Approaches and Their Critics." *American Political Science Review* 85, no. 1 (1991): 77–96.

Moore, Sally Falk. *Social Facts and Fabrications: "Customary" Law on Kilimanjaro, 1880–1980*. Cambridge: Cambridge University Press, 1986.

Moskowitz, Kara. "'Are You Planting Trees or Are You Planting People?' Squatter Resistance and International Development in the Making of a Kenyan Postcolonial Political Order (*c.* 1963–78)." *Journal of African History* 56, no. 1 (2015): 99–118.

———. "From Possibility to Postcolony: The Politics of Decolonization, Development, and Inequality in Kenya (*c.* 1950–1980)." PhD diss., Emory University, 2014.

———. "Sweating to Help Themselves: Self-Help and the Contradictions of Citizenship and Development in Decolonizing Kenya." *International Journal of African Historical Studies* 50, no. 1 (2017): 35–58.

Mosley, Paul. *The Settler Economies: Studies in the Economic History of Kenya and Southern Rhodesia, 1900–1963*. Cambridge: Cambridge University Press, 1983.

Mutongi, Kenda. *Matatu: A History of Popular Transportation in Nairobi*. Chicago: University of Chicago Press, 2017.

———. *Worries of the Heart: Widows, Family, and Community in Kenya*. Chicago: University of Chicago Press, 2007.

Mytton, Graham. *Mass Communication in Africa*. London: Edward Arnold, 1983.

Nally, David, and Stephen Taylor. "The Politics of Self-help: The Rockefeller Foundation, Philanthropy and the 'Long' Green Revolution." *Political Geography* 49 (2015): 51–63.

Ndegwa, Stephen N. "Citizenship and Ethnicity: An Examination of Two Transition Moments in Kenyan Politics." *American Political Science Review* 91, no. 3 (1997): 599–616.

Nottidge, C. P. R. *The Million-Acre Settlement Scheme, 1962–1966*. Nairobi: Department of Settlement, 1966.

Oboler, Regina Smith. "Whose Cows Are They, Anyway? Ideology and Behavior in Nandi Cattle 'Ownership' and Control." *Human Ecology* 24, no. 2 (1996): 255–72.

———. *Women, Power, and Economic Change: The Nandi of Kenya*. Stanford, CA: Stanford University Press, 1985.

Ocobock, Paul. *An Uncertain Age: The Politics of Manhood in Kenya*. Athens: Ohio University Press, 2017.

Odhiambo, E. S. Atieno. "Ethnic Cleansing and Civil Society in Kenya, 1969–1992." *Journal of Contemporary African Studies* 22, no. 1 (2004): 29–42.
Odinga, Oginga. *Not Yet Uhuru: The Autobiography of Oginga Odinga*. New York: Hill and Wang, 1967.
Ogot, Bethwell A., ed. *Kenya before 1900*. Nairobi: East African Publishing House, 1976.
Ogot, Bethwell A., and William R. Ochieng', eds. *Decolonization and Independence in Kenya, 1940–93*. London: James Currey, 1995.
Okia, Opolot. *Communal Labor in Colonial Kenya: The Legitimization of Coercion, 1912–30*. New York: Palgrave Macmillan, 2012.
Okoth-Ogendo, H. W. O. *Tenants of the Crown: Evolution of Agrarian Law and Institutions in Kenya*. Nairobi: ACTS Press, 1991.
Omosule, Monone. "Kalenjin: The Emergence of a Corporate Name for the 'Nandi-Speaking Tribes' of East Africa." *Geneve-Afrique* 27, no. 1 (1989): 73–88.
Osborne, Myles. "'The Cat with Nine Lives': Paul Ngei and the Making of Modern Kenya." *Journal of Eastern African Studies* 6, no. 2 (2012): 196–210.
Parsons, Timothy. *The African Rank-and-File: Social Implications of Colonial Military Service in the King's African Rifles, 1902–1964*. Portsmouth, NH: Heinemann, 1999.
Peters, Pauline E. *Dividing the Commons: Politics, Policy, and Culture in Botswana*. Charlottesville: University Press of Virginia, 1994.
———. "Inequality and Social Conflict over Land in Africa." *Journal of Agrarian Change* 4, no. 3 (2004): 269–314.
Peterson, Derek R. *Creative Writing: Translation, Bookkeeping, and the Work of Imagination in Colonial Kenya*. Portsmouth, NH: Heinemann, 2004.
———. *Ethnic Patriotism and the East African Revival: A History of Dissent, c. 1935–1972*. Cambridge: Cambridge University Press, 2012.
Phillips, Kristin D. "Dividing the Labor of Development: Education and Participation in Rural Tanzania." *Comparative Education Review* 57, no. 4 (2013): 637–61.
———. *An Ethnography of Hunger: Politics, Subsistence, and the Unpredictable Grace of the Sun*. Bloomington: Indiana University Press, 2018.
Presley, Cora Ann. "The Mau Mau Rebellion, Kikuyu Women, and Social Change." *Canadian Journal of African Studies* 22, no. 3 (1988): 502–27.
Reid, Richard. "Past and Presentism: The 'Precolonial' and the Foreshortening of African History." *Journal of African History* 52, no. 2 (2011): 135–55.
Rich, Paul B. "Bernard Huss and the Experiment in African Cooperatives in South Africa, 1926–1948." *International Journal of African Historical Studies* 26, no. 2 (1993): 297–317.
Robertson, Claire C. *Trouble Showed the Way: Women, Men, and Trade in the Nairobi Area, 1890–1990*. Bloomington: Indiana University Press, 1997.
Robertson, Claire C., and Iris Berger, eds. *Women and Class in Africa*. New York: Holmes and Meier, 1986.
Rossi, Benedetta. *From Slavery to Aid: Politics, Labour, and Ecology in the Nigerien Sahel, 1800–2000*. Cambridge: Cambridge University Press, 2015.
———. "What 'Development' Does to Work." *International Labor and Working-Class History* 92 (2017): 7–23.
Ruthenberg, Hans. *African Agricultural Production Development Policy in Kenya, 1952–1965*. Berlin: Springer, 1966.

Ruto-Korir, Rose. "The Faint Voice in Academia, Including the Excluded: An Analysis of the Psychology of Nandi Proverbs and Its Place in Critical Psychology." *Annual Review of Critical Psychology* 5 (2006): 328–41.

Sabea, Hanan. "Mastering the Landscape? Sisal Plantations, Land, and Labor in Tanga Region, 1893–1980s." *International Journal of African Historical Studies* 41, no. 3 (2008): 411–32.

Saeteurn, Muey Ching. "'A Beacon of Hope for the Community': The Role of Chavakali Secondary School in Late Colonial and Early Independent Kenya." *Journal of African History* 58, no. 2 (2017): 311–29.

Sang, Godfrey K. *Just for Today: The Life and Times of Jean-Marie Seroney*. Coventry: Dolman Scott, 2015.

Sayer, Derek. "Everyday Forms of State Formation: Some Dissident Remarks on 'Hegemony.'" In *Everyday Forms of State Formation: Revolution and the Negotiation of Rule in Modern Mexico*, edited by Gilbert M. Joseph and Daniel Nugent, 367–78. Durham, NC: Duke University Press, 1994.

Schmidt, Elizabeth. *Cold War and Decolonization in Guinea, 1946–1958*. Athens: Ohio University Press, 2007.

Schneider, Leander. *Government of Development: Peasants and Politicians in Postcolonial Tanzania*. Bloomington: Indiana University Press, 2014.

Schroeder, Richard A. *Shady Practices: Agroforestry and Gender Politics in the Gambia*. Berkeley: University of California Press, 1999.

Scott, James C. *Seeing Like a State: How Certain Schemes to Improve the Human Condition Have Failed*. New Haven, CT: Yale University Press, 1998.

Sen, Amartya. *Poverty and Famines: An Essay on Entitlement and Deprivation*. Oxford: Clarendon Press, 1981.

Shadle, Brett L. "Bridewealth and Female Consent: Marriage Disputes in African Courts, Gusiiland, Kenya." *Journal of African History* 44, no. 2 (2003): 241–62.

Shaffer, Jack. *Historical Dictionary of the Cooperative Movement*. Lanham, MD: Scarecrow Press, 1999.

Shanguhyia, Martin S. *Population, Tradition, and Environmental Control in Colonial Kenya*. Rochester, NY: University of Rochester Press, 2015.

Sharma, Aradhana, and Akhil Gupta, eds. *The Anthropology of the State: A Reader*. Malden, MA: Blackwell, 2006.

——. "Introduction: Rethinking Theories of the State in an Age of Globalization." In Sharma and Gupta, *Anthropology of the State*, 1–41.

Sheldon, Kathleen E. *Pounders of Grain: A History of Women, Work, and Politics in Mozambique*. Portsmouth, NH: Heinemann, 2002.

Shepard, Todd. *The Invention of Decolonization: The Algerian War and the Remaking of France*. Ithaca, NY: Cornell University Press, 2006.

Shipton, Parker. *Mortgaging the Ancestors: Ideologies of Attachment in Africa*. New Haven, CT: Yale University Press, 2009.

Skinner, Kate. *The Fruits of Freedom in British Togoland: Literacy, Politics and Nationalism, 1914–2014*. New York: Cambridge University Press, 2015.

——. "Who Knew the Minds of the People? Specialist Knowledge and Developmentalist Authoritarianism in Postcolonial Ghana." *Journal of Imperial and Commonwealth History* 39, no. 2 (2011): 297–323.

Smith, James H. *Bewitching Development: Witchcraft and the Reinvention of Development in Neoliberal Kenya*. Chicago: University of Chicago Press, 2008.

Smith, Lahra. *Making Citizens in Africa: Ethnicity, Gender, and National Identity in Ethiopia*. Cambridge: Cambridge University Press, 2013.
Snell, Geoffrey S. *Nandi Customary Law*. London: Macmillan, 1954.
Somers, Margaret R. *Genealogies of Citizenship: Markets, Statelessness, and the Right to Have Rights*. Cambridge: Cambridge University Press, 2008.
Sorrenson, M. P. K. *Land Reform in the Kikuyu Country: A Study in Government Policy*. Nairobi: Oxford University Press, 1967.
Southall, Aidan W. "The Illusion of Tribe." In *The Passing of Tribal Man in Africa*, edited by Peter C. W. Gutkind, 28–50. Leiden: Brill, 1970.
Spear, Thomas, and Richard Waller, eds. *Being Maasai: Ethnicity and Identity in East Africa*. London: James Currey, 1993.
Spencer, Ian. "Settler Dominance, Agricultural Production and the Second World War in Kenya." *Journal of African History* 21, no. 4 (1980): 497–514.
Staples, Amy L. S. *The Birth of Development: How the World Bank, Food and Agriculture Organization, and World Health Organization Changed the World, 1945–1965*. Kent, OH: Kent State University Press, 2006.
Staudt, Kathleen. "The Effects of Government Agricultural Policy on Women Farmers: Preliminary Findings from Idakho Location, Kakamega District." Working Paper No. 225, University of Nairobi Institute for Development Studies, 1975.
Strobel, Margaret. *Muslim Women in Mombasa, 1890–1975*. New Haven, CT: Yale University Press, 1979.
Sutton, John E. G. "The Kalenjin." In Ogot, *Kenya before 1900*, 21–52.
Tanui, Priscilla J. "A Gender Analysis of the Influence of Colonial Policies on Access to Land and Agricultural Technology among the Nandi in Kenya, 1895–1954." *International Journal of Humanities and Social Science* 5, no. 9 (2015): 217–29.
Terretta, Meredith. *Nation of Outlaws, State of Violence: Nationalism, Grassfields Tradition, and State Building in Cameroon*. Athens: Ohio University Press, 2014.
Thomas, Lynn M. *Politics of the Womb: Women, Reproduction, and the State in Kenya*. Berkeley: University of California Press, 2003.
Thomas-Slayter, Barbara P. *Politics, Participation, and Poverty: Development through Self-Help in Kenya*. Boulder, CO: Westview Press, 1985.
Thomson, Joseph. *Through Masai Land: A Journey of Exploration among the Snowclad Volcanic Mountains and Strange Tribes of Eastern Equatorial Africa*. London: Sampson Low, Marston, Searle, and Rivington, 1887.
Throup, David. *Economic and Social Origins of Mau Mau, 1945–53*. London: James Currey, 1988.
———. "Elections and Political Legitimacy in Kenya." *Africa* 63, no. 3 (1993): 371–96.
Tibbetts, Alexandra. "Mamas Fighting for Freedom in Kenya." *Africa Today* 41, no. 4 (1994): 27–48.
Tignor, Robert L. "The Maasai Warriors: Pattern Maintenance and Violence in Colonial Kenya." *Journal of African History* 13, no. 2 (1972): 271–90.
Tilley, Helen. *Africa as a Living Laboratory: Empire, Development, and the Problem of Scientific Knowledge, 1870–1950*. Chicago: University of Chicago Press, 2011.
Tilly, Charles. "Epilogue: Now Where?" In *State/Culture: State Formation after the Cultural Turn*, edited by George Steinmetz, 407–20. Ithaca, NY: Cornell University Press, 1999.
Van Beusekom, Monica M. *Negotiating Development: African Farmers and Colonial Experts at the Office Du Niger, 1920–1960*. Portsmouth, NH: Heinemann, 2002.

Viner, Jacob, George Meany, Fowler Hamilton, Otto Passman, and Paul Hoffman. "The Report of the Clay Committee on Foreign Aid: A Symposium." *Political Science Quarterly* 78, no. 3 (1963): 321–61.

Waller, Richard D. "Emutai: Crisis and Response in Maasailand, 1883–1902." In *The Ecology of Survival: Case Studies from Northeast African History*, edited by Douglas H. Johnson and David M. Anderson, 73–112. London: Lester Crook Academic, 1988.

———. "Interaction and Identity on the Periphery: The Trans-Mara Maasai." *International Journal of African Historical Studies* 17, no. 2 (1984): 243–84.

———. "The Maasai and the British, 1895–1905: The Origins of an Alliance." *Journal of African History* 17, no. 4 (1976): 529–53.

Wallerstein, Immanuel M. *Africa: The Politics of Independence*. New York: Vintage Books, 1961.

Wanja, Josephine H. "Land on Loan: An Analysis of the Factors Affecting Loan Repayment on the Million Acre Schemes." Working Paper No. 355, University of Nairobi, 1979.

Wasserman, Gary. *Politics of Decolonization: Kenya, Europeans and the Land Issue, 1960–1965*. Cambridge: Cambridge University Press, 1976.

Weitz, Eric D. "Self-Determination: How a German Enlightenment Idea Became the Slogan of National Liberation and a Human Right." *American Historical Review* 120, no. 2 (2015): 462–96.

Weitzberg, Keren. *We Do Not Have Borders: Greater Somalia and the Predicaments of Belonging in Kenya*. Athens: Ohio University Press, 2017.

West, Harry G. *Kupilikula: Governance and the Invisible Realm in Mozambique*. Chicago: University of Chicago Press, 2005.

White, Luise. *The Comforts of Home: Prostitution in Colonial Nairobi*. Chicago: University of Chicago Press, 1990.

———. "Separating the Men from the Boys: Constructions of Gender, Sexuality, and Terrorism in Central Kenya, 1939–1959." *International Journal of African Historical Studies* 23, no. 1 (1990): 1–25.

———. *Speaking with Vampires: Rumor and History in Colonial Africa*. Berkeley: University of California Press, 2000.

White, Luise, Stephan F. Miescher, and David W. Cohen, eds. *African Words, African Voices: Critical Practices in Oral History*. Bloomington: Indiana University Press, 2001.

Widner, Jennifer A. *The Rise of a Party-State in Kenya: From "Harambee!" to "Nyayo!"* Berkeley: University of California Press, 1992.

Wiemers, Alice. "'It Is All He Can Do to Cope with the Roads in His Own District': Labor, Community, and Development in Northern Ghana, 1919–1936." *International Labor and Working-Class History* 92 (2017): 89–113.

Willis, Justin. *Mombasa, the Swahili, and the Making of the Mijikenda*. Oxford: Clarendon Press, 1993.

Winans, Edgar V., and Angelique Haugerud. "Rural Self-Help in Kenya: The *Harambee* Movement." *Human Organization* 36, no. 4 (1977): 334–51.

Wipper, Audrey. "The Maendeleo Ya Wanawake Organization: The Co-Optation of Leadership." *African Studies Review* 18, no. 3 (1975): 99–120.

Woods, Dwayne. "The Politics of Organising the Countryside: Rural Cooperatives in Côte D'Ivoire." *Journal of Modern African Studies* 37, no. 3 (1999): 489–506.

Youe, Christopher P. "Settler Capital and the Assault on the Squatter Peasantry in Kenya's Uasin Gishu District, 1942–63." *African Affairs* 87, no. 348 (1988): 393–418.
Young, Crawford, Neal P. Sherman, and Tim H. Rose. *Cooperatives and Development: Agricultural Politics in Ghana and Uganda*. Madison: University of Wisconsin Press, 1981.

ORAL INTERVIEWS BY AUTHOR

Interviews were conducted from 2012 to 2018 in eight small communities on the edge of the western Rift Valley highlands. See map A.2.

Agatha, Difina. Lumakanda, 3 November 2012; 6 June 2015
Alulu, Ainea. Lumakanda, 5 November 2012; 14 November 2012; 20 July 2016; 18 July 2018
Arusei, John. Leseru, 15 January 2013
Barno, Selena Chelimo. Leseru, 28 November 2012
Bir'geng, Joseph arap. Sosiani, 20 November 2012
Birir, Eunice. Leseru, 27 November 2012
Bitok, Daniel Kebeney. Leseru, 26 November 2012; 10 June 2015; 21 July 2016; 17 July 2018
Boit, Joseph. Eldoret, 18 July 2018
Boit, Wilson Cheruyot. Sugoi, 10 January 2013
Bulimu, Benjamin. Lumakanda, 30 October 2012
Busianey, Kibet arap. Sosiani, 29 November 2012
Busianey, Selena. Sosiani, 29 November 2012
Bwalei, Chebagui. Leseru, 23 November 2012
Chanzu, Fanike. Lumakanda, 9 November 2012
Chepkuto, Helen. Sosiani, 30 November 2012
Chepkwony, Kimeli arap. Sosiani, 30 November 2012
Chepng'ok, Joachim Kirua. Leseru, 30 November 2012
Cheptekeny, Ruth Malakwen. Leseru, 9 January 2013; 11 June 2015
Cherotich, Christina. Tapsagoi, 12 January 2013
Choge, Stephen Kimeli. Tapsagoi, 12 January 2013
Esipeya, Manasi. Chekalini, 11 January 2013
Iboso, Deina. Lumakanda, 12 November 2012
Jarenga, Theresa. Lumakanda, 3 November 2012
Kagode, Ismael. Lumakanda, 12 November 2012
Kamonya, Gladys. Lumakanda, 8 June 2015
Karanja, James. Webuye, 11 July 2013
Kasigene, Nora. Lumakanda, 30 October 2012; 7 November 2012; 5 June 2015; 18 July 2016; 17 July 2018
Keino, Chelimo Martha. Leseru, 19 November 2012
Keter, Hoseah arap. Sosiani, 21 November 2012
Keter, Michael. Sugoi, 14 January 2013
Ketera, Zipora. Sosiani, 21 November 2012
Kihinga, Jamin Maneno. Lumakanda, 8 November 2012; 9 July 2013; 5 June 2015; 18 July 2016
Kili, Jemosbei Kirwa. Tapsagoi, 12 January 2013

Kili, Jepkosgei Kirwa. Tapsagoi, 12 January 2013
Kipkalum, Anna Chelimo. Leseru, 28 November 2012
Kipkurui, Ruth Jepng'eno. Tapsagoi, 12 January 2013
Kiplagat, Samuel Kimeli. Sugoi, 10 January 2013
Kirua, Helen. Sosiani, 3 December 2012
Kitur, Mary. Leseru, 19 November 2012; 9 June 2015
Koech, Nelson Kiplagat. Sugoi, 14 January 2013
Kogo, Sally. Leseru, 23 November 2012; 11 June 2015
Konyonyi, Florence. Lumakanda, 7 November 2012
Korir, Kimeli. Nairobi, 13 July 2018
Kuto, John arap. Sosiani, 30 November 2012
Lagat, Dorcas. Sugoi, 10 January 2013
Leleli, Chepsiror arap. Tapsagoi, 12 January 2013
Libapu, Jairo Murunga. Lumakanda, 3 November 2012; 19 July 2016
Lilan, Christopher Lelei. Leseru, 26 November 2012; 21 July 2016
Limo, Simon. Leseru, 27 November 2012; 10 July 2013
Lukorito, Joseph Juma. Webuye, 12 July 2013
Machasio, Fred. Webuye, 12 July 2013
Machayo, Alfred. Chekalini, 30 October 2012; 1 November 2012; 11 January 2013
Machayo, Florence. Chekalini, 1 November 2012
Macheso, Joab Siundu. Webuye, 11 July 2013
Maikuma, Alan. Lumakanda, 3 November 2012
Maina, Kiptoo arap. Leseru, 23 November 2012; 11 June 2015; 22 July 2016
Maiyo, Eunice Tele. Leseru, 9 January 2013; 11 June 2015
Maneno, Rebecca Aliviza. Lumakanda, 6 November 2012; 9 July 2013; 5 June 2015
Masista, Aaron. Lumakanda, 2 November 2012; 20 July 2016
Masiza, Veronica. Lumakanda, 12 November 2012; 5 June 2015
Matifali, Aston. Lumakanda, 5 November 2012
Matunda, James Musamusi. Lumakanda, 2 November 2012; 14 November 2012; 9 July 2013; 19 July 2016
Mbailu, Festus. Lumakanda, 6 November 2012
Meiyo, Esther. Sosiani, 29 November 2012
Metto, Phillip. Leseru, 15 January 2013
Misavo, Karen. Lumakanda, 31 October 2012; 14 November 2012; 6 June 2015; 19 July 2016; 18 July 2018
Muchai, Peter. Lumakanda, 6 November 2012
Mulwa, Deputy. Chekalini, 1 November 2012
Munge, Joseph Dugere. Mautuma, 11 November 2012
Munyatta, David. Chekalini, 17 November 2012
Murei, Priscilla. Sugoi, 14 January 2013
Muriga, Solomon Ndeche. Lumakanda, 9 November 2012
Mutungu, Ngome. Chekalini, 17 November 2012
Mwangi, Elizabeth Wambui. Sugoi, 10 January 2013
Mwangi, Jotham Njau. Lumakanda, 5 November 2012; 20 July 2016; 17 July 2018
Nagaine, Shadrock Ngetich arap. Sugoi, 14 January 2013
Nasambu, Felistas Muriga. Lumakanda, 9 November 2012
Nasimiyu, Grace. Lumakanda, 12 November 2012
Ngetich, Pauline. Sosiani, 21 November 2012

Ngetich, Steven Kiplemai. Sosiani, 4 December 2012
Ngososei, Kipkugat arap. Leseru, 27 November 2012
Ngososei, Theresa. Leseru, 27 November 2012
Noyi, Mareb. Lumakanda, 8 November 2012
Nyanya, Margaret Wanjiru. Mautuma, 11 November 2012
Olindo, Jotham. Lumakanda, 13 November 2012
Omamo, Rastos. Lumakanda, 9 November 2012; 16 November 2012
Oyalo, Wilberforce. Chekalini, 11 January 2013
Rongei, Tororei arap. Leseru, 15 January 2013
Rono, Susan. Leseru, 22 November 2012
Sabatia, James. Lumakanda, 31 October 2012
Sawe, Tiengik arap. Tapsagoi, 12 January 2013
Serem, Rael. Leseru, 3 December 2012; 10 June 2015; 22 July 2016; 17 July 2018
Serem, Selena. Leseru, 28 November 2012
Serem, William. Leseru, 3 December 2012; 10 June 2015; 22 July 2016; 17 July 2018
Shioani, Muzole. Lumakanda, 13 November 2012
Sing'ari, Sylvester Barngetung. Leseru, 19 November 2012; 10 June 2015
Sitiene, Paul. Sosiani, 21 November 2012
Sitienei, Laban Kipkurir arap. Tapsagoi, 12 January 2013
Songok, Stanley arap. Sosiani, 20 November 2012
Sumba, Samson. Lumakanda, 13 November 2012
Tanai, Philomon. Leseru, 9 January 2013
Tanui, Nauma Jeptarus. Tapsagoi, 12 January 2013
Teregin, Solome. Leseru, 26 November 2012
Terigin, Benjamin Kirwa. Tapsagoi, 12 January 2013
Tororei, David. Sosiani, 3 December 2012
Tum Kaptulus, Frederick Kemboi arap. Leseru, 22 November 2012; 10 July 2013; 9 June 2015; 21 July 2016; 17 July 2018
Tum, Pauline. Leseru, 22 November 2012; 10 July 2013; 9 June 2015; 21 July 2016; 17 July 2018
Visyafua, Coretta. Lumakanda, 7 November 2012
Wairimu, Ann. Mautuma, 11 November 2012
Wanyonyi, Samson. Chekalini, 17 November 2012
Wechuli, Aaron Juma. Lumakanda, 31 October 2012; 14 November 2012; 6 June 2015; 18 July 2016
Zarembka, Dave. Lumakanda, 8 June 2015
Zieze, Patrick. Lumakanda, 7 November 2012

Index